THE FIGHT FOR PEACE:
THE SECRET STORY BEHIND
THE IRISH PEACE PROCESS

Also by Eamonn Mallie

Tom Carr: an appreciation
The Provisional IRA (with Patrick Bishop)

Also by David McKittrick

Despatches from Belfast
Endgame
The Nervous Peace

THE FIGHT FOR PEACE

THE SECRET STORY BEHIND THE IRISH PEACE PROCESS

Eamonn Mallie
and
David McKittrick

HEINEMANN : LONDON

First published in Great Britain 1996
by William Heinemann
an imprint of Reed International Books Ltd
Michelin House, 81 Fulham Road, London SW3 6RB
and Auckland, Melbourne, Singapore and Toronto

Reprinted 1996

A CIP catalogue record for this title
is available from the British Library
ISBN 0 434 00308 5

Phototypeset by Intype London Limited
Printed and bound
by Clays Ltd, St Ives PLC

*This book is dedicated to
the memory of our mothers,
Eileen Mallie and Rita McKittrick*

CONTENTS

INTRODUCTION

This book represents a first, or perhaps a second, draft of the history of a remarkable period. Its great highlight was the IRA cessation of August 1994, followed closely by the loyalist ceasefire which followed two months later. The great moment of disappointment and dismay was, of course, the collapse of the republican ceasefire in February 1996, the disappointment being all the greater because of the great surge of hope engendered in 1994.

As journalists we have covered events in Belfast, London and Dublin since the 1970s, but we were frankly astonished by the unexpected complexity of the process described here, in particular the hidden labyrinth of secret contacts that lay beneath it. Some of the twists and turns of the saga are scarcely believable, some of the human tragedies enough to draw tears from a stone.

The extraordinary thing was that so many of the clandestine contacts described here were successfully kept secret for so long. Many people were involved in many ways, but the fact is that hardly any individual, and quite possibly no one, had as complete a picture as that contained in these pages.

We offer our sincere thanks to a wide range of people, many of whom wish to remain anonymous. Those who can be named include Philippe Bernes, Mary Holland, Conor Lenihan, Michael Lillis, Mark Lyons, Eamonn McCann, Rory O'Hanlon and Brian Rowan. We would like to thank the family of Paddy McGrory, the late Belfast solicitor, for giving us access to his papers and Sean Duignan for permission to quote from his informative and entertaining memoirs.

Journalistic friends were invaluable. Robert Bell and Tom Bradby provided great encouragement; David Davin-Power read the manuscript and provided insightful criticism; Deric Henderson read an early draft and made useful observations. Ed Moloney readily allowed us use of a highly detailed chronology and analysis of events; his journalism throughout this period proved immensely valuable for its accuracy. Conor O'Clery, doyen of the Irish foreign correspondents, read sections dealing with the US and, from his vantage point in Washington, suggested many improvements. Fionnuala O Connor provided both encouragement and a highly detailed critique of the manuscript. John Ware gave us access to voluminous research material. We count ourselves exceptionally fortunate to be able to draw on such funds of friendship and journalistic expertise.

A special word of thanks to Vivienne Napier and Claudia Bradby, who cheerfully took so many hours of dictation and transcribed so many tape-recorded interviews. We also wish to express appreciation to the *Independent* newspaper and to David Sloan and Harry Castles of Downtown Radio for their understanding attitude during the writing of the book.

The following people were interviewed on-the-record. In some cases the interviews were quite brief, while others were interviewed again and again over a period of many hours.

David Adams	Ulster Democratic party
Gerry Adams	president, Sinn Fein
Bertie Ahern TD	leader, Fianna Fáil
Dermot Aherne TD	Fianna Fáil
Bill Barry	Irish-American businessman
Peter Brooke MP	former Northern Ireland Secretary
Austin Currie TD	Fine Gael minister and former SDLP member
Dr Cahal Daly	Catholic primate of all-Ireland
Jeffrey Donaldson	honorary secretary, Ulster Unionist party
Mark Durkan	former chairman, SDLP
Dr Robin Eames	Church of Ireland Archbishop of Armagh

Fergus Finlay	aide to Dick Spring, Irish Labour party
Bill Flynn	Irish–American businessman
Maire Geoghegan-Quinn TD	former Fianna Fáil Minister for Justice
Denis Haughey	international secretary, SDLP
John Hume MP, MEP	leader, SDLP
The late Brian Lenihan	former deputy leader, Fianna Fáil
Richard McAuley	press aide to Gerry Adams
Rev. William McCrea MP	Democratic Unionist party
Martin McGuinness	Sinn Fein executive member
Rev. Roy Magee	Belfast Presbyterian minister
Michael Mates MP	former Northern Ireland Office minister
Sir Patrick Mayhew MP	Northern Ireland Secretary
Martin Meehan	Sinn Fein member, former IRA prisoner
James Molyneaux MP	former leader, Ulster Unionist party
Fr Raymond Murray	Catholic priest, Armagh
Rev. Ken Newell	Belfast Presbyterian minister
Niall O'Dowd	publisher, *Irish Voice* (New York)
Des O'Malley TD	former leader, Progressive Democrats
Martha Pope	assistant to former US Senator George Mitchell
Albert Reynolds TD	former Fianna Fáil Taoiseach
Kathleen Reynolds	wife of Albert Reynolds
Nancy Soderberg	US National Security Council
Dick Spring TD	leader, Irish Labour party, Irish Minister for Foreign Affairs
David Trimble MP	leader, Ulster Unionist party
Trina Vargo	advisor on Irish affairs to Senator Edward Kennedy
Andy Wood	Director, Northern Ireland Information Service

A number of the above, in addition to giving their on-the-record comments, privately helped with other information, opinions and guidance. In addition, more than a dozen significant figures declined to speak on-the-record but were much more forthcoming in private. Some of these gave lengthy interviews; several spent many hours outlining what they knew of the peace process. Some had the patience to answer repeated queries. A number, while insisting on anonymity, nonetheless allowed the interviews to be tape-recorded for greater accuracy. They include senior figures involved in the republican movement, Northern Ireland politics, Anglo-Irish relations and the security field in Belfast, Dublin, London and elsewhere.

The previously unpublished confidential documents which appear in the text emanated from five separate sources, to whom we are especially grateful.

To our keen regret Father Alec Reid, the Redemptorist priest who was one of the prime movers in the peace process, declined several requests for an interview. Readers of this book will gain an insight into the value of his efforts, almost all of which take place far from public view. While disappointed, we can understand his reasons for deciding not to step out from behind the veil.

Great support came from Helen Fraser of Heinemann, Jim and Ann Aiken, and Wilhelm and Sally Bourdonge.

Finally, we wish to thank our families – Detta, Pat, Ciara, Julie, Kerry, Laura Kate and Michael – for their endurance, understanding and love.

Belfast 1996

PROLOGUE:
DEATH IN THE
AFTERNOON

Other members of the IRA squad were urging the gunman, 'Do them in the head, do them in the head,' as he pumped bullets into the bodies of the two soldiers who lay on the rough ground off Andersonstown Road in west Belfast. The gunman, the hood of a duffle-coat pulled over his head in a cruel caricature of a monk's cowl, clinically pointed his weapon at the heads of the soldiers, shot them, then walked away.

Minutes later, Father Alec Reid, a Redemptorist priest from the nearby Clonard Monastery, knelt in the dirt beside the spread-eagled semi-naked body of one of the soldiers. Although he knew there was little or no hope, he bowed and, amid the mud and the blood, attempted to give him the kiss of life.

It was March 1988. Father Reid, a slightly stooped, middle-aged priest, came from peaceful Tipperary, far from the grim back-streets of Belfast's republican ghettos. He had arrived in the city two decades earlier, a year before the Troubles broke out, and all that time had lived in the Falls Road, in the midst of the violence, in the midst of people condemned through the years by other priests and bishops.

The month of March 1988 had brought a series of extraordinary incidents beginning with the SAS killing of three IRA members in Gibraltar. Mairead Farrell, Daniel McCann and Sean Savage had been plotting to blow up a military band, but were unarmed when the SAS shot them twenty-nine times.

The three were given a huge solemn funeral in west Belfast, but as their coffins were being lowered into the earth in Milltown cemetery, an unprecedented attack occurred. A loyalist gunman, Michael Stone, single-handedly launched a near-suicidal attack on mourners with gunfire and hand-grenades, killing three men and injuring dozens of others.

Three days later, the coffin of one of Stone's victims, Kevin Brady, was being taken to Milltown. The atmosphere was already highly charged, with dozens of republican stewards on the lookout for another loyalist attack, when a silver Volkswagen car suddenly reversed at speed into the funeral.

Mourners immediately surrounded the car, assuming it contained more loyalist attackers. In fact, it contained two army corporals who had chanced into the cortège. One of the corporals fired a warning shot but in a frenzied attack dozens of men swarmed over the car and dragged them from it. They were then beaten, shoved and pushed into a nearby sports ground and park where they were again beaten and partially stripped by some members of a smaller crowd. After five and a half minutes in the park they were, sickeningly, thrown over a nine-foot-high wall, bundled into a black taxi and driven away. They were taken to the waste-land where after a struggle they were shot. It later emerged that an army surveillance helicopter had recorded on film, in harrowingly graphic detail, the actual moment of their deaths.

An IRA member later recalled: 'After the Michael Stone attack three days earlier, it was decided that several people would carry [i.e. carry weapons] on the periphery of Kevin Brady's funeral. Four or five were armed, with another squad floating about with access to an arms dump nearby. We came to the gate of the park and one volunteer handed us the soldiers' identity cards. We established they were SAS. [In fact, the soldiers were Signals engineers.] We commandeered a black taxi. We brought the taxi round to the wall where the soldiers were lying. They were pushed over the wall and put into the taxi. There were two people in the taxi. The remaining members of the squad jumped into a car and followed the taxi. The soldiers were taken out of the taxi and shot with their own gun. To the squad of men it was a good hit. They were SAS to all intents and purposes. The fact that Dan McCann and Mairead were colleagues meant we felt we were getting something back for the Gibraltar shootings.'

Father Reid leaned down and pressed his mouth to that of the soldier; when he straightened up, after his hopeless effort, his lips had the soldier's blood on them. Journalist Mary Holland, who witnessed the scene, wrote: 'His courage and compassion redeemed us all. It sent one image of Ireland across the world that spoke of human pity in the face of death rather than the savagery of the mob.'

But in that ghastly tableau Father Reid was also the picture of helplessness, a living symbol of the impotence of organised religion and indeed of rational argument in the face of a determined, merciless gunman. Many would have given up; yet that same priest, spurred on by this awful experience, was to play a hidden but vital part in bringing about the IRA cessation of violence in 1994.

A Presbyterian clergyman described the qualities of the priest: 'Alec Reid's ministry is like an electrician. He gets two wires that are not connecting and he brings them together and he wraps his concern around them. He is the masking tape until the current begins to flow. He is a spiritual spark: he brings the light on.'

Despite that moment of despair, the priest went on with his work for peace. On that dark day in west Belfast, Father Reid was powerless to save that soldier's life; but his work for peace eventually bore fruit, saving many others from premature graves.

I

TALKING TO
TERRORISTS

'You always wondered what was going on in
that little mind'
   – Gerry Adams's former teacher, Brother
Bosang

'The island of Ireland could become a Cuba off
our western coast. What on earth would we
do?'
   – former Northern Ireland Secretary James
Prior

On a bright Saturday morning in April 1993 Gerry Adams, president of Sinn Fein, emerged from a car and took a few strides up
to the door of a high terraced house in West End Park, on the
edge of the republican Bogside area of Londonderry city. Behind
him came a Catholic priest. At the black double-fronted door of
the Victorian house stood John Hume, leader of the Social Democratic and Labour party and Adams's rival for the leadership of
Northern Ireland's half a million nationalists. Hume greeted the
two men civilly, showed them inside and closed the door.

Since the front room of Hume's house was packed with books,
papers, documents and political bric-à-brac, he led the republican
and the priest upstairs to a first-floor sitting-room. The bay window
of the room overlooks the Bogside and affords a panoramic view of
the city's historic walls, as formidable and forbidding today as they
were when the Protestant defenders repelled Catholic assailants
three centuries ago.

Inside, Hume's wife Pat brought coffee for Adams and her husband and tea for the priest, Father Alec Reid. She then left them to one of those conversations which Irish nationalist politicians follow closely but which to outsiders can seem so theoretical as to be almost theological. The three men, all of whom were to play a key part in bringing about the IRA's cessation of violence in August 1994, talked of national reconciliation, of internal settlements, of self-determination. But as they rummaged through the abstractions they were intent not on political point-scoring but on finding a basis for peace. The two party leaders were deadly political rivals: Adams's party, Sinn Fein, was in essence the political wing of the Provisional IRA, which for more than two decades had been trying to bomb the British out of Ireland. It regularly won 30 per cent of the Catholic nationalist vote, while Hume's non-violent SDLP represented the major part of northern nationalism.

But as their discussion continued that day in Londonderry both men sensed they were making progress. Hume had long accepted Adams's assertion that the Irish people as a whole had a right to national self-determination: now they were agreeing that this self-determination had to be exercised in an agreed way. This apparently obscure distinction would in time prove to be one of the foundations of the seventeen-month IRA ceasefire of August 1994, which brought Ireland so tantalisingly close to a permanent peace.

These were two of Ireland's finest political brains. Hume, the leading nationalist theoretician of his generation, had a conventional education, studying at Maynooth seminary, taking an MA in history and teaching before going into politics. Adams was self-taught, a one-time barman and lorryman's helper who honed his formidable conceptual and debating skills while interned for IRA activities in Long Kesh prison camp near Belfast. Because of its inmates' fondness for debate and argument Long Kesh had once been called the IRA's university: Gerry Adams was its brightest graduate.

As the conversation went on, a personal process was under way: a sense of trust was gradually developing between these two men, in spite of their different beliefs and their direct political rivalry. This relationship was to prove vital in the fraught months ahead, for they developed a sense of trust in each other in those tense and often murderous times.

The conversation was the latest in a long line of secret meetings between them: they preferred to talk in private, believing they made more progress away from the glare of publicity. What they did not realise, as they talked on, was that the secret of their contacts had been blown.

In the few seconds Adams took to leave the car and walk into Hume's house he had been spotted by a local man, Tony Gillespie, who had immediately recognised the tall, bearded bespectacled Sinn Fein president. Shortly afterwards Gillespie walked into Londonderry city centre where he spotted Eamonn McCann, the well-known left-wing journalist and civil rights activist. McCann was selling copies of *Socialist Worker* outside a shop in Shipquay Street. 'Here,' said Gillespie, 'you'll never guess who I just saw going into John Hume's house.'

McCann rang the Dublin *Sunday Tribune* newspaper and broke the story of the meeting. Within hours, a range of political figures were issuing statements condemning Hume for consorting with the mouthpiece of terrorists. The media clamoured at Hume for explanation. No one accused him of sympathising with terror: his twenty years as a man of peace had won him an international reputation, especially in Europe and the United States, as an implacable opponent of violence. But what, the critics demanded to know, was he doing talking to Adams, the despised mouthpiece for terrorism?

The question of mainstream politicians talking to men of violence or their representatives was intensely controversial. Over the years, many politicians, including British governments, had taken part in such contacts, usually in conditions of strict secrecy. On the occasions when they were uncovered the reaction tended to be a storm of condemnation.

The biggest fear was that such meetings would actually worsen things by encouraging the IRA to believe it was winning. The former Irish Taoiseach, Garret FitzGerald, spelt this out in condemning meetings between the British and republicans in the 1970s:

'The contacts had the effect merely of prolonging the violence by deluding the IRA into believing that a British government would eventually negotiate a settlement with them.'

In fact, as this book will show, under the surface of Irish politics there existed a whole labyrinth of secret talks and contacts. The disclosure of the West End Park meeting was in fact only the tip of a very large iceberg.

But in April 1993 the heat on Hume was all the fiercer because IRA violence was raging at a high level. Just three weeks earlier the IRA had set off a bomb in a litter-bin in the Lancashire town of Warrington, fatally injuring two young boys. A wave of revulsion at the killings, which seemed at once particularly poignant and particularly meaningless, had swept both Britain and Ireland. And thirteen days after the meeting the IRA set off a huge lorry-bomb in Bishopsgate, killing a man and causing many millions of pounds' worth of damage to the City of London financial district.

It was true that Gerry Adams had for many months been appropriating the language of peace, signalling that his republican movement was interested in dialogue. But he was still a political pariah, and while the bombs continued to go off his talk of peace seemed to most people the rankest of hypocrisy, a mere attempt to lend a political veneer to sheer terrorism.

A further shock came eleven days after the West End Park meeting when Adams and Hume issued the first of a number of agreed statements. Critics denounced it as 'Provo-speak' because it mentioned self-determination, which was regarded as Sinn Fein language. Others, however, noted that the statement concluded: 'We both recognise that [such] a new agreement is only achievable and viable if it can earn and enjoy the allegiance of the different traditions on this island, by accommodating diversity and providing for national reconciliation.' Such language was much more Hume-speak than Provo-speak, and it held out the tantalising possibility that he had been the first to spot that a genuine rethink was under way within the republican movement.

The SDLP leader was almost alone in believing Adams was sincerely interested in seeking peace, that he could bring his profoundly militaristic movement along with him, and that the conditions could be created for a permanent stoppage of the IRA campaign. Hume had a dominant position within his party, but even some of the faithful wondered whether he was making a major misjudgement, and whether Adams was leading him up the garden path.

No one could be certain of Adams's real intentions. But if anyone had the power to sell the idea of peace to the Provisionals it was Gerry Adams, with his impeccable republican credentials and his decades of commitment to the republican movement. Few ever really knew what his real thoughts were, for even as a child, according to one of his teachers, Brother Bosang: 'He was a meditative sort of fellow, very quiet, almost taciturn. You always wondered what was going on in that little mind. He would be in the class and you would barely be aware of his existence but you knew when you looked at him that he was taking everything in.'

For many people in Britain and Ireland Gerry Adams was – and still is – a hate figure. His television appearances, until his voice was outlawed from the airwaves in 1988 under the broadcasting ban, caused much anger. He was seen as the evil, murder-justifying public mouthpiece of the IRA. He could be heard mournfully intoning that he regretted all deaths in the conflict; then he would add, apparently more in sorrow than in anger, that more deaths were inevitable until Britain took its troops home. His self-assured articulacy and his capacity to deal with the most hostile of interviewers infuriated his enemies all the more.

It is unquestionably true that for a quarter of a century Adams has been a key figure in the republican movement, and for much of that time has been its most important personality. His militancy and his willingness to be associated with the campaign of terrorism was obvious to all. But he has other qualities too, which his admirers list as pragmatism, flexibility, an ability to inspire loyalty, a taste for dialogue and an openness to innovation. Together these were to play a large part in bringing about the IRA cessation of 1994.

The story of his life is the story of the Provisional republican movement. He was born in 1948, into a Falls Road family which might be described as part of the west Belfast republican aristocracy, a small cluster of families who had passed on their republican faith down through the generations. His father, known in later life as 'Old Gerry', was an old-time republican activist while his mother, Annie, was a Hannaway, one of the most prominent of the small number of Falls families who kept the republican flag flying during the lean years of the 1940s and 1950s.

Adams passed his 11–plus and his GCE O levels, but dropped out of the sixth form of St Mary's Christian Brothers grammar school to become a barman. By his late teens he was already highly politicised, involving himself in local housing and unemployment campaigns. He also joined the IRA. He was twenty-one when the first serious violence erupted in 1969, much of it centring around the streets where he had been born and brought up. According to Adams the last wages he ever picked up were on 15 August 1969: since then he became in effect a full-time republican activist. His IRA career is said to have included the ranks of intelligence officer, battalion quartermaster and battalion commander, before he was picked up in 1972 and interned without trial.

Although he was still in his early twenties, his importance in republican ranks was emphasised later that year when he was chosen by the IRA to be one of its team to take part in secret talks with the British government. Adams was plucked from Long Kesh internment camp and, with his later close friend Martin McGuinness and others, was flown to London in a military aircraft. Escorted through London by the Special Branch, they were driven to Chelsea to meet the then Northern Ireland Secretary, William Whitelaw, for talks which were the forerunner of the secret contacts of the 1990s. A revealing description of Adams in his early twenties was recently given by Frank Steele, a retired British official who was present at those talks with Whitelaw. Steele said later:

> I'd been briefed that although Adams was a young man, he was a senior member of the Belfast battalion and that battalion had been murdering and shooting and bombing and therefore I expected – putting it frankly – an aggressive streetwise young tough and I was therefore pleasantly surprised when instead a

very personable, likeable, intelligent, articulate and persuasive young man appeared.

At one point I said to him: 'You're a young man, you've got your life ahead of you. Do you really want to spend it on the run from us British?' He replied that he didn't and I said: 'Well, what would you like to do?' and he said: 'I'd like to go to university and get a degree.'

So I said: 'Well, we're not stopping you, all you've got to do is renounce violence and you can go to university.' To which he said: 'Well, I've got to help to get you British out of Northern Ireland first.'*

When those talks failed Adams stayed out of prison for a time, but in 1973 he was again arrested and spent the following four years behind bars. If his first spell in Long Kesh was his degree course, this period was when he took his Ph.D. Other inmates recall his air of authority, his debating skills and above all his inner conviction that he knew the way ahead. One of his closest friends and confidants, who spent hours walking with him inside the perimeter walls, recalled: 'He studied every colonial situation in the world. He knew more about revolution around the world than anybody else. He started lectures and debates in jail.' Under the pen-name 'Brownie' he contributed a series of thoughtful columns to the Provisional newspaper, *Republican News*. He had his critics too, however, one prisoner writing of his 'arrogance and overbearing posture, his sarcastic and devious ways'. In the years following his release in 1977 he not only rose to senior rank within the republican movement but, with a group of like-minded colleagues, came to dominate its entire approach and philosophy.

Until the late 1970s the movement had essentially been run from the south, with middle-aged, often rural-based, southerners such as Ruairi O Bradaigh and the late Daithi O Conaill holding sway. The southerners had important support roles, but the front line of the IRA's war was not in the south but in the north, in the fields

*NB: It is most unlikely that Adams used the phrase 'Northern Ireland', since republicans traditionally do not recognise the state and do not use its name.

of south Armagh and on the back streets of west and north Belfast. By the late 1970s the IRA looked to be on the ropes, its shooting and bombing attacks dramatically reduced as a new hard-line security policy wore it down.

Adams and his supporters put into effect a well-organised coup and, with surprising ease, ousted the O Bradaigh-O Conaill faction. Power shifted to a faction headed by Adams, the Londonderry republican Martin McGuinness and other northerners such as Danny Morrison, many of whom would play a part in the peace process of the 1990s. But in the late 1970s they saw things very differently, aiming then not for peace but for eventual victory over the British. They criticised the ceasefire which O Bradaigh and O Conaill had agreed to in the mid-1970s, arguing that the old leadership had been duped by the British. There could be no short cuts to peace, they declared: the British had no intention of withdrawing, and it would take many years to shift them. But if it took years rather than months, or even decades rather than years, then so be it. Together they constructed the theory of the long war, accepting that their campaign would be long and difficult. The IRA was reorganised and tightened up while, in the early 1980s, Sinn Fein was developed as its significant political adjunct. Adams became Westminster MP for West Belfast in 1983, symbolising Sinn Fein's new-found political strength: the party showed it could regularly win more than a third of the nationalist vote in Northern Ireland. In the same year he emphasised his commanding position in the movement by replacing O Bradaigh as Sinn Fein president. An IRA associate said of Adams: 'He's the best there is. He's terrific at meetings – the rest of us can be flapping around and he just stays cool and calculating.'

One who worked closely with him during the peace process noted: 'Patience is his strength.' Richard McAuley, one of his closest aides, summed him up: 'He is very good at listening to other opinions before taking a decision. It's rare for Gerry to lose his temper – I don't remember when it last happened, though there are times when he is irritated if he is tired.'

In 1984, after one of his many brushes with the law, Adams was required to appear at a magistrates' court in Belfast city centre. He and four other men were driving back to the Falls district after the hearing when they were fired on by gunmen from the loyalist Ulster Defence Association who riddled their car with bullets. Four of the republicans were injured, while Adams himself was hit three times in the neck, shoulder and arm. He might have been killed had the attack been pressed home with more precision, but it was a confused incident – one of the loyalist gang shot another in the hand.

Adams quickly recovered from his wounds, but it was a salutary reminder that he could never relax. In the following years a number of other plots to kill him came to light: in one incident a British squaddie went AWOL and went looking for him with murderous intent, but was intercepted by the security forces. The republican movement supplied Adams with an armoured black taxi, and he often wore a flak jacket.

He once outlined something of his family history. The British army had shot dead his brother-in-law, he said, and shot and seriously injured his brother. 'I had a cousin picked up, tortured and stabbed to death by loyalists, and most of my immediate family have been in prison. I've a brother in prison at the moment.' In May 1995 a cousin, arrested in a hijacked van with weapons and a bomb, was jailed for twenty-five years. Eight months after the IRA ceasefire, in May 1995, Adams said that he still changed where he slept at night: 'Republicans always stay on the run. It's factored into your subconscious when you live life on the edge. It's part of life.'

One of the aims of this book is to help explain why and how Adams and his associates developed from their 1970s militancy to become sponsors of the 1990s peace process. In the 1970s they fashioned a machine to wage the long war; in the 1980s that clinically efficient machine claimed many lives. Then in the 1990s they built a process aimed at turning off that machine. In other words, the architects of the long war were also the creators of a strategy for peace.

Even after the 1994 IRA ceasefire, workmen in Belfast continued

13

to build more of the 'peacelines' which criss-cross and deface the city – high brick and metal walls designed to separate Protestant and Catholic districts. This is not some government effort to impose segregation: the walls were put up by community demand, and are generally popular in the districts they divide. They are a symbol of ancient and lasting community divisions. They are a sign of the difficulties which Protestants and Catholics have of co-existing with each other, a sign that after centuries northern Protestants have not assimilated into Ireland.

The ancestors of most of the Protestants arrived in Ireland in the seventeenth and eighteenth centuries, encouraged to emigrate from England and Scotland by Elizabeth I and other English monarchs who wanted to stock the troublesome island with a loyal garrison community. Ireland was a perennial nuisance and worry to England, local leaders continually rising against the Crown and threatening to make dangerous alliances with England's traditional enemies, France and Spain.

Although there was some intermarriage between the Catholic natives and Protestant settlers, the two communities, especially in the north, continued down through the years to regard themselves as separate entities. The communities were differentiated primarily on the basis of conflicting national identities, but there were other important points of difference – religious, territorial, economic and social. The existence of these kept communal divisions fresh and potent.

Protestantism was by no means synonymous with Unionism, by which is meant allegiance to the union with Britain. There have been many prominent examples of Protestants who became Irish nationalists: in 1798, for example, many northern Presbyterians themselves unsuccessfully rose against the British. In the decades that followed, however, the Presbyterians and the Anglicans made common cause, becoming a solid phalanx for the union with Britain.

In the nineteenth century Catholic Ireland produced a series of movements seeking to cut or lessen the ties with Britain, led by nationalist heroes such as Daniel O'Connell, Thomas Davis and

Charles Stewart Parnell. But most of the Protestants, who were largely concentrated in the north-eastern corner of the island, were hostile to such movements. While most of the island was rural, the north-east had been built into the British economy and had become heavily industrialised, resembling Liverpool and Glasgow more than Limerick and Galway. Protestants tended to have the better jobs, and their poor community relations with Catholics expressed themselves with sporadic rioting and sectarian clashes.

The Protestants wished to keep their advantages and to stay part of the British economy. They also regarded themselves as British and were fiercely proud of the British empire, and wanted no part of any new independent or semi-independent state. Another strong factor was that they feared, in their potent slogan, that Home Rule would mean Rome Rule, picturing a nightmare state in which their Protestant heritage would be actively attacked.

By the end of the nineteenth century they had organised formidable bodies such as the Ulster Unionist Council (the forerunner of today's Ulster Unionist party) and the Orange Order to oppose any weakening of the link with Britain. All this was in direct opposition to the nationalist home rule movement, which pressed for a measure of autonomy for Ireland. The tide of history seemed to favour the nationalists, for various British administrations were in favour of home rule. The Unionist response to what they saw as a threat to their British citizenship, religious traditions and economic well-being was to pledge their determination to oppose home rule by 'all means which may be found necessary'. In the spring of 1914 the Unionist establishment smuggled 25,000 rifles and three million rounds of ammunition into the north of Ireland from Germany. They proclaimed their readiness to act outside the law and a major military confrontation seemed inevitable, but the outbreak of World War One intervened and the home rule issue was put on ice for its duration.

Nineteen sixteen saw the Easter Rising in Dublin, with a small number of republicans staging an armed rebellion. The rising itself was quickly put down, but the action of the British government of the day in shooting many of its leaders rebounded: London was deemed to have over-reacted and a wave of sympathy for the republicans ensued. Within a few years, faced with an onrush of strong republican sentiment, London was ready to give Ireland a large measure of autonomy. But the determination of the northern Protestants to stay British was recognised, and the six north-eastern counties were allowed to remain under British rule. Thus was the state of Northern Ireland born.

Its creation did not bring happiness or security for the Protestants who made up two-thirds of its population of a million and a half, for it was clear that London was not as committed to the union as they were. They constantly feared a 'sell-out' – a switch of British policy in favour of a united Ireland. They also remained deeply suspicious of the half-million Catholics who found themselves within the boundaries of the new Northern Ireland state. Those Catholics considered themselves trapped in this new state, denied their Irish identity, cut off from their co-religionists in the south and politically powerless. Their plight was worsened by their belief that the Unionist establishment, which was to run the state on the basis of strict majority rule for the following half-century, actively discriminated against them in terms of jobs, housing and political rights.

Today northern nationalists have formidable political leaders in Hume and Adams, as well as considerable influence in Dublin and in Washington, but between 1921 and the early 1970s the Catholic community was politically isolated. The system was then based on Protestant rule, to the virtual exclusion of Catholic and nationalist influence. The Stormont parliament had a built-in Protestant majority, as had most local councils. In many places Protestant and Unionist control was artificially contrived by devices such as distortions of electoral boundaries. Thus 32,000 Catholics elected seven members of Fermanagh county council, while 25,000 Protestants elected thirteen and hence took power. The government, the judiciary and the security forces, the Royal Ulster Constabulary and Ulster Special Constabulary, were either exclusively or overwhelmingly Protestant. The system survived for so long because of Unionism's monolithic strength, aided by divisions within nationalism and Westminster indifference. It may not have been a fair arrangement, but in London's terms it worked: the Protestants kept the Catholics in line and a potentially vexatious state remained reasonably quiet. In effect Britain considered the Irish question closed.

The Catholic community's fortunes did not materially improve until the late 1960s when, inspired by Martin Luther King in the United States and by student agitation in Paris, northern Catholics launched a civil rights movement. Some of the movement's leaders were merely trying to wrong-foot Unionism, but many others were motivated by an urge to participate in the business of the state. The civil rights campaign was thus a major departure from the old-style nationalist politics which were characterised by boycott and doleful complaint.

But the Unionist system could not cope with demands which were by most standards modest. Unionism split into moderates, who were prepared to consider concessions to the nationalists and those, such as the fundamentalist preacher and politician the Rev. Ian Paisley, to whom the idea of any compromise was anathema. Civil rights demonstrations produced Paisleyite counter-demonstrations; some marches degenerated into violence and it was not long before street disruptions were common. Widespread rioting in the cities of Belfast and Londonderry overwhelmed the police force, the largely Protestant RUC, and in August 1969 the British army had to be sent in to restore order.

They failed, and the quarter-century that followed was one of the most remorselessly violent in centuries of Irish history. Protestant attacks on Catholic ghettos in Belfast led to the re-emergence of the IRA: at first it professed to be a defensive organisation but it quickly became a terrorist organisation of fearsome force. By 1972 large Protestant paramilitary organisations had emerged, with tens of thousands of men marching around the streets of Belfast. A violent hardcore of these groups was not content to remain as defensive vigilantes and in the summer of 1972 began killing substantial numbers of Catholics.

Political crisis followed political crisis; terrorist outrage followed terrorist outrage. In 1972 the British government dismantled the Unionist system, and then spent two decades attempting to replace it with a new arrangement in which Unionists and nationalists could work together. In the early days the general view was that the issue was reasonably straightforward: the problem was defined as one of helping the Catholics who had suffered for decades under a discriminatory Protestant government. The question became much more complicated, however, as violence steadily increased, reaching its peak with a death-toll of almost 500 in 1972. The fact that many of the deaths were caused by the IRA reduced British and international sympathy for the Irish nationalist point of view, leading many observers to re-define the problem as one of terrorism rather than civil rights. The authorities found themselves attempting to deal with two major factions on the Catholic side, one prepared to participate in politics, the other intent on overthrowing the state by violent means. Hume was prominent in the former, while Adams was active in the latter.

London remained focused on ways of securing Catholic participation in government. This appeared to have been achieved when, early in 1974, Hume's SDLP came together in a power-sharing devolved administration in partnership with moderate Unionists. Within months, however, extreme loyalists organised a Protestant general strike which brought down the new arrangement. That element of Unionism which had been prepared to share power with nationalists disappeared virtually overnight. Thereafter, the principle that Catholics must be got into government was matched by the belief that Protestants would not have them. Much hope had been vested in the power-sharing initiative, and its collapse meant that disillusion developed in many quarters. The IRA was clearly not interested in any such settlement, and was intent only on forcing the British out through a military victory. Similarly the Rev. Ian Paisley and a strong body of Protestant ultras were implacably opposed to sharing power with Catholics. The British government was not about to give in to the IRA and withdraw from Northern Ireland; nor was it going to buckle to the loyalist extremists and reinstate another version of majority rule. It seemed obvious that the way ahead was to bring Catholics to identify fully with the state, and that this could only be done by offering them participation in government; yet the bulk of the Protestant community consistently made clear its determination – and its ability – to frustrate any attempt to do so.

At this stage most British politicians concluded that nothing could be done and lost interest. The decline in sympathy for the Catholics continued, largely because the IRA kept up its campaign while loyalist killings, which had always received less publicity and attention than republican violence, decreased sharply after 1977. The upshot was a stalemate which lasted for many years. The death-toll dropped from an average of 275 deaths per year to 85 per year. IRA violence significantly decreased in the face of a tough new security policy adopted by the then British Labour government. This approach included the abandonment of internment without trial, which had gained the republicans considerable domestic and international sympathy, and a concentration instead on extracting confessions from IRA suspects in specially designed interrogation centres, principally at Castlereagh in Belfast. The confessions were usually enough to secure convictions in court, and a steady stream of IRA members was imprisoned. Another facet of the policy was the increased use of the SAS (Special Air Service) who killed a number of IRA members in a series of carefully laid ambushes.

Little political progress was made, while recurring security crises buffeted Northern Ireland and occasionally Britain and the Republic: one incident among many was the IRA assassination of Lord Mountbatten as he relaxed on his boat off the Sligo coast in 1979. By the early 1980s a form of surly stalemate had been established: a large security apparatus was holding the violence down to certain levels, but was unable to eradicate it completely.

Then in 1981 came an event which brought the republicans perhaps as close as they ever came to their aim of destabilising both parts of Ireland. A long-running dispute at the Maze prison (as Long Kesh had been renamed) over the status of republican prisoners led to months of protests: the inmates wanted what was in effect political status, to differentiate themselves from non-paramilitary prisoners. The authorities, headed by a Margaret Thatcher still in her early and most uncompromising days as prime minister, refused to give way. She laid down that terrorists should not be treated differently from other prisoners.

The dispute escalated into a hunger strike which brought many deaths on the streets and a dangerous degree of polarisation throughout Northern Ireland. The starkness of the deepening division was shown when the principal IRA hunger striker, Bobby Sands, stood in a Westminster by-election and was elected MP for Fermanagh-South Tyrone. Other hunger strikers were elected to the Dáil, the Irish parliament in Dublin. Many nationalists who did not support the IRA none the less reacted against what they saw as British inflexibility, and were prepared to show emotional sympathy to the prison protest. Sands died in May 1981, after sixty-six days on hunger strike, entering republican mythology as one of its most revered martyrs. Nine other republicans also starved themselves to death, six of them members of the IRA and three from the smaller Irish National Liberation Army. Their funerals were attended by tens of thousands of people as both communities were affected by the intensity and trauma of the time. The protest itself eventually petered out but the after-shocks lingered, in particular a surge of anti-British feeling among nationalists. Large numbers of young people came forward to swell the ranks of the IRA: for the terrorist organisation the hunger strikes brought a period of renewal, expansion and new possibilities.

Adams and the other republican leaders had always been wary of what they reviled as 'electoralism', believing that entering the political processes would blunt the edge of the IRA. But when they saw the masses of nationalists prepared to go to the funerals of hunger strikers, and the 30,000 who voted for Sands, they realised that the basis existed for a sizeable broad-based movement. As a result they transformed Sinn Fein from little more than a flag of convenience for the IRA into a political organisation with a life of its own, an entity in its own right. Many people who baulked at joining the IRA itself were ready to join its political wing and work for it politically. It contested elections in earnest, with spectacular initial success. In four elections between 1982 and 1985 it averaged around 12 per cent of the total vote and 40 per cent of the nationalist vote. Its best performance came in 1983 when it took more than 100,000 votes and, in a victory of great symbolic significance, had Gerry Adams elected as Westminster MP for West Belfast. Adams's election victory won him new allies among the British Labour left, and he made several trips to England, attracting saturation publicity. The election of almost sixty Sinn Fein representatives to councils all over Northern Ireland brought widespread Unionist protests and often disruption at council meetings. Sinn Fein was the focus of all attention and there was much worried talk that its foray into politics was poisoning the wells of political processes. The republican movement was on the up and up: its strategy, and the scale of its ambitions, was revealed when Danny Morrison, one of Adams's closest confidants, asked a Sinn Fein ard-fheis (annual conference): 'Who here really believes that we can win the war through the ballot box? But will anyone here object if, with a ballot paper in this hand and an Armalite in this hand, we take power in Ireland?'

Emboldened by their advances in the north, the republicans turned their eyes south. In 1981, at the height of the hunger strikes, a number of republican prisoners put themselves forward in southern elections and two, Kieran Doherty and Paddy Agnew, were elected to the Dáil, the first Dáil seats won by republicans since 1961. This was taken as a sign that a great potential for republican growth existed in the south. Sinn Fein hoped to pick up votes from the border counties, from the disaffected poor in Dublin and from voters who generally inclined to the left. Furthermore, party politics in the south was particularly fragmented at that stage, as a decline in the fortunes of the largest party, Fianna Fáil, prevented it from securing an overall majority. There was a distinct possibility that just a small number of Sinn Fein members of the Dáil could find themselves in a pivotal position. All of this was alarming for southern politicians, who feared their settled polity was about to be invaded by republican revolutionaries intent on overthrowing the system from within. An Irish Labour party minister, Barry Desmond, spoke fearfully of the prospect of 'IRA army council deputies [members of the Dáil] stalking the corridors of Dáil Eireann, holding the balance of power'. At that moment many republicans believed, with Danny Morrison, that the new strategy of combining IRA violence and political sabotage offered a route to victory, and enthusiastically set about building up Sinn Fein.

There is a huge historical irony here. Someone once said that when revolutionaries become involved in discussion and debate they cease to be revolutionaries. So it proved in Ireland: the republican leadership which built up Sinn Fein had, probably unwittingly, laid the groundwork for the intensive years of internal debate in the late 1980s and early 1990s. What was initially designed as an instrument of subversion and sabotage eventually evolved into a mechanism of entry into politics, and instead of complementing the armed struggle eventually almost displaced it. But all that lay in the future. In the early 1980s Sinn Fein's foray into politics was seen by conventional politicians not as an opportunity but as a source of alarm and dismay.

One of those southern figures most perturbed by the Sinn Fein advance was Dr Garret FitzGerald, who during the 1970s and much of the 1980s played a commanding role both in domestic southern politics and Anglo-Irish relations. The son of a southern nationalist father and a northern Presbyterian mother, he devoted more time, energy and thought to the questions of the north and relations with Britain than any other southern political figure. He made a significant contribution, both in terms of his actions during his two spells as Taoiseach, and intellectually as one of the key thinkers who helped re-define modern Irish nationalism. He had personal memories of the threat gunmen could pose to the Irish Republic. In the dangerous 1920s his father's post as the first Foreign Minister of the new Irish Free State gave the young FitzGerald an early insight into Irish political realities: he remembered the family travelling in an army car with soldiers with machine-guns guarding against Sinn Fein supporters.

Sixty years on, FitzGerald's nightmare was that the same Sinn

Fein might actually overtake John Hume's SDLP as the principal voice of nationalism in the north. He viewed Sinn Fein as a malignant dry rot in the northern body politic, a rot which threatened to spread south. He feared, as he later explained in his memoirs, that 'the situation there could get out of control and threaten the whole island, for in those circumstances the IRA might seek a violent confrontation with the Unionists and try to follow this by an attempt to destabilise the Republic.'

FitzGerald was not alone in this assessment, for the British government of the day, headed by Margaret Thatcher, also regarded the rise of Sinn Fein as a dangerous development. In public Mrs Thatcher affected to believe that FitzGerald's fears were exaggerated, but privately her ministers were intensely worried. In 1983 James Prior, then Northern Ireland Secretary, warned a private meeting of Conservative MPs that the island of Ireland could become 'a Cuba off our western coast'. Prior too had a nightmare vision. According to a reliable source who attended the meeting, he predicted that Sinn Fein could overtake the SDLP – 'What on earth would we do?' Prior asked. If it happened, he said, one could foresee the whole of Ireland being taken over by the Marxists of Sinn Fein. Prior's immediate response was to fashion a plan which led to the establishment of a new assembly in Belfast, but in the event his initiative was boycotted by all shades of nationalism and came to nothing.

The main British aim at this time was to contain a dangerous situation and restore as much stability as possible. The failure of the Prior assembly put paid to the idea of making progress through the devolution of power to Northern Ireland politicians. Attempting to integrate Northern Ireland with Britain, as advocated by some Unionists, was rejected because it would have wrecked relations with the Republic. Withdrawal was not favoured because it would inevitably be viewed as a defeat for Britain at the hands of terrorism, and because in any event it could well result in a level of violence worse than anything yet experienced.

Constitutional nationalists, meanwhile, went back to basics. Acting on an idea put forward by Hume, FitzGerald convened a

'New Ireland Forum' to act as a think-tank for all shades of constitutional nationalist opinion. Senior figures from FitzGerald's Fine Gael and Hume's SDLP sat for several months with Fianna Fáil, under the leadership of Charles Haughey, and the Irish Labour party, headed by Dick Spring. Sinn Fein was excluded on the grounds that it supported violence. The forum took submissions and heard evidence from a wide range of sources, including leading Protestant and Catholic church figures and a few northern Unionists. Its report, published in May 1984, reproached the British government for allegedly insensitive security policies and for concentrating on crisis management. Calling for a major reassessment by Britain, it warned: 'Constitutional politics are on trial. This requires priority attention and urgent action to halt and reverse the constant drift into more violence, anarchy and chaos.' In the report the four parties made it clear that their first preference was for a united Ireland in the form of a sovereign, independent Irish state, achieved peacefully and by consent. They also examined the options of a federal Ireland and of Northern Ireland coming under the joint authority of London and Dublin. And they also mentioned, in what looked like a throw-away line, that 'the parties in the forum also remain open to discuss other views which may contribute to political development'.

All shades of Unionist opinion in Northern Ireland summarily rejected the three forum options. So too did Mrs Thatcher, though she did so with such brusqueness that she caused a crisis in Anglo-Irish relations. A unitary state, she told the media, was out; a federal Ireland was out; and joint authority was out. Her words, which became known as 'Out, out, out', were taken as an insult even by moderate opinion in the Republic. It was the latest in a series of difficult moments in Mrs Thatcher's handling of Anglo-Irish relations. Ireland had few pleasant connotations for her: during the campaign which successfully made her prime minister in 1979 her close friend and office manager, Airey Neave MP, had been killed just outside the Commons by an INLA booby-trap bomb. Later that year she had to deal with a major security crisis when Lord

Mountbatten and eighteen British soldiers were killed on the same day.

In 1980, making a determined effort to put Anglo-Irish relations on a constructive new footing, she flew to Dublin with an unprecedentedly strong team of ministers which included not only the Northern Ireland Secretary but also her Foreign Secretary and the Chancellor of the Exchequer. She and the then Taoiseach, Charles Haughey, had a meeting which went exceptionally well. A communiqué issued afterwards said the two governments had agreed to examine 'the totality of relations' between their two countries, a phrase which alarmed Unionists but which Haughey described as a historic breakthrough. A follow-up meeting in London later that year went equally well. This came to be known as 'the tea-pot summit' because Haughey gave Mrs Thatcher an antique Georgian tea-pot. An eyewitness said: 'She was charmed by the tea-pot. He was an extraordinarily charming man when he wanted to be and he exercised all his charm on her. The relationship just grew from there.'

Within months, however, this promising relationship fell apart amid bitterness and acrimony. First Haughey was critical of Mrs Thatcher's handling of the hunger strike; then his Foreign Minister, Brian Lenihan, predicted a united Ireland could emerge within ten years from the 'totality of relations' studies. Mrs Thatcher wanted closer Anglo-Irish relations but a united Ireland was not on her horizon, and she felt betrayed by what she regarded as a gross distortion emanating from Dublin. When she and Haughey met at a European summit at Maastricht in March 1981 she delivered what was described as 'a monologue, a diatribe' by one of those present – 'she couldn't speak coherently, she was in such a rage. Lenihan had put the cat among the pigeons and she just said in no uncertain terms what she thought.'

When FitzGerald succeeded Haughey as Taoiseach it seemed to Mrs Thatcher to offer a second chance of building up London-Dublin relations and of increasing cross-border security co-operation. But the 'Out, out, out' furore looked like jeopardising her hopes; so, taken aback, she asked FitzGerald how she could make amends. With hindsight it can be seen that this was a crucial moment in Anglo-Irish relations. Over the years one of the specialities of Irish diplomacy was to turn apparent reverses to Dublin's advantage, and that is precisely what happened at this juncture.

FitzGerald's response was that the two governments should work together on a far-reaching new agreement designed to bolster constitutional nationalism against the menace of Sinn Fein and the IRA. He was supported in this not only by Hume and other constitutional nationalists but also, more unusually, by a number of key British civil servants. The initiative which developed thus originated in Dublin but was endorsed and indeed crafted by senior British civil servants and diplomats.

Chief among these was Sir Robert (now Lord) Armstrong, who was then Cabinet Secretary; also important was Sir David Goodall, a senior Foreign Office official then on secondment to the Cabinet Office; a third was Sir Alan Goodison, then British ambassador to Dublin. These three formidable mandarins, all of whom were convinced something needed to be done, were put to work on an Anglo-Irish committee with an equally formidable and experienced team of Irish diplomats, Michael Lillis, Sean Donlon, Dermot Nally and Noel Dorr. The approach of containment and crisis management was left behind as the team went to work in a determined attempt to seize the initiative from the republicans.

Mrs Thatcher was particularly keen on increasing security co-operation with the Republic, of which she was privately critical, but she also accepted that political action was necessary. One of the British team later said privately:

Perhaps Mrs Thatcher had a less than comprehensive grasp of Irish history, but she's an intensely pragmatic politician. She was conscious of the need to do something – not to solve the situation, but to move it forward from the impasse which it had reached. It was logical to explore the possibilities of the Anglo-Irish dimension. Those of us negotiating were under a clear political direction to reach an agreement. We were aware of history but we were not cowed by it. We met on equal terms.

We were able to meet with a degree of personal commitment to achieving something, and in an atmosphere of trust and friendship. We were aware of national obligations but we shared a common commitment and a common sense that we were engaged in a very important and very exciting and rather new stage in the long history of relations between Britain and Ireland.

Another of the British negotiators said: 'One of the main purposes of the deal was to try to enable the Catholic population of the north to participate in the instruments of government and the general fabric of society. The watchword was Catholic alienation, and the agreement was intended to help in overcoming it.'

The forum report's line that the constitutional nationalists 'remain open to discuss other views' now came into its own as the civil servants got down to discussing something completely different from the three forum options. A complex negotiation followed as, between March 1983 and November 1985, the civil servants took part in thirty-six meetings. British and Irish ministers, including Mrs Thatcher and FitzGerald, met regularly to review progress.

This negotiation was ultimately successful, in the eyes of both governments, in that it produced the Anglo-Irish Agreement of November 1985. But the process of negotiation was itself important in that key figures in London and Dublin developed relationships of trust and friendship. Anglo-Irish relations had often been difficult and many more rocky periods lay ahead; but the mid-1980s were a significant turning-point in that Dublin, and important figures in London, came to regard the Northern Ireland question as a common problem which was best managed jointly. This was by no means the joint authority suggested in the forum report; rather, it was the beginning of a partnership relationship. In the 1990s this would be useful for the peace process, in that it established a precedent for Dublin and London working closely together, and with some success. Garret FitzGerald later described the changing nature of Dublin–London relations:

The IRA have one positive achievement, but only one: they have transformed the Anglo-Irish relationship. In the 1970s we were thought to be pursuing different policies with different attitudes, because the focus of attention in people's minds was on Irish unity versus Northern Ireland remaining part of the UK. It was therefore thought to be a conflict of interest. But the reality, because of the IRA, has been that that long-term divergence of interest has been subordinated to the common concern, the restoration of peace. The fact is that the two governments are pursuing the same policy in cooperation with each other – although most Irish people, most Irish governments, feel that British governments don't do it as intelligently as we'd like, and they make many mistakes. That change from a position of polarised attitudes to one of common purpose has been the fundamental change of Anglo-Irish relations in the last twenty years.

But while constitutional nationalism was intent on making progress through peaceful negotiations, the IRA went on prosecuting its war. In one of many incidents, nine RUC officers, two of them women, were killed when an IRA mortar scored a direct hit on an RUC canteen in the grounds of the police station in Newry, County Down. In October 1984 a bomb meant for Margaret Thatcher exploded at the Grand Hotel in Brighton during the Conservative party's annual conference. The blast, which took place early in the morning, demolished much of the façade of the old building. It missed its primary target, the Prime Minister, but killed five other people. These were two Tories, including an MP, and the wives of three more Conservatives. It was the closest the IRA ever came to striking at the heart of the British political establishment, and the shock-waves reverberated throughout Britain and Ireland; but the long, careful Anglo-Irish negotiation inched painstakingly onward. Just over a year after the Brighton attack it was ready.

2

ANGLO-IRISH
AGREEMENT

'They tell you that the war against British rule
will be run down. Shame − shame − shame.
Our position is clear and it will never, never,
never change: the war against British rule must
continue until freedom is achieved'
  − Martin McGuinness of Sinn Fein

On a chilly November morning in 1985 a group of loyalist protesters, including several Unionist MPs, pushed and jostled RUC
officers outside Hillsborough Castle in Co. Down. Inside the ornate
building, once the residence of Northern Ireland governors,
Margaret Thatcher and Garret FitzGerald formally put their signa-
tures to the Anglo-Irish Agreement.

   The document they signed was by any standards a historic one,
giving the Republic as it did a significant role in the running of
Northern Ireland. The Agreement opened with a statement by the
two governments that any change in Northern Ireland's status could
only come about with the consent of a majority of its people. It
added that if in future a majority clearly wished to have a united
Ireland, that decision would be respected and put into effect. The
Agreement then unveiled intricately crafted new structures, at the
heart of which was an intergovernmental conference, to be jointly
chaired by the Northern Ireland Secretary and the Dublin Minister
for Foreign Affairs. This was to be serviced by a small secretariat
of British and Irish civil servants based at Maryfield, a closely
guarded office building on the outskirts of east Belfast. At the

intergovernmental conference the Irish government could put forward views and proposals on almost any subject: the Republic was given no executive power, but the Agreement committed the two governments to making determined efforts to resolve their differences within the conference.

Almost everyone was surprised that Mrs Thatcher was prepared to sign such a document. She had a reputation of being one of the few British politicians to retain any personal commitment to the union between Britain and Ireland; and, as the European Community had ample cause to know, she was famously jealous and protective of British sovereignty. That sovereignty was technically untouched by the Anglo-Irish Agreement, yet its green nationalist tone was obvious to everyone.

It was certainly evident to the loyalist protesters outside Hillsborough Castle, who were absolutely appalled by its contents. So too was every other Unionist in Northern Ireland, for to a man they believed the document – 'the Diktat', as Unionist newspapers called it – weakened Northern Ireland's place within the union. Their opposition was so deep, in fact, that it lasted for years. Protests took many forms, ranging from political boycotts to mass rallies and demonstrations, and an increase in loyalist paramilitary killings. Unionists objected not just to the Agreement itself but also to what a Protestant clergyman described as 'all the stuff in there between the lines'. Many nationalists also believed they detected a barely hidden agenda on the British side, with London signalling that it did not expect for ever to be in charge of Northern Ireland. One of the Irish architects of the accord said:

> As far as we were concerned it looked as though the British government was giving us a voice in the affairs of Northern Ireland so as to educate us, in a sense, in the sort of problems there were in running the country. It could be viewed as a sort of long-term apprenticeship in how to run the place when they were going to go. They never mentioned that they were going to go and if we had ever asked 'Are you going to leave Northern Ireland?' the answer would doubtless have been 'No, never, that is not on our agenda'. But the people we were dealing with

don't think in the short term, they think in the long term. And our perception of their actions and what they were agreeing to, was that they were saying, 'Look, we will go some time in, I don't know, fifty years, a hundred years; but when we are gone we would like to go in agreement, knowing we would leave behind a responsible administration.'

Unionists saw the Agreement as a victory for constitutional nationalism; and constitutional nationalism agreed with them. It represented in fact a historic new partnership between the British government and the non-republican nationalists. In the following years that partnership had tense and difficult moments during many political and security crises, but though battered it was not broken. Southern politicians, though generally wishing the accord could be strengthened and built on, showed themselves fiercely protective of it, regarding it as a standing affirmation by Britain of the legitimacy of Irish nationalism, and a reassurance that the north was not, as Mrs Thatcher had once asserted, as British as Finchley. The Agreement greatly reduced the practice of megaphone diplomacy, Irish politicians no longer stomping the US and Europe censuring Britain. London, for its part, seemed glad to have the south as an active ally in running the north.

This was partly because important sections of the British establishment came to appreciate that constitutional nationalism had, since the 1960s, been in the business of re-defining itself. This was first evidenced in the civil rights campaign of the late 1960s, which represented a major departure from old-style nationalist politics. Traditional nationalism held that the heart of the problem was the British presence, which was said to have deliberately divided Ireland in order to control it. The conventional nationalist recipe for solving the problem was therefore to persuade the British to leave – or, in the view of the IRA, to force them to do so. The assumption was that Unionists, faced with an imminent British withdrawal, would embrace a new destiny as a majority in a united Ireland. Some of them might fight for a time and some might leave for Scotland or England; but after a while the majority of Protestants would settle down and become reconciled to their new circumstances.

The new nationalist theory, as evolved by Hume, FitzGerald and others, rejected many of the old assumptions. In this revised view the key to the problem was not Britain but the Protestant community. The import was that the British presence was not imperialist but neutral, that the border was maintained not because of British interests but at the insistence of the Unionists, and that Irish unity could only come about with Protestant consent. The real border, it was now said, was not geographical but in men's minds. Though very different from conventional Irish nationalism, this doctrine by no means jettisoned the idea that a united Ireland was the ultimate solution. Rather, it envisaged unity as coming about not through compulsion but almost naturally, after a long period in which Protestant and Catholic would gradually learn to live with each other. Unity, the rhetoric had it, would come through reconciliation rather than coercion.

As the years of violence dragged apparently endlessly on, there was a steady convergence of London and Dublin opinions and of interests. The Republic no longer saw itself as warring with the British over the fate of the north: instead, the two governments came to view it as a difficult and dangerous problem for both. The emphasis thus switched to joint management and containment. This new approach provided one of the foundations for the Anglo-Irish Agreement, which was an acknowledgement by non-violent nationalists that the British presence would remain for the foreseeable future. A British withdrawal had quietly slipped off the agenda of all nationalist parties except Sinn Fein, partly because of an acknowledgement of Unionist rights and partly due to an appreciation of the enormous risks involved, for many feared withdrawal could lead to a bloodbath.

The Agreement reflected the fact that the constitutional nationalist thrust had shifted away from separatism and towards accommodation. The peaceful nationalists accepted, if grudgingly, that a united Ireland was not on the horizon. But in the meantime the accord gave Irish nationalists a say in the formulation of British policy and formally acknowledged the legitimacy of their tradition.

Unionists were appalled by the idea of Dublin having any say in their affairs, and in the immediate aftermath of the signing of the Agreement most attention was focused on Protestant attempts to bring it down. Unionist-controlled councils adjourned their meetings in protest; the Northern Ireland Secretary, Tom King, was attacked by loyalists when he visited Belfast city hall; there were violent clashes between protesters and police. In one incident a Portadown loyalist was killed by a plastic bullet fired by a police officer. Loyalist paramilitants launched a systematic campaign of intimidation against RUC personnel, petrol-bombing the homes of police officers: more than 500 police homes were attacked, with 150 officers forced to move house. Unionist politicians boycotted government ministers, and there was much loyalist rhetoric threatening the use of force. The fifteen Unionist MPs resigned their seats to force by-elections, a move which backfired when one of the seats was lost to the SDLP. A loyalist 'Day of Action' brought much of Northern Ireland to a standstill, but the widespread intimidation and riots which accompanied it dismayed many Protestants.

Unionism was plainly in crisis, but the Agreement also presented a formidable challenge to the republican movement, since it seemed to undermine many of the assumptions which had kept the IRA campaign alive for so long. The accord was a momentous development, and at first Sinn Fein did not know how to deal with it. The Agreement certainly contained a counter-insurgency function, promising as it did closer security co-operation between London and Dublin. This aspect of it was embodied in the new range of huge border watch-towers which the army built across the south Armagh landscape.

But the accord had much deeper implications. Sinn Fein had always characterised the Unionist tradition as a British creation, saying that London relied on the Protestant population to help administer Northern Ireland as a British colony. The republican charge was that Unionists had developed a veto on British policy and that London would not dare challenge Protestant strength. But this old pattern was now shattered. Britain was clearly intent on forging a new deal with constitutional nationalism and in doing so was prepared to stand up to fierce Unionist opposition. The daily-expressed rage of Protestants at the Agreement was an unmistakable sign that Britain was prepared to press ahead even in the teeth of Unionist anger.

Furthermore, the Agreement demonstrated that the republican view of the southern state was, in the eyes of the world, ludicrously out of date. Since its inception republican purists had refused to acknowledge the legitimacy of the southern state, arguing that it was a British creation, a puppet state economically dominated by London which was not a truly independent entity. Sinn Fein always refused to use the south's formal names, the Republic of Ireland or the Irish Republic, on the grounds that the real republic did not yet exist. Practically everyone regarded this as a ludicrously far-fetched characterisation of the southern state: certainly 99 per cent of its residents, whatever their views about the north, regarded themselves as citizens of a free and independent country. The signing of the Agreement was a further body-blow to the republican stance, for the accord was very obviously a deal struck between two sovereign states on equal terms. Britain's formal acceptance of the legitimacy of Irish nationalism, including its recognition that many people in Northern Ireland did not feel they owed allegiance to the United Kingdom, caught Sinn Fein off-balance.

This was reflected in Adams's early reactions to the accord. He prophesied, wrongly, that it would lead to the banning of Sinn Fein and the reintroduction of internment. He said, at various times, that it was a most dangerous document; that republicans would not openly oppose it; that its benefits were really due to republican activities; and that it had produced no benefits. Such a note of uncertainty was unusual in the man whose quality of inner certainty had been so evident to his fellow-prisoners in Long Kesh. The Agreement was clearly posing the most fundamental of questions to all concerned: on one reading, it had re-defined the whole Irish question. The IRA had traditionally regarded itself as being engaged in an anti-colonial, anti-imperialist freedom struggle: suddenly the supposed imperialist power had made an important move which suggested it did not expect to stay in Ireland for ever. This raised the issue, in thoughtful republican minds, of whether a continuation of violent action represented the best way ahead.

Nine years separate the Anglo-Irish Agreement of November 1985 and the IRA cessation of August 1994. It is difficult to point to a precise moment when the peace process was born within the republican movement, but there is at least an argument that its genesis is to be found in the document which, to the angry sound of loyalist clamour, Mrs Thatcher and FitzGerald signed on that frosty November day in 1985.

Sinn Fein turned its attention to examining a document which one party strategist described as 'the biggest challenge we ever faced'. The party set up a special team to examine the Agreement's implications. One member of the team said: 'We saw the coming together of Dublin and London, and this proved London could be shifted. Another view was that it was the first time the British had to recognise a form of joint authority on the island of Ireland — that was a minority view at the time. The fact that Britain moved unilaterally was pivotal. They hit the Unionists a kick in the balls, saying to them "We've tried to work with you but that failed". That didn't go unrecorded in republicanism. At the same time, as we looked at the isolation and marginalisation of Sinn Fein, we realised Sinn Fein's vote was going down. There was a realisation Sinn Fein could not overtake the SDLP and that we were losing ground electorally.'

In the 1985 council elections the Sinn Fein vote slipped from its 1983 high point of 102,000 votes to 76,000. While the party still retained a 40–per-cent share of the nationalist vote, its overall share dropped from 13.4 to 11.8. This was not a disastrous performance but it was certainly a decline, and a far cry from the heady days when the republicans aspired to eclipse the SDLP and become the main voice of northern nationalism.

Adams asked a leading member of Sinn Fein, Mitchel McLaughlin, to write an internal paper on the Agreement's real significance. McLaughlin, who has held a series of high offices in Sinn Fein, is a republican from Londonderry's Bogside who became close to both Adams and Martin McGuinness, and who over the years developed into one of the movement's most important theoreticians and strategists. He produced a paper, which was adopted by Sinn Fein, in which he noted that Britain was now prepared to embrace constitutional nationalism as part of the political landscape. He argued that republicans should welcome many aspects of the Agreement as steps along the road to what they wanted, a constructive and progressive reduction of the British presence. He explained: 'There is a negative counter-insurgency dimension to it, but in fact as a result of it the British government position has changed and changed irrevocably. They have actually indicated, in terms of historical perspective, that they can be moved along.'

The architects of the Anglo-Irish Agreement built into it an incentive function for Unionists, offering to reduce its scope if they would agree to a new power-sharing arrangement. Unionist leaders rejected this idea, however, denouncing it as a snare and a trap to draw them into the Anglo-Irish web. There followed several difficult, violent and politically fitful years. Unionists complained about the continuing existence of the Agreement while Dublin and the SDLP grumbled that it was being implemented too slowly. They were none the less prepared to support it because of its potential. In the vacuum the IRA campaign, and the British response to it, appeared to move back to centre-stage, though beneath the surface the Agreement's longer-term implications continued to sink into the general consciousness.

It was partly because of the republican movement's attempts to modernise itself that a year later, one Sunday evening in November 1986, Ruairi O Bradaigh, life-long republican and former president of Sinn Fein, stepped up to the rostrum in Dublin's Mansion House to address that year's Sinn Fein ard-fheis (annual conference). The large hall was packed to the doors: O Bradaigh looked out on more than 600 delegates, mingled with hundreds of observers and media personnel. They waited expectantly to hear what many expected, correctly, to be his last-ever speech as a member of Sinn Fein.

Behind him on the platform sat Gerry Adams, who several years earlier had displaced him as head of Sinn Fein. O Bradaigh was momentarily nonplussed to feel a tap on his shoulder: he turned to find Adams, a broad grin on his face, leaning down from the platform, offering a handshake. The older man, taken aback, briefly shook hands and turned to his task of warning the party that dropping abstentionism from its constitution would spell the beginning of the end for the republican struggle.

Abstentionism was the decades–old rule, which traditional republicans regarded as a point of high principle, that if elected to the Dáil or Westminster Sinn Fein representatives should not take their seats. If the prohibition on Sinn Fein deputies entering the Dáil was dropped, he warned, 'Haughey, FitzGerald and Spring will say, "We waited sixty-five years but we have them at last".' It was a tense moment in a highly charged debate, recognised by all as critical in setting the future direction of republicanism.

The debate, which would indeed have profound results, also had profound historical echoes. Sinn Fein had often contested elections to the Dáil and had occasionally won seats in it; but for more than six decades it had been an article of faith that its members should not actually take their seats in what it viewed as an illegitimate institution. Over the years various splinters had broken away from the movement, taken Dáil seats and been absorbed into the political system: republicans denounced these as traitors and mentioned their names with scorn.

The Provisional movement itself had been born when its founder-members, including O Bradaigh himself, walked out of an ard-fheis in 1970 partly because the then leadership favoured taking Dáil seats. The Provisionals therefore regarded themselves as the keepers of the sacred republican abstentionist flame. Now the Adams leadership was advancing a proposition of historic import, arguing that the IRA campaign could be carried on while Sinn Fein deputies took their seats and pursued their aims politically.

The irony was that Adams and his people had once favoured boycotting elections and been highly suspicious of what republicans term 'electoralism'. But the surge of support during the hunger strike showed that in the right circumstances they could collect large numbers of votes. They contended they could exploit the political system without being drawn into it. They specified that they only advocated taking seats in the Dáil, and did not want to lift the ban on Westminster or any new assembly in Belfast.

They recalled that two IRA prisoners held in the Maze had been elected to the Dáil during the 1981 hunger strike. Although the prisoners lost their seats the following year, the Adams faction believed there was a substantial vein of support to be tapped in the south. Martin McGuinness publicly predicted that Sinn Fein could win up to five Dáil seats, but only if abstentionism was dropped. Southern voters expected an efficient constituency service from their Dáil representatives, and time after time republican canvassers had been rebuffed on the doorsteps with the question – 'But what can you do for us if you won't take your seats in the Dáil?'

For some months the abstention debate had been raging within Sinn Fein and in the media. Many of the exchanges had a bitter edge, partly because O Bradaigh and his supporters had never forgiven the Adams faction for ousting them from the leadership of Sinn Fein and the IRA. In the mid-1970s the O Bradaigh faction had called a ceasefire under what turned out to be the mistaken assumption that the British government was thinking of withdrawing from Northern Ireland. During the ceasefire the security forces reorganised and regrouped, putting into place a system which later placed the IRA under severe pressure. Adams claimed O Bradaigh and his associates had almost lost the war, saying later that the British 'probably came as near at that time to defeating the republican struggle than at any time during the last fourteen years'. Since Adams was in effect accusing O Bradaigh of an almost criminal degree of incompetence, personal relations between the two republican figures were understandably poor. O Bradaigh argued that abstentionism was not a historical hangover but an essential point of principle for republicans. In the run-up to the ard-fheis he wrote: 'The armed struggle and sitting in parliaments are mutually exclusive. The one is about absolute demands – parliament is the world of compromise, the art of what is possible. The two cannot exist, side by side, in the same house. Accept an end to abstentionism and the balance will have been tipped decisively in the direction of purely political campaigns that wind up in establishment parliaments. Parliament is a substitute for a national liberation struggle. It is there to contain and draw off revolutionary fervour.'

Much of what he was saying would turn out to be eerily prophetic: the movement would indeed, eight years later, move in the direction of politics. But that evening in the Mansion House the tide of opinion was against him. As he spoke he was perspiring and over-emotional, his words tumbling out not always in sentences. In contrast to the young, confident, self-assured men who made up the new leadership, he looked old-fashioned, desperate: a loser. They seemed to look forward while he looked back. His hands could be seen quivering with the tension of the moment as he took the delegates back through history: 'The destabilisation of this state, we are told, will result and the movement will be strengthened. Always it has been otherwise, the movement suffered and the state was strengthened. Four times since 1922 it happened – all ended in failure and ultimately in the degradation and shame of collaborating with the British.'

In the debate Gerry Adams made a strong contribution but the key intervention came from Martin McGuinness, speaking with what was clearly the authority of the IRA. Within the republican movement McGuinness was regarded as the military man. Gerry Adams stood at the head of the movement, its philosophical and political leader and chief strategist; McGuinness was his indispensable partner and implicitly trusted associate, regarded as the movement's primary militarist. Many who had anxieties about Adams's penchant for innovation were reassured by McGuinness's presence at his side: for many militants, if it was all right with Martin, then it was all right with them. His reputation was particularly important in this debate, for there were reports that if abstentionism was abandoned O Bradaigh would lead a walkout from the hall.

McGuinness, Adams and their supporters had made careful preparations for the crucial vote, travelling all over Ireland to meet key activists to persuade them of the case for change. In particular, they had asked the IRA army council to issue a statement endorsing the end of abstentionism. IRA volunteers had gathered at a rare 'army convention' to discuss the proposition: not all were in favour, but all agreed to go along with the majority decision. The army council issued a statement supporting the end of abstentionism, thus immeasurably strengthening Adams's hand.

Because the exact origins of the peace process have always been unclear, some observers have speculated that as far back as 1986 the Adams–McGuinness leadership was secretly working to steer the movement away from violence and towards a political path. It has to be said that McGuinness's speech on this occasion gave absolutely no indication that this was in his mind. He was highly supportive of the IRA campaign, insisting that it would continue and that the movement would not be side-tracked into pure politics. The Martin McGuinness who stood in the Mansion House in a sleeveless jumper was a figure radiating certainty, absolute determination and complete commitment to the armed struggle. This was a very far cry from the Martin McGuinness who, eight years later in 1994, donned a clean shirt, neat jacket and tie to meet British ministers in Belfast for political talks. McGuinness responded in the strongest terms to the accusation from O Bradaigh and others that the move would mean the end of the IRA campaign:

> They tell you that it is an inevitable certainty that the war against British rule will be run down. These suggestions deliberately infer [sic] that the present leadership of Sinn Fein and the IRA are intent on edging the republican movement on to a consti-tutional path. To bolster their arguments, they draw a comparison between a pre-1970s leadership of the republican movement, which had surrendered before the war began, and the present leadership of this movement. Shame – shame – shame.
>
> I reject the notion that entering Leinster House [the Dáil] would mean an end to Sinn Fein's unapologetic support for the right of the Irish people to oppose in arms the British forces of occupation. Our position is clear and it will never, never, never change: the war against British rule must continue until freedom is achieved. The British government fear this movement, they fear this leadership. They have every right to fear us because, in or

out of Leinster House, we led the most dangerous and committed revolutionary force in Ireland for sixty-five years. If you allow yourself to be led out of this hall today, the only place you are going is home. You will be walking away from the struggle. Don't go, my friends. We will lead you to the republic.

The vote in favour of dropping abstentionism was 429 to 161. When the result was announced O Bradaigh rose from his seat, shouldered his way through the close-packed crowd and made his way out into the November cold. Sixteen years after he had walked out of the old Sinn Fein in 1970, the wheel had turned full circle and he was walking out again. The difference was, however, that this time only a few dozen followed him, and the majority stayed in the hall. He went on to found a new breakaway organisation styled 'Republican Sinn Fein' which never rose above the status of a minor splinter group. This was for two principal reasons: one was that Adams and McGuinness clearly won the argument, while the other was that the IRA did not split on the issue. The organisation stayed together, leaving O Bradaigh a marginalised figure without a military wing.

The bulk of the members stayed in the Mansion House with Adams and McGuinness, and would travel with them as they steered the movement into new and uncharted waters. Observers will continue to wonder whether or not they knew, at that 1986 ard-fheis, where they were heading; Ruairi O Bradaigh, after his subsequent years in the wilderness, could perhaps be forgiven for crying, when the 1994 ceasefire came, 'I told you so.'

Years later, one of Adams's closest lieutenants explained that the dropping of abstentionism had represented the abandonment of the policy, enunciated by Danny Morrison, of the republicans seeking to take power with an Armalite in one hand and a ballot paper in the other. Sinn Fein had moved away from the concept of undermining the south, this source said, and instead wished to forge a relationship with it. He explained: 'Dropping abstentionism allowed republicans to involve ourselves in the building of broad-front politics. We also needed to convince the Irish government it was not our intention to destabilise the South.'

The Taoiseach, Garret FitzGerald, drew no such message from the abstention decision: on the contrary, he made it plain that he regarded it as laden with menace. Within hours of the ard-fheis decision he issued a dramatic warning that Irish democracy was endangered by a move which had no precedent in the history of the state. He declared: 'For the first time a party which is engaged actively in a brutal campaign of violence, and which requires from all its elected representatives a specific commitment to support this murder campaign, has committed itself to seeking, and, if elected taking, seats in Dáil Eireann.'

Some observers were notably far-sighted in suggesting that the political processes might have more effect on Sinn Fein than Sinn Fein would have on the political processes. Michael Farrell, a civil rights activist and lawyer, wrote with some foresight on the day after the debate: 'When the movement was almost purely military-orientated, its leaders and members had little contact with the mass of the population, being restricted to the republican hardcore. Political campaigning inevitably brings them into contact with a much wider spectrum of opinion. That may make them more sensitive to the effects of IRA actions on the public at large, and may lead to changes in the IRA's strategy.'

Farrell was correct, although it took some years for the process he described to take effect. One of Hume's aides, Denis Haughey, also took the long view, charting the progress of Sinn Fein and predicting the path it would follow. He wrote:

> I remember Provo sympathisers snarling 'traitor' at those of us in the SDLP who had the temerity to fight elections on an attendance basis back in the 1970s. I remember frantic Provo sympathisers blocking roads to try to prevent voters going to the polling stations. I suppose we should be glad that the Provos are now showing signs of wakening up from the long sleep of blind adherence to old dogmas. I suppose we should be thankful that they are now taking the first tentative steps along the hard road of real politics. As they travel down that road, and face up for the first time to harsh realities, their approach to things will evolve further. It offers us hope of an end to the campaign of violence.

We must welcome the conversion of the Provos to constitutional politics, and I do. It will lead in the end – and quickly,
I hope – to the abandonment of the Armalite. What a tragedy
that they had to wade through so much blood to reach the
conclusion that we in the SDLP reached years ago. Their problem
is to persuade enough of the hard men to follow them past the
point of no return, before they twig where exactly they are
going. It will be interesting to see whether they succeed.

Denis Haughey was correct in suggesting that the ard–fheis decision
on abstentionism would eventually lead to an increasingly political
path – a path which would eventually lead to the ceasefire of
August 1994. But he was also right to worry about the hard men,
and to predict a long argument between the politically-minded and
those who, in February 1996, brought that ceasefire to an end.

3

FROM LIBYA TO ENNISKILLEN

'She was a great wee lassie. She was a pet, and she's dead. But I bear no ill-will. I bear no grudge'
  – Gordon Wilson, whose daughter Marie died in the Enniskillen Poppy Day bombing

'[We don't want] to wake up some morning and find 1,000 automatic rifles being paraded down O'Connell Street or through Government Buildings'
  – Irish Justice minister

In October 1986, exactly one month before Martin McGuinness promised the ard-fheis that the armed struggle would go on, a former oil-rig vessel bumped to a halt at the Roadstone Pier, a jetty by a remote beach in Co. Wicklow on the east coast of Ireland. The ship had been re-registered in Panama as the *Villa*. Crewed by three IRA members and two seamen, it had come from Malta and was loaded down with the biggest consignment of illegal weaponry to be smuggled into Ireland for three-quarters of a century.

Thirty men toiled for many hours to transfer hundreds of wooden boxes into a fleet of lorries and vans which dispersed the cargo to specially prepared hiding places all over the Republic. The boxes held nearly 100 tons of high-quality military hardware – not only rifles and pistols but also RPG-7 rocket launchers, SAM-7 surface-to-air missiles, heavy machine-guns and a ton of Semtex plastic explosive. Martin McGuinness spoke to the ard-fheis of leading the most dangerous and committed revolutionary force in Ireland for sixty-five years: the *Villa*'s consignment at a stroke doubled its capacity for waging war.

The authorities knew nothing of the consignment, or of three previous smaller shipments from the same source. It was the greatest British intelligence lapse for many decades, for all the surveillance of the RUC, military intelligence, MI5 and MI6 had failed to uncover the Libyan connection. It would take the authorities a full year to discover what was going on.

The *Villa*'s cargo was a gift from Colonel Gaddafi's regime in Libya. The erratic Colonel supplied the IRA with such thoroughness that he transformed it from a struggling group short of guns into one of the world's best-equipped terrorist organisations. His regime had been linked with the IRA in the early 1970s when he had given them money and sent an arms shipment, but this was intercepted by the Irish navy and the relationship faded. It was renewed in 1984, however, as Britain's relations with Libya plummeted. In April of that year a gunman inside the Libyan embassy fired a shot into a London street, killing a policewoman, WPC Yvonne Fletcher, in an incident which led to a prolonged siege of the building. Relations between Libya and Britain, never warm, reached a new low. Shortly after this Gaddafi agreed to supply more guns to the IRA, Britain's enemy.

To bring them into Ireland the organisation, needing maritime front-men, turned to two Irish freebooters with sailing experience, Adrian Hopkins and Henry Cairns. Hopkins, in a series of confessions to the authorities after he was caught, said his relationship with the IRA was strictly financial: he was in debt and needed cash. Hopkins had had what could be termed a chequered career. After ten years as a radio operator in the Merchant Navy, he returned to Ireland in 1966 to help run the family business. Two years later it failed, its offices burning down. He next launched a holiday business but this also was not a success. Its offices also burnt down. His next venture, a travel company, grew into a substantial enterprise before collapsing spectacularly at the start of the 1980s. Once again, fire struck at its premises. In 1982 Hopkins, then in his forties, set up a company buying and selling boats, but by 1984, when he came into contact with the IRA, it too was in financial difficulties. His link man with the IRA was his friend and associate Henry Cairns, whom he had known since their schooldays. Cairns, in his late forties, had worked in casual building jobs in London and in the Republic as a petrol-pump attendant and a driver, and at one stage ran a second-hand bookshop near Dublin.

Cairns was contacted by a member of the IRA who said they needed a means of transporting arms. He put the IRA man in touch with Hopkins who was quickly attracted by the large sums of money mentioned. Hopkins and Cairns worked in the venture with three IRA men: Gabriel Cleary, who was a senior figure in the organisation, James Coll and James Doherty. Cleary told Hopkins they wanted to transport several tons of weaponry into Ireland. In London Hopkins bought a 65–foot converted yacht for around £50,000, and in August 1985 set sail from Malta with a member of the IRA on board. Off the Maltese island of Gozo he rendezvoused with a Libyan ship.

The Libyans on board included one man from the Libyan embassy in Malta, together with a senior figure who was to act as the IRA's main contact. This man was believed to be the number two or number three man in Libyan intelligence. He was a close associate of Gaddafi, whom the Colonel had sent to London in 1984 to negotiate the ending of the Libyan embassy siege. Ten tons of arms, including Kalashnikov rifles, pistols and grenades, were transferred to Hopkins's ship. Hopkins and others then sailed the vessel close to Roadstone Pier, and the consignment was ferried ashore in high-speed rubber dinghies, to be ferried away by IRA teams. Hopkins said he was paid £100,000 for his part in the enterprise, half of which went on buying the ship. Another shipment was quickly arranged for October 1985, using the same ship. The rendezvous off Gozo was repeated, with another ten tons of arms transferred and ferried again to Wicklow. The third shipment, this time of fourteen tons, followed in similar fashion in July 1986. On each occasion Hopkins was paid £50,000.

It was the huge fourth shipment delivered by the *Villa* in October 1986, which gave a new lease of life to the IRA and left it better armed than ever before in its history. It previously had limited resources and had spent much money, time and effort attempting to smuggle in small amounts of weapons from the United States and the European arms market. At a stroke the Libyan connection solved almost all of the IRA's weaponry problems: suddenly it had more guns than members.

But until a year later, close to the end of 1987, the authorities knew nothing of this. They mistakenly believed that the fight against the IRA was going rather well, for the death-toll was down and the IRA seemed, if anything, to have a shortage of weapons. No one realised that the organisation was simply keeping its powder dry by not using any of the heavy weaponry, in case its appearance should disclose its Libyan source and cut the supply route.

In 1986 the leaderships of the IRA and Sinn Fein sat back and systematically took stock of the new political and military facts of life. Sinn Fein was committed to the attempt to make major inroads into the south's political system, but critical decisions were also taken on the terrorist campaign. It is now known that the IRA army council (the organisation's ruling body) seriously considered what senior republicans described among themselves as 'the Tet offensive' option. This was a reference to the sudden Vietcong switch of tactics in the Vietnam war from guerrilla hit-and-run actions to standing and fighting pitched battles. The Americans had been taken by surprise; the IRA wondered if they could surprise the British in the same way.

The era of the hunger strike and the anti-British sentiment which it generated had provided a stream of new recruits to the republican cause. The huge Libyan arsenal then gave the IRA unprecedented potential for wreaking havoc. It had a virtually unlimited number of rifles; it had heavy machine-guns firing armour-piercing rounds which could cut through even protected police vehicles; it had powerful Semtex plastic explosive; it had SAM-7 missiles and anti-aircraft guns capable of downing helicopters and planes; it even had flame-throwers, which could propel a jet of Napalm-like flame up to 80 yards, generating a heat of 1,200 degrees Centigrade. A senior police officer said later of this weapon: 'It is frightening. It could be used against anything – police land-rovers, army sangars [concrete shelters], anything. It would simply cremate any police officer or soldier – it is absolutely horrendous.'

With such weapons at its disposal, the army council examined the option of changing the nature of its campaign and escalating it into a more open form of warfare. A republican source said: 'Consideration was given to open confrontation. Ground-to-air missiles were now coming in and there was a view that with all this gear [weaponry] the campaign should be stepped up. A Tet offensive was a runner. They very seriously tested it – they put different areas on full alert on seek-and-destroy missions. The idea was to take on the army on roads and at fortifications with fifty to sixty IRA members involved at a time, and to attack helicopters.' The option was, however, discarded, a senior IRA member explaining: 'We could do, say, six months' intense fighting, with heavy casualties on both sides, but the consensus in the IRA is that it wouldn't work. The big bang wouldn't do it.'

Another consideration weighed in the balance was the potential reintroduction of internment without trial both in Northern Ireland and in the Republic. In the 1970s internment had been a public relations disaster for the British authorities: many of the wrong people had been locked up, often in a heavy-handed way, giving rise to a storm of human rights protests and much criticism from Dublin. At that time Dublin had refused to introduce internment, which meant wanted republicans could take refuge south of the border. But following the signing of the Anglo-Irish Agreement, Britain and the Republic had drawn much closer together, and the IRA's worry was that an all-out offensive might spark off a joint London–Dublin security initiative. The IRA had put in place a second and indeed a third line of leadership, standing by to take over if its leaders were rounded up, but the republican conclusion was that internment implemented on both sides of the border could amount to a pincer movement which might beat the IRA. An IRA source summed up: 'Internment could be terrible or it could get us right to a united Ireland.'

The republicans also carefully weighed up Britain's will and capacity to stand up to such an offensive. A republican strategist explained: 'There was a tactical consideration – would it shorten the war? There was clear evidence that Thatcher and company were willing to resist, and the bottom line was that we couldn't defeat the British army. For every helicopter we would shoot down they could have brought in five more – they could have put 100,000 soldiers on the streets. They were clearly very determined. That validated the political analysis – that it was not about a military victory, it was about a political victory.'

In the end the IRA's conclusion was that a Tet-style offensive would amount to risking everything on one throw of the dice, and the idea was shelved. They did, however, take the fateful decision to intensify the violence, both at home and abroad – a key decision which in the following years was to cause many deaths in Ireland and further afield.

The plans were laid. First, the Republic was to be exempt from the planned escalation: since it was targeted for political expansion, it was thought best that voters there should not be subjected to off-putting violence. The killing of a number of Gardai (Irish police) there in 1984 by the IRA and the INLA had brought sharp anti-republican reactions. Ruairi O Bradaigh, who lived in the south, explained before he left Sinn Fein: 'Each time a Garda is shot I have to recoil – no one wants to know me.' But in Northern Ireland the traditional attacks on British soldiers would continue; so would attacks on members of the RUC and the Ulster Defence Regiment, the locally raised militia, both on duty and off duty. The bombing campaign in Northern Ireland would be stepped up.

The organisation's Belfast brigade was given a complete overhaul, with new commanders appointed, following a three-year period in which IRA activity in the city had dropped to an all-time low. Between January 1985 and August 1986 the IRA killed around seventy people in Northern Ireland, but only seven died in Belfast and of these only two were members of the security forces. The Belfast IRA had suffered, in the words of one republican source, from a crisis of confidence because of the widespread belief that city units had been penetrated by informers. The army council was intent on making a fresh start in the city.

Right across Northern Ireland a new offensive would be launched to wreck RUC stations and army barracks with bomb and mortar attacks. The civilian workers called in to repair the damage would themselves be designated 'legitimate targets', liable to be killed; so too would anyone who supplied building material to the security forces, or worked in their bases. An expanded 'engineering department' would work on improving the design and manufacture of the IRA mortars, rockets and grenades which, though home-made, were often highly effective against the security forces. High-technology research into making radio-controlled bombs would go on. Meanwhile the 'security department' was to continue to comb the ranks of the IRA for informers, and to kill any they found. A new front was to be opened against loyalist extremists, who in the wake of the Anglo-Irish Agreement had increased their killings. Others would also be on the 'legitimate target' list – army and naval recruiting officers; judges; so-called 'anti-social elements' such as alleged petty criminals; and, occasionally, prison officers.

It was further decided to prioritise, and devote huge resources to, mounting a campaign of unprecedented intensity in England. The IRA had attacked targets in Britain ever since the early 1970s, causing a series of multiple deaths. Eight soldiers and four civilians were killed in February 1974 when a coach was bombed on the M62; bombings of pubs frequented by off-duty service personnel in Guildford and Woolwich claimed seven lives in November 1974; more than twenty people were killed when bars were blown up in Birmingham in the same month. Another series of bombings in the early 1980s had claimed many lives, culminating in the Brighton bombing in October 1984.

But the army council ordered a new type of offensive. Previous campaigns had tended to come in waves, with flurries of activity followed by periods of comparative quiet. The new concept was to establish an ongoing IRA presence in Britain, with IRA personnel and closely vetted supporters waging a sustained and in effect permanent offensive. This approach was to prove such a danger that, according to official figures, the British Ministry of Defence was forced to spend £126 million on anti-terrorist security measures at military bases in Britain and in West Germany.

The thousands of British servicemen who lived, often with their families, in West Germany were not to be spared. Unlike soldiers in Northern Ireland they lived relaxed lives, their bases often open to the public. The army council hoped that, with luck on its side, the IRA could stage a night attack on lightly guarded sleeping quarters, inflicting mass casualties. In this they would fail, but their attacks were to take a dozen lives on the continent, leading a British minister to comment that servicemen and their families abroad were at greater risk from the IRA than those actually stationed in Northern Ireland.

Many deaths followed those strategic decisions of 1986. Listing the hundreds of deaths and thousands of gun and bomb attacks would be wearisome, but the following illustrate something of the resulting upsurge in violence.

Private Iain O'Connor, a twenty-three-year-old soldier from Preston in Lancashire, died on 30 March 1987, when a new type of 'impact grenade' was dropped from a walkway in Divis Flats in the Falls Road district of Belfast on to the roof of his land-rover. He was one of 200 members of the security forces killed between 1986 and 1994.

William 'Frenchy' Marchant, a leading loyalist activist who was a member of the Ulster Volunteer Force, died in a hail of bullets on the Shankill Road on 28 April 1987. He was among fifty alleged loyalist extremists killed between 1986 and 1994.

Seventy-four-year-old Lord Justice Maurice Gibson, Northern Ireland's second most senior judge, died in a huge explosion when a land-mine was detonated underneath his car close to the border on 25 April 1987. His wife, Lady Cecily, died with him in the blast. This was one of many attacks on members of the judiciary.

Charles McIlmurray of Andersonstown, west Belfast, was found shot dead near the border on 12 April 1987. Aged thirty, he was married with two children and his wife was pregnant. The IRA said he was a former member of the organisation and claimed he was an informer. The Belfast *Irish News* reported: 'Speaking only a few hundred yards from the victim's home, Sinn Fein president Gerry Adams said: "I think that Mr McIlmurray, like anyone else living in west Belfast, knows that the consequence for informing is death." ' The IRA killed at least twenty alleged informers between 1986 and 1994.

James Oldman, a part-time member of the Ulster Defence Regiment in Fermanagh, was shot dead in his car as he arrived at the shop where he worked in the town of Ederney on 3 April 1987. The IRA gunmen ordered his cousin, a thirteen-year-old schoolgirl, out of the car before they opened fire. He was one of many members of the security forces to die while off duty.

Harry Henry, a fifty-eight-year-old County Londonderry man with six children, was killed on 21 April 1987 by five men who forced their way into his home. The IRA said he was killed because the firm he worked for, which was owned by his brother, carried out construction work for the security forces. Between 1986 and 1994 the IRA killed more than thirty people for this reason.

William Mullan, aged seventy-two, was one of eleven Protestants killed when a bomb went off on 8 November 1987, as they waited in the street to watch a Remembrance Day ceremony in Enniskillen, Co. Fermanagh. They were among dozens of civilian casualties of IRA bombs and bullets.

Twenty-four-year-old musician Mick Ball, a member of the Royal Marines band, was one of eleven bandsmen killed when a bomb exploded on 22 September 1989 at the Marine school of music in Deal, Kent. Many other people were killed and widespread destruction was caused by the IRA's large-scale offensive in Britain, which opened in 1987 and went on until 1994.

In the German town of Wildenrath, close to the Dutch border, RAF Corporal Maheshkumar Islania was killed on 26 October 1989 when IRA gunmen opened fire on his car. Their bullets also killed his six-month-old baby daughter. The Islanias were among a dozen people – servicemen, members of their families and uninvolved bystanders – killed by the IRA on the continent.

The IRA itself suffered many losses in the years after 1986. Jim

Lynagh, thirty-two, one of the IRA's most valued activists, died along with seven other IRA members in the act of blowing up what they mistakenly believed was an undefended RUC station at Loughgall, Co. Armagh, on 8 May 1987. SAS men lying in ambush wiped out the entire IRA squad, together with an unfortunate civilian who happened to be parked nearby. The IRA sustained many other casualties, for example the three members shot dead by the SAS in Gibraltar on 6 March 1988.

Until the Libyan arsenal arrived the IRA had a limited amount of arms which it used as sparingly as possible: the rule was that an operation would be called off if it exposed weapons to the risk of loss. In the early 1980s the organisation's basic bottleneck was weaponry: it always had a certain number of weapons and a large amount of home-made explosives, but its resources were finite and had to be carefully marshalled. Guns obtained from the United States and from the European arms market cost a great deal of money and in the 1980s many were seized, particularly by the FBI. Gaddafi changed all that. Although the authorities and outsiders had at best only a hazy idea of the IRA's internal economic workings, the signs were that its finances were also transformed by Gaddafi. Instead of paying out large amounts of cash for material which might or might not reach Ireland, his gift of guns freed IRA money for other purposes.

The linchpin of the escalation was Semtex explosive. Apart from Kalashnikov rifles, this was almost the only part of the Libyan consignments to be used by the IRA before its Libyan connection was revealed. They calculated – correctly, as it turned out – that the detection of Semtex by the security forces would not necessarily lead the intelligence agencies to the Libyan connection, since it could have been obtained from a variety of other sources.

Semtex is a plastic explosive, which is to say a mixture of standard explosive and a plasticiser to create malleability. Though light, it is extremely powerful, ranking one and a half times more powerful than TNT. It is also stable, long-lasting, odourless and difficult to detect, even in airport security machines. Palestinian terrorists used Semtex in the bomb which killed an Israeli military attaché in

London in the early 1970s, and again in an abortive attempt to blow up an El Al jet *en route* from London to Tel Aviv in 1986. It was also incorporated in the device which blew up a Pan-Am 747 jet on its way from London to the United States in December 1988, causing the plane to crash, with the loss of almost three hundred lives, on the Scottish village of Lockerbie.

Semtex had first turned up in an IRA device in Belfast in 1981, but it was not until 1987 that the organisation began to use it in quantity. Its arrival gave its bomb-makers a new cutting edge, lending a completely new dimension to their campaign.

Semtex was one of the mainstays of the renewed IRA campaign in Britain and on the continent. The three IRA members shot dead by the SAS in Gibraltar in 1988 intended to set off a Semtex device during a changing of the guard ceremony there. In July 1990 a Semtex booby-trap bomb killed Ian Gow, a prominent Tory MP who was a close personal friend of Margaret Thatcher.

The IRA showed itself to be extraordinarily inventive in exploiting to the full the fact that Semtex was easy to conceal, more powerful and more penetrative than home-made explosive and was effective in very small quantities. It was employed in, among other things, booby-traps, grenades, rockets, mortars and roadside bombs. In 1986 a British army general said privately: 'The IRA's secret weapon isn't SAM-7 missiles. The thing that has made the single biggest difference to them is the Semtex – it's impossible to over-emphasise the flexibility it has given to them. Semtex is so easy, and so little of it has such a devastating effect.'

The IRA also switched to using Semtex in its frequent mortar-bomb attacks on army and police bases. A half-pound of the explosive was placed in the missiles, which were made and assembled in unofficial mortar factories in the Republic. These were well-made devices, as a Garda Chief Superintendent described after the discovery of more than sixty mortars in the Republic in 1988: 'Home-made would be a misnomer for these bombs. They were not commercially manufactured, but they were expertly finished to a high standard. '

Another menace faced off-duty members of the security forces and other potential IRA targets – under-car Semtex bombs. The IRA and other groups had for years used booby-traps beneath cars: one such device, planted by the INLA, killed the Conservative party's Northern Ireland spokesman Airey Neave, at the House of Commons in 1979. But the older, larger devices often failed to explode, or fell from the car, or were spotted because of their bulk. The advent of the plastic explosive meant the IRA could considerably refine such bombs. Only two pounds of Semtex was needed, so that the entire device could be fitted into an ordinary plastic lunchbox and fixed unobtrusively beneath a vehicle with a magnet. Such devices were usually fitted beneath the driver's seat or under a wheel-arch. According to a British general: 'It changed the way they make the booby-traps. Now the device is just a small box with a little magnet underneath it. It can be planted in a second by a guy bending over.'

Off-duty troops, policemen and others at risk were regularly warned to check their vehicles, but none the less the devices claimed many lives. In June 1988 six soldiers, travelling in an unmarked van, were killed by a booby-trap in the Co. Antrim town of Lisburn. Two months later a Semtex device, left at the side of a road at Ballygawley, Co. Tyrone, was detonated as an unmarked coach was passing carrying several dozen soldiers back to their base after a leave in England. Eight of them were killed and twenty-eight injured. An eyewitness described the horrific scene: 'There were bodies strewn all over the road, and others were caught inside the bus and under it. There were people running around stunned, screaming and bleeding and shouting for someone to come to their aid. If they had been animals it would have been bad enough, but these were people.'

On television, Ulster Unionist MP Ken Maginnis emotionally described how he had gone to the scene and found a badly injured young soldier who had managed to crawl several hundred yards before dying in a cow shed. 'Like any other soldier, he used his training to crawl undercover into hiding after the blast, but he lay there dying in front of us,' Maginnis said.

In spite of the step-up in violence, 1987 was a bad year for the republicans. After all the excitement of the November 1988 decision to drop abstentionism, the general election held in the Republic three months later saw them polling less than 2 per cent of the vote. Their candidate won a paltry 33,000 votes – much the same total as Bobby Sands had polled in a single northern constituency during the hunger strike. Many candidates lost their deposits. Gerry Adams had specified that he did not expect to win seats so soon after the abandonment of abstentionism, but even so such a dismal performance dismayed party activists: the clear message was that people in the south, even those with republican sympathies, did not want the northern troubles spilling over into their territory.

In the north Sinn Fein had a sound grasp of the state of opinion in the Catholic ghettos which were their strongholds: they knew what their people wanted, and knew what they would tolerate. But they found the south much more difficult to read, and overestimated their potential attraction there. Much of the problem lay in the fact that almost all the key analysts in the republican movement – Adams, McGuinness, Morrison, McLaughlin – were northerners with a different life experience and no instinctive feel for opinion in the south. Those southerners who were prominent in Sinn Fein were not members of the southern political mainstream, and lacked a feel for how opinion was flowing in Dublin, Cork and Galway.

In April 1987 the IRA assassination of Judge Maurice Gibson created a major impact in terrorist terms, receiving world-wide publicity and causing a large-scale security review in the wake of its demonstration that it could kill the most closely guarded figures. But republican celebrations were short-lived, for two weeks later the SAS inflicted on the IRA its heaviest-ever loss when undercover soldiers ambushed and wiped out a heavily armed IRA unit which was attacking Loughgall RUC station in Co. Armagh. Eight IRA men, led by the highly experienced Jim Lynagh, were killed in the incident. The then Chief Constable of the RUC, Sir John Hermon, estimated in a private report to ministers that those killed had been involved in between forty and fifty killings. The organisation was clearly shaken by the loss: the *Republican News*, normally a determinedly cheerful propaganda sheet, spoke candidly of shock and disbelief at the incident. Gerry Adams, grim-faced after carrying so many republican coffins, vowed at one of the Loughgall funerals: 'Margaret Thatcher and all the other rich and powerful people will be sorry in their time for what happened in Loughgall.'

Adams could not know it at the time, but 8 November 1987 would bring an even more crushing shock to republicanism. No IRA members died in the incident, but the eleven civilian fatalities represented a hammer-blow to the IRA's support and Sinn Fein's prospects for political expansion. This was the Enniskillen bombing.

That Sunday morning crowds of people, most of them Protestants, gathered in the Fermanagh town in readiness for the annual Poppy Day parade and service. Among those waiting were William Mullan, seventy-two, and his wife Agnes, seventy; Kitchener Johnston and his wife Jessie, both aged seventy; Wesley Armstrong, sixty-two, and his wife Bertha, fifty-three; and sixty-year-old Gordon Wilson, standing with his daughter Marie, a twenty-year-old nurse known in the town for her cheerfulness and vitality.

Without warning, an IRA device containing 40 lbs of gelignite hidden in a community hall just behind them exploded, demolishing a wall, bringing down tons of masonry and crushing them against a steel barrier. A man who lived nearby said: 'The explosion itself seemed to last about fifteen seconds. Then there was a dead silence for two seconds. Then there was sobbing and crying.' As the dust cleared, the disbelieving survivors made frantic efforts to dig victims from the rubble.

The Mullans, the Johnstons and the Armstrongs were all killed. Gordon and Marie Wilson were buried in the rubble: they were unable to move but they held hands and could speak to each other. Gordon Wilson's account in a radio interview of how he lay trapped in the debris holding his daughter's hand was one of the most poignant and affecting moments in Irish history. They talked for a while, but then Marie said, 'Daddy, I love you very much', and fell silent. Mr Wilson survived the ordeal; Marie did not. After her death he summoned the strength of character to say: 'She was a great wee lassie. She was a pet, and she's dead. But I bear no illwill. I bear no grudge.'

The local hospital was almost swamped with the casualties. The final death-toll was eleven, but more than sixty other people, aged from two to seventy-five, were injured, nineteen of them seriously. Five of the dead were women. The IRA had desecrated an occasion set aside for the remembrance of the dead, and the entire world condemned them for it. Republicans were supposed to be fighting for recognition of their national identity and rights, but they had killed Protestants engaged in a solemn act of remembrance and reaffirmation of their heritage.

Two themes flashed round the world in the wake of the bombing: one was that the IRA had killed eleven Protestant civilians as they gathered on Remembrance Day; the second was the almost superhuman display of Christian charity and forgiveness shown by Gordon Wilson. The savagery of the bombing, the tragedy and futility of the deaths of Marie Wilson and the ten others, and Gordon Wilson's personal victory over bitterness showed up even more starkly the viciousness of the bombers. (In 1994, after the IRA ceasefire, he showed his forbearance by sitting alongside Sinn Fein in the Forum for Peace and Reconciliation in Dublin.)

In many instances when its bombings went wrong the IRA openly admitted its errors and issued public apologies. This time, however, the reaction was so strong that it took refuge in a straight lie. An IRA statement said the device had been aimed at members of the security forces patrolling in connection with the Remembrance Day service. It accused the army's electronic countermeasures, which were designed to keep patrolling soldiers safe, of triggering the bomb, insisting: 'The bomb blew up without being triggered by our radio signal. In the past some of our land-mines have been triggered by the British army scanning high frequencies, and other devices have been jammed and neutralised.'

In 1995, IRA sources admitted that this 'explanation' was just nonsense. They acknowledged that the device was not radio-controlled, as had been claimed, but was to be set off by a pre-set timing device. They said that it was supposed to go off to catch soldiers and police carrying out a security sweep of the area before the parade. When it failed to go off, however, members of the unit omitted to take steps to alert the public about the presence of the bomb. Several years later, after other incidents which also inflicted civilian casualties, the IRA announced that the unit involved had been disbanded.

But no 'explanation', genuine or falsified, could have sheltered the republicans from the force of public anger and indignation about the Enniskillen attack. A few days after the bombing a senior IRA source acknowledged the damage it had inflicted on his movement.

> Politically and internationally it is a major set-back. Our support is in concentric rings. The centre is the republican movement, the next is the nationalist community in the north, followed by the south then solidarity groups, left groups and finally international sympathy. Our central base can take a hell of a lot of jolting and crises, with limited demoralisation. But the outer reaches are just totally devastated. It will hurt us really badly in the Republic more than anywhere else. We were trying to convince people there that what's happening in the north is a legitimate armed struggle. But the obloquy we've attracted cuts the ground from under us. It allows the Brits to slot us into the category of terrorists and that's bad. People in the IRA just feel sick. This is probably the worst year the IRA has had for five years.

These sentiments were echoed by Gerry Adams, who said: 'What is clear is that our efforts to broaden our base have most certainly been upset in all the areas we have selected for expansion. This is particularly true for the south and internationally. Our plans for expansion will have been dealt a body-blow.' Republicans were correct in realising the profound effect of the Enniskillen attack in the south. A section of southern opinion seemed prepared to tolerate attacks on British troops, clearly regarding these as legitimate acts of war; but the killing of non-combatants was not acceptable, and in the Enniskillen attack the nature of the target, and the scale of the killing, caused a strong wave of revulsion. A minute's silence in tribute to the victims brought the south to a virtual standstill, silent television screens showing a white dove of peace. In Dublin's

Mansion House, where Sinn Fein held its ard-fheis each year, fifty
thousand people queued, often in wind and rain, to sign a book
of condolence. The then mayor of Dublin, Carmencita Hederman,
personally took the book to Enniskillen, and wept as she handed
it over.

A senior intelligence source later remarked that the opportunity
to strike at a military target was very tempting for an IRA unit:
'The intention was to hit a military target but probably gross
negligence is a fair description of it. It was a gross miscalculation.
At that time each incident wasn't as finely tuned at local level as it
later became, they were much more careful afterwards.'

Enniskillen was clearly a grave set-back for the republican movement, but two other almost simultaneous events combined with it
to make the month of November 1987 a historic watershed and
turning point in the history of the troubles. Just seven days before
Enniskillen a French customs patrol had intercepted a battered old
trawler named the *Eksund* off the coast of Brittany and put a stop
to the flow of arms from Libya. Customs officials, on the look-out
for drugs, went on board and were amazed to find enough weaponry to equip a small army. They also found the IRA's Libyan
delivery team – Cleary, Coll, Doherty, Hopkins and Cairns.

When the authorities in London, Dublin and Belfast were
informed that five Irishmen had been picked up with 150 tons of
military hardware, they at first refused to believe that it could be
destined for Ireland: it seemed too large an amount, beyond the
IRA's requirements. Perhaps, one early theory went, the IRA
intended to share the cargo with militant Basques or other terrorist
groups. It took some time for it to be accepted that all of it was
bound for Ireland. In a French jail the IRA men – Cleary, Coll
and Doherty – would answer no questions, but Hopkins gave police
a full account of the episode. He said he had been contacted in
January 1987 about a proposed shipment of 200 tons, and set about
finding a boat capable of holding such a load. He saw the *Eksund*
in Sweden in May, bought her in June and had her brought to
Malta by an unsuspecting delivery firm in August.

The ship left Malta in October of that year, making for Tripoli.

A pilot boat guided the vessel first into the civil port and then to the military section, where it tied up between the quayside and a military patrol boat. The loading, which was carried out by crane and by thirty Libyan sailors, took two days and was chaotic: at one stage Hopkins was concerned that it had not been stowed evenly, and might unbalance the ship. With 150 tons of armaments on board, the *Eksund* headed for Ireland. The trip did not, however, go as smoothly as the others had. On three occasions – off Spain, off Bordeaux and off Brittany – small planes overflew the ship, leading the crew to believe they were under surveillance.

They decided to abandon the mission. The first plan was to steer to a deep spot in the Channel and blow up the ship. Explosive charges were placed around the vessel. Later, however, they decided instead simply to open the valves and scuttle her. They would then head for France in a rubber dinghy. By this stage, however, the ship itself was giving trouble. The *Eksund* was an elderly vessel in poor condition: Hopkins had been overcharged in paying £50,000 for her. The delivery firm which brought her from Sweden to Malta had trouble on the way with both the engine and the steering. By this stage the weather was stormy, and once again the steering gave problems, hindering Hopkins's efforts to reach a deep spot. Repairs were necessary, but were difficult because the steering fault meant the vessel was rolling and pitching, and he told the others they needed to steer towards more sheltered waters closer to France to carry out repairs.

Anxious not to enter French waters, they then discussed what the territorial limits were. Hopkins assured the others the limit was 3 miles, and told Cairns to stay in the wheelhouse and make sure the ship did not approach closer than 5 miles from the French coast, so as to leave a safety margin. Cairns dutifully monitored the radar, which had a digital read-out showing their distance from the coast. But the French limit is in fact 12 miles, and a French customs vessel was on its way to board the *Eksund*. When it arrived the radar showed they were 5.6 miles from France. Customs officers found three of the men in diving outfits, and in the wheelhouse discovered five loaded Kalashnikovs, a machine-gun and a bayonet. But for some reason they made no attempt to scuttle the ship.

The five crew members of the *Eksund* were held in France for between five and seven years, on their release returning to the Republic. The seizure of the *Eksund* marked the end of the Libyan connection, but by then the damage was done. The initial relief of the security forces that its cargo had been seized turned to shock and dismay when Hopkins disclosed that four previous shipments had got through.

For the first time the authorities north and south of the border realised the scale of the threat posed by the IRA, and that it possessed weaponry of unprecedented power. The Dublin government was particularly alarmed by the revelation, realising that the IRA now owned weapons which might even match those available to the Irish army itself. Irish ministers were especially concerned at a report that the IRA was considering using the heavy weaponry to launch a frontal assault on Portlaoise prison, the southern jail which housed republican prisoners.

Within weeks of Hopkins's revelations the Irish government ordered a search operation of unprecedented scale, sending 7,000 Gardai and soldiers into border counties. Thirty-three republicans were rounded up while in the north the RUC arrested forty people, including Mitchel McLaughlin of Sinn Fein. The Irish Justice Minister, Gerry Collins, declared in a sombre television broadcast: 'No state can tolerate a situation where arms of the volume and power we are talking about are held by any group other than the lawful security forces.'

The search operation turned up a number of weapons as well as unearthing five underground bunkers, two of them on a large scale. One found in Co. Wicklow was the size of a small house — 55 feet long, 11 feet wide and 9 feet high. Gardai had firm information about where it was but even so it took detectives more than an hour actually to locate it: it had been covered over with reinforced concrete, and was only reached after a drill was used to break through into it. The bunker was estimated to be big enough to house the entire cargo of the *Eksund*. Another bunker was found under a field in a remote area of Co. Galway, in the west of Ireland. Equipped with electricity and ventilation and consisting of three separate chambers, it reminded one person who inspected it of the network of tunnels built by the Vietcong in Vietnam. Neither of these constructions contained any guns or explosives: the bulk of the Libyan supplies were not found, then or later. In all, the southern security forces searched more than 50,000 homes, saying such an operation was better than 'to wake up some morning and find 1,000 automatic rifles being paraded down O'Connell Street or through Government Buildings'.

This sense of alarm in the south was heightened even more by an extraordinary episode over which the IRA had no control. A northern man, Dessie O'Hare, who was aged twenty-eight at the time, was one of those renegade republican figures who periodically emerged during the troubles, maverick to the point of finally becoming uncontrollable. A one-time member of the IRA who broke with the organisation after finding its discipline not to his taste, he went on to join the INLA. His madcap activities led to a reputed thirty killings, repeated brushes with death and a series of jail sentences.

In October 1987 he assembled a small gang and set out to kidnap for ransom a well-known Dublin medical figure. The man they kidnapped turned out not to be their target but a dentist, John O'Grady. They held him captive for several weeks but then, in an action which appalled the entire country, O'Hare cold-bloodedly hacked off two of the dentist's fingers with a chisel. Shortly afterwards John O'Grady was rescued, but for the following three weeks O'Hare and other gang members were pursued by police over large stretches of Ireland, twice shooting their way out of roadblocks and injuring several Gardai in the process.

He was eventually captured after a shoot-out in which he was seriously injured and a fellow gang-member killed. But the fact that he had been able to remain at large for weeks, and his ability to out-gun Gardai in their clashes, sapped public confidence in the police. The *Irish Press* newspaper declared: 'The spectacle of armed desperadoes running amok across the country, thumbing their noses at the law and the Garda and enforcing their demands at the point of a gun is one that threatens the very basis of civilised society.' A Dublin judge later reflected the level of public concern about the episode when he jailed O'Hare and an associate for forty years, the heaviest sentences ever handed down in the Republic.

The combination of the Enniskillen bomb, the *Eksund* seizure and the O'Hare dragnet created widespread alarm that the northern conflict was spilling across the border and threatening the stability of the entire island. Together they were traumatic enough to close off the south to the IRA and Sinn Fein. From that point on expansion was not a possibility; instead, attitudes hardened against the republicans. The republican ambition of having up to five Sinn Fein members holding the balance of power in the Dáil vanished in the month of November 1987.

A telling sign of this new mood came on the day Dessie O'Hare was finally apprehended. Moves to facilitate the extradition of republican suspects from the south to Northern Ireland had proved controversial, with Charles Haughey's government set to block the measure. But on that day Haughey told the Dáil: 'The recent combination of events – the seizure of a massive shipment of arms by the French authorities, the kidnapping of John O'Grady and the slaughter at Enniskillen – bring the whole question of subversive threats to the security of this state into a new and urgent focus. We are not soft on terrorism, domestic or international, and we must give a clear and unequivocal signal to that effect.'

No one knew it at the time, but even as he made the extradition of IRA suspects easier, Haughey was himself in indirect secret contact with the leadership of the republican movement. And within months the man whose Justice Minister feared the IRA might march down O'Connell Street with 1,000 automatic rifles would be sending emissaries to sit across the table from Gerry Adams.

4

THE PERSISTENT
PRIEST

'Anyone unwilling to accept a united Ireland
and wishing to leave would be offered re-settlement grants to permit them to move to Britain'
   – Sinn Fein document, 1987

'They were people who were on a hook and
wanted to get off the hook. It came out very
strongly from Gerry Adams himself that he was
endeavouring to ensure that his children and his
children's children didn't go through that'
   – Southern Irish politician who took part in
a secret meeting with Sinn Fein, 1988

Father Alec Reid, the priest who in 1988 had wept over the body
of a dying British soldier on waste ground in west Belfast, might
have been forgiven for despairing of ever making progress towards
peace. He had worked for years in the Falls Road district, one of
Europe's most dangerous areas, to bring the troubles to an end. Yet
there were more and more bodies on the streets as republicans,
loyalists and the British remained locked in their three-way war.
That day in 1988 was one of the lowest points of the troubles. The
violence was appalling, but the IRA and the other violent groups
were evidently intent on fighting on indefinitely, whatever the cost.
It would take a further six years to achieve the August 1994 ceasefire: when that happened, few realised what a crucial role the
publicity-shy priest had played in the process.

In the late 1980s the gulf between the violent republicans and
the constitutional nationalists seemed unbridgeable, but Father Reid
was endlessly prepared to try to bridge it. He had a gift for over-

coming discouragement, a rare faith in the value of talking and personal encounters, and an unquenchable hope that dialogue might provide a way out.

Born in Tipperary in the Republic, he had arrived in Belfast in 1967, two years before the bloodshed broke out. He was based in Clonard monastery, which is run by the Redemptorist Order in the heart of the Falls. When he arrived the Falls was the poorest part of Belfast; within two years it had become the most violent. The monastery itself was one of the earliest flash-points of the troubles, for loyalists in the neighbouring Shankill and Woodvale districts regard it as an unwelcome bastion of Catholicism and republicanism on their doorsteps. The mean streets surrounding the imposing building became one of the fiercest battlegrounds of August 1969, when the first serious violence broke out.

A Protestant crowd invaded the district, shooting dead a republican youth, destroying almost fifty houses in the adjoining Bombay Street with petrol bombs, and trying to burn down the monastery. Many people were injured in pitched street battles. A Clonard priest later described the scene to an official tribunal: 'I was terribly afraid there was going to be a holocaust and that the whole area was going to be wiped out. I was absolutely convinced that this was an attempt not merely to wipe out the monastery but the whole area. I was really in desperation for help.' He testified that he came across two armed locals, whom he regarded as reliable men, in a lower corridor of the monastery. They told him they would defend the building and, because of the fear of an attack and the absence of police, he gave them permission to stay. He instructed them to use their weapons as a last resort if the monastery was attacked, and then only to fire in the air. The monastery survived August 1969, but the district was scarred both psychologically and physically. Fifty houses lay in ruins, and a high 'peaceline' wall was built to keep the loyalists out. A quarter of a century later that wall, meant as a temporary expedient, was still in place, a lasting monument to division.

The battle of Clonard monastery and Bombay Street was in a real sense the birthplace of the Provisional IRA, which a short time later broke away from the main IRA. One of its first posters featured a phoenix and the slogan 'From the ashes of Bombay Street rose the Provisionals'. The Irish Catholic hierarchy could denounce the IRA as evil terrorists and gunmen who should be shunned; but as Father Reid looked out over the parishioners attending mass in the monastery he knew he was looking at those gunmen, and at their children, their wives and their parents. He also knew this was a district which considered itself under siege, which regarded the loyalists, and later the British army, as tormentors, and the IRA as legitimate and necessary defenders.

For the following quarter of a century Father Reid had to face the reality that he was living in and serving a community of which the IRA was an integral part. Another Catholic priest once explained how people in the ghetto viewed members of the IRA: 'They don't see them as terrorists. They see them as the fellow next door who took their wee lad by the hand to school.' Gerry Adams once said privately: 'The IRA will only be beaten when the wee women on the Falls throw the guns out on to the street.' But to the rest of the world this was an outlaw community, beyond the pale because it was prepared to condone terrorism and to support the men of violence. Father Reid would come to see it as part of his mission to try to persuade the world, against all the odds, that these were decent, self-respecting people who should not be treated as pariahs.

The priest first became known as a man who was prepared to work with the paramilitaries and mediate between them in the deadly feuds which periodically broke out in the republican underworld. In 1975 he helped bring to an end a feud between the INLA and the Official IRA, the rump of the movement left after the Provisionals broke away in 1970. Six people were killed before the dispute was settled.

He also helped end a short but vicious battle between the Official IRA and the Provisionals in 1977. A bomb exploded at an Official republican Easter parade in Belfast, and the Officials accused the Provisionals of planting it. It was in fact a loyalist bomb, but it took some time for this to emerge, and in the meantime Gerry

Adams invited a number of priests to help resolve the crisis. Father Reid made himself available as a 'facilitator', helping to end the feud and in the process striking up a relationship with Adams. They worked closely together during the prison protests which led up to the 1981 hunger strike. Father Reid played a central role in efforts to avert the hunger strike, but in doing so he burned himself out and suffered a nervous breakdown. Later, in 1987, he played a part in ending an internal INLA feud which had led to twelve deaths.

In addition to his mediation work within the republican community, Father Reid worked to bring republicans into contact with the outside world. In the late 1970s he brought two leading Sinn Fein members to meet the Catholic primate of all-Ireland, the late Cardinal Tomas O Fiaich. O Fiaich knew many republicans, coming as he did from Cullyhanna, close to Crossmaglen in south Armagh border territory: but holding formal meetings with the republican movement was a controversial proposition and the contacts took place in secrecy. Father Reid was a regular visitor to Long Kesh prison ministering to republican prisoners there. In 1980 he wrote lengthy letters to the government warning that unless a more lenient regime was introduced republicans could go on hunger strike. In December 1979 and February 1980 he helped arrange meetings between Sinn Fein and the Cardinal. They were a forerunner of later meetings which he would organise between the Cardinal and Gerry Adams. On the surface there seemed little scope for politics and dialogue amid the din of the explosions and the gunfire. Yet beneath the surface things were stirring. The years ahead would be full of violence but they would also hold many talks, most of them taking place in strict secrecy. Though hardly anyone knew it then, a peace process was slowly taking shape.

In the mid-1980s Father Reid arranged for the Cardinal to speak directly to Adams, and the cleric and the Sinn Fein president held a series of private meetings. Adams also met another Catholic bishop, but the hierarchy's foremost political brain, Dr Cahal Daly, would not see him; and of all the bishops Dr Daly was the sharpest critic of violent republicanism.

To many Northern Ireland Protestants, Cardinal O Fiaich was a 'sneaking regarder' (a covert sympathiser) of Sinn Fein and the IRA. His repeated condemnations of IRA violence cut little ice with Unionists, who viewed them in the context of other comments which they saw as backing Sinn Fein policy. On several occasions he called on Britain to declare its intention of leaving Northern Ireland. The fact that he came from south Armagh increased loyalist suspicions. The Rev. Ian Paisley growled: 'He comes from Crossmaglen. You can take him out of Crossmaglen but you can't take Crossmaglen out of him.'

The Cardinal was an unabashed nationalist, but he was very clear in his own mind on the distinction between wanting a united Ireland and trying to achieve that end by force. Cardinal O Fiaich died in May 1990 but in 1986, in an unpublished interview with Eamonn Mallie, one of the authors, he gave an insight into his conversations with the Sinn Fein leader. Asked what he would say to a man like Adams, the Cardinal responded:

> There was a famous phrase used by my predecessor Cardinal Conway – that you can't bomb a million Protestants into a united Ireland. And of course I agree with that and it is morally wrong to try to do so. But I think it's also true – and it's a statement that's very rarely made – that you can't bomb or hold by force half a million nationalists out of a united Ireland. That's a corollary of the other. If the first is a correct statement, and I believe it is, it's also a correct statement to say it's wrong to prevent half a million Catholics from being united with the rest of the country. I basically have always looked upon partition as being almost the worst possible solution, and I don't believe it is ever going to provide a peaceful and happy and satisfactory solution to the Irish problem.
>
> But if I were talking to a man like Gerry Adams I would be inclined to dwell primarily on the difficulty, as I see it, of uniting people by force. I feel there's a contradiction in that – you can unite people by showing your interest in them, by caring for them, by loving them. But you can't unite them by using violence on them. Therefore I would argue with a man like Gerry Adams that, in fact, instead of bringing people together the violence is widening the gap between them.

Even if force should succeed in overthrowing the northern state, and it was forced against its will into a united Ireland, you are simply going to have a continuation of the present situation – except that instead of having republicans in rebellion you are going to have possibly a considerable number of loyalists rebelling. If partition had never been instituted, if we were talking about getting the British out of Ireland, if Ireland were a single entity and you had therefore the vast majority of the people who wanted the British out, then it would be much easier to justify it morally.

But why take the view of the majority within the six counties and give it all the importance, and not give any importance at all to the view of the Irish people as a whole, or even the viewpoint of the people of Britain? They're involved too. If they were in favour of pulling out from Ireland what would be so sacrosanct about the six counties [of Northern Ireland] as an entity?

IRA violence has lost the sympathy of a considerable number down south for the concept of a united Ireland. In the north in 1968–9 when the civil rights movement started, an awful lot of journalists for instance from England, were very sympathetic, and they accepted without any difficulty that the Catholics of the north didn't get fair play with regard to jobs, housing, and all the rest. But now because of the IRA, northern Catholics have lost a considerable amount of the world's sympathy. Probably the only hope of getting the IRA to desist from the campaign of violence is to try to sell the idea, to them and to their supporters, that a united Ireland is attainable – but by peaceful methods and by gradual advance towards it.

As the dialogue between the Cardinal and Adams was going on, Father Reid was meanwhile pressing Fianna Fáil leader Charles Haughey to open a line of contact with the republicans. He sought and received permission from his Redemptorist Order to pursue what now became a one-man peace initiative. He also had the blessing of Cardinal O Fiaich, with a number of other priests involved along the way. Principal among these was his Clonard colleague, Father Gerry Reynolds. Father Reid's approach was explained by Father Raymond Murray, a County Armagh priest who was involved in human rights activities and was a constant critic of the authorities and the security forces. In an interview conducted for this book, Father Murray said of Father Reid:

> His motive was a humanitarian one – bluntly, to stop the killing. He came to Armagh to see me in a mood of great anxiety. He said to me a number of times: 'When you are faced with this problem you must face it in a realistic way. How do you get the republicans to stop the war – what would tip the balance to get the IRA to stop?' His main plan was to help Sinn Fein to gain complete control over the republican movement, and then to build an alliance of nationalist parties, respecting party differences but all working for peace.
>
> Gerry Adams met Father Reid and myself in the Sinn Fein office in Belfast. There was a lot of general discussion and what was emerging was that he would need a high-level meeting with the Irish government, which would act as an authentic proof that a seriousness attached to this, that it wasn't merely ephemeral. That essentially boiled down to a meeting with Haughey. Father Reid was continually putting together position papers on common nationalist grounds that might meet with the approval of three sides – the Irish Government, the SDLP and Sinn Fein – and was continually refining these position papers. The emphasis was on trying to persuade Haughey to meet Adams and thus give the project real credibility.

It was in 1986 that Father Reid's venerable Volkswagen Polo first arrived at Charles Haughey's grand mansion at Kinsealy, north of Dublin. The old Volkswagen and its thin, ascetic, black-clad owner were in stark contrast to the grandeur of Kinsealy with its sweeping lawns and its pheasants. Haughey, then leader of the opposition, greeted his visitor and gave him a flavour of the fine paintings and *objets d'art* which abounded in the sumptuously furnished house. Then they got down to business.

Father Reid made his points in his quiet but insistent low-pitched voice. He said the Catholic church and others could not stand aside and simply condemn the IRA: they had to become involved, to engage them. He spoke of the tragedy and loss of life and human misery he had seen, and said everyone had a duty to intervene to try to end it. He sought to convince the Fianna Fáil leader that, although most people did not believe it, Sinn Fein was actually different from the IRA. He argued: 'Sinn Fein is trying to build a political front – the IRA are at war.'

He said Gerry Adams believed there was a stalemate and that neither the British nor the IRA could win the war. He described Adams and his associates as the most visionary leadership in the history of the republican movement, and argued that Adams possessed a personal strength which should be exploited. The way ahead was to persuade the British government to make a historic statement which would enable Adams to go to the IRA and argue that there was an alternative to violence. Haughey should start the ball rolling by meeting Adams.

Haughey listened with great concentration as the clergyman made his case. He gave the idea of meeting Adams serious consideration, but in the end decided against it. The principal problem with the idea, he concluded, was his own past. In 1970 he had been charged with conspiring to import guns which might have ended up with the IRA. Although he was acquitted of the offence in what became known as 'the arms trial', something of a whiff of sulphur still clung to him. He concluded that meeting Adams, even in secret, was too risky: word might leak, and if it did all the old charges would be dusted off and hurled at him again. It smacked of political suicide, and he would not do it. Father Reid, disappointed, drove dejectedly back north to tell Adams the bad news. Adams, reflecting later on his reasons for wanting to meet Haughey, explained: 'The politics demanded the building of a consensus. Sinn Fein had by that point developed a position which saw dialogue as the main vehicle for resolving this problem. We thought it was an important step for Dublin to meet us. It was required in terms of their persuading us they wanted to move the process forward. It came as no surprise when he didn't meet me. He missed an opportunity which he may have since regretted.' Although Haughey declined to meet Adams, he instructed his adviser on Northern Ireland, Martin Mansergh, to keep in touch with Father Reid. Haughey and Cardinal O Fiaich also from time to time dined together at Kinsealy, and on these occasions the cleric kept the Fianna Fáil leader briefed on his talks with Adams.

Fianna Fáil formed a government in February 1987, with Haughey as Taoiseach. Bertie Ahern, who went on to become leader of Fianna Fáil and was then a senior Cabinet Minister, said later: 'When we returned to government I remember Charlie talking about connections and movements and views within republicanism, things that would move things on. I remember Father Reid's name being mentioned. I was aware that on the public surface it seemed there was no official contact between the government and Sinn Fein, but Charlie always knew what Adams was thinking about, and on what road he was moving.'

In the spring of 1987 Reid opened a new avenue of contact by writing to John Hume asking him to consider meeting Adams. For advice Hume turned to one of his aides, Mark Durkan. Durkan, a former student leader, worked full-time in Hume's Londonderry office and had become party chairman. Although he was one of the youngest of the party's activists, his considerable political talents meant he was often spoken of as a possible successor to Hume as party leader. Durkan and Denis Haughey, a veteran SDLP official also based in Hume's office, and Hume's astute wife Pat formed a kind of unofficial 'kitchen cabinet' for the SDLP leader. Durkan advised Hume to be careful, since a British general election was in the offing.

Durkan met Father Reid, and said later: 'Father Reid spoke in gospel terms, spoke of people being treated as lepers, spoke of how Jesus had always been prepared to speak to everybody. He said he believed intensely that the church couldn't simply hide behind condemnation of the IRA, and added, "Nor of course can you people." ' Hume waited until the election had taken place, in June of that year, before meeting Father Reid. The priest said he believed dialogue should take place with Sinn Fein, saying that his contacts with the republican movement had led him to sense that changes were taking place within it. Hume had a series of meetings in Belfast, Londonderry and Donegal with Father Reid, before agreeing to his request to meet Adams face to face.

Hume's decision to go ahead was, in retrospect, a historic one. It was the beginning of an extraordinary relationship between the two dominant figures in northern nationalism, two figures who have already, in very different ways, left their mark on Irish history. The two were direct rivals for the nationalist vote; indeed they were rivals for the leadership of the nationalist north, and their parties contested many hard-fought battles. Yet through all the bruising conflicts the two men forged a personal relationship of some trust, and came to develop a sense of pursuing a common purpose.

Hume and Adams had a series of meetings, agreeing that their parties should meet formally in 1988. The detailed arrangements were left to be worked out between Father Reid and Durkan. Hume had had contacts with the IRA and Sinn Fein dating back to the early 1970s and was no stranger to republican personalities or the republican mind-set. He had been closely involved in arranging an IRA ceasefire in 1972, but his most recent public brush with the IRA had been singularly unproductive. It had taken place in February 1985, following a radio confrontation with Adams. When Adams put it to Hume that he should meet Sinn Fein, the SDLP leader replied that he was prepared to talk to those who really made the decisions in the republic movement, the IRA army council, in order to ask them to stop their violence. Within days the army council issued a public invitation to Hume and, amid a chorus of condemnation from Unionist politicians and others, he agreed to a meeting.

On a Friday evening Hume was collected from his Londonderry home and driven a considerable distance to an unknown location. He was kept there for twenty-eight hours, then informed the meeting was about to take place. Moments before it was due to start he was told it would be filmed. He then met three persons, one of whom described himself as a spokesman for the IRA. Hume said he did not approve of this, pointing out that he would have no control over any future use of the material. The spokesman then said: 'Then the meeting is off.' Hume arrived back at his home in the early hours of Sunday morning.

The IRA issued a statement saying it believed the SDLP leader had been engaged in a propaganda exercise to avoid the issue of talking to Sinn Fein. It added: 'There was never any peace initiative. Genuine peace initiatives have to confront the British government and have to be based on British disengagement and national self-determination.' Hume responded: 'Since the IRA has now confirmed beyond any shadow of doubt that they believe that only an "armed struggle" can solve the problems of this community, there is no point whatsoever in discussing politics with their political wing.'

Two years on from this unpromising precedent Hume and Adams committed themselves to trying again. Since the fiasco of 1985 there had been several important developments. The Anglo-Irish Agreement had changed much of the political landscape. Bombs were still going off, but Sinn Fein was thinking in a political way. While many viewed their entry into politics as a dangerous development, Hume was intent on seeing whether the positive aspect of this trend could be encouraged and exploited. Besides, Sinn Fein had by this stage established itself as a part of the political landscape too sizeable to be ignored: in the Westminster election of June 1987, for example, Adams had retained his West Belfast seat and the party as a whole collected 83,000 votes.

Several different and contradictory themes had become evident in republican pronouncements. The IRA was as belligerent as ever, promising menacingly that its campaign would go on until Britain agreed to leave Ireland. In some ways, Sinn Fein's political stand seemed as hard-line as ever: for example, the only hopeful feature about its May 1987 policy document, 'Scenario for Peace', was its title, for its contents offered little sign of any new approach. The document did not depart in any significant way from the standard republican 'Brits Out' demand, defining the conflict as a struggle against colonialism. Much of it was little more than a wish-list: Britain should depart, but before doing so it should disband the locally raised security forces, the RUC and Ulster Defence Regiment, and disarm their members. All republican prisoners were to be unconditionally released.

Sinn Fein assured Protestants that their rights would be respected in a new Ireland, but there was little sign that the republicans had thought seriously about the Unionist position. It even offered to facilitate the repatriation of Unionists: 'Anyone unwilling to accept a united Ireland and wishing to leave would be offered re-settlement grants to permit them to move to Britain.' This might have proved insulting to Protestants, but since few of them bothered to read 'Scenario for Peace' none really took offence.

The document laid out that Britain, after withdrawing, should pay reparations – substantial sums of money to atone for the wrongs it had done the Irish. The scenario for peace looked, in short, very much like a scenario for surrender by Britain, and seemed to confirm that republicans continued to pin their hopes on eventual victory over the British. Adams, however, was clearly applying his flexible mind to reassessing the position. As early as 1979 he had told republicans he believed their aims could not be achieved by military means alone. In 1980 he said the British realised there could not be a military victory, but added it was time republicans realised it too. He later wrote:

> While Irish republicans could prevent a settlement on British government terms, we lacked the political strength to bring the struggle to a decisive conclusion. Military solutions were not an option for either side. The conflict had been militarised by the British, but it remained essentially political and demanded a political solution. Republicans could block British strategy, could survive a long stalemate, but the political goals of republicanism meant we needed to do much more than either of these things if our struggle was to be successful. For our part we needed to consider how a negotiated settlement could be secured and how we could further our objectives in this light. If we were serious in our search for a settlement, we needed to engage our opponents, our rivals and our enemies in debate on these matters and especially so on the issue of peace.

This line of thought led him on to think in terms of a 'broad front' of nationalists to put concerted pressure on the British.

A republican source commented: 'The weakness with the struggle wasn't in its armed militarisation – it was in its lack of politics. What we decided to do was to go on a political offensive to engage our opponents about peace.' A former prisoner added: 'Our own assessment was that military struggle could take us so far, but it couldn't deliver long-term peace or a real settlement.' It was from this perspective that Adams and Sinn Fein made approaches to almost all points of the political compass, even making overtures to Unionist and Protestant church sources. There were many rebuffs, and in almost all the meetings which did take place there was no endorsement for the republican contention that the way ahead was to use violence to force a British withdrawal.

So although there were some small signs of fresh thinking within republicanism, there were many statements of the old hard-line position, and the violence continued without let-up. It was therefore highly risky for Hume to contemplate talking to Adams, since past experience had shown he could expect a barrage of criticism for doing so.

Although the two leaders differed fundamentally in their analysis of the problem, and above all disagreed on the methods for resolving it, they actually had a considerable amount in common in their backgrounds. Hume, like Adams, came from a Catholic working-class background, from a family which was not well off. Born in Londonderry in 1937, one of a family of seven squashed into a two-bedroomed house, his father fought with the British army in France in the First World War. He was later unemployed for many years. The family had little money for education, but Hume passed the 11–plus examination, which provided free grammar school education, in its first year of existence.

He attended St Columb's grammar school in Londonderry and then Maynooth College in the Republic, where for several years he trained as a priest. He became a teacher, then went full-time into self-help community projects such as the Credit Union. He married a local girl, Pat, and had five children. He came to public prominence with the emergence of the civil rights movement in the late 1960s, always on the moderate side of the many arguments within the movement and always advocating a peaceful and non-confrontational approach.

Years later Douglas Gageby, a former editor of the *Irish Times*, encapsulated in a short letter Hume's role in defusing many tense situations in those often fraught times. He wrote: 'Many years ago my wife Dorothy and I were observing the progress of a large civil rights crowd across Craigavon bridge in Derry. [Nationalists refer to the city not as Londonderry but as Derry.] On the west side we were stopped by the RUC. A young man in a check jacket turned round and motioned us all to sit down. He went forward to speak to the police. I was told his name was John Hume. He was unperturbed, cool and steady. I will never get that picture out of my mind. The demonstrators on the bridge, the wall of police and the young man crossing the open space on his own.'

Nineteen seventy saw the launch of the Social Democratic and Labour party, bringing together in one organisation almost all sections of non-violent Catholic and nationalist opinion. The party's first leader was Gerry (later Lord) Fitt, but from the start everyone was aware that Hume, his deputy, was its chief strategist. He went on to become party leader in 1979.

His unique feature was his ability to combine theory with practical politics. He was foremost in challenging the traditional nationalist assertion that the root of the problem was the British presence in Northern Ireland. He argued that the heart of the Irish question was not the British but the Protestants; that the problem was the divisions between Unionist and nationalist; and that partition was not the cause of division but a symptom of it. The historic mission of nationalism, he argued, was not to drive out the British but to convince Unionism that its concerns could be accommodated in a new agreed Ireland.

He successfully fended off the challenge from Sinn Fein, maintaining the SDLP as the principal party of northern nationalism. He also built up an international reputation as a man of non-violence and an opponent of the IRA. He accumulated a considerable amount of clout outside Northern Ireland, especially in the Republic and, as a European MP, on the continent. In particular he wielded great influence in Washington, where powerful Irish–American figures such as Senator Edward Kennedy looked to him for advice and guidance. A bronze bust of Kennedy's brother, the late President John F. Kennedy, has pride of place in Hume's Donegal retreat, overlooking the waters of Lough Foyle.

Hume was the most influential nationalist politician in Northern Ireland and indeed one of the most important political figures on the island of Ireland. He had access to sources of power that no Northern Ireland politician had ever reached before. As 1988 opened he embarked on a mission to reach out to the republican movement.

On a sunny morning early in 1988 an elderly black taxi chugged its way up the steep hill to St Gerard's, a retreat house run by Father Reid's Redemptorist Order. St Gerard's sits above Belfast's Antrim Road on the northern outskirts of the city, on an imposing site with sweeping views of Belfast lough and the rolling County Down countryside beyond. Its elevation helps give visitors a sense of being above the fray, even though it is only a mile or so from the deadly sectarian battlefields of north Belfast.

The taxi drew to a halt and out stepped Gerry Adams and three other senior Sinn Fein members. One was Mitchel McLaughlin, the one-time refrigeration engineer who had become one of the republican movement's leading intellectual forces, and who lived a stone's throw away from Hume in Londonderry's Bogside.

Another was Danny Morrison, the gifted propagandist whose name would be linked for ever with the phrase 'the Armalite and the ballot box'. Morrison was a man of many parts. A former internee, he was one of the group led by Adams which had wrested control of the movement from the O Bradaigh old guard. The fact that he was generally affable and pleasant but also had a quick temper earned him two very different nicknames – 'Smiler', because of his ready grin, and 'Bangers', because on his first day behind the wire in Long Kesh he was involved in a fight with another internee. He had contested a number of elections for Sinn Fein, in one instance coming within seventy-eight votes of a Westminster seat. He listened to Mozart and Schubert, read Tolstoy and Dostoev-sky, and wrote two novels about life in west Belfast. Within two years he would be arrested next door to the house where an IRA team was holding an informer. He was later jailed, the judge describing him as clever and astute but untruthful.

The third member of the team, Tom Hartley, was another key theorist who has held a series of senior positions within Sinn Fein and had two short spells in prison. His brooding and occasionally morose personality earned him the nickname of 'Hate the world' in republican circles; his brusqueness on the telephone led the children of one journalist to christen him 'Billy Goat Gruff'. Hartley's facial characteristics changed constantly over the years: at some stages he was clean-shaven; at others he sported a moustache reminiscent of Stalin; sometimes he affected a Karl Marx-style beard.

John Hume's team arrived at the retreat house in private cars. With him was Seamus Mallon, the MP for Newry-South Armagh and deputy leader of the party. Mallon was a skilled debater and public speaker but his relations with Hume had sometimes been difficult: Hume made many 'solo runs' in politics and Mallon often felt excluded. In debate he had a tendency to lecture, and to take no prisoners in argument. Also on the team was Sean Farren, an economics lecturer who was one of Hume's closest confidants in the party and who had served as party chairman for five years. The SDLP team was completed by Austin Currie who had been close to Hume ever since the 1960s, when both were prominent in the civil rights movement. The following year he would leave the SDLP and join the Fine Gael party in the south, going on to become a minister in Dublin. In an interview for this book Currie recalled that first meeting:

> There was a certain amount of tension at the beginning. It was a very sparse room, and there was nobody in the chair; we sat opposite each other at the table. Father Reid was present and just before the meeting started he sat down at the table and invited us to join him in prayer. He prayed to the effect that he wished God's blessing on our deliberations, and he himself added that he

thought it important that there should be a degree of unity between the parties of the nationalist tradition. He then withdrew.

I hadn't met any of the others apart from Adams, once during the hunger strike, and I had a certain amount of apprehension. We had coffee before we started, and there was no intrusion from the outside between that and lunch-time. The thrust of our dialogue was essentially building on the argument, which we had been making publicly since the Anglo-Irish Agreement, that the British were now neutral on the question of remaining in Ireland. Sinn Fein challenged that, of course.

We went on from that basic point to point to the futility of violence. We said violence was demonstrably futile – the British were no nearer to leaving Ireland than on the first day shots had been fired at them, and in fact it was reinforcing division. These were what you might call the classic SDLP arguments.

Sinn Fein had, as I understand it, two immediate objectives. One was to identify a number of practical local objectives on which the two parties could co-operate. Fair employment was one they suggested, but we made it clear that even on those more immediate social and economic issues there could not be any co-operation as long as the IRA campaign continued and as long as Sinn Fein was condoning or endorsing it. Their second, more important objective, which I suppose had been implied by Father Reid's opening reference, was the creation of a broad agreement, a broad front, across the nationalist family, the nationalist parties in Ireland. Again, we in the SDLP would not go along with that, or even consider it, as long as the campaign of violence continued. So in a sense you could say that for the rest of that meeting, and the subsequent meetings, we were almost logjammed from the start.

The main point on which we felt that we could begin to make any real contact with them was on one phrase that we had identified in their document 'Scenario for Peace'. It referred to the wishes of people indigenous to, or domiciled in, the island of Ireland. And that in a sense was the embryo from which the thinking on self-determination would evolve in the future. We picked that out of their document as something on which we might be able to build some kind of common understanding.

We were saying the British were disengaging – it was no longer in the British interest to stay. They didn't accept that because there wasn't sufficient movement, and it was clear something from the British side was necessary. We sought to persuade them that there was a political way ahead, that the continuation of their campaign was self-defeating, that the British wanted to go anyhow – that the job we had to do was to persuade the Unionist people that their future lay in an agreed Ireland.

The proposition the SDLP was putting forward was what Sinn Fein later agreed to – that the IRA should give up their violent campaign, that they should embrace the constitutional way forward. I had no doubt that Adams wanted an alternative strategy: I got the impression from both him and McLaughlin that they wanted an alternative.

The meeting was one of a series which stretched on throughout 1988, before coming to an end in September. The two parties took the exercise seriously, exchanging a series of detailed policy papers. The lengthy debate went to the heart of the differences between violent republicanism and constitutional nationalism. One of the major themes of the exchanges concerned the nature of the British presence, an issue which was to be much debated in the years that followed. Sinn Fein argued that the British presence was colonialist and imperialist: Hume responded that Britain was actually neutral and agnostic on the question of Irish unity. This was much more than a purely academic point. The IRA was fighting what it characterised as an anti-colonialist war. If it could be shown that the basis of the British presence was not colonialist or imperialist, this would invalidate the republican justification for prosecuting their 'armed struggle'. It would show that the main conflict was not, as Adams argued, between 'the liberation forces and the occupation forces'.

Sinn Fein produced a document, 'Towards a Strategy for Peace', which was more detailed than its 'Scenario for Peace' document of a year earlier. It argued strongly that the British presence was malign because it continued to be based on Britain's own self-interests.

It declared:

Given the lengths to which Britain goes to remain here and indeed to consolidate its position, one can only conclude that it believes it is in its interests to maintain the union, to finance the union, to let its soldiers die for the union, to be internationally scandalised at times for the union. Britain's actions totally contradict SDLP claims that Britain somehow is now neutral since the signing of the Treaty [i.e. the Anglo-Irish Agreement].

Britain's continuing involvement in Ireland is based on strategic, economic and political interests. Strategic interests are now the most important consideration in Britain's interference in Ireland. Quite apart from the very real, if somewhat exaggerated, fear among the British establishment that an Ireland freed from British influence could become a European Cuba, even the prospect of a neutral Ireland is regarded as a serious threat to British, and NATO's, strategic interests.

Although the annual British subvention to the north is £1.6 billion-plus, it would be wrong to conclude that this level of spending negates any British economic interest in Ireland. British involvement in Ireland serves a wider role in securing the interests of Britain's multi-national capitalist allies from the potential or perceived threat posed by an independent Irish state.

Though less important than strategic or economic considerations, there remains a significant historical and political commitment on the part of the British establishment to the union. This stems from Britain's historical role as an imperial power and an inherent reluctance to see either its territories or its influence diminished. There is also – particularly within the Conservative party – a political loyalty to the union, if not to the Unionists themselves.

Hume replied by pointing to Article 1 of the Anglo-Irish Agreement, with its formal declaration that, if a majority in Northern Ireland wished to have a united Ireland, Britain would support that wish. He declared: 'Britain has no interest of her own in remaining in Ireland. She has no strategic, military or economic interests and if Irish people reached agreement among themselves on, for example, Irish unity, then Britain would facilitate it, legislate for it and leave the Irish to govern themselves.' In other words, Hume was telling the republicans that they were fighting the wrong battle.

The republican argument was that the only solution was the ending of partition, British disengagement from Ireland, and the restoration to the Irish people of 'their right to sovereignty, independence and national self-determination'. The demand for self-determination would be achieved, they predicted, 'when the will of the British government to remain in Ireland will be eroded'.

Hume responded that the strategy of trying to drive Britain out, even if successful, could result in chaos. He declared:

> This route is the route of maximum risk. In such a vacuum the likelihood is that the British army would become inactive. In the knowledge that their government has decided to withdraw all responsibility, does anyone think that soldiers would be prepared to risk their lives? Each section of the community would seize its own territory and we would have a Cyprus or Lebanon-style formula for permanent division and bloodshed.
>
> What would the 12,000 armed members of the RUC do? What would the 8,000 armed members of the Ulster Defence Regiment do? Is it not likely and natural, in the emotionally charged atmosphere that would obtain, and in the absence of any acknowledged authority, that they would simply identify with the community from which most of them come and become its military defenders? And what would happen to the Catholic community in such circumstances, particularly in those areas where they are most vulnerable? Is the risk involved in such a military policy not an awesome one, and likely to ensure that the peace and unity of Ireland will never come?

Adams addressed this point by arguing that an irreversible intent by the British to withdraw would minimise any loyalist backlash 'and would go a long way towards bringing around to reality most loyalists and their representatives genuinely interested in peace and negotiation'.

During the talks Sinn Fein suggested that they and the SDLP should together accept 'the internationally established principle of the right of the Irish people to self-determination'. Republicans had used the phrase 'national self-determination' so often that it had come to be regarded as 'Provo-speak', and there was some surprise when Hume readily endorsed the view that the Irish people as a whole had the right to national self-determination. He also offered a route into politics for Sinn Fein: if IRA violence ended, he suggested, the Irish government could establish a conference of all parties to reach agreement on self-determination. If Unionists refused to attend it, the nationalist parties would seek agreement among themselves: the republicans would thus gain entry to the political processes.

The formal meetings ended in September 1988, both sides saying they regretted not reaching agreement in the talks. But Hume, in a statement to the media, used some of the language which six years later would help bring about the 1994 ceasefire: 'The Irish people as a whole have the right to national self-determination, but since there is a very deep division among the people of this island as to how that right is to be exercised, it is the search for agreement on the exercise of that right that is the real search for peace.'

The formal talks were brought to a close without agreement, but private meetings between Adams and Hume would continue. Adams wanted to keep talking to Hume; Hume believed seeds had been sown in the talks, and wanted to cultivate them. Durkan noted 'a genuine chemistry' between the two. Hume said later: 'I remember the seriousness of the talks, and noticing how my points struck them – not so much by anything they would say, but how they were clearly taking points on board. I think that for the first time, sitting face to face, they realised that we believed in what we were saying, that there was a rationality and a logic to what was being said to them. I said, "You wouldn't run a corner shop today the way it was run in 1912 or 1916 – times have changed, the nature of the problem has changed." ' The formal talks had been conducted in the glare of publicity, against a background of criticism from British and Unionist politicians and, often, of violence. There had been much ritual restatement of positions but neither had given ground on any major point. It suited both men for their future talks to be conducted privately.

One of the best-kept secrets from this time was the fact that, unknown to the outside world, the Dublin government opened its own parallel direct contacts with republican leaders. Before the 1988 SDLP–Sinn Fein talks, Hume informed Haughey of his intention to meet Adams, and Haughey had given his approval. But secretly he went further, sending his own emissaries to meet Sinn Fein. The key man in this contact was Haughey's principal adviser on Anglo-Irish relations and the north, Martin Mansergh.

Mansergh, who would play a key role at many points in the developing peace process, is one of the most unusual and apparently incongruous characters in Irish politics. He was close both to Haughey and his successor, Albert Reynolds, and is known as a passionate and committed nationalist and non-violent republican. Yet he is a Protestant, English-born and Oxford-educated, speaking with a distinct English accent.

His father, Nicholas, was an influential Irish historian, and Mansergh himself holds a doctorate in pre-revolutionary French history. He began his career as a diplomat in the Irish Department of Foreign Affairs but was talent-spotted by Haughey and persuaded to leave government service to work directly for the Fianna Fáil party. Described as reclusive and painfully shy, he has a reputation as one of the most astute analysts in Dublin.

An exuberant description of him is given in a fascinating and informative 1995 book by Sean Duignan, one of Irish broadcasting's most respected political journalists, who served as Reynolds's government press secretary and kept a diary of events which he published under the title *One Spin on the Merry-go-round*. Duignan wrote: 'Fianna Fáil positively delighted in their very own Protestant republican, complete with distinguished Anglo-Irish pedigree and Oxford honours. They might joke about him being a cross between Dr Strangelove and Dr Mengele – "Mansergh pronounced as in Panzer" – but they would brook no criticism of him by outsiders.'

Mansergh had kept in touch with Father Reid, and was now chosen by Haughey to act as his chief contact with Sinn Fein. Haughey also involved in the exercise Fianna Fáil deputy Dermot Ahern, who is today a senior party figure but who was then a young and inexperienced member of the Dáil. Ahern, a solicitor, represented the border town of Dundalk, which though just south of the border had been much affected by the troubles – in the 1970s so many IRA men on the run ended up there that it was nicknamed 'El Paso'.

Ahern had represented Fianna Fáil at a number of conferences in 1987, but he was surprised when the phone rang in his Dáil office on a Friday evening and he was summoned to Haughey's office. In an interview for this book he recalled:

I went into the office and he explained to me that he had been asked by Father Reid of Clonard monastery to in effect mirror what John Hume was doing at the time. He added that Cardinal O Fiaich was involved in the request to him. He said he had been asked by the priest to set up a meeting with Sinn Fein in the Republic so that they could be given a southern nationalist perspective from Fianna Fáil. He asked me to take part in this.

He explained that two other people would be with me, Martin Mansergh and another Fianna Fáil member, though not a politician. But he explained that because of the sensitivities of it, if it ever came out that meetings were going on then, in effect, I would be on my own. I didn't give him any commitment one way or the other. I told him I would think about it over the weekend and get back to him. After speaking to people over the weekend I felt that I had a duty to do it. I went back to Haughey and agreed to do it, but I said to him: 'You said to me I'd be out on my own, but yet Mansergh will be with me. Surely if anything comes out people will say Haughey must have known what was happening because Martin Mansergh was part of it?'

His response to me was: 'We'll be able to get over that one.' A meeting was arranged shortly afterwards in the Redemptorist monastery in Dundalk, and I attended. When I drove up to it I didn't really know what I was supposed to do other than to go to the monastery. I think it was 11 o'clock on a Monday morning – I drove up and looked for cars and I couldn't see any, though I do recall that there was a Special Branch car outside the monastery grounds. They obviously knew something was happening – I don't know how they knew, whether they were following people or whether they were told to be there.

I was met by a priest who brought me to a waiting room. I didn't recognise the priest: I got the impression that he wasn't from the Dundalk monastery. I was brought into a waiting room and shortly after that Martin Mansergh and this other man came along and we were brought to a larger room by the priest.

We were now in a typical monastery room – a wood-panelled

room with a large table, with nothing on it. Shortly thereafter Gerry Adams, Pat Doherty and Mitchel McLaughlin arrived into the room and we were introduced. [Pat Doherty, one of the most senior figures in the republican movement, was born in Scotland of Irish parents. He moved to Ireland in the late 1960s.]

There was very little small talk, and then we sat down. We sat on one side of the table and they sat on the other and the priest that was with us said: 'I'll be leaving you in a minute but I'd just like you to pause a moment for a short prayer to help you in your deliberations.' I remember during the prayer I felt it was very eerie in the way it was being done, but I was very conscious that it was a momentous occasion because it was obviously top secret.

It was obviously being done in effect to try and convince Sinn Fein and those that they represented that Irish nationalism had moved on since 1918. I felt that we were able to get across the view that Ireland had moved on, that the feeling in the Republic had progressed in such a way that people realised that there was a section of the population on the island [the Unionists] who, no matter what happened, had to be accommodated and their views had to be taken into account. The talks lasted around two hours. Most of the talking was done by Adams and Mansergh.

Adams made a point of stressing to Mansergh that the IRA was not in the business of attacking the southern state, and that the fears of Fianna Fáil Justice Minister Gerry Collins, who had spoken of his nightmare of finding 1,000 automatic rifles being paraded down O'Connell Street, were groundless. In a lecture Mansergh later reported what Adams and the other republicans said:

The point was made that northern nationalists were alienated from Dublin. They claimed that if British troops were stationed in Dundalk the popular reaction would be the same as in the north. They needed an alternative political strategy, if violence were to stop. The view was expressed that the Anglo–Irish Agreement was not worth the candle, as the cost of the provocation of Unionists was not commensurate with any substantial gain. We naturally stressed the total unacceptability of violence to the people of the south, and pointed out that it was the single most potent divisive factor weakening Irish nationalism, with northern nationalists, nationalists north and south, and the Irish–American community all divided on the question of the legitimacy of violence, thus preventing a political combination for electoral or other purposes.*

Interestingly, Fianna Fáil stopped short of endorsing Hume's argument that Britain was neutral, believing that Britain had an interest in preserving the unity of the United Kingdom, particularly at times when the question of a measure of self-government for Scotland was on the British political agenda.

Mansergh and Ahern held only two sessions of talks with Sinn Fein, in March and June of 1988. Haughey brought the meetings to a close because he concluded that there was no real chance, at that point, of the IRA being persuaded to call off its campaign. Like Hume, he was not interested in forming any alliance or broad front with Sinn Fein while IRA violence continued. But although the talks ended Father Reid remained as a channel of communication.

In one sense the Dundalk meetings could be written off as encounters which had no positive outcome. Adams had been given the chance to come face to face with Mansergh, who reported back directly to Haughey: yet nothing he said was intriguing or interesting enough to persuade the Taoiseach to maintain and develop the dialogue. Yet on another level Adams had conveyed the strong impression that he meant business. Thus Ahern was left with this abiding memory of the talks:

All during the discussions it was quite obvious to me that Adams, Doherty and McLaughlin were people who were on a hook and wanted to get off the hook, while at the same time not giving on the core principles they felt very strongly about. One of the things that I think convinced us was something which came out very strongly from Gerry Adams himself: that he was going into his forties [Adams's fortieth birthday was in October 1988], that he'd seen nothing but violence from his early life. He was endeavouring to ensure that his children and his children's children

*Paper read by Dr Martin Mansergh at international symposium, University of Rennes, 16 September 1995.

didn't go through that in the years ahead. I got the impression that he and the others could see that the violent campaign was not progressing the cause of Irish republicanism or nationalism.

But I was never convinced, and we were never convinced, that he and the others had the wherewithal to stop the atrocities. We felt that while their intentions were good in that regard they just were not able to convince the people who were pulling the triggers or planting the bombs to stop.

Ahern was right in sensing the tensions within republicanism. As we shall see, the signs are he was correct in his judgement that Adams and his close associates were genuine in seeking a way out of the violence. But he was also correct in questioning their ability to persuade the gunmen and bombers to stop: the events of 1994–96 would show that a halt was achieved, but that it did not last.

By the end of 1988 Sinn Fein had been in contact with the Dublin government, the head of the Catholic church and the SDLP, representing most of the source of power and influence in nationalist Ireland. In republican eyes the fact that such meetings had taken place was itself significant, yet the net result of the encounters was not particularly encouraging.

Cardinal O Fiaich had told them that while partition had been a disaster, the use of force to remove it was morally wrong, and would probably create a Protestant mirror-image of the IRA. Both he and Fianna Fáil had stressed that violence was counter-productive. John Hume had agreed that the Irish people had the right to self-determination, but he and the others would clearly never condone the use of violence. The IRA campaign, he argued, could result in Lebanon-style chaos. He had agreed to maintain a private dialogue with Adams but his party, like Fianna Fáil, plainly had no intention of forming public alliances or broad fronts with Sinn Fein.

Thus contacts had been made, but most had been in secret and the continuing violence ensured that Sinn Fein officially remained political outcasts. The broad front of which Adams had often spoken was not coming together, and even those prepared to enter into dialogue with him showed no sign of adopting the republican agenda he was putting forward. Adams said later that the most important outcome of the talks was 'that John Hume and I kept talking. We kept talking before and we kept talking afterwards.' Over the next few years the fighting would continue, but so too would the talking.

5

BRITISH
INTENTIONS

'The British government has no selfish strategic
or economic interest in Northern Ireland'
– former Northern Ireland Secretary Peter
Brooke

'Nothing I say should be interpreted as condemnation of the IRA. As I remind them of
their responsibilities, I salute them as freedom
fighters'
– Gerry Adams

'I believe the violence could be ended, as far as
the nationalist side is concerned, within any
given six-month period, provided it were
handled properly'
– Father Alec Reid

It was not only Adams and Hume who kept talking in the years
after 1988. The Unionist parties, which in the wake of the Anglo-
Irish Agreement had boycotted political talks, gradually relaxed
their prohibitions on discussions, opening the way for a number of
contacts, some overt and some clandestine, to take place. One
of the most unusual, which was never revealed to the public in any
detail, took place between Charles Haughey and Unionist elements.
It came about when the Fianna Fáil leader and Taoiseach explored
the possibility of doing business with the then Ulster Unionist party
leader, James Molyneaux.

It was never a particularly promising avenue, since Molyneaux
was dedicated to strengthening Northern Ireland's links with Britain
while Haughey's ambition was to loosen them. But Haughey had

expressed interest in finding some alternative to the Anglo-Irish Agreement, and Molyneaux certainly wished to replace it with something else. The optimistic theory developed that something might be built on this tenuous area of possible common ground.

Haughey tried by several routes to reach Molyneaux, making approaches through a senior Church of Ireland figure and through Quaker contacts. He also sent Mansergh, only months after his secret meetings with Adams, to London for private talks with Enoch Powell, the former Unionist MP who was Molyneaux's mentor. Mansergh the passionate nationalist and Powell the quintessential Unionist had two sessions of talks which were described as long and animated discussions, Mansergh urging a direct meeting between Haughey and Molyneaux. Haughey was encouraged when, during an illness in 1989, Molyneaux wrote to him wishing him a speedy recovery; but in the event personal courtesy did not extend to political common ground, and after several meetings the Mansergh–Powell dialogue proved unproductive.

One Dublin source described the exercise as 'a sort of courtly minuet at a distance', adding: 'What we were trying to achieve was the opening of direct communication between Haughey and Molyneaux. There was an idea to meet, maybe in Britain or further afield. It nearly came about but then there was a leak in the *Irish Times* which blocked it.'

Haughey was at this stage a major disappointment to Sinn Fein. He was leader of the greenest and most nationalist of southern parties, and he personally was probably the most nationalist individual in the ranks of his party. But after the experimental 1988 contacts with the republicans he saw little value in continuing them.

Instead, he placed more and more store on the Anglo-Irish Agreement. Although he had originally opposed the Agreement in 1985, when he was in opposition, in office he carefully maintained it. Both London and Dublin saw it as a valuable instrument. The accord helped keep Anglo-Irish relations on an even keel, especially during the occasionally difficult periods when the south disapproved of aspects of British security policy, or when London was critical of Dublin's extradition arrangements. The Agreement was especially useful in soothing and regulating the potentially explosive relationship between Margaret Thatcher and Charles Haughey, two leaders who plainly did not care for each other. A senior diplomatic source said: 'I've seen the notes on their meetings together. With one slight exception, which was a little difficult [a diplomatically couched reference to the 'diatribe' delivered by Mrs Thatcher in March 1981], they've all been relatively sober and businesslike – respectful on both sides, no pretence at tremendous affection, but a sense that "we have a common operation going, let's get on with it." '

Republicans, who instinctively preferred to see London and Dublin at odds with each other, thus watched uneasily as relations grew steadily more ordered and composed. Haughey represented their best chance of establishing a broad front with other nationalist parties, but to Sinn Fein's dismay he was plainly more concerned with his relationship with Britain than with building bridges to them.

The obstacle to Haughey doing business with Adams was quite plain: the violence. Had Adams been in a position to halt the IRA campaign, even on a temporary basis, the situation might have been transformed. But although there were occasional reports that the IRA might consider a ceasefire, these were repeatedly and firmly denied by both Sinn Fein and the IRA. On one typical occasion an IRA spokesman said: 'We can state absolutely, on the record, that there will be no ceasefire, no truce, no cessation of violence short of a British withdrawal. That, as blunt as that, is our position. Having said that, should the British government at any stage genuinely seek dialogue, then we are more than willing to engage in dialogue with them.'

One useful point of contact for the republicans was removed from the scene with the death of Cardinal Tomas O Fiaich in May 1990. Though he was a stern critic of IRA violence he had been prepared to meet privately with Gerry Adams, who caused a stir by attending his funeral. O Fiaich, the old-style gut nationalist, was replaced as head of the Irish church by the more cerebral Dr Cahal Daly. This was a set-back for Sinn Fein, since the new Cardinal was the hierarchy's most unambiguous and trenchant critic of the republican movement.

O Fiaich had several times called for Britain to say it was withdrawing from Ireland; Daly, in sharp contrast, was one of the leading voices on that wing of nationalism which saw the Protestants and not the British presence as the real problem. According to one admirer of Dr Daly: 'He has a philosophical basis for opposing the violence. He sees the government as being a lawfully constituted government and democracy. The Thomist conditions [as specified by Thomas Aquinas] for any sort of violence do not exist, therefore it's evil and it's wrong. He and Gerry Adams are engaged in a public dialogue for hearts and minds – Cahal might say souls. They're competing.' Despite repeated public challenges from Adams, Daly would not meet Sinn Fein representatives.

But although the leader of the Catholic church in Ireland was perceived as taking a sterner line towards the republicans, out on the ground Father Reid was still trying to make progress. In one venture he was instrumental, in great secrecy, in bringing together a collection of northern politicians in West Germany. Those present in the town of Duisburg included members of the SDLP, the Ulster Unionists, the Rev. Ian Paisley's Democratic Unionists and the Alliance party. The purpose of the meeting was to break the talks stalemate, for Unionists were still insisting they would not enter formal discussions unless the Anglo-Irish Agreement was suspended, but they failed to lead to a breakthrough.

The republican sense of isolation was increased in the autumn of 1988 when Mrs Thatcher responded to an upsurge in IRA violence by banning Sinn Fein from the airwaves. From then on Adams could not be heard making his arguments: his words were either spoken by an actor or, on occasion, appeared as sub-titles at the bottom of the screen. This attracted much criticism from human rights groups, but Sinn Fein acknowledged that in practical terms it harmed their propaganda efforts.

By early 1989 the IRA campaign was causing so many civilian casualties that Gerry Adams, speaking at the Sinn Fein ard-fheis in January of that year, stood at the Mansion House podium and appealed to IRA volunteers: 'At times the fate of this struggle is in your hands. You have to be careful and careful again. The morale of your comrades in jail, your own morale and of your comrades in the field, can be raised or dashed by your actions. You can advance or retard the struggle. Nothing I say should be interpreted as condemnation of the IRA. As I remind them of their responsibilities, I salute them as freedom fighters.'

The accidental deaths which led to Adams's appeal to the volunteers to be careful brought home the lesson that civilian casualties were an inevitable consequence of the expanded campaign. The deliberate killings also continued. In Britain eleven military bandsmen died when the IRA blew up a band school in Deal, Kent, while in Northern Ireland and on the continent there were numerous shootings and bombing incidents. Such violence did not deter John Hume from continuing to talk to Adams. During 1989 they met four times, usually in rooms made available by Father Reid in Clonard monastery, but the encounters did not inhibit Hume from publicly attacking the IRA's methods and mind-set. In one fierce attack in late 1988 he told his party's annual conference:

> They are more Irish than the rest of us, they believe. They are the pure master race of Irish. They are the keepers of the holy grail of the nation. That deep-seated attitude, married to their method, has all the hallmarks of undiluted fascism. They have all the other hallmarks of the fascist – the scapegoat – the Brits are to blame for everything, even their own atrocities! They know better than the rest of us.
>
> I had discussions with them recently. The talks were designed to explore whether they were willing to lay down their arms and join the rest of the people of this island in the lengthy and difficult search for peace based on real self-determination. I put some questions to them about the price of their means and method, about the consequence of victory for their viewpoint, about peaceful alternatives which already exist.
>
> They replied with sheaves of paper reiterating well-worn declarations about nationhood and the rights of the Irish people to self-determination while ignoring the single most self-evident fact that strikes every human being in the world as they look in at

Ireland – the Irish people are divided on that very question, the question of how to exercise self-determination. Agreement on its exercise will never be brought about by force and violence but only by dialogue.

The sluggish political scene was enlivened in mid-1989 by the replacement of Tom King as Northern Ireland Secretary by Peter Brooke. King's years as Northern Ireland Secretary had been dominated by the Anglo-Irish Agreement and the furious loyalist reaction to it. The frigid political atmosphere offered little hope of bringing the parties together and King had been forced to adopt a defensive posture.

When Peter Brooke took his place in July 1989 the atmosphere had lightened a little and something of a thaw set in with the political parties, in particular the Unionists, adopting a less confrontational stance. On the republican side, meanwhile, Gerry Adams and the IRA were still talking about peace while at the same time waging war. The question was whether Brooke had the skills and creativity to make progress in such a delicate and uncertain situation.

The first impressions he left were not particularly promising. He looked and sounded old-fashioned and gave the appearance of being slightly bumbling; some early slips of the tongue were seized on by the media and described as gaffes. The fact that his family had something of an Irish background did him few favours, for his forebears had been firmly Unionist. He was a descendant of the Rantaven, Co. Cavan, branch of the family, who were linked to the Brookes of Colebrooke, Co. Fermanagh. In the 1920s the Fermanagh branch provided the first prime minister of Northern Ireland, Sir Basil Brooke, whose name was a nationalist byword for inflexible Unionism. Brooke thus arrived in Belfast against a background of nationalist suspicion.

The widespread early impression was that this was a scion of the old ascendancy, a quasi-aristocrat who would be out of his depth in the shark-infested waters he had been despatched to manage. His upbringing had been the picture of establishment orthodoxy: he was educated at Marlborough and Balliol College, Oxford, and his father, Henry Brooke, had been a Tory Home Secretary. In fact, he would turn out to be one of the most intelligent and imaginative, if not always the most deft, of the many Englishmen who have been given the task of running Northern Ireland.

He brought a sense of history to the job, once outlining some of his antecedents: 'My family lived here for some two and a half centuries, primarily in County Cavan and County Armagh, but also in Dublin and County Kildare, with an Irish ancestry going back much further. We were Church of Ireland parsons, soldiers, artists, farmers, writers, preachers, manufacturers, Indian civil servants, scholars and at least one MP.' He proudly claimed that an ancestor, the eighteenth-century poet Charlotte Brooke, had been the first writer to use the word 'Fenian' (meaning republican rebel) in the English language.

Brooke was a complex man. He could at times be quiet, but could deliver uproariously hilarious after-dinner speeches, often featuring himself as the butt of jokes. He had also known grief in his life, having lost an invalid son and his first wife in a tragic accident. He was capable of the occasional indiscretion, as for example when he was once asked his opinion of Margaret Thatcher. He replied: 'It has been enjoyable working with her, but if you are asking me would I like to spend three weeks on holiday with her, I'm not so sure.'

A studious man, he drew up a reading list which included three books on the IRA and a whole series of works on international terrorism. His study repaid him well, for even Sinn Fein would concede that he came closer than probably any other minister to understanding the republican mind-set. As a result he was able to make several statements which were important in helping along the developing peace process. Gerry Adams, years later, was to pay him this back-handed tribute: 'Brooke was one of the more interested and thoughtful ministers, compared to some of the dimwits they have sent.'

The first major stir of his tenure came in November 1989, when he gave interviews to journalists on the occasion of his hundredth day in office. This was not particularly out of the ordinary, but what began as a routine event turned into something which both electrified the republican movement and drew a furious political response. The question which produced a most unexpected response came from Deric Henderson, a Tyrone-born correspondent with the Press Association who had reported most of the troubles and was regarded as one of Belfast's best-informed journalists. Henderson put it to Brooke that the British and republicans were 'basically in a Mexican stand-off' and asked him if he could ever imagine a British government talking to Sinn Fein.

The standard ministerial response to this was usually that there was no question of the government talking to terrorists, to denounce the IRA as mindless terrorists or financially motivated 'godfathers', and to call on the IRA to lay down its weapons.

Brooke, however, said this:

I'll need to give you a slightly elaborate answer to that because there are obviously a number of factors which weigh with it. The first factor is that in terms of a terrorist organisation as well organised as the Provisional IRA have become, it is difficult to envisage a military defeat of such a force because of the circumstances under which they operate – though the security forces can exercise a policy of containment to enable, broadly speaking, normal life to go on within the Province. So in that sense it would require a decision on the part of the terrorists that the game had ceased to be worth the candle, that, considering the life-style they have to adopt, the return which they were securing from their activities did not justify the costs that it was imposing in personal terms.

There has to be a possibility that at some stage debate might start within the terrorist community. Now, if that were to occur, then you would move towards a point, if in fact the terrorists were to decide that the moment had come when they wished to withdraw from their activities, then I think the government would need to be imaginative in those circumstances as to how that process should be managed. I think it would be foolish to be making statements today about what would happen then, but I hope that because of the welcome which would be given to a return to peaceful conditions in the province by everybody living

here, I hope that the Government at that stage would be imaginative in how it responded.

When Henderson said it was remarkable for a minister to indicate
he might consider speaking to Gerry Adams and Danny Morrison,
Brooke went on: 'Let me remind you of the move towards independence in Cyprus, and a British Minister stood up in the House of
Commons and used the word "never" in a way which within two
years there had been a retreat from that word. All I'm saying is that
I would hope that the British government on a long-term basis
would be sufficiently flexible, that if flexibility were required it
could be used, but I am in no way predicating or predicting what
those circumstances would be.'

Within hours of Henderson filing his story a political storm had
developed. One Tory MP said: 'I was hoping for a quiet weekend.
This is appalling.' Kevin McNamara, Labour's Northern Ireland
spokesman, reproached Brooke: 'Careless talk costs lives.' Brooke's
emphasis on being 'flexible and imaginative' if IRA violence should
stop was all the more striking since Mrs Thatcher had only just
dismissed the IRA as 'common murderers', while the Foreign Secretary, Douglas Hurd, had spoken of the need to 'extirpate' (i.e. to
annihilate) the organisation.

Brooke's approach, by contrast, clearly set out that he believed
not in crushing the IRA but in making a 'flexible and imaginative'
response to a republican ceasefire. No government figure had ever
before spelt out such a scenario, so his comments represented
something new in terms both of tone and of style. His mention of
Cyprus also excited much republican interest in that it presented
an example of an island which had been a British possession, but
which in 1959 had been granted its independence following a
campaign which included both political agitation and terrorist
violence.

Sinn Fein, intrigued by Brooke's comments, reacted quickly. The
'Scenario for Peace' document, which had first appeared two and
a half years earlier, was dusted off, tidied up, and sent to all major
political parties in Ireland and the UK. (The section offering

resettlement grants to those unwilling to accept a united Ireland was quietly removed.) Adams, McGuinness and McLaughlin met the media together to express interest in his words, Adams saying they had sparked off what he described as 'some partial debate' within the movement. There had been various rumours and newspaper reports that the IRA was considering a ceasefire: the republicans were anxious to deny these, while expressing interest in Brooke's words. All three spokesmen were adamant that no one in the ranks was talking about ending the IRA's campaign of violence. Martin McGuinness said:

> Our attitude to the struggle for freedom is the same now as ever it was. Gerry Adams and I went to London, I don't know, it's like a lifetime away, seventeen years ago, when we were only children really, and we talked to William Whitelaw. We talked to him on the issue of Britain's disengagement from Ireland. We're here seventeen years on, and we're still talking about Britain's disengagement from Ireland, and nothing Peter Brooke says about the republican movement not winning the struggle is going to convince us that we can't win. We're absolutely convinced that at some time in the future some British government will talk to the republican movement, that some British government will disengage from Ireland. We're absolutely confident about that.
>
> The question is, is there a group of people within the republican movement or within Sinn Fein who believe that the freedom of Ireland can be won only through political involvement in constitutional politics or in elections. I have heard absolutely no discussion from any group or any person within Sinn Fein along those lines – so it's a total and absolute nonsense.

The storm of protest led Brooke to issue a stream of clarifications, corrections and amplifications designed to palliate Unionist opinion: in particular he said he regretted making his reference to Cyprus. In an interview for this book he reflected on his controversial remarks.

> The question did catch me slightly by surprise and I gave a pretty honest answer to it. I have to say it was instinct rather than a process of rigorous analysis, and it would be wrong to say that it was all premeditated. My view was that we were not going to

make any larger progress unless we got the IRA to engage in a ceasefire, because until you got a ceasefire you couldn't have negotiations.

But although I ran into absolutely major media criticism for saying it, a whole series of soldiers who had served in the province separately sent me messages to say that they basically wholly agreed. They particularly agreed that any solution was ultimately going to be political rather than military.

Although my remarks were carefully worded, saying it was difficult to envisage a military defeat of the terrorists, I was making an admission that had not hitherto been made. But it always seemed to me that if you were actually going to get into negotiation you had to make it feasible for the terrorists and their political front to feel they had an honourable method of doing so. There is an old Chinese principle that you must always leave your opponent an honourable method of retreat.

There were unquestionably some intelligence suggestions that there was a debate going on within the republican community. I have often quoted Wellington's remarks that one of the problems is knowing what is going on on the other side of the hill, and I was genuinely interested because it seemed to me that the Mexican stand-off observation was a fair analysis.

So something had to happen: the ice had to break up. I'd been asked a question about a stalemate. What I was seeking to say, since I'd started down this particular line of communication, was that a ceasefire would be a fruitful thing to do. I couldn't have just said that we can't have a conversation until a ceasefire, and even then there's not much that is likely to happen. That is not a particularly sensible message to send.

Almost a year and a half later, late in 1990, Brooke took a telephone call from a senior officer in MI5, the Security Service. The officer said he wanted to talk to him on an important matter; Brooke told him to drop round.

The officer was John Deverell, an MI5 veteran who had risen to senior rank and who for more than a decade had been concerned with monitoring and combating the IRA in Northern Ireland, Britain and on the continent. Deverell was head of intelligence in Northern Ireland, a position in which he oversaw and co-ordinated the activities of the RUC's Special Branch, military intelligence, and MI5 itself. This meant he was at the centre of a vast web of clandestine activity. Hundreds of Special Branch officers and hundreds of army intelligence operatives were targeted on the IRA, trying to find out all they could about the republican movement. His job was to put all the pieces together.

The security forces had their successes against the IRA. Just days before Deverell's meeting with Brooke, for example, an intricate intelligence operation had led to the setting of an ambush in a County Armagh farmyard near the village of Loughgall. When two seasoned IRA operatives, Desmond Grew and Martin McCaughey, arrived to move some rifles, SAS men lying in wait killed them both. Grew was one of the IRA's most valuable activists, having helped organise its campaign in mainland Europe. He was wanted by West German police in connection with the killings of RAF Corporal Maheshkumar Islania and his baby daughter. McCaughey, a former Sinn Fein councillor, had previously been seriously injured in a fierce firefight with undercover soldiers. In security force terms it was an excellent 'clean kill', one of the occasions in which sound information was used to deprive the IRA of experienced and valuable operatives.

But the intelligence world's record was patchy. Its failure to detect the Libyan connection meant the IRA had been able to assemble its deadly new arsenal. Intelligence had also failed to act as an early-warning system and had not detected the IRA's intention to launch a full-scale and sustained campaign in Britain; it had taken some years to realise the extent of the threat.

In addition to watching the IRA, it was also part of Deverell's remit to chart political currents within the republican movement. It was clear enough that Sinn Fein was exploring political paths while the IRA maintained its violence, but it was difficult to work out exactly what was going on in that closed world. In the years to come the authorities would often display an unsure touch in reacting to the republicans' moves. This, taken together with the Libyan fiasco and the unexpectedness of the campaign with Britain, amounted to telling signs that none of the various intelligence agencies had succeeded in penetrating the high command level of the republican movement, where the key decisions were made.

Ironically, John Deverell would, after all his years of combating the IRA, meet his death in June 1994, just two months before the organisation's cessation of violence. He was one of twenty-five senior intelligence figures who died when an RAF Chinook helicopter crashed into the Mull of Kintyre in fog while flying to Scotland for a conference to discuss the latest anti-terrorist measures.

John Deverell had worked in the Colonial Service before joining MI5. In Belfast he mixed in the community, going under the alias 'John Devon'. A close colleague said of him: 'He was a big, bluff, hearty, very nice guy. I never heard him say a bad word about anybody. Some people thought in fact that he was too genial a boss. He was a large man, very able, a very big man with a big personality to go with it, well-liked by everybody.' Brooke had a close working relationship with Deverell, whom he counted as a friend. Deverell regularly brought security warrants for him to sign to permit telephone tapping and postal checks, an activity they always carried out on a one-to-one basis. They would also discuss the wider intelligence picture. Deverell was not however Brooke's only source of information on political trends within republicanism. The Northern Ireland Secretary made a point of doing his own research on the republicans, reading every issue of the weekly Sinn Fein paper, *Republican News*. He also held regular discussions with Hume, who kept him briefed on his continuing contacts with Gerry Adams.

Deverell's message to Brooke, on that day in 1990, was a most sensitive and potentially important one: that a line of communication was open to the republican leadership. He said he believed there was potential for progress, and sought permission to explore it further. Brooke was most interested.

An occasional channel of contact with the republicans had existed throughout most of the troubles. It had been operative in the 1974–5 period, when the republicans and the British government of the day had been in frequent contact, and again in 1980–1 during the period of the hunger strike. But it had lain dormant since then, though the person who had acted as go-between was still available to do so again.

The question of when the back-channel was reopened has been one of continuing dispute between Sinn Fein and the British government. The republicans say the contact dated back to 1990, while the government said it restarted in 1993. The precise testimony of Brooke himself, however, is that he gave the go-ahead in 1990, at a time when Mrs Thatcher was still prime minister. Brooke talked the issue through with Deverell and a small number of senior aides, including his permanent secretary, the self-effacing but astute Sir John Chilcot. As the most senior British civil servant in Northern Ireland, Chilcot would play a leading role in many of the negotiations and manoeuvring which lay ahead.

Chilcot was described by a colleague as 'the best Home Office type of mandarin, really quite outstanding of his generation, an immensely subtle mind'. Like many other senior NIO officials, he began his career in the Home Office, moving to the NIO in 1990. It was always expected that he would return to the Home Office to run that much larger and more complex department as permanent secretary, but at the last moment ministers had a change of heart and he stayed at the NIO. A senior NIO source commented in 1995: 'Fate worked to everybody's benefit in the end, for John has been so good in the Belfast post. He played a key role, which meant it hasn't all been left to people in the Foreign Office and the Cabinet Office, many of whom had no idea of the subtleties of the Northern Ireland situation – and didn't really care, actually.'

Chilcot's key deputy also played a pivotal part in putting government policy into effect. Quentin Thomas, another official whose background lay in the Home Office, was slightly unusual in that he departed from the standard bureaucrat's penchant for being inconspicuous: with his sharp suits, blue shirts, gold-rimmed glasses and close-cropped hair he came, in fact, to resemble a stereotype of a CIA agent. This was perhaps an eminently suitable impression to give since, as will be seen, the roles of Chilcot and Thomas were to include a fair amount of the art of deception. A colleague said of him:

He's an amazing character. He's very relaxed, very genial in nature, but he has a really, really original mind – more so than Chilcot. When you discuss an issue with Quentin you're never quite sure how he's going to come at you, which direction he's going to come at you with the answer. He's quite outstanding, has got a tremendous brain. He's also the master drafter: he can produce a piece of paper that is given to three conflicting parties and they all think they've got something good out of it. He and John Chilcot are very close – both Home Office backgrounds, they mix very closely, they have a very supportive relationship, they're very good with ministers.

Brooke gave political permission to proceed with the contact, but stipulated that the exercise should be carried out on the basis of 'deniability' – that is, if questioned, he would feel free to issue public denials that he was talking to terrorists. He considered the fact that a go-between would be involved meant he felt he could say, with some degree of truth, that there was no direct contact. He said later:

It was bound to be a risk – it couldn't be but a risk because you were engaged, even indirectly, in conversation and the whole thing could obviously blow up in your face. But equally if you were actually going to make any progress, that was a risk you were going to have to take. It seemed to me to be totally unreasonable of politicians to expect the soldiers and the policemen to be risking their lives, to be holding the ring while the politicians produced the solution, if the politicians weren't making any effort to produce a solution. I wanted to end the shooting that was producing absolutely pointless tragedy for lots of families when it wasn't going anywhere, and I therefore was perfectly happy to run a risk myself.

We had a substantial debate about it. It was a debate which among other things discussed the identity, the process by which the linkage would occur. I mean – were we making statements which were not strictly true, in terms of responding to the House of Commons? I certainly believed, in the context of the conduit which existed, that we could continue to say that we were not in direct contact. The conduit was a voluntary one. There was somebody in place who had been involved for quite some time, and he had the advantage of retaining the confidence of both sides.

It was not negotiation. I was not sanctioning a whole series of things – it was the opportunity to carry on conversation. I mean it was essentially an Intelligence process. It would be totally wrong for me to suggest that I was in day-to-day, fingertip contact with the process. The process might well take place with intervals of three weeks or a month and I might easily not know until another three weeks or a month had gone by what was occurring. The process of intelligence would have been to sift through what was coming back and apply meaning to it. But there was so much else going on that I didn't spend my time being impatient and saying, 'What on earth is happening?' You waited until somebody felt it necessary to tell you something.

The secret contacts were so sensitive that only a very small number of officials knew about them. All of these were British-born: the decision was taken that no civil servants born in Northern Ireland should be aware of the secret in case they concluded the union was being betrayed and blew the whistle on the exercise. One senior minister later explained: 'It would test the Unionist-minded civil servant to the point of destruction.' (This was a prophetic remark: the contact was in the end to be exposed by a Northern Ireland-born official.)

In November 1990 Peter Brooke delivered a speech in his Westminster constituency which dwelt on the nature of the British presence. With its final paragraph he wrote a small part for himself in Irish history. He declared: 'The British government has no selfish strategic or economic interest in Northern Ireland: our role is to help, enable and encourage. Britain's purpose, as I have sought to describe it, is not to occupy, oppress or exploit, but to ensure democratic debate and free democratic choice. That is our way.' Even today, most republicans would not accept the assertion that Britain has no selfish or economic interest in Ireland. But his remark, like his earlier reference to Cyprus, aroused intense interest within the republican movement. His characterisation of the connection with Britain was strikingly different from Mrs Thatcher's one-time assertion that Northern Ireland was as British as Finchley.

His statement was to prove to be one of the central building blocks which led to the IRA cessation of violence in August 1994.

Brooke, it is now known, made the statement at the prompting of Hume, who had been arguing on this point in his talks with Adams. The SDLP and Sinn Fein had spent much time in their 1988 talks on this argument, with Hume characterising Britain as neutral. Brooke's statement, while by no means regarded by republicans as conclusive, was none the less strong evidence in support of Hume's contention. It would play an important part in the embryonic peace process.

World events had also punched a large hole in the Sinn Fein analysis. In their 1988 talks with the SDLP they had argued that while Britain had economic advantages and economic interests in staying, strategic interests were the most important consideration. They argued that the prospect of a neutral Ireland was viewed as a threat by Britain and by NATO. This is clearly a reference to the threat posed by the Soviet Union, and the potential value of Northern Ireland to British forces protecting Atlantic sea and air routes. Since then, however, history had moved on in a dramatic way. In May 1989 the Berlin Wall had been torn down, with the collapse of the Warsaw Pact quickly following. With no Soviet Union there could be no Soviet threat, leaving Sinn Fein in need of a new argument. In his speech Brooke did not even mention the strategic question. According to Brooke the setting and substance of what he said in his speech were carefully considered. He later related:

> That was a premeditated statement. Firstly, in conversation with John Hume he shared the view that there was potentially a misunderstanding on their part of where reality was. Secondly, I had been reading *Republican News* for the whole of the previous year and, while I didn't necessarily believe that they believed everything that they were writing, they did go on and on and on about it being a colonialist struggle and the motivation of the British Government being imperialist. That just seemed so hopelessly inaccurate that it was important that one should make a statement about it. And thirdly I actually deliberately made it

in my own constituency rather than in Ireland so that it would in fact have a London ring to it rather than a Belfast ring.

The republicans responded to Brooke's speech in several ways. Gerry Adams issued a nine-page statement saying the onus was on those who believed there was an alternative to the 'armed struggle' to prove it. Mitchel McLaughlin contributed two lengthy analytical articles to the Belfast *Irish News* questioning whether Britain really was neutral but conceding that the remarks were worthy of consideration.

The Brooke speech was followed by one of Father Reid's extremely rare public utterances. By this stage he felt his private efforts to open dialogue between the republicans and the constitutionalists were not bearing fruit. In a long, closely reasoned article printed in the *Irish Times* he appealed to political parties and especially to his own church to open lines of communication to the republicans. He made the startling claim that, if dialogue were opened, republican violence could be ended within any given six-month period.

In the article he carefully laid out his arguments, and his sense that dialogue could bring the IRA campaign to an end. He said the IRA was convinced it had the right to take up arms. But at the same time, the republicans were also convinced that their campaign could not of itself achieve their aim and therefore believed that political methods must also be used. He argued:

> They are saying, in effect, that they are using armed force not because they want to but because, as they see the situation, they have to . . . If, as they say, armed force is simply a tactic to pressurise the British authorities into giving the people of Ireland their democratic rights, then you can immediately enter into a dialogue with them about replacing the pressure of armed and violent force with the pressure of political and diplomatic force . . .
>
> I believe that the church must enter into direct communication and dialogue with the republican movement if she wants to persuade it to abandon the gun and to follow the ways of peaceful politics. My own experience has taught me that, if the church

does this, she will find that the republican movement is open, not only to communication and dialogue, but also to such persuasion. I believe, for example, that, given the necessary communication with the other political parties or authorities that would be concerned, the republican movement could be persuaded to end its strategy of armed force in favour of a strategy of political force or even of new, realistic ways of defining and applying the democratic principles that should govern the just resolution of the present conflict.

I am convinced, however, that the republican movement will not be persuaded to give up its armed strategy for a political strategy unless it has first been satisfied that such a strategy would be organised enough and strong enough to pursue the traditional aims of Irish nationalism in the political setting of the 1990s. Such an efficacious political strategy could, I believe, be set up, but only if the main nationalist political parties and the main republican movement agree to pursue it together, because only then would it have the kind of political force behind it that would satisfy the republican movement.

The problem, he argued, was that while republicans were open to a new political strategy as a replacement for violence, such a strategy could not be constructed because no one would talk to them. The republican movement was interested in a political path, but would not lay down its arms until it had been able to verify the political viability of proposals for an unarmed strategy. The result was an impasse.

The priest added: 'I am pointing out all this to explain why I believe the violence could be ended, as far as the nationalist side is concerned, within any given six-month period, provided it were handled properly. But it would have to be handled properly, patiently and with diplomatic skill.'

Father Reid's article aroused little or no obvious interest. He was writing some months after Cahal Daly had replaced Tomas O Fiaich as head of the Catholic church in Ireland, and was clearly worried by Dr Daly's action in ending his predecessor's secret contacts with Sinn Fein.

It is perhaps not surprising that Father Reid's arguments, for all their cogency, were not taken more seriously. The IRA campaign in Britain was raging at a high level, with senior Conservative MP Ian Gow assassinated only a few months earlier. Media reports that the IRA might consider a ceasefire were consistently denied by the republican leadership. Just a month before Father Reid's article, for example, an IRA spokesman had reiterated, in an interview with the *Independent*, that there would be no ceasefire short of a British withdrawal.

Yet the fact is that Father Reid was right in arguing that there was much more to the republican movement's position than the hardline assertions of the IRA spokesman. The IRA would, in the end, declare a ceasefire with no British withdrawal in prospect. Sinn Fein would be seen to pursue exactly the type of pan-nationalist front which he described, as an alternative to violence. He was right in saying the republicans wanted to talk, and that if someone talked to them they would consider stopping the violence. In his article he contended that the Christian approach was to reach out to everyone, even the worst of sinners; but what he wrote was clearly informed by a detailed sense of the state of thinking within the republican leadership. The 1994 cessation would be a long time in coming, but when it did it was based almost exactly on the propositions put forward by the Clonard priest.

The sense within republicanism that some movement might be possible was sharply enhanced in the same month, November 1990, with the resignation of Margaret Thatcher as leader of the Conservative party and prime minister. Sinn Fein and the IRA had long since concluded that the chances of Mrs Thatcher making any move in their direction were remote, and had resigned themselves to simply outlasting her term of office. They welcomed her successor, John Major, in three ways.

First, the IRA declared a three-day Christmas ceasefire, its first for fifteen years. The terrorists habitually took a Christmas break but traditionally no official announcement was made: the fact that a formal declaration was made was clearly meant to send a signal to the British government that the IRA could be flexible. A senior republican explained shortly afterwards:

The Christmas ceasefire was a gesture, but one should not have the impression that the IRA are casting about to get out of a dilemma. The armed struggle can go on indefinitely, but there is a willingness to examine possibilities which Brooke is exploring. He must move beyond what he has said or else things won't go anywhere. We want him to go beyond shadow boxing. If he is serious then he has to take risks. He should be talking to Sinn Fein. He made a statement to the effect that the British had no selfish or economic interest in staying in Northern Ireland: republicans must examine that. Why not move forward to convince republicans that he is serious, to try and reach agreement with Sinn Fein? The British Government needs to set the objective of a united Ireland.

The fact that Brooke said what he did is positive. The present leadership can't sit around and say just because it criticised Ruairi O Bradaigh over the 1975–6 talks it cannot undertake a debate with the Brits – but it must guard against making the same mistakes. That experience is a problem but our criticism of it is not a big enough obstacle to prevent the examination of any avenue towards peace.

The second Sinn Fein gesture towards Major came in February 1991 when Gerry Adams wrote asking him to talk to Sinn Fein about peace. The third gesture came when, five days after Adams sent his reasonably phrased letter to Downing Street, the IRA fired a volley of mortar bombs at the new British prime minister.

6

MORTARS IN DOWNING STREET

'The IRA terrorists are better equipped, better
resourced, better led, than at any time before.
If we don't intern, it's long haul'
   – senior British army officer

'The traditional objective of Irish nationalism –
the exercise of self-determination by the people
of Ireland as a whole – cannot be achieved
without the agreement of the people of
Northern Ireland'
   – draft declaration by John Hume

In the official minutes of a meeting of Cabinet ministers held in
10 Downing Street on 7 February 1991 a terse little note records:
'A brief interruption to the war committee of the Cabinet took
place.' The Gulf War with Iraq was under way and the new prime
minister, John Major, was discussing the handling of the struggle
for Kuwait with senior colleagues.

The 'brief interruption' was not a knock at the door but a
violent explosion in the back garden, a grim reminder that the
Middle East was not the only conflict facing the British government. The explosion went off only 15 yards from where ministers
sat, but the blast was absorbed by the room's strengthened windows
and heavy protective curtains. Windows were shattered in 10
Downing Street and adjoining buildings, and while no one was
injured many, including ministers, were shaken. The Prime Minister
and the others ducked when the explosion went off and John Major

said: 'I think we had better start again somewhere else.' They quickly left the room, later resuming their meeting in a more secure underground bunker.

The IRA had succeeded in exploding a substantial mortar bomb within yards of the Prime Minister, one of the most closely guarded people in Britain. The attack achieved major international publicity for the IRA and represented a serious embarrassment to British police. After the 1984 Brighton bombing Margaret Thatcher's protection had been stepped up dramatically, and in 1989 security around Whitehall was again increased, with high Gothic gates erected across Downing Street, streets and alleys blocked off and new electronic surveillance installed. Yet despite all the precautions the IRA had struck right in the nerve centre of government, achieving a 'spectacular' which caused jubilation among its supporters.

The breach of Whitehall security was achieved in the space of a few moments. A white Transit van drew up at the corner of Whitehall and Horseguards Avenue; the driver got out, jumped on the pillion-seat of a waiting motor cycle and was driven away. A few minutes later three large mortar bombs shot out of the top of the van and went soaring across the roof-tops of Whitehall towards the rear of Downing Street. The concept of the attack was relatively simple, but the planning had been lengthy and meticulous. It was in fact conceived as another attack on Mrs Thatcher, but when Major replaced her the IRA decided to make him their target. The van had been bought for cash in London the previous July, and work then began on cutting a hole in its roof, making the mortars, and calculating the exact distance and angle of fire.

After the attack the IRA boasted that the Cabinet was being forced to meet in bunkers. Gerry Adams, whose letter proposing peace talks had arrived a few days before the mortars, said the incident underlined that 'as Peter Brooke agrees, the IRA cannot be defeated, that there is no military solution'. The overall message from the republicans was that, while they were interested in talks, they were also intent on prosecuting their campaign. The Armalite and ballot-box strategy had, it seemed, been superseded by one of operating with a talks invitation in one hand and a mortar bomb in the other.

The Downing Street incident and the many other IRA attacks in Britain during this period did not deflect Brooke and Major from keeping open the government's secret lines of communication to the republicans. But during 1991 Brooke concentrated most of his attention on a political initiative which excluded the republicans.

He believed he saw a window of opportunity among Northern Ireland's constitutional parties. None of the three major parties – the Ulster Unionists, SDLP and Democratic Unionists – was particularly keen to get round the table, but Brooke none the less embarked on a long process of nudging and persuading them towards talks. He cleverly played on the fact that none of the parties wished to be viewed as obstructive. Sinn Fein watched these moves from the sidelines, since the government laid down that the party's endorsement of IRA violence should exclude them from the talks process, and they were not involved. Many months of political activity followed as Brooke met the parties on a bilateral basis and edged them towards round-table talks. He began the effort in January 1990, and it took him more than a year to get agreement from all sides to sit down together. By that stage Margaret Thatcher had lost the Conservative party leadership and John Major had taken her place: the new Prime Minister had little previous track record on Ireland, north or south, and no one knew quite how he felt about the problem.

The talks dealt with three 'strands' – internal Northern Ireland matters, north–south relations and overall Anglo-Irish relations. Brooke's insistence on pressing ahead with these talks had introduced new strains into London–Dublin relations, since Haughey suspected Unionist parties were more concerned with sabotaging the Anglo-Irish Agreement than with genuinely searching for a new understanding.

However, confidential personal correspondence which passed between Haughey and Major, which has been obtained by the authors, shows clearly that the two premiers were careful to work closely together to ensure that the political talks would not undermine the Agreement and thus harm Anglo-Irish relations. One way in which Major sought to reassure Haughey was by briefing him on what was said in his supposedly confidential meetings with Unionist leaders. The letters also show that Haughey and Major were paying minute attention to the smallest detail. On 16 May 1991, for example, Major wrote to Haughey:

I realise the difficulties that have been caused for the other participants in the talks by the obstacles that have been raised by the Unionist leaders, particularly when the others had accepted the document [a paper produced by Brooke] without difficulty. But I felt it important to explore whether the Unionist objections were substantial roadblocks to future progress or whether we could find a way through.

They wanted clarification that the paper which Peter Brooke circulated to party leaders on 14 May applied to the talks in Strands 2 and 3 and not to Strand 1. I was able to confirm this. They also wanted an assurance that the appointment of an independent chairman did not mean that the issues in Strand 2 would be open to international adjudication. I was able to give them that assurance . . .

They indicated that they could not give full agreement to the document until the location of the talks in Northern Ireland had been settled, and until the name of the chairman had been agreed, but they said they were willing to go ahead with the talks and, as they put it, 'to work the procedure' set out in the May document.

I look forward to remaining in close touch as the talks continue and to having a meeting with you as we discussed when we last met.

The following day Haughey replied:

I very much appreciated the message which you sent me last night and your generous words about the efforts of Gerry Collins, in cooperation with Peter Brooke, to formalise the basis on which the three strands of talks would begin. For our part, we are very conscious of, and would like to pay tribute to, the patient and painstaking efforts of Peter Brooke over past weeks to move the process forward.

I very much hope that we can get agreement on these

remaining issues so that the talks in Strand 1 can begin as soon as possible. I am therefore asking my officials to begin at once to explore the names of possible chairmen and suggestions on venue.

Despite the close attentions of London and Dublin the 1991 talks ran into the sands after a few months. With much distrust in the air, the discussions stalled on procedural points and barely touched on substantive issues. Brooke indicated that he regarded the talks process as paused rather than closed, and indeed later his successor as Northern Ireland Secretary, Sir Patrick Mayhew, would restart the exercise.

Although Hume, as leader of the SDLP, played an important part in the Brooke talks, part of his mind was preoccupied with the idea of helping move the IRA away from violence. He doubted that inter-party talks, held as they were against a backdrop of continuing violence, could succeed. But he sensed, from his analysis of republicans in general and in particular his personal contacts with Adams, that the IRA might be persuaded to stop.

Hume's aide, Denis Haughey, described how intently Hume studied republican documents: 'I remember once on a flight to Berlin noticing that John was completely preoccupied. He reached down into a carrier bag and pulled out a sheaf of papers and started to read them in such an intensive way that it looked as though he was trying to inhale them. They were the Sinn Fein papers presented to us in 1988. Several years later there he was, trying to get into the minds of the people who wrote them and get to the wellspring of their thinking.'

Hume's inhalation of the Sinn Fein papers was to pay dividends, for it led him to begin a process which helped lead to the IRA's 1994 cessation of violence. The central political demand of Sinn Fein was for Irish self-determination; Hume thus set out to consider whether, and how, this demand could be reconciled with the positions of the other parties to the conflict, including the British and Irish governments, the Unionists and the SDLP.

As far back as 1988 Father Reid had been pushing the idea of crafting a statement, to be made by the British government alone, which might have the effect of stopping the IRA campaign. The priest produced a series of position papers in the hope of attracting the approval of Sinn Fein and the constitutional nationalists. This idea was now evolving into that of a joint London–Dublin statement.

Hume, who was in regular contact with Gerry Adams, Charles Haughey and Father Reid, had a fair idea of what might be feasible. On 6 October 1991, he picked up a pen and a piece of lined white paper and did something which was to prove a vital step in the peace process. He wrote out a draft declaration to be made jointly by the British and Irish governments. It was to prove the first in a long line of such drafts which would, in December 1993, culminate in the Downing Street Declaration. Few realised at the time of the Declaration's appearance that it represented the final draft in a process which had secretly been under way for years. The intention was to find common ground in everyone's ideological positions, and to reconcile what had always appeared irreconcilable. Under the heading 'A Strategy for Peace and Justice in Ireland', Hume wrote as follows:

Aim: A joint declaration by both British and Irish Prime Ministers.

1 Leaving the past aside and regretting the pain and suffering caused by past failures to settle the relationships of the people of both islands satisfactorily.

2 Recognising that the implementation of the Single Market and the coming into being of European Union with the effective removal of all borders fundamentally changes the nature of British/Irish relationships. Further recognising that future developments which leave both parts of Ireland as the only part of the new Europe with no land links with the other regions, will intensify the common ground between both parts of Ireland and intensify the need for maximum co-operation to achieve maximum benefit from European Union.

3 Regret, however, that there remains a serious legacy of past relationships – a deeply divided people on the island of Ireland. This is a major concern of both governments and both deeply regret that these are the last remaining such divisions in the new European order.

4 Both governments recognise that these divisions can only end with the agreement of the people North and South in Ireland.

5 Both governments therefore commit themselves to using the maximum resources to create the atmosphere in which such agreement is made easier. Both governments find it unacceptable that these are the last remaining divisions in a Europe that has already ended many more deep and bitter quarrels. They will, therefore, promote intensive co-operation at all levels in order to strengthen the process of agreement.

6 The British Government reiterate yet again that they no longer have any selfish political or strategic interest in remaining in Ireland. Their sole interest is to see peace and agreement among the people who inhabit the island and will devote all their available resources to that end.

7 For its part the Irish Government recognises that the traditional objective of Irish nationalism – the exercise of self-determination by the people of Ireland as a whole – cannot be achieved without the agreement of the people of Northern Ireland. It would, therefore commit itself to working for institutions of government North and South which would respect the diversity of the people of Ireland but allow them to work their substantial common ground together in order to build the necessary trust for an agreed future.

In order to pursue that strategy the Irish Government would set up a permanent Irish Convention in order to plan and implement the steps and policies required to break down the barriers which divide the people of Ireland and which prevent the exercise of agreed self-determination. If the British Government refuse the joint declaration, the Irish Government would proceed to set up the Convention with the additional objective of planning and implementing the policies required to persuade the British Government to adopt our strategy and objectives. Membership of the Convention would consist of elected representatives of all parties in Ireland who share the objective of a united self-determined Ireland.

This draft contained many of the key features of what would, after many changes, become the Downing Street Declaration, including self-determination, an assurance from Britain that it had no selfish interest in remaining in Ireland, and a heavy emphasis on the need for agreement. In setting out these points Hume was building on a number of elements, one of which was material from his 1988 debates with Sinn Fein.

The document set the Northern Ireland problem firmly in an Anglo-Irish context, drawing on the Anglo-Irish Agreement and envisaging the two governments working ever more closely together. It also stressed the European dimension. Peter Brooke had set out, in his speech of November 1990, that Britain had no selfish strategic or economic interest: Hume augmented this by saying it had no political interest either.

The offer of a convention to be set up by the Irish government was another element which could be traced back to the 1988 SDLP–Sinn Fein talks. In those discussions Hume suggested that an IRA ceasefire would be followed by a conference, convened by the Irish government. The document did not explicitly demand an IRA ceasefire, but it was obvious that it was intended to produce one. It was also implicit that Sinn Fein would be admitted to mainstream Irish political life, for the proposed offer by the Irish government to set up an Irish convention was an open invitation to give up violence and enter constitutional politics. Hume's pro-Europeanism, meanwhile, was reflected in the heavy emphasis on the European dimension.

None of this amounted, in terms, to fulfilment of the traditional republican demand for a British declaration of intent to withdraw from Ireland. But it cast Britain in a very different light from the colonialist and imperialist power of Sinn Fein's standard analysis. On the contrary, it made clear that Britain was anxious above all to secure agreement; that it viewed the problem in an Anglo-Irish context; and that it intended to manage the problem jointly with Dublin. It also, arguably, amounted to a strong signal that Britain did not expect to be in Ireland for ever and a day.

The crucial part of Hume's draft lay in its seventh point, in which he sought to address the republican demand for Irish self-determination. This could not be achieved, he wrote, without the agreement of the people of Northern Ireland. This was a very subtle concept, for in effect it entwined the principles of self-determination and consent. It thus combined, at least in theory, that which republicans sought with the Unionist demand that the majority opinion should prevail within Northern Ireland.

The importance of this was that it offered republicans something which they had never had before: a chance to fit the northern Protestants into their theoretical scheme of things. Although, as we shall see, republican thinking was evolving quite fast, it still lacked any way of rationalising the very obvious divisions between Unionist and nationalist. Sinn Fein had strayed so far away from the original eighteenth-century republican vision of uniting Protestants and Catholics that it had actually suggested giving resettlement grants to those who did not want to live in a united Ireland.

Hume was offering a way of making the reality of the division more digestible in terms of nationalist doctrine. The principles of self-determination would be recognised and acknowledged, but nationalists would be conceding that Unionists had rights. Partition would still be in place, for the moment at least, but it would continue not because Britain insisted on it, but because Irish nationalists were, in the exercise of self-determination, granting Unionists the right to choose it. The border would therefore exist by nationalist choice rather than British imposition. It was not an easy concept, but it was obviously a serious attempt to address republican concerns.

A few days later Hume took the piece of paper with him to Dublin and showed it, still in long-hand, to Haughey, explaining his thinking behind each point. The Taoiseach listened attentively: he was fully aware of Hume's continuing contacts with Adams, and realised that the document had been put together in the hope of meeting republican concerns. After a while Haughey pressed a buzzer and the two men were joined by his adviser, Martin Mansergh. Mansergh took the document and embellished it with diplomatic language.

Shortly afterwards two more key figures were drawn into the process. One was Dermot Nally, a senior official who had played a leading role in Anglo-Irish relations as far back as the Sunningdale negotiations of 1973 and had guided Irish ministers through the

Anglo-Irish rapids for decades. Nally had served for years at the highest levels of the Dublin administration as secretary to the government. In this capacity he attended almost every Irish Cabinet meeting for more than a decade, as well as dozens of summit meetings. After his official retirement he was almost immediately asked to return to play a leading role in Anglo-Irish relations – 'he was brought back as a wise man,' as one Dublin source put it.

The other was Sean O hUiginn, a senior diplomat in charge of the Anglo-Irish division of the Department of Foreign Affairs (DFA) who for years has been at the centre of Anglo-Irish relations. He had worked in its Anglo-Irish division in the 1970s before becoming Irish consul in New York, where he had to cope with the turbulent Irish-American backwash of the hunger-strike crisis. He went on to serve as ambassador to Saudi Arabia and as senior Irish representative in what the DFA called 'the bunker' – the Maryfield secretariat on the outskirts of Belfast established under the Anglo-Irish Agreement. His nickname was 'the dark prince', partly because of his complexion and partly because of his some-times brooding manner.

Although O hUiginn and Nally were virtually unknown to the general public, they were important figures who would play import-ant parts in the developing peace process. In one way Dublin had a permanent advantage over London in Anglo-Irish relations, for many of the best and the brightest Irish officials tended to specialise in London–Dublin relations. The result was a high quality of Irish representation.

One of Ireland's shrewdest journalists said of O hUiginn: 'He is the most formidable exponent of nationalism that I've ever encount-ered. I would put him well ahead of Hume or Cardinal Daly. Hume is powerful and a *tour de force* and so on, but in terms of exposition and application O hUiginn is stronger.'

Another source who has had many dealings with him said: 'Sean has one of the finest minds of his generation, and he has a number of strengths. First is his intellectual formulation and analysis of the problem. Then there's his grasp of what is possible, what's practical politics, north and south on a day-to-day level, as well as his vision about the direction we should all be heading in. Then there's his abilities as a negotiator, especially in dealing with the British. And last there's his passion, unusual in an official, his passion about trying to get the violence ended and to move to a civilised new settlement.'

For British officials, by contrast, Northern Ireland and Anglo-Irish affairs were and are relatively unfashionable areas of specialis-ation. This has meant that the quality of the Irish diplomats has not always been matched on the British side.

This Dublin team set to work on Hume's draft. First Mansergh produced an alternative document, then Hume and the Dublin team amalgamated them into one. This document (which is repro-duced as Appendix 1) retained the structure of Hume's and dealt with the same subjects in the same order, but was slightly longer and contained more verbal flourishes.

The crucial section on self-determination read: 'The Taoiseach, on behalf of the Irish Government, accepts that the exercise of self-determination by the people of Ireland as a whole cannot be achieved except with the agreement and the consent of the people of Northern Ireland.'

Hume proposed to take this back north and give it to Gerry Adams. The fact that it had the endorsement of Haughey as Taoise-ach, even if only unofficially, enormously enhanced the status of the joint declaration idea. Hume said later: 'I said to Haughey, "I am talking to these people and I am going to give this to Adams – since it's a joint declaration have you a problem?" Haughey said: "Good luck to you." ' Not long afterwards Hume arranged to meet Adams. They discussed the origins of the document, and Hume handed it over. Adams promised to consider it.

He did not study it alone; rather he brought it to the small tight coterie which makes up the collective brain of Sinn Fein. Adams was the undisputed leader of the party, but he had strong intellectual support from what was in effect a republican Cabinet.

In 1987 Chief Superintendent Brian Fitzsimmons (who later died in the same Chinook helicopter crash which killed John Deverell) said privately that three figures essentially dominated the entire republican movement. He listed these as Gerry Adams, Martin McGuinness and Pat Doherty of Donegal. The three did not necessarily always occupy the top positions, he explained, because they did not need to. McGuinness, for example, was then reportedly second in charge in the north, he went on. The IRA's chief of staff was none of these three, he explained, but he was 'an Adams man' and under the influence of the three men.

The signs are that in the years after that assessment was given the Adams-McGuinness-Doherty triumvirate came to concentrate more and more on Sinn Fein and lost their reported tight control over the IRA. Certainly, the 1996 resumption of IRA violence seemed to confirm that although the IRA and Sinn Fein were in many ways closely entwined, a distance existed between the leaderships of the two entities.

Within Sinn Fein, a vital figure was Londonderry republican Mitchel McLaughlin. Another key figure, Danny Morrison, had been jailed and was therefore to a large extent out of commission, but there were other important members including Tom Hartley and Jim Gibney. One of the few southerners on the team was Sean McManus, a long-time republican from County Sligo who had visited Libya on behalf of Sinn Fein in the early 1980s. His son Joseph, a member of the IRA, would later die when an Ulster Defence Regiment member he was trying to kill returned fire. These were the men who sat down to consider the draft declaration.

Haughey was hopeful enough about the exchanges to mention them when he met Major in Dublin in December. According to a reliable source: 'Haughey gave John Major a broad outline and said that there was something that might come to fruition. Major replied, in effect: "Very interesting, but let's wait and see." '

At this time some of Major's senior security advisers were pushing him not towards the idea of bringing the republicans into politics, but instead towards a concentrated security initiative in the face of the continuing violence from both the IRA and the militant loyalist groups. Some senior army officers were arguing that the authorities had little option but to take the drastic step of bringing back internment without trial.

In the early 1970s internment had been an unmitigated disaster, failing to improve the security situation while providing the IRA with a valuable propaganda weapon. It was brought to an end in 1975. But in late 1991, to senior officers in army headquarters at Lisburn, County Down, it seemed things were so bad that desperate measures were needed. The IRA was mounting numerous attacks in England, while in Northern Ireland it was killing members of the security forces, people who supplied building materials or worked for them in any way, alleged loyalist extremists and others. Large bombs were causing extensive damage to towns and cities. In one month, November 1991, the IRA killed two soldiers working in the military wing of a Belfast hospital, two members of the Ulster Defence Regiment and six alleged loyalists, some of whom were in fact uninvolved civilians. Two of the loyalists were killed by a Semtex bomb smuggled into Belfast's Crumlin Road. The IRA also lost two of its own members killed in a premature explosion in St Albans: this was a set-back but it did not stop the campaign in England.

The IRA displayed lethal ingenuity in inventing new ways of attack. It adopted mortars, already a dangerous weapon, by digging them into the side of the road and firing them, at point-blank range, into army or police vehicles using remote control. A number of soldiers and police officers were killed by these 'horizontal mortars'. It was also deploying one of the most merciless tactics ever seen in Northern Ireland, the 'human bomb'. In the first instance of its use a Londonderry man, Patsy Gillespie, was taken from his home by the terrorists. The fact that Gillespie worked in the canteen at Fort George army base in his home city meant he qualified for the IRA's list of 'legitimate targets'.

While his wife and family were assured he would be returned safely, he was taken outside, chained into a hijacked vehicle, and ordered to drive it to an army checkpoint on the border. The vehicle contained a 1,000-lb bomb; when Gillespie arrived at the checkpoint the IRA detonated the bomb. The checkpoint was heavily fortified but little defence was possible against such a powerful device, and five soldiers were killed. For many hours the security forces were unsure whether Gillespie himself had escaped or not, for no trace of his body could be found. Eventually it was determined that he had died in the huge blast: his coffin was nailed tightly shut when it was delivered to his family.

Loyalist violence was also running at a high level and contributing to a rising death-toll. As a result some senior army officers concluded that existing security policy was inadequate, that they were not winning the war, and that even worse violence was on the way. In November 1991 a senior army officer, forecasting an IRA escalation, privately said the following:

> The IRA terrorists are better equipped, better resourced, better led, bolder and more secure against our penetration than at any time before. They are absolutely a formidable enemy. The essential attributes of their leaders are better than ever before. Some of their operations are brilliant, in terrorist terms. The fact is that the IRA are very, very good. When you're a terrorist and a good one you don't make many mistakes. They've had twenty-two years' experience – most soldiers are here for eighteen months then they're away again. We know the guys who are doing this mayhem – we know them well. If we don't intern, it's long haul. The argument is on whether there are acceptable short cuts to peace.
>
> Some important people are thinking of ceasefire – or, alternatively, maybe they are floating the idea to see if it would be picked up by the government. I accept there are people in the movement who want to spend more time with their families, who would like to stop if they could get what they would regard as some honourable arrangement. But a lot of them aren't interested. I mean, what the hell do you offer them? They absolutely enjoy being a terrorist. I have no doubt they find it very stimulating and challenging.
>
> There are different types. There are people, I suppose Gerry Adams and Martin McGuinness are examples, who do have a burning zeal about getting Britain out and who wish to see a United Ireland. But there are equally people who enjoy the power that terrorism gives them. There is a lot of extortion and racketeering, and some make money. There are others who actually get a thrill from killing and assassination. And then at the

bottom end there are minions, who join from family tradition and so on. It's heady stuff for them. You can break up the command structure by picking up key individuals. The quarter-masters, for example, are the only ones who know where the arms dumps are. They might in time perhaps re-equip and re-muster their efforts, but the command structure won't be there.

I would say to Peter Brooke, we can deliver, given a favourable or at least not unhelpful climate in the south; and if you can keep the Americans off our backs, and deal with the EC and the human rights people and so on, and ensure it does not become a *cause célèbre*, then yes, we can deliver. Some say to me, 'But you might only get half of them on the first day.' I say to them – 'That's all right, we'll get them in the following days.' They'll go on the run, but that will disrupt the command structure. And if you do that, you've brought peace. Wouldn't people then say, 'This is better, this is a climate in which we'd prefer to live?'

7

DEATH AND
DIALOGUE

'The scene was horrific, with bodies everywhere. In that confined space there was a smell
from the gunfire and all the bleeding and whatever that you couldn't describe'
   — Ambulance officer describing the aftermath
of a loyalist attack on a Catholic betting shop

'He had a growing respect for the Presbyterian
and Protestant tradition. There is a side of him
that is very reflective and warm, and he deeply
believes people should be together and not
apart'
   — Presbyterian minister who held a series of
confidential talks with Gerry Adams

The cold bleak dawn broke over Teebane crossroads, a remote part
of County Tyrone, to reveal the first results of the escalation of
violence predicted by the army officer. The grey January morning
light revealed the full horror of the scene. A blue van, or what was
left of it, lay upside-down on a roadway strewn with dirt, debris,
pieces of clothing, personal possessions. It was said to be a Mercedes,
but not enough of it was left to be certain.

The grey morning illuminated a damp, lonely countryside of
green and brown. The van had been travelling along the road in
the previous evening's twilight, packed with working men on their
way home to their families on a Friday evening. They were looking
forward to the weekend. The attack that killed eight of those men
had obviously been planned with precision. Some of the gang had
placed the bomb in the hedge at the roadside. Others unrolled a

command wire, running it along the shelter of another hedge to set up a firing point on a rise overlooking the road.

When the van appeared, an IRA man pressed his finger on the firing button, sending an electric current along the wire and detonating the bomb. The vehicle took the full force of the blast. The van's upper part was torn asunder, but instead of being blown into a field its momentum kept it tumbling along the road until it came to rest 30 yards on. Seven men were killed outright, an eighth dying shortly afterwards. The scene at that point was hellish, with dead, dying and injured bodies scattered on the road, in a field, and trapped under wreckage. Some passers-by who stopped to help were sent into shock by the sight of terrible mutilations. It took the emergency services a considerable time to work out how many had been killed. Looking at the shredded remains of the van in the grim early light, it seemed inconceivable that anyone who was inside could have survived. Yet seven men were left alive, though they would carry physical and mental scars for the rest of their lives.

The men in the van, all Protestants, had been working on refurbishing an RUC station and were thus, in IRA terms, 'legitimate targets'. At the station itself they worked under heavy guard, but the unmarked van was travelling without an escort. The security forces believed it had escaped the attention of the IRA, but they were wrong.

Just over two weeks later came another shocking and unprecedented attack from another source. A twenty-four-year-old RUC constable, Allen Moore, arrived in plain clothes at the Sinn Fein press office on the Falls Road. He talked his way past Paddy Loughran, who was manning the electrically controlled security door, pretending he was a journalist, but once inside produced a pump-action shotgun and turned it on three men in a ground-floor office. Paddy Loughran, a fifty-one-year-old father of five, was killed; so was Pat McBride, another republican; so was Michael O'Dwyer. O'Dwyer, who was aged twenty-one, had two children, and had called at the office to complain to a Sinn Fein councillor about local youths who were making a nuisance of themselves.

Eighteen years earlier his mother had been killed by a loyalist bomb left at a Catholic pub. Constable Moore then drove out of Belfast to a secluded spot and shot himself dead.

The following day came yet more violence as loyalists exacted a grim revenge for the Teebane attack. Two members of the Ulster Defence Association walked into a quiet betting shop frequented by Catholics on the Ormeau Road in south Belfast. The UDA men coolly opened fire, systematically shooting as many men as they could. The attack only took a matter of minutes, but when it was over the room was filled with dead and dying. Five men were killed in the incident. An ambulance officer called to the scene described what he saw: 'I went in and had a quick look inside the building. The scene was horrific, with bodies everywhere. In that confined space there was a smell from the gunfire and all the bleeding and whatever that you couldn't describe. It has an effect on you as an individual. I get flashbacks to it, I get visions of what was going on. Even now talking about it, I get flashbacks to the original scene as I walked through the door – the smell, the feeling of being there. For other ambulancemen it was worse: they were knee deep in it, dealing with the dead and dying.'

Less than two weeks later the SAS was back in action, laying an ambush for IRA members who attacked an RUC station in the town of Coalisland in County Tyrone. The authorities allowed the attack on the heavily fortified station to go ahead, with the IRA men commandeering a lorry and firing a heavy machine-gun from the back of it. The security forces took no action at that point, but when the IRA unit drove into the car-park of a church some distance away, to dump the lorry and disperse in getaway cars, the SAS was waiting for them.

In the church car-park the undercover troops had the advantage of surprise, and of operating in a much less populated area where the risk of civilian casualties was low. When the lorry slewed into the car-park there was a call for the gang to surrender, followed by intense, prolonged gunfire. When it was all over four IRA members lay dead, with two others injured. The authorities celebrated the incident as a clean, clinical strike against the IRA.

The funerals of the four brought the spectacle of Adams and McGuinness engaging in a public argument with the RUC, a tableau which gave an insight into the bitterness between official-dom and republicanism. Thousands of people attended the funeral, watched by hundreds of police: the hatred between them was palpable. At one point police halted the funeral, a phalanx of several hundred officers in full riot gear forming a line across the road. A senior officer stepped forward and spoke to Adams, saying he wanted an assurance there would be no paramilitary trappings: Adams replied that he didn't like the officer's tone.

The policeman courteously explained that his concern was to prevent any paramilitary display. Adams turned and made his way through the crowd to find the parents of the dead men. While he was away Martin McGuinness stood face to face with the officer, who was clad in dark uniform, flak jacket, protective leggings, helmet, visor, black gloves and swagger stick. McGuinness needled him: 'You're standing there like a big child. You're as bigoted and sectarian as ever youse were.' The officer did not respond.

Adams and other Sinn Fein members came back with the fathers of the dead IRA men, and the officer explained that he wanted the coffin moved forward to the front of the mourners so that police could keep a closer eye on those around it. 'We want an assurance that there will be no shooting or paramilitary trappings. As soon as there are any signs of marching, stamping feet or para-military trappings we will stop it,' the officer said. 'Are there regu-lations for funerals?' Adams asked. The policeman said he was not going to get into any arguments. He agreed with the father of one of the dead IRA men that the proceedings had so far been very dignified, and accepted his assurance that there would be no para-military trappings. The police line moved back, and the coffins made their way through the little town and up to the small graveyard on the hill. In the graveyard, while the police were momentarily occupied elsewhere, the republicans surreptitiously staged their little ceremonial, a dozen or so youths, men and women in black leather jackets and white shirts carrying the coffin a few yards. But it took place out of public view, and both sides reckoned honour was satisfied.

At the time it seemed virtually inconceivable, in the middle of such a cycle of violence, that meaningful political activity could be under way; yet once again behind the scenes there were what turned out to be significant stirrings. For one thing, a major new actor appeared on the Anglo-Irish scene in January when Haughey, who had survived so many upheavals in his career, finally fell victim to one crisis too many. His successor as Taoiseach and leader of Fianna Fáil was an unknown quantity in Anglo-Irish relations, Albert Reynolds, who despite his previous inexperience would play a pivotal role in the developing peace process.

Known sometimes as 'the Rhinestone Taoiseach' because of his fondness for country-and-western music, Reynolds presented himself as a business wheeler-dealer. Where Haughey always professed strong nationalist beliefs, Reynolds belonged to the pragmatic, non-ideological wing of Fianna Fáil. Coming from the unfashionable Irish midlands county of Longford, he made a fortune for himself in the unlikely areas of pet-food, dance-hall management and bingo. Where Haughey was noted for his sense of dignity and even pretensions, Reynolds was a no-nonsense poor boy made good, a self-made millionaire who prided himself on having no airs and graces, but always with an eye for a deal.

He entered the Dáil relatively late, at the age of forty-four, but rose quickly, serving in a variety of economic departments including the senior post of finance minister. He and Haughey were close for many years, but their relationship cooled when Haughey made it known that his preferred successor was not Reynolds but Bertie Ahern. Late in 1991 he had taken part in what Irish politicians call a 'heave' – a move to oust Haughey. It was not a success and Reynolds was sacked for his pains. Within a few months, however, Haughey was brought down by a scandal unconnected with the north. Ahern took soundings and, concluding that he would not win the leadership contest, stepped aside, thus allowing Reynolds to become leader of Fianna Fáil. He brought to the job a directness and willingness to take risks which Haughey lacked: in the end he would write himself into Irish history by making the republicans an offer, almost along the lines of a business deal, which in the end they felt they should not refuse.

Haughey handed on to Reynolds the ongoing business of the joint declaration. Reynolds, in the course of extensive on-the-record interviews for this book, said Haughey, when briefing him, mentioned the joint declaration only in passing. According to Reynolds: 'He wasn't saying there was a breakthrough or anything like that. He said there were off and on contacts behind the scenes from time to time, but it hadn't been brought far enough that we were ready for a breakthrough. He said that he had discussions with John Hume off and on, that John Hume had been speaking with Sinn Fein off and on and no doubt John Hume would be bringing me up to date on where it was at – very little more.'

Reynolds's assertion that Haughey gave him only a peremptory briefing on the declaration is disputed by sources close to Haughey and others in Fianna Fáil. Bertie Ahern said later: 'I spoke to Haughey just before Christmas, and it was clear to me that he was not going to stay around too much longer. He mentioned key items to me, and the one that he put number one was the north. He actually told me he thought progress could be made on it and that it could be significant, and it was something in which I should take a big interest. I have no doubt he told Albert the same things he told me because he said he would be totally co-operative – and I know from Albert Reynolds he was totally co-operative.'

Whether or not Haughey stressed the importance of the joint declaration to Reynolds, Hume certainly did when the two met within days of his election as Taoiseach. Reynolds later said of that meeting: 'John Hume believed there was a window of opportunity to be exploited, that the mood within Sinn Fein was changing towards trying to find a political solution rather than continuing with the violence. He was convinced that if the government became involved and were prepared to take initiatives, we could take it quite a distance down the road. He asked me was I going to raise it with John Major. I said I was going to make it the very first item with Mr Major, which I did when I met him, within a matter of days after I met Hume.'

It was on 26 February that Reynolds flew to Downing Street for his first prime ministerial meeting with Major. The two premiers were not strangers, having become acquainted at EC meetings when Major was Chancellor of the Exchequer and Reynolds was Finance Minister. According to Reynolds: 'I told him straight what my priorities were, but he wasn't very familiar with the complexities of Northern Ireland and the historical background and we talked it through. We talked about twenty-five years of violence and we said together that we were prepared to try and change the scenario if that was possible. We agreed we'd give it our best shot to see if we could save the next generation from another twenty-five years of violence, and we said we were prepared to go the whole distance in trying to do this.'

According to Reynolds he did not mention the declaration to Major, since at that stage he himself had not seen any of the drafts. But he was happy that he and the British prime minister had started with a reasonable understanding, and had agreed to give priority to the northern problem: 'I knew that between us we had a relationship, that we could lift the phone and talk to each other, which we did time and time again. The relationship was as close as that, all through, right the whole way, no question about it. Even the civil servants didn't necessarily know we were talking to each other. Many a time too when we met we would have a tête-à–tête to ourselves with nobody present, for maybe ten, fifteen, twenty minutes. You'll find that not everything was on the record.'

Amid all the violence of early 1992, something was stirring within the leadership of Sinn Fein. Looking back three years later, a Protestant minister who was involved in lengthy secret contacts with Gerry Adams said simply: 'In spring 1992 we noticed Sinn Fein were prepared to make peace.' With hindsight a number of straws in the wind can now be seen as significant, though at the time their importance was largely masked by the din of battle.

Something of the evolution of the thinking of Adams can be traced through the eyewitness accounts of that minister, the Rev. Ken Newell of Fitzroy Presbyterian church in south Belfast. Mr

Newell is an evangelical Protestant, but unlike many such he was prepared to work with and worship with Catholic priests; he was also prepared to go further and meet republicans. This brought him into contact with Adams and others.

The clergyman is tall, silver-haired, blunt and straightforward, confident in his own views of religion and of life. Once, speaking to a mainly Catholic audience, he spelled out his philosophy: 'We need to talk to each other. Because we haven't been talking, a lot of pressure and anger and bad feeling has built up on both sides. I certainly feel there are enormous misconceptions, and the challenge for me is how you take this discussion out into the grassroots. We have to work out where to go together from here, because at the moment we're not friends, we haven't got the emotional bonding that we need if we're going to build a community that is worth living in. There's no future if we can't become friends.'

Mr Newell's church had a connection with Clonard monastery going back to the early 1980s, and in 1990 a senior Presbyterian minister suggested to him that Presbyterians should be working to understand Adams and Sinn Fein. The idea was taken up and, starting in September 1990, meetings were held in the monastery library. Mr Newell was accompanied by the Rev. Sam Burch from west Belfast and another senior Presbyterian from the north of the city. Father Reid and Father Reynolds attended, together with Gerry Adams, who brought with him Aidan McAteer and Theresa Holland, two members of his personal staff who were also related by marriage. Meetings were held twice and sometimes three times a month, on terms of strict confidentiality, with those present speaking frankly to each other.

All of them were chaired by Father Gerry Reynolds, who opened the proceedings with a reading from Psalm 85:

> I will hear what the Lord God has to say,
> a voice that speaks of peace,
> peace for his people and his friends
> and those who turn to him in their hearts.
> His help is near for those who fear him
> and his glory will dwell in our land.

Mercy and faithfulness have met;
justice and peace have embraced.
Faithfulness shall spring from the earth
and justice look down from heaven.

The Lord will make us prosper
and our earth shall yield its fruit.
Justice shall march before him
and peace shall follow his steps.

At first the meetings were fairly stiff, partly because positions were so far apart, but in time they came to speak frankly, and in doing so Adams showed a side of himself not usually seen by outsiders. Mr Newell recalled later:

At the time it was high-risk stuff. We told our own stories. We told how we grew up as Protestants, how we became ministers, Adams told how he became a republican: it was like exploring each other's life experiences. We explored and we analysed their ard-fheis statements, particularly one which addressed the concepts of freedom, justice and unity. I made a response to that, and we looked at the need for resolving problems through a democratic resolution. We took a pastoral approach to Sinn Fein: we weren't there to condemn, we were there to listen.

Many of the people being killed were Presbyterians, and they felt the emotional hurt through us. Many of the members of the RUC being killed were from our flocks. Gerry Reynolds and myself were going to RUC funerals and we were bringing back to those meetings in Clonard the raw hurt of them. The assaults on our communities were felt as raw assaults on us as pastors: those hurting them were hurting us.

During our first year and a half we were still polarised because we were meeting with a general defence of the armed struggle. We reached a point where we knew each other very well but didn't touch each other. We then suggested we should pull out of the talks because we were not going anywhere – we were looking over our shoulders at the loyalist paramilitaries as well as at our own congregations. Suggestions were then made on the republican side that if they couldn't connect with us they couldn't connect with Unionists at all. The input of one of the republicans was fairly static – you were talking to an answering machine, it was set in concrete. That was the view eighteen months into our talks: we had reached an impasse. We knew each other's geography but there wasn't a willingness to work towards a cessation, an end to violence, and some proposed we should stop in the absence of a peace process.

Then, after eighteen months of meetings, in the next couple of meetings there was a definite shift. In spring 1992 we noticed Sinn Fein were prepared to make peace. What we noticed was Adams's growing commitment to make peace and bring the violence to an end. When we first met Adams he was emotionally distant, quite nervous, but that didn't last long. He had a growing respect for the Presbyterian and Protestant tradition, especially its rugged independence of spirit, its sense of fairness, its democratic tendency and its willingness to take risks – embodied in the people who were there before him. There is a side of him that is very reflective and warm, and he deeply believes people should be together and not apart.

There was a feeling of a genuine willingness to try to make peace on the basis of the principles of self-determination of the Irish people, consent, and a democratic resolution of the conflict. There was a new agenda. The old frozen stereotype of republican responses was giving way to the impact of genuine friendship and real concern for each other. The emotional warmth of the meetings began melting the iceberg of traditional responses. If you attack an iceberg it just bounces back at you. The language now being used was – how do you get rid of an iceberg – you tow it into warmer water.

From Adams we got warm appreciation because we were talking. Ideas were floated such as how Sinn Fein could replace lost military influence if a ceasefire was called. One idea, mooted by the Protestants, was for Sinn Fein to mend relationships with the SDLP, Dublin etc. We knew for nearly two years that Adams was committed to peace, but he had to bring his party with him, and it would take all his skills as a leader to do this and not to split. Eighteen months before the ceasefire we knew it was coming, but it was full of risks in terms of his leadership.

Those meetings have left a legacy of real friendship. Adams suggested a second group of republicans should become involved in meetings and that is still [in 1995] going on, involving Presbyterian, Church of Ireland, Methodists and Catholics.

In February 1992, during a British general election campaign and in the midst of the security crisis, Sinn Fein launched a discussion document entitled 'Towards a Lasting Peace in Ireland'. Coming as it did so soon after the carnage of Teebane and all the other violence of the time, the title seemed little more than a mockery. Sinn Fein was speaking of peace but with the IRA using civilian workers as human bombs it was hardly surprising that few politicians and analysts paid much attention to the document.

It can now, however, be viewed as a document of great significance. In 1987 the document 'Scenario for Peace' had in effect set out demands for a British withdrawal. Five years on, this new paper showed a much more analytical, more thoughtful and more realistic republican movement. A new ideology was being born, one in which the republicans were seriously examining the possibility of pursuing their aims by political means alone. A republican source involved in the internal debates of the time later explained:

There was no 'road to Damascus' change. People didn't go to bed without a political strategy and wake up the next morning with one. It took time for the leadership to develop a strategy, and it took time for the activists to accept it – it took years. We were educating ourselves. We were learning. It was a learning curve for us. When you talked to republicans of the 1920s, or even the 1950s, you realised that they didn't really believe they could win – they saw themselves as keeping the flame alive and passing it on from one generation to another. If you are a small group of people, and if you are so certain of yourself, you tend to become élitist, condescending even, with a political philosophy which doesn't advance. Sinn Fein had to be modernised. Abstentionism, for example, wasn't relevant any more, but it took us two or three years to get rid of it.

The importance of 'Scenario for Peace' was that for the first time in fifteen years Sinn Fein had sat down and sought to explain its motivation and its objectives, and to spell out how its objectives could be achieved. Okay, it might have been naive, but it was a strategy. People involved in producing it knew it was flawed, but it was still early days when it was put together. After that it was a question of almost adopting a scientific approach to the issue of political development. Sinn Fein had to be modernised, the politics had to be brought into the 1990s, it had to be relevant. In 'Towards a Lasting Peace' we sought to identify problems, address them realistically, producing a strategy which had some prospect of success because it was based on realpolitik rather than simply a list of demands.

The republican team which wrote 'Towards a Lasting Peace' laboured for a full year before producing the document. In their deliberations the republicans had to face up to many new and changing factors. It was a time of great change in many areas: the world had moved on, posing a challenge for many of the old republican certainties.

To begin with, there was the question of the nature of the British presence. Although Sinn Fein would not accept that Britain was neutral, London had unquestionably changed the way it looked at the problem. The idea of returning to a Stormont-type system of Unionist domination was clearly long gone. So too was the idea that Northern Ireland was 'as British as Finchley': the Anglo-Irish Agreement had survived against all challenges for more than six years, and had become a permanent fixture of the political landscape. Dublin's part as an important player had been firmly established. Even if Sinn Fein's accusation that Britain was enlisting Dublin and the SDLP to help it control Northern Ireland was true, this in itself clearly represented a sea-change in British policy which had to be taken into account. The British had, after all, been prepared to face down all the loyalist protests over the accord. This made it much more difficult for republicans to argue that London was cynically manipulating the Unionists to maintain the British presence.

Furthermore, the unsuccessful Brooke talks had been based firmly on the three-stranded approach of defining the problem in terms of three relationships: those within Northern Ireland, the north-south relationship, and relations between the British and Irish governments. The republicans had been impressed by the fact that Hume and Dublin remained adamant about one point – that there could be no question of an 'internal settlement' under which

Dublin would largely fade out of the picture. Even the Unionists had accepted this framework, if reluctantly: the basic point was made, however, that constitutional nationalism, north and south, was not prepared to allow the British to treat the issue as a domestic British problem.

Peter Brooke's statements also represented a radical departure from the traditional British attitude. He had intrigued republicans with his reference to Cyprus and his assertion that Britain had no selfish strategic or economic interest in Northern Ireland. While he had proceeded under Unionist pressure to make comments which heavily qualified his remarks, he had not withdrawn them, and republicans were impressed by this. It was also noticed that the British Labour party had gone further, adopting a policy of Irish unity by consent.

Brooke's statement that a military defeat of the IRA was difficult to envisage, coupled with his indication that a cessation of violence would generate an imaginative and flexible British response, also suggested that London was not seeking an abject IRA surrender. Brooke had, after all, referred to the 'old Chinese principle that you must always leave your opponent an honourable method of retreat'. He had accepted, on behalf of the British, that no military solution looked possible just as Adams had, years earlier, begun saying the same thing on behalf of the republican movement. The clear implication of this, for both sides, was that they should be seeking a political solution.

In 1990, two years earlier, republican spokesmen continued to argue, in spite of the fall of the Berlin Wall, that Britain still regarded Northern Ireland as having significant strategic importance. The collapse of the Warsaw Pact had, however, made this contention distinctly threadbare as time went on, eventually leading Sinn Fein to concede that the breakup of the USSR 'opens up a completely new phase of history'. This had immensely weakened the case, made by Sinn Fein during the 1988 talks with the SDLP, that Britain's primary interest for remaining in Ireland was strategic. Those talks, together with the continuing private contacts between Hume and Adams, clearly had a profound effect on republican thinking, for many of the ideas advanced by Hume, and much of the language, would come to be adopted by Sinn Fein.

It is interesting to reflect that over the quarter-century of the troubles literally thousands of statements of condemnation of the IRA were issued: they were like water rolling off a duck's back. In the end it was not ritual rejection but intellectual engagement which helped bring the Sinn Fein leadership along the political path: dialogue was effective where denunciation was not.

From the Unionist side, however, came only continuing condemnation and a refusal to contemplate doing business with republicans. This was hardly surprising, for many loyalists viewed the conflict primarily in sectarian terms. The IRA could argue that the eleven people killed at Enniskillen had died accidentally, and that the eight who died at Teebane crossroads were killed because they were part of 'the British war machine'; but all Unionists could see were the bodies of nineteen dead Protestants. They never accepted the IRA explanation that such incidents were not sectarian. Yet if Protestants were not in the business of reassessing republicanism, Sinn Fein itself was re-examining its view of Unionism. Little about it appealed to them, yet the sense was growing that Unionists were an important feature of the landscape who could not simply be dismissed as people with no national rights.

Sinn Fein's theorists also had to come to grips with the profound social and political changes taking place in the south of Ireland. They had to face the harsh reality that they were making no significant electoral inroads into the southern political scene. Martin McGuinness's ambition of winning up to five Dáil seats had, post-Enniskillen, vanished: it was by now abundantly clear that there were to be no Sinn Fein representatives in the Dáil. Furthermore, nobody agreed with the traditional republican accusation that the south was a less than fully independent state dominated economically and in other ways by Britain. Its citizens regarded it as a sovereign independent country.

That country was going through momentous internal transitions. For decades economic and political change had been resisted in what was traditionally a conservative society, but at the beginning of the 1990s the floodgates suddenly opened and a new era of modernisation dawned. The comfortable old rural Catholic value system was challenged by a new outward-looking spirit as the south's strikingly young population – the youngest in Europe – came to the fore. The question of change and modernisation became the keynote of Irish politics, the Republic taking stock of itself and, more and more, coming to the conclusion that change rather than continuity should be the order of the day.

The first major political manifestation of this came in 1990 when Mary Robinson, a liberal feminist lawyer, turned tradition on its head by winning the presidential election campaign. Voters responded to her message that change should be the order of the day, sending seismic shocks through the old system. An advocate of liberal values and pluralism, she held out a vision of 'a future Ireland which can be open, generous, pluralist and tolerant'. She was nominated as president by the Irish Labour party, an elderly institution which remodelled and remarketed itself, under the leadership of Dick Spring, as the party of change and progress. This new approach resulted in a rich harvest of votes.

The trouble for Sinn Fein was that this strong new tide of opinion ran directly against their interests. The new breed, even more than the old, spoke of building a new Ireland and a new Europe, but when they did so they thought in twenty-six county terms, that is to say excluding the north. Northern Ireland was increasingly seen not as unfinished national business but rather as a nightmare, a place of endless, senseless, barbaric violence. The fear that Sinn Fein might make inroads into southern politics had by this stage practically disappeared, since it was obvious Sinn Fein could not win votes.

The violence had cut down on north–south social and economic contacts, many southerners not daring to venture north into what they viewed as a war zone. The IRA's campaign of violence seemed inexcusable and unjustifiable, the work of unfathomable northern strangers. Mainstream southern nationalism came to be expressed less and less in traditional terms; in fact nationalism itself began to be seen as outmoded. The south increasingly saw itself as European, and was far more interested in Brussels than in Belfast. This too told against Sinn Fein, which almost alone among Irish nationalist parties was anti-EC.

The national focus, in other words, tended to be not on the north but on the continent. This turning away from the north was strongly reflected by the south's intelligentsia, in particular newspaper columnists, who in Dublin tended to be much more influential than their counterparts in Britain. By the 1990s no reputable columnist or intellectual defended the IRA or Sinn Fein or pleaded their cause. The closest thing the republicans had to a sympathetic ear was the distinguished *Irish Times* columnist, Mary Holland. She strongly opposed their methods but persistently made a case for attempting to wean them away from violence and bring them into the political system. She attracted heavy criticism for doing so. For the most part, however, republicans were scorned, reviled and rejected by the south. All the political parties had become noticeably less nationalist in their outlook, while the resignation of Haughey as leader of Fianna Fáil had removed from the scene perhaps its 'greenest' politician. Old-style republicanism, preoccupied as it was with territorial conquest and self-determination, simply had no place in the new dispensation, with its emphasis on the pooling of sovereignty in the quest for a European ideal.

Even worse from Sinn Fein's point of view was the growth of a new southern trend to regard Unionists and Protestants as the real victims in the north. A few Unionist figures, headed by Ken Maginnis, the personable and popular MP for Fermanagh-South Tyrone, regularly travelled to the Republic, and in doing so had some success in winning friends and influencing people. This was anathema to the republicans, who found themselves losing their treasured victimhood. They were viewed as the real problem, not as a symptom of it, left behind by the tide of history, a murderous throwback to times gone by. The south's rejection of Sinn Fein was symbolised early in 1992 when the party was denied the use of the traditional venue for its ard-fheis. Instead of the Mansion House's admittedly fading grandeur, Adams found himself addressing the faithful in a run-down community centre in Dublin's unfashionable

Ballyfermot housing estate. The political message was clear. If Sinn Fein was to have any prospect of harnessing the south's considerable influence, it could not be done by winning votes and penetrating the system. If it was possible at all, it could only be by reaching out to the Dublin authorities and persuading and lobbying them.

The importance of this was that in being prepared to work with Dublin, republicans were recognising that they were unlikely to shift British policy on their own. They were also coming to terms with the fact that working with others would necessarily mean some compromise on their part. A Taoiseach might, as Haughey had done, send secret emissaries for furtive meetings behind closed monastery doors, but no Dublin government would openly co-operate with Sinn Fein while IRA violence persisted.

Something of this was later acknowledged by Adams when he wrote: 'We were mature enough to understand that because it was a consensus it wouldn't be the 1916 Proclamation [the declaration made by republicans during the Easter Rising of 1916]. It would have to reflect the view of John Hume and of the Irish government.' The vital importance of this is that republicans were beginning to think in terms of moderating their position in order to take account of the views of others. For a movement which had always thought in absolutist terms of victory, this was a crucial development, and one which paved the way for much that followed.

The 'Towards a Lasting Peace' document reflected a great many of these considerations, the much longer and more complex paper reflecting how much internal debate had taken place since the old simplicities of 'Scenario for Peace' in 1987. The new document contained much familiar republican rhetoric but instead of laying down conditions and demands it described itself as 'a responsible and realistic contribution to the debate on peace in Ireland'. Its first sentence was: 'The heart-felt aspiration of most people in Ireland is for peace.' It went on to acknowledge that Dublin had a major role to play, calling on the Irish government to persuade Britain and the Unionists of the benefits of unity. It continued to contest the concept that Britain was neutral, asserting that London actively wished to preserve partition. But it accepted that the collapse of the Warsaw Pact had profound implications. It mentioned the question of Unionist consent to unity, calling on a British government to 'join the ranks of the persuaders in seeking to obtain the consent of a majority of people in the north . . . for a united Ireland'. This was a long way from the old policy of demanding withdrawal irrespective of Unionist feelings.

There were several other indications that the republicans were by now thinking in terms of negotiation. Launching the document in Belfast, Adams said they might have to accept 'interim phases and interim arrangements' while still clinging to their aspiration of a united Ireland. Another Sinn Fein strategist, Jim Gibney, added in an important speech: 'We know and accept that the British government's departure must be preceded by a sustained period of peace and will arise out of negotiations involving the different shades of Irish nationalism and Unionism.' Clearly, traditional republican thinking had undergone a major overhaul.

Most tellingly of all, the document defined 'armed struggle' as 'an option of last resort'. It specifically said: 'There is an onus on those who proclaim that the armed struggle is counter-productive to advance a credible alternative . . . the development of such an alternative would be welcomed by Sinn Fein.' It also spoke of convincing a British government to adopt a policy of withdrawal 'either by continuing armed resistance or by an effective unarmed constitutional strategy'. All this illustrated a real evolution in republican analysis. For Adams and his associates it represented a marked shift away from simple utopianism, a lowering of the sights from absolutism towards the realms of the possible, a definite move towards political action and the possibility of an unarmed strategy. A senior republican, speaking at the time, described the new thinking:

> The long-term goal is still the same in terms of a united Ireland, but the period of time over which that might be achieved could be flexible. There is no necessary upper limit. It's a matter of trying to balance how far you can push the Unionists without forcing them over the edge. We have to be mindful of their fears and their concerns, and to deal with this in a time frame that minimises the risk of them going over the edge. There is potential

for greater pragmatism, but it should be possible without diluting Republican goals and objectives. We accept nobody in this situation is going to get everything they want. It's a question of accommodating each other. In the short term we may have to accept things we don't like but in the long term Britain must disengage.

The document represented a sea-change in republican thinking, but for a number of reasons its significance was not appreciated at the time. One was that Danny Morrison's 'Armalite and ballot-box' dictum meant that any move by the republicans in the direction of politics was automatically viewed by their opponents as designed to subvert the system rather than participate in it. Another was that the document was launched during a British election campaign, and on the day after the election the IRA exploded, in the heart of the City of London, a bomb which caused extraordinary and unprecedented devastation.

8

MEETINGS IN
MONASTERIES

'It involved nobody in my department except
Martin Mansergh and me – nobody else, no
records. To be successful it had to be kept so
tight'
   – former Taoiseach Albert Reynolds, describing secret contacts with republicans

Between 1969 and 1992 almost 10,000 bombs went off in Northern
Ireland, some large and some small. But on 10 April 1992, a single
IRA attack in London inflicted more financial damage than all the
bombs which had ever exploded in Northern Ireland.

As John Major was celebrating his re-election as prime minister
a huge bomb blast shook much of London. When the smoke and
dust cleared it was found that two IRA bombs, placed in the
heartland of the financial City district, had caused damage of more
than £700 million. The total paid out in compensation in Northern
Ireland at that point was just over £600 million. The device had
been placed near the Baltic Exchange and the tall buildings around
it created a canyon-like effect, preventing the blast from escaping
and instead funnelling it into the surrounding buildings. British
newspapers were so mesmerised by the extent of the destruction
that they carried full-page photographs of the devastation. The
damage was so severe that the fact that the bomb had also killed
three people, one of them a fifteen-year-old girl, was almost over-
looked.

The spectacular destruction grabbed the attention of the world.

Republican sources made no secret of the fact that they were both amazed and delighted at the extent of the damage and by the extraordinary bill for repairs. The idea of placing large bombs in the City, where so many expensive prestige buildings cluster in a tightly packed area, came late and largely by accident to them. Since 1988 they had carried out scores of attacks, but it took four years before they hit on the idea of bombing the financial quarter.

The scale of the Baltic Exchange chaos opened a new avenue, the possibility of inflicting serious damage on the entire British economy. In the 1970s the IRA had naively held such a belief, but the idea faded as the government showed itself able to absorb, without great difficulty, the cost of dealing with terrorism and disorder. However, the fact that a single attack could cost Britain more than half a billion pounds lent a whole new dimension to the IRA campaign. The authorities were desperate to prevent any recurrence, and worried that if the IRA could strike again major financial institutions might relocate to other countries not subject to such a terrorist menace. The government's nightmare was that Britain's entire billion-pound financial sector could be undermined.

The republicans wondered whether they had accidentally found the Achilles' heel of the British, and immediately laid plans to repeat the Baltic Exchange attack. But even as the 'active service units' in England set about targeting large buildings such as Canary Wharf in London's docklands, the republican theorists back in Ireland were busy working on a form of words which might have the power to bring their campaign to an end. Once again, violence and politics were proceeding in tandem.

Late in 1991 Hume had given to Adams the joint declaration which he, Haughey, Mansergh, O hUiginn and Nally had put together. On 6 February 1992, a response came back from the republicans, Father Reid bringing copies to Dublin and to Hume.

This was a document of potentially historic significance, since it represented the IRA laying out precise terms for bringing its campaign to an end. In a cover note with the draft the republicans said they had accepted the draft sent to them with minimum rewording on a timeframe, on the collective right to self-determination, and on the British being persuaders for unity.

The declaration process had by now produced three documents: the first drawn up by Hume; the second as expanded by Mansergh and Haughey, and now this, a substantive response from the republican movement. The document (which is reproduced in Appendix 1) kept to the general format of the Hume–Dublin document but radically altered its import by inserting what was in effect a declaration that Britain would depart from Ireland within a certain period. The document's focus was not on agreement but on a proposed unilateral move by the British government, which would commit itself to Irish unity and to withdrawal from Ireland, within a period to be agreed. Ireland would be united as an independent country. The consent of Unionists was to be sought for such an arrangement, but was not held to be a prerequisite: Britain was to attempt to secure consent, but if it was not forthcoming the British withdrawal would proceed in any event.

The key section said: 'The British government, consequently, commits itself to such unity (within a period to be agreed) and to use all its influence and energy to win consent for this policy.' On one reading this was simply a slightly softened restatement of standard Sinn Fein policy, but from another perspective it was a major change in republican thinking. The principle of consent was not given priority, but nor was it brusquely brushed aside. Instead, the republicans acknowledged that it was a real factor in the equation.

It was still, however, a long way from the Hume–Dublin formula, which had envisaged an all-Ireland context but not a British withdrawal. It had not been thought, however, that the republicans would sign up for the joint declaration on the basis of the first wording offered to them: it was to be expected that they would attempt to alter it to make it a much more republican document. Hume was very hopeful, while from Dublin's point of view the response was not so extreme as to close down the approach of seeking a joint declaration. The process of working towards an agreed text therefore continued.

Dublin and Hume set to work in an attempt to reconcile the

text they had sent to Adams with the text he had sent back. Reynolds, on learning of the initiative, had from the start been most enthusiastic, putting the full weight of his office behind the effort. Reynolds and Hume spoke often on the phone, and Hume frequently journeyed to Dublin for work on the declaration. Father Reid was also highly active, conveying messages between Adams and Dublin. The pace of movement quickened, and in April 1992 Hume and Dublin formulated a reply, much of which was drafted by Sean O hUiginn, to the February text (see Appendix 1). This contained no reference to a time-scale for unity, though it proposed the British government should declare its readiness to give legislative effect to unity if this had the consent of a majority in Northern Ireland.

The republicans replied to this with a document which has already entered Irish history. Delivered in June 1992, it was what came to be known as 'Hume–Adams' (see Appendix 1). With very few changes, this document would a year later be sent to London as the proposed basis for an IRA cessation and thus the opening of a new period of Irish history. It was an uneasy compromise between the republicans and the constitutional nationalists: both sides were nervous about it, for different reasons, and each had reservations. Yet it was enough to establish a thin ledge of common ground on which both violent and non-violent nationalism could stand.

The June 1992 document revealed movement on the part of the republicans, in effect confirming the Rev. Ken Newell's observation that 'in spring 1992 we noticed Sinn Fein were prepared to make peace'. The republicans shifted from their February 1992 position, which sought to commit Britain to Irish unity within a period to be agreed. The principle of consent was now given much more emphasis, with the British asked to commit themselves not to unity but to self-determination. Furthermore, the republicans accepted, for the first time ever, Hume's formulation that self-determination must be achieved and exercised with the agreement and consent of the people of Northern Ireland.

All this amounted to a masterpiece of what a senior British official referred to, in another context, as constructive ambiguity.

The traditional republican attitude was that self-determination meant a vote of all those in both parts of the island, taken after a British commitment of intent to withdraw. Here they were accepting that self-determination could only be exercised with the consent of people in the unit of Northern Ireland.

Did this latest document contain, in its fourth paragraph, the British declaration of intent to withdraw so sought after by Sinn Fein? The language used was woolly and vague enough to occupy politicians and lawyers for days if not weeks; the deft use of ambiguity made it, in practical terms, all but impossible to say. The bottom line was that it was unclear; but it might be enough. This document was to prove a vital landmark in the peace process, as a text which Sinn Fein could live with and which Dublin could accept, albeit with reservations.

Both Hume and Dublin were concerned about the phrase 'within a specified period to be agreed', for on one reading it had overtones of a British declaration of intent to withdraw. In the months that followed there would be many contacts between republicans, Hume and Dublin, with the constitutional nationalists attempting to iron out the ambiguity.

Throughout 1992 absolutely none of this was known to the general public. The notion of talking to Sinn Fein, even indirectly, remained a highly sensitive issue guaranteed to produce a hail of protest and condemnation. With IRA violence running at a high level, including many high-profile attacks in England, the general assumption was that the republicans were interested only in pursuing a military victory over the British. Equally, many people, especially Unionists and Conservatives, held the view that the only way to deal with the republicans was by inflicting a military defeat on them. The evolution of Sinn Fein thinking, as illustrated in 'Towards a Lasting Peace' and other republican statements, was not generally regarded as particularly promising, and not seen as forming any new basis for talks with the republicans.

Instead, the public focus was in an entirely different direction, as John Major pursued a policy of reviving the talks, involving the constitutional parties and the two governments, which Peter Brooke had unsuccessfully conducted in the spring of 1991. He did so without Brooke himself, who left the Cabinet following the general election in April. He had spent three arduous years as Northern Ireland Secretary, during which time he had set in motion both the talks process and the back-channel contacts with the republicans. He would be remembered as one of the most imaginative and thoughtful British ministers, though he had made a serious *faux pas* in February 1992 after the Teebane crossroads bombing. On the evening after the bombing he had gone ahead with a previous arrangement to appear on Gay Byrne's *Late Late Show* on RTE, the Irish television service. The fact that during the show he sang a party piece, 'Oh My Darling Clementine', brought a storm of Unionist protest and led him to offer Major his resignation.

Later he recalled: 'I went and saw the families of seven of those who were killed. My wife was with me: that was our first wedding anniversary, and we spent the whole of the anniversary visiting seven homes, because they all said they would like to see me. It was a very moving experience.' Major declined Brooke's resignation offer at the time, but from then on his days in the office were numbered and it came as no surprise when he was not re-appointed three months later.

John Major's choice as the new Northern Ireland Secretary was welcomed by Unionists but caused dismay in Dublin. Sir Patrick Mayhew, as his name suggested, came from an Irish background, but in his previous post as Attorney-General he had been locked in a series of often acrimonious disputes with the Irish government. He was at the centre of long-running wrangles over extradition arrangements, causing many in Dublin to characterise him as arrogant and high-handed. One Dáil backbencher commented: 'He has raised haughtiness to an art form.'

He also angered nationalists with his part in what became known as the Stalker affair, when a senior English policeman, John Stalker, was called in to examine the 1982 deaths of five republicans and a civilian at the hands of the RUC. During the protracted affair Mayhew, as Attorney-General, told the Commons that evidence had been found of attempts to pervert the course of justice. He added, however, that in the public interest and due to 'particular considerations of national security', there would be no prosecutions. The resulting storm of protest from the Irish government plunged Anglo-Irish relations into the deep freeze. Gerry Collins, then Irish Foreign Minister, said anyone who believed there was a conspiracy but thought there should be no prosecutions 'is not fit for public office'. He added: 'Only the paramilitaries will benefit. The British Attorney-General has given a new lease of life to the IRA.' The Foreign Office lodged an official protest against the remarks. The combination of the extradition disputes and the Stalker controversy meant Mayhew was something of a hate figure in Dublin political circles, where he was characterised as anti-Irish. A Dublin government source said: 'His attitude to even the existence of our state would seem to be odd.' Although his background was Irish, he came from an Anglo-Irish landowning family and was viewed as leaning towards the Unionist cause. Mayhew had had some direct brushes with the IRA. He had been sitting close to John Major when the mortars were fired at 10 Downing Street, and he knew he was on an IRA assassination list: his name was one of a hundred on a target list found concealed in a flat in Clapham.

In the event, Mayhew's record as Northern Ireland Secretary would not please Unionists as much as they had hoped. But neither were nationalists to be impressed: their criticism would be that he was too stiff and that Brooke's political skills were to be missed. Their view was largely shared by a senior British source who had contact with both Mayhew and Brooke: 'I think Brooke had the more subtle mind and was perhaps prepared to think of what you might call high-risk ways of taking the process further. I'm not sure he's got quite the subtlety of intellect that Brooke had.'

Within weeks of his arrival in Belfast Mayhew pushed ahead with a revival of the Brooke talks, an undertaking which would occupy the constitutional politicians for many months. Sinn Fein was again excluded because of its identification with the IRA. This session of talks would ultimately prove unsuccessful, but it did get beyond the procedural points which had defeated the Brooke discussions, and some serious debate did take place. Thus the peace process, based on the joint declarations, ticked over in the background while the talks process occupied public attention.

As the Mayhew talks progressed at Stormont the Unionist parties were primarily concerned to reduce the influence which Dublin had been given by the Anglo-Irish Agreement. They also wished to get rid of Articles 2 and 3 of the Irish constitution, which since 1937 had laid legal claim to Northern Ireland. Some Unionists wanted a strong new devolved government re-established in Belfast, while others preferred to aim for closer links with Westminster, accompanied by a less powerful Belfast assembly. The first priority of Hume and the Irish government, on the other hand, was to protect the Anglo-Irish Agreement and if possible develop stronger north-south and Anglo-Irish links. As the talks were starting Hume met Adams to assure him the SDLP was not interested in an internal settlement. He told Adams: 'We're not trying to get a few jobs at Stormont – we're not going for an internal solution.'

The Unionist parties wanted to concentrate on discussing a new assembly, while Hume and Dublin were more interested in dealing with north-south relations. Hume's analysis was that the Mayhew talks would not reach agreement since Sinn Fein was not involved in them, and because Unionists were not ready for the type of far-reaching new arrangements he envisaged. His approach was to discuss the issues but to regard the exercise as essentially an overture to later all-inclusive talks in which he hoped Sinn Fein would take part, following an IRA cessation. A number of those involved in the talks, including some in his own party, remarked on Hume's demeanour at Stormont, saying they often found him irascible and difficult to work with. There were several reasons for this. One was the fact that his sister, a well-known health worker in Londonderry, was dying of cancer. His approach was also heavily influenced by what an associate described as 'the bigger picture' – his hope that the work on the declaration might bear fruit and supersede the limited nature of the Stormont talks.

According to Unionist politicians, during the talks Hume's aide, Mark Durkan, agreed with them on the outline of a new assembly, but was shortly afterwards overruled by Hume. This, they claimed, showed Hume was not serious about reaching agreement with them. Hume and Durkan both denied this, but for years afterwards Unionists claimed the SDLP leader was in the business of overruling more reasonable elements in his party. However, the fact that Durkan knew about the declaration work, and agreed with Hume that it held more potential than any assembly plan, makes it unlikely that he would commit himself as the Unionists claimed he did.

When Hume unveiled the SDLP's proposal for new structures it established once and for all that he was not interested in an internal settlement. Under his plan, power would be divided between a new assembly and a panel of six commissioners – three from Northern Ireland, one each from the British and Irish governments, and one from the EC. This controversial and innovative proposal dismayed Unionist politicians, some of whom had perhaps naively hoped the SDLP would settle for a Northern Ireland-centred arrangement with modest links to Dublin and elsewhere. The talks sparked some interest when Molyneaux became the first Ulster Unionist leader to head a delegation to Dublin for discussions with the Irish government, but in the end nothing emerged to bridge the gulf between the SDLP and the Unionists, and in November 1992 the exercise was wound up. Hume later said: 'I was very interested in those talks but they didn't lead anywhere. I was working on both fronts. I wanted the declaration to move forward, but I was in talks and it was obvious the Unionists weren't moving an inch.'

The British government's approach continued to be that it would hope for an agreement among the constitutional parties with the purpose of isolating the republican and loyalist extremists. But after the best efforts of Brooke and Mayhew it was plain enough that there was no immediate prospect of this coming about.

As the Mayhew talks ran their course, other events were taking place in strict secrecy behind the scenes. Work was going on in parallel on the joint declaration while, as we shall see later, the British government was in frequent contact with the republicans via the back-channel. Everyone knew about the Mayhew talks;

very few knew about the declaration; hardly anyone knew about the back-channel. The British government was aware of much of what was happening, for John Hume told John Major of the declaration work, also mentioning it to Mayhew in May, during the Stormont talks. He found Mayhew aloof and not greatly interested in the declaration. In the summer of 1992 Hume held detailed discussions on the discussion work with Chilcot of the NIO. London was clearly interested in it, but tended to regard the declaration idea as one fraught with difficulties, likely to stir up the extreme loyalists and standing little real chance of triggering an IRA cessation.

Against the background of the failure of the Mayhew talks, more Dublin attention became focused on what was unofficially called 'the JD document' – the joint declaration drafts. Dublin regarded the version arrived at in June 1992 as flawed and unfinished: it clearly contained ambiguities and it went to what one involved called 'the outer limits of what was acceptable'.

Dialogue was continuing between Hume and Adams while Mansergh was in contact with Father Reid, who in turn spoke to Adams. The republicans wanted a clear definition of self-determination, a clear timetable, and a clear commitment that the British would act as persuaders for Irish unity. The constitutional nationalists, by contrast, were stressing the need for agreement, and wanted the declaration to be clearly in line with the Anglo-Irish Agreement in relation to Unionist consent and other matters. While the republicans hoped to dilute the concept of consent, Reynolds regarded himself as effectively bound by the Agreement's clause that Dublin and London agreed that any change in Northern Ireland's status could only come about with the consent of a majority of its people.

With many points still not cleared up, Reynolds took an important decision: to open direct contact with the republican movement. As Charles Haughey had done five years earlier, he asked Martin Mansergh to sit down face to face with Sinn Fein. This followed a personal letter written to Reynolds by Adams in the summer of 1992, in which he said it would be best to discuss the declaration drafts face to face with someone from the Irish government. He conceded in the letter that such meetings would be a risk for Reynolds, but promised him that republicans could keep a confidence and assured him there would be no breach of security. Adams wrote again in September 1992 repeating his request. In a 1995 interview for this book Reynolds explained:

> The question arose – how did you build Sinn Fein's confidence so they would accept that I was prepared to take an initiative and to run with it? By my own actions I had to build confidence between us so that they were prepared to come along the road with a declaration that had some possibility of success. The dramatic decision to put my man to meet intermediaries – you could call it a gamble, I called it a calculated risk to move the peace process forward. I didn't consult with anyone. I listened to the various messages being brought to me by various people, Father Alec Reid, Martin Mansergh and others coming to me independently. I thought about it quite extensively, I thought about it at home, I thought about it in the office, I evaluated where we were at. We weren't going anywhere. We didn't seem like we were going to get anywhere, so the question was, do I shut it down altogether or do I try and break the deadlock. We had to do something otherwise you were only going to continue on using up time and energy and not getting anywhere.

Reynolds did not even inform the leader of the Progressive Democrats, Des O'Malley, his coalition partner in the Irish government. He said he believed the PDs would have disapproved of the secret talks – 'they would probably have burst it wide open anyway if I'd discussed it'. He intended, he says, to bring them into the secret at a later stage if progress was made. O'Malley, interviewed in the course of research for this book, confirmed that he had not been told of the contacts with republicans. He also confirmed that if he had been informed he would have expressed reservations about the approach. He said: 'We weren't told, and I gather most Fianna Fáil ministers weren't told either. It was a kind of solo run by Reynolds. I would have been in two minds about the contacts. I am very doubtful that I would have encouraged it. It wouldn't have been a policy I would have advocated.' According to Reynolds:

My intention was that if it went wrong I would resign my position and walk away from it and that's why I didn't involve others in it. I mean it was a major risk, a total shift in direction, a total shift in policy, and it was so sensitive that it had to be kept very tight. That's why it involved nobody in my department except Martin Mansergh and me – nobody else, no records. Secrecy had to surround it, for to be successful it had to be kept so tight. That's the only way I saw it having any chance of success. I told Mansergh, 'You tell me if you're happy with that and if you're not, say so.' I didn't want to involve the guy to that extent if he didn't want to be involved, and if he didn't feel happy. But I said I would carry the can at the end of the day anyway – 'it's my responsibility, it's not yours, you are here doing a job'. He said he thought it was an extremely courageous decision, and he said, 'I don't know of anybody else who would do that.' I said, 'Well, I've made up my mind to do it.'

I took the view that, whatever views you might have on Sinn Fein, IRA or otherwise, the one thing about them is that they were very highly confidential people. I didn't feel they would ever sell me down the river and I'd no intention of selling them down the river. Now I could leave myself out of a job, but then I'm not the type of politician, I'm not the traditional politician, I'm not the career politician. I come in, I want to do a job, I want to do something decent with the time I'm there and if I fail I walk away and I can live without politics the following week.

A little later Reynolds informed some senior colleagues about the declaration and the talks. Bertie Ahern, who was then Finance Minister, said later: 'The document wasn't circulated generally but there was some discussion on it. I understood it was a distillation of the conversations of Gerry Adams and John Hume which arrived with the Taoiseach. It was seen at the time as significant. It was very risky. It had the huge political risk of the Taoiseach moving out and taking that chance without having anything cleared at the Cabinet table, or keeping colleagues directly informed and directly briefed.'

Reynolds also told Mrs Maire Geoghegan-Quinn, a close colleague who as Justice Minister was responsible for policing and security in the Republic. She said later in an interview conducted for this book: 'Martin Mansergh was going to be Albert's spokesperson so that if anybody asked questions as to whether Albert was meeting anybody, nobody could say that he was. Knowing Albert as a risk taker over the years when he was in various government departments, he had taken risks and they had paid off. I suppose I felt that whatever risk he was going to take, he would pull it off.'

Reynolds said that he never considered informing the Gardai that the government was talking to Sinn Fein, but when Mrs Geoghegan-Quinn learnt of it she informed the Garda assistant commissioner responsible for security matters. She said later that the police officer's reaction was 'one of surprise, but not one of shock. This was on the basis of a comment that Albert had made very early on when he became leader of the party, to the effect that he meant business about Northern Ireland, and they knew that had to mean that people had to talk to the Provos. Nobody should take it that during all this dialogue we went soft on the Provos, because we didn't. If anything over that period of time the Guards were even tougher in relation to searches and finds.'

One person who was not informed of the Mansergh–Sinn Fein talks was Hume: he was himself still in touch with Adams but knew nothing of Mansergh's activities in meeting senior Sinn Fein figures. The meetings were arranged through Father Reid and Father Reynolds. Almost all of them were held in the Redemptorist monastery in Dundalk, the same venue where in 1988, on the instructions of Charles Haughey, Mansergh had met Gerry Adams, Mitchel McLaughlin and Pat Doherty. Only one of the meetings took place elsewhere, in a monastery in Dublin. Most of them involved Martin McGuinness and Aidan McAteer, an important activist not known to the general public. McAteer had a strong republican pedigree: he is the son of Hugh McAteer, a one-time IRA chief of staff. He spent most of the 1970s in prison on IRA offences, became a full-time republican worker on his release in 1981 and in 1985 joined Gerry Adams's personal staff. For security reasons the meetings were kept to a minimum. According to Reynolds, he told John Major about the approach he was taking. He said later: 'I told him I was not going to expose him at all to it unless I arrived at a situation where I believed a breakthrough was possible. I told him I was going to work behind the scenes to try to produce some kind of formula that had the potential to get peace in Northern Ireland, but that I wasn't asking him to be part of any of that operation. I would continue it and would present it to him at a given point in time if I thought there was potential for success, and if there wasn't he would hear no more about it. I said I had my own contacts, my own intermediaries.'

9

TWO BALLS OF
ROASTED SNOW

'If you are talking in terms of success rates, yes, this week has been a success – and it is still only Thursday'
   – UDA leader, speaking after the organisation had killed four Catholics

'He impressed me as one of the most serious and intellectually gifted political people that I have met. Adams is, thank God, a person of considerable brains'
   – former Irish diplomat who held confidential talks with Gerry Adams

'You're on your own, Albert'
   – reported reaction of Albert Reynolds's new Foreign Minister, Dick Spring, when briefed on the joint declaration idea

'If the Arabs and the Israelis can do it, why can't we?'
   – Albert Reynolds, in a private letter to John Major

Mansergh twice met McGuinness and McAteer of Sinn Fein in Dundalk in October 1992, but the following month brought a sudden and potentially fatal interruption to the talks on the declaration when, with some ill-chosen words, Reynolds unexpectedly brought down his own government. Although he and Des O'Malley of the Progressive Democrats were coalition partners, they had long been at odds over a long-running issue concerning alleged irregularities in the important Irish beef industry. Giving evidence to a tribunal investigating the issue, Reynolds described O'Malley as dishonest, apparently in the belief that the word was part of the normal vocabulary of political abuse. But, since O'Malley's party was actually founded on a platform of raising standards of integrity and honesty in Irish political life, he would not accept the word. When Reynolds refused to withdraw it the government collapsed and an election was called.

The episode caused many to question Reynolds's judgement, for while there had been tensions in the coalition there seemed no reason why it should not continue in office for much longer. Yet after less than a year he essentially talked himself out of government. There were also criticisms of Reynolds's style and his use of language. In one broadcast interview, for example, he had used the words, 'That is crap, absolute pure crap.' Many felt a Taoiseach should refrain from such undignified expressions. A former Fianna Fáil deputy said of Reynolds at the time: 'He's a nice guy but he hasn't grown into the office. Whatever you'd say about Charlie Haughey, he could go up there and sound good. But Albert doesn't express himself in the way you would expect a Taoiseach to do, and he's produced this election out of thin air.'

The result of the election came as a shock to everyone and as a personal disaster for Reynolds. His Fianna Fáil party lost many seats, slumping to its worst defeat since 1927, while the other large traditional party, Fine Gael, also fared badly. The accidental election turned out to be a real watershed, for the voters switched in large numbers to parties advocating reform and modernisation.

Principal among these was the Irish Labour party, led by Dick Spring, who in 1990 had come up with the inspired idea of nominating Mary Robinson in the presidential election. The election result showed her victory in that contest was more than a flash in the pan, the huge rise in Labour's support confirming the country's appetite for change. Of most immediate importance to Reynolds was the fact that it gave Labour the balance of power in the Dáil, making Dick Spring the kingmaker. It initially seemed that Spring would link up with Fine Gael but, after weeks of negotiation, he opted, to general surprise, for a Fianna Fáil–Labour coalition.

Reynolds, who had seemed destined for opposition, against all expectations found himself re-elected Taoiseach. Republicans breathed a sigh of relief at this, for Reynolds had a proven commitment to the joint declaration work whereas John Bruton of Fine Gael, the other contender for the job of Taoiseach, took a much sterner line against the republicans and was thought likely to abandon the whole declaration process.

In the negotiations before the Fianna Fáil–Labour coalition was formed Reynolds briefed Spring fully on the declaration work. When the two men met in the Berkeley Court hotel in Dublin on 13 December, public and media attention was focused on a huge IR£8-billion deal for the Republic which Reynolds was negotiating with the European Community. The two men were closeted for some hours, with everyone assuming they were discussing the European money. In fact, most of the time was spent on Anglo-Irish affairs, Reynolds giving Spring a full run-down on the declaration work. He did so in the strictest secrecy on the basis that if they did not form a coalition together, Spring would take the knowledge 'to his grave'.

In an interview conducted for this book, Spring explained: 'In our negotiations Mr Reynolds was absolutely honourable, putting all cards on the table, facing upwards. There was nothing hidden. He showed me the draft of a document: what they were drafting up was a position that Sinn Fein could live with, a position that would trigger Sinn Fein into a peace process. At that stage Mr Reynolds said there was a prospect of a breakthrough, of an end to the violence. Sinn Fein were engaged, they were looking for an avenue, a way to come in. I kept knowledge of it very tight. I didn't tell others.'

Dick Spring had driven a hard bargain, extracting many concessions from Reynolds before agreeing to enter into a coalition with him. Reynolds had to sign up for a fifty-eight-page 'programme for a partnership government', much of it effectively dictated by Spring. Labour took six of the fifteen Cabinet seats, Spring himself becoming both Tanaiste (deputy Taoiseach) and Minister for Foreign Affairs, with responsibility for the north and Anglo-Irish relations.

Soon after the new Reynolds–Spring coalition took office it became apparent that Spring was pursuing his own line on Northern Ireland. One theory on why the Mayhew talks had not got further was that Dublin had not been generous enough in considering changes to Articles 2 and 3 of the Irish constitution. Spring believed Dublin should reach out to Unionists by holding out the prospect of greater movement on the Articles. This approach greatly interested Mayhew, who believed such movement might help break the inter-party logjam and could draw a reciprocal response from Unionists. Spring had been given a huge vote and a mandate for change. Opinion in the Republic was clearly more anti-republican than ever, with a new appreciation of Unionist sensitivities and wishes. He believed the emphasis should be on attempts to reach out to Unionists rather than on concentrating on the republicans. The programme for government drawn up during the coalition negotiations made no mention of the joint declaration, reflecting instead Spring's priority of seeking a resumption of the type of talks conducted by Brooke and Mayhew. His approach was a departure, but it was not necessarily at odds with Reynolds's work on the joint declaration. This was primarily because, to begin with at least, the declaration work was being conducted in complete secrecy. Spring was focusing on Unionism while Reynolds concentrated on republicanism: the two approaches might eventually conflict, but in the meantime the Irish government pursued them in tandem. Spring explained in an interview conducted for this book: 'We had to have a twin approach and different things had to be done. There was a prospect of the republican contacts working and the obvious thing was to nurture that, and that was the Taoiseach's bag. We divided the brief, so to speak. He kept me informed on a daily basis. It was very much part of our daily focus.'

Fianna Fáil sources would later say bluntly that Spring did not really believe the declaration process could deliver peace: sources close to Spring retort that neither did most Fianna Fáil ministers.

Fergus Finlay, Spring's shrewd personal adviser, confirms that Spring was sceptical of the declaration work. Interviewed in the course of research for this book, he explained: 'Dick instinctively took the view that too rapid a movement in one direction would result in alienation in the other and decided his role ought to be to address the concerns of Unionism – to try to set a more open agenda where Unionism was concerned. From that moment, really for the remainder of the year, he was the counterweight, I suppose. It wasn't a "good cop – bad cop" kind of strategy, it was just the way things evolved. He had trouble with the speed with which Albert wanted to move, and I think he argued several times that enough time had to be given to enable private dialogue to bring Unionist opinion around.'

A more vivid description of how Reynolds and Spring arrived at this division of labour is given in the memoirs of Reynolds's press officer, Sean Duignan. In March 1993, early in the life of the new government, Reynolds showed Duignan and another close aide, Bart Cronin, a draft of the declaration: Duignan said the risks Reynolds was taking 'scares the bejasus out of us'. In his book he recounts:

> I subsequently asked him [Reynolds] if Spring knew about pulling in the Provos. I made a diary note of how Reynolds responded: 'Yes, I told him.'
> 'And what did he say, Taoiseach?'
> 'You're on your own, Albert.'

Finlay, it should be recorded, disputes that Spring said this about the declaration work, contending that Duignan is mistaken and that Spring in fact used the words on a later occasion in a different context. It should also be noted that Finlay himself became one of the small group of senior officials who handled the declaration work, taking part in many Anglo–Irish negotiations.

A Dublin source used a striking image to describe the different approaches of Reynolds and Spring to the peace process.

> In terms of Dick Spring's cautious political approach, Albert was sort of the joyrider from hell. As it turned out Albert was actually

a very sure driver, but it was a nerve-racking journey for someone who is more cautious by temperament. Spring very deliberately saw himself as being the insurance policy for the outfit if things went wrong.

He wanted the thing to work, but he was more cautious and felt his role was not to out-Albert Albert, but rather to stay those few steps behind in case it went off the rails. If it had become unstuck Spring at that point would have just moved into the driving seat, as somebody who wasn't compromised by an earlier policy that had failed.

Reynolds, it should be noted, had a highly individualistic prime ministerial style and approach: he was a hands-on Taoiseach, much given to sorting things out on a one-to-one basis. Bertie Ahern, his eventual successor as leader of Fianna Fáil, later gave a flavour of the unique Reynolds approach:

> Albert doesn't follow notes in the formal way of accounting to the Cabinet. Albert would say, 'Well I've been in touch with that fellow, I've been in touch with him and I'll ring him' – that's his style, he'd do it himself. Albert would come in with the sheet [agenda] and the civil servants, but then he would never look at the sheet. He'd be saying, 'Well I'll be on to your man, I'll have those two down to the office – those two fellows met me and I met them in a room and I had to get rid of my car and my bodyguards, then I had to get my daughter to give me a lift down and the security guys were going the other way.' He'd say these kind of things, it was very horrific, but I mean that's the way Albert went on.

The road towards peace was proving long, slow and tortuous. The Anglo-Irish Agreement was signed in 1985; the IRA's Libyan armoury arrived in that year and in 1986; the simplistic 'Scenario for Peace' was published in 1987, the same year as the Enniskillen bombing. The Sinn Fein–SDLP talks took place in 1988. The following year Peter Brooke made his Cyprus speech; in 1990 he said Britain had no selfish interest in Northern Ireland and opened the back-channel to the IRA. In 1991 the IRA attacked Downing Street with mortars, and John Hume wrote the first draft of the joint declaration. In 1992 the IRA killed eight Protestant workers at Teebane crossroads, while loyalists killed five Catholics in a betting shop and the SAS killed four IRA members in Coalisland. In the same year Sinn Fein had produced the more thoughtful 'Towards a Lasting Peace', while Albert Reynolds had arrived on the scene and added energy to the peace process.

The peace process was so painfully slow that many doubted whether it was in any way meaningful. If the process was worthwhile it was nevertheless taking years to come together: meanwhile, out there in the back streets of north Belfast and in the country lanes of east Tyrone, people were still dying.

But after all the years of moving at a snail's pace, the spring of 1993 ushered in a new phase of often frantic activity, with the public for the first time glimpsing a little of what had for so long been going on in secrecy. From then on, incident followed incident and development followed development in an often bewildering blur of events. Ahead lay moments of public interest and tremendous excitement; of hope and exhilaration; but also of near-despair. The sudden burst of pace made the course of events difficult to follow, but behind the scenes things also began to move much more quickly. Hardly anyone knew the full story. In the course of researching this book it became obvious that many of the leading players knew much of it, but that few, if any, knew it all.

As always, there was violence, and there were innocent victims. One of the saddest incidents came in Warrington, near Liverpool, when two IRA bombs placed in litter bins in a shopping precinct killed two young children and injured fifty-six other people. Jonathan Ball was only three years old, and an only child. Timothy Parry, aged twelve, had gone into the town to buy a pair of football shorts: he suffered severe head injuries and died some days later. His father said: 'We produced a bloody good kid, one of three, he was a fine lad. He had his moments. He could be a cheeky, impudent pup, but a good kid. The IRA – I have no words for them at all.' The killings led to a wave of revulsion throughout Britain and especially in the Republic, where tens of thousands attended a Dublin peace rally. The IRA, undeterred, within weeks staged another huge bombing in the City of London, repeating their Baltic Exchange attack of April 1992 by setting off a large bomb at Bishopsgate in the heart of the financial district. Again the damage was extraordinary, with estimates of the cost ranging as high as a billion pounds.

Loyalist violence also continued at a high level. In March Ulster Defence Association gunmen attacked a van used by Catholic building workers in Castlerock, Co. Londonderry. Four men were killed, one of them a member of the IRA. At the same time the UDA petrol-bombed the homes of several SDLP politicians. After the Castlerock shooting a UDA spokesman remarked conversationally to a Belfast journalist: 'If you are talking in terms of success rates, yes, this week has been a success – and it is still only Thursday.'

Following the deaths of the two Warrington children Gordon Wilson, who had lost his daughter Marie in the 1987 Enniskillen bombing, asked to meet the leadership of the IRA to appeal to them to end the violence. The meeting, as he recounted later, was a poignant one:

> I had a copy in my hand all the time of the book I wrote about Marie, if nothing else to reinforce me and to give me the strength of mind and body to go through with it. We had a friendly meeting. I was given a statement from the IRA, which seemed to me to be simply saying no to my request for peace. They were saying to me that they would not abandon the armed struggle, that the armed struggle was not their initiative, it was their response to the British presence in Ireland. Voices were not raised. I spoke at some length as Marie Wilson's dad, as one who had suffered at their hands. I told them about the suffering in Northern Ireland and in Warrington. I said there was no excuse for the killing of innocent civilians, including Marie Wilson and the two innocent little children in Warrington and dozens of others. I made it very clear that I was aware that they had their losses. I was very aware, and said so, that they were not the only ones who were in the business of shedding blood and killing and shooting people. They apologised once again for Enniskillen and for Warrington. They said they do not condone, nor indeed do they set out to kill innocent civilians, men, women or little children. I tried with all the sincerity and honesty and integrity

I could muster to get over my simple request with as much conviction as I could. They listened, but they made no change in their position. Perhaps it was naive of me to imagine that because it was me they would. That word naive has been used: I have to live with that. I left disappointed and indeed saddened.

Gordon Wilson's meeting was apparently futile and he was to know more tragedy in his life. His son Peter later died in a traffic accident, and he himself died after a short illness in 1995.

In this same period, two secret meetings took place which seemed to give more hope of progress than Gordon Wilson had detected in his encounter. These meetings involved Gerry Adams and Michael Lillis, the former Irish diplomat who had distinguished himself in the intensive negotiations leading up to the 1985 Anglo-Irish Agreement. By the spring of 1993 he had left the Department of Foreign Affairs to pursue a career in business, but when the opportunity arose of a meeting with Adams he agreed. Lillis, like Wilson, wanted to condemn the violence and to make the case for a cessation. His description of the meetings gives an insight into the thinking of Gerry Adams:

> I began my conversations with Gerry Adams by telling him in very strong terms that I disagreed with the use of violence by the Provisional IRA and was ashamed of it as an Irish person. But I said I was extremely glad to have an opportunity to explain any political issues to him, as part of an effort which people of goodwill might make to persuade those involved in violence to reconsider it. I started with a very vehement statement of opposition to violence and he listened to it with patience; it wasn't the first time he had heard it. I could not have expressed myself more strongly – I mean these were two Irishmen speaking to each other, and in our more intimate occasions Irishmen are pretty good at expressing ourselves forcefully. I have rarely spoken with such passion.
>
> I did not lecture him, that's not our style, but I spoke with passion about how it demeaned all of us who come from a noble tradition of seeking to free our country. I dwelt on the suffering and the extreme damage that it had caused, and he acknowledged that this caused him considerable concern. But he made it quite

clear he was proud to be part of what he represented as the tradition of resistance, as what he saw as a justified, necessary and noble tradition. It would be inaccurate to suggest that he was in any way ashamed of the campaign of violence. On the contrary, he believed that it had produced useful political effects and had produced whatever progress they were prepared to see in the attitude of Britain.

I'm quite prepared to believe, and do believe, that he felt a good deal of grief and concern about the suffering that had been caused. I think his view, which I absolutely rejected, was that this is a war situation, that these things happen, they are terribly regrettable but they are unavoidable. I think that had he been convinced that it was necessary to continue to support a campaign of violence he would have been ready to do that. But I think it's fair to say that he had moved intellectually quite a distance in his analysis of the problem. I think he had moved to a position much closer to the analysis which Hume had put before us, all of us, for most of the past generation, which is that this is a divided community which requires a more complex response than simply the imposition of one nationality over another.

The impression I had of this man, in serious lengthy private conversations, was that he was very concentrated, very sincere, very serious in the questions that he asked. I am someone who has spent a great deal of my life talking and listening to politicians, and he impressed me as one of the most serious, and intellectually gifted political people that I have met. I think that people in both Britain and Ireland are very lucky to have, in Adams and Hume, people of unusual intellectual gifts. Adams is, thank God, a person of seriousness and considerable brains. It is a great advantage to find yourself dealing with a person of seriousness and intelligence who is capable of listening to you, listening to new ideas and responding to them. Believe me, that's unusual.

Other talks were also under way, with three different channels of communications in existence between Adams and Dublin. Mansergh held occasional meetings with Martin McGuinness and Aidan McAteer, and sometimes with Gerry Adams. By this stage Adams and Reynolds were in regular contact by letter, while Father Reid remained active as a go-between. Sean Duignan relates:

I was becoming increasingly aware of comings and goings around the Taoiseach's department. Mansergh would disappear at intervals for a day or two at a time – it was considered indelicate to refer to his absences – and Nally would suddenly materialise from what were called 'roving missions' for private meetings with the Taoiseach. Reynolds repeatedly told me that their contacts were always through intermediaries. Then there was the man Reynolds referred to only as 'the priest'. Slightly built, almost wraith-like, he would 'appear' and invariably make a bee-line for Mansergh's room. When we first met there, he did not introduce himself, merely shook hands. I recognised Father Alec Reid from the famous photograph of him kneeling over the bodies of two British soldiers shot dead by the IRA in Belfast. I knew from the way Reynolds referred to him that he was a vital link to Sinn Fein and the IRA.

Hume and Adams meanwhile remained in touch, and it was in April 1993 that Adams was seen entering the SDLP leader's house. Unionists and others issued strong statements of condemnation of Hume for talking to Adams: their reaction, had they known that this was just the tip of an iceberg of secret contacts, can only be guessed at. The criticism of Hume intensified when, eleven days after their meeting was revealed, he and Adams issued the first of a series of joint statements saying they were involved in a search for agreement. More criticism was levelled because the statement was faxed to newspaper offices on Sinn Fein notepaper: Hume, it turned out, had no secretary available and had left it to Adams to distribute the statement. Members of his own party wondered if the whole thing was wise: 'Oh, I just don't know,' said one. 'I trust John Hume's judgement but my stomach's been churning all day, sick with worry whether it's the right thing to do.'

The disclosure of the talks put the joint declaration work under great strain. The original hope had been that it would continue in secrecy, coming into public view only with the publication of an agreed declaration which would then trigger an IRA ceasefire. But the revelation caused real shock in Dublin. Reynolds and his advisers had always been preoccupied with secrecy, for two reasons. The first was that talking to republicans was such a sensitive and difficult issue for Irish governments; the second was that it was even more problematic for the British. Both Dublin and London were desperate to mask the fact that the republicans had a large input into the work. A Dublin source described the reaction there:

> There was a great deal of consternation because it was always understood that the key to British engagement was a complete disavowal of any extreme nationalist [i.e. republican] involvement. At that stage things were done in a fairly unstructured way – there wasn't an active Cabinet sub-committee, for example. Officials communicated with each other in a fairly loose sort of way, so there was never a meeting at which people sat down and said, 'Oh, what in the name of God is going on here?' There was just a great deal of wringing of hands and a great deal of people saying, 'This sets us back, this doesn't help.' There were a lot of worried messages from the Brits. I know that Sir P [as Dublin ministers and officials referred to Sir Patrick Mayhew] was extremely upset. I don't think he complained officially, but the atmosphere just noticeably soured and there was a kind of a hands-off sense.

Reynolds said later: 'When the news broke of the dialogue taking place between Adams and Hume, it just brought more tensions and pressure on the situation. I would have preferred to have dealt with the whole lot nice and quietly behind the scenes – you make more progress that way. But it burst into the open and I had no control over it. It didn't help.' Hume later commented: 'The price of that leak has been quite enormous. Without it we would have had peace sooner, without all the distrust from the Unionists. If the two governments had quietly reached agreement then a ceasefire would have followed.'

For almost a year Dublin had been trying to persuade the republicans to accept changes in the June 1992 version of the declaration. This was vital work, since Dublin felt it had to produce a document which would attract London's attention and interest, and which would form the basis of further negotiations between the two governments. Reynolds said later: 'Questions such as setting a time limit for political agreement, the British government accepting the

role of persuaders, and the principle of consent, all caused difficulties.' The judgement was that as it stood, the June 1992 declaration
had little chance of being accepted by London. Dublin's ideal
position was to agree a document which in principle would be
immediately acceptable to the British government.

Mansergh's talks with the republicans also ranged over other
important matters. From the outset he and Sinn Fein discussed how
long it would realistically take for a united Ireland to come about.
Reynolds sent Adams a note saying the emergence of a united
Ireland could take a generation; he defined a generation, rather
loosely, as something between fifteen and forty years.

Then in April 1993 came an important development. For many
months Hume and Mansergh had separately been holding discussions with the republicans aimed at removing ambiguities from
the June 1992 Hume–Adams declaration draft. Hume and Dublin
had together formulated three alternative versions of the key statement on self-determination and attempted to persuade the republicans to accept these in preference to the June 1992 wording. (The
text of these is set out in Appendix 1.) Hume and Adams had met
regularly, while Mansergh met McGuinness and McAteer in the
Dundalk monastery in February and early April 1993. But after
the best part of a year of considering the drafts and the arguments, the republicans sent a message saying they would not accept
any of the alternative formulations, and were falling back on the
June 1992 document. This effectively ended negotiations on the
text. The republicans said, as a Dublin source put it: 'That's it –
it's the 1992 document or nothing.'

The message came from the army council of the IRA. The text
of it is as follows:

1 Thank you for your latest draft and other documentation. We have
   examined all of this, the draft joint declaration/steps/timetable and
   discussed them at length, hence the relatively lengthy period in
   coming back with a response.
2 We are very serious about this project. We recognise that what it
   requires is a package that creates what is a political dynamic for

irreversible change, and whose objective is the exercise of the right to national self-determination. We see this as the basis for democracy and the beginning of the process of national reconciliation and a lasting peace. This is the standpoint from which we approach your latest submission.

3 While accepting the integrity of BAC's [BAC = Baile atha Cliath, the Irish for Dublin, which is the army council's way of referring to the Irish government] seriousness about the project we are nevertheless unable to convince ourselves that the outline package proffered, or joint declarations/steps/timetable and BAC's 'understanding' of a 15/40 years timescale would produce the necessary dynamic.

4 We earnestly believe that the position put by us in the June draft is the surest way of providing what is required. We remind you that in coming to the June position we've accepted the concepts which form no great part of our traditional political vocabulary. We offer this as proof of our willingness to be flexible.

5 In this context we remain open-minded about our realisable alternative. We ask only that this seeks to fulfil the criteria outlined in paragraph 2, and we believe that this requires an agreement with London to do this in the shortest possible time, consistent with obtaining maximum consent to the process involved. Our preference is for a joint declaration which embodies a clear and specified time for achieving this, but we are prepared to consider various options for dealing with this, and these could involve public and/or private elements to the joint declaration.

This could include a private agreement on a specified timescale underwritten by independent, international guarantors or a delayed public statement to be released sometime – 6/12/18 months? – after the joint declaration and as part of agreed implementation of the joint declaration.

6 We await with interest your response. We wish to express concern at the protracted nature of this process and the degree of looseness* about it which is most unhelpful to the search for a peace settlement. We believe that this demands that we approach our task with increased urgency.

7 Finally, as we conclude our consideration of this section of our project we have been informed that Gerry Adams and John Hume have reached agreement on most of the June draft and have isolated the one part of disagreement so that this can be given separate consideration. They have agreed in principle to all parts of this document except the 'within a period [to be specified in advance by both Governments]' section. John Hume has made some suggestions on this about structures, measures and time which have to be further developed by him and Gerry Adams. We believe that this agreement between Gerry Adams and John Hume is an important breakthrough at this time and propose that we endorse the Gerry Adams/John Hume agreement on the June draft.

*Since this draft was prepared there have been media disclosures about Gerry Adams/John Hume dialogue. These increase our concern.

The republicans meanwhile sought assurances on a number of important points concerning how the Irish government would react to an IRA cessation. Adams was concerned with securing the early release of the more than fifty prisoners with IRA associations in prison in the south. He also wanted details of how the proposed convention, which had been mentioned in the various drafts of the declaration, would function. In May 1993 Reynolds sent a confidential document entitled 'Steps Envisaged' to Adams via Father Reid to reassure him that Dublin would react positively to a cessation. The text is as follows:

1 Statement to be agreed by two priests.
2 Discussion on statement by the two Prime Ministers.
3 Finalise statement and consultation with all sides and agree a date for it to be announced and become operational for all sides.
4 Engage in procedural discussions with a view to establishing a convention within three months along the parameters set out in the statement.
5 Since the convention, unlike the New Ireland Forum, will be a standing body, it would meet in plenary one or two days a month

except August on the model of the European parliament, but committees could meet in the interim between sessions. It would be complementary to any other institutions either already in existence or to be established.

6 Section 31 would be lifted simultaneously with the announcement at 3, coming into operation for all sides. [This was a reference to the order banning Sinn Fein representatives from speaking on Irish TV and radio, which had been in effect since the early 1970s.]

7 Once public confidence in peace had been established, every effort would be made to deal expeditiously with issues such as long-standing prisoners, excepting cases of serious violence, particularly against the person; and arms and equipment,* so that the legacy of the past 20 years and the cost could be put behind us as quickly as possible.

Clarifying points such as the above posed no real problem for Reynolds, but the republican stipulation that the June 1992 document stood gave him a real dilemma, since both he and Hume regarded it as unsatisfactory and had been trying for almost a year to make important changes to it. In spite of the army council stipulation that June 1992 was the only document acceptable to them, further attempts were made to change it. A document produced by Hume and Dublin on 3 May did not find favour. Another produced by Hume alone on 1 June was laid aside, though it may be said to contain echoes of the eventual Downing Street Declaration. Yet another document, finalised on 3 June 1993, was at length agreed as an advance on the June 1992 document. (See Appendix 1 for texts.)

This was the last in the sequence of documents negotiated by Hume, Reynolds and the republicans, though from that point on

---

*In the wake of the 1994 August ceasefire the question of the 'decommissioning' of IRA weaponry became a major issue. Dublin sources confirm that the term 'arms and equipment' here refers to the question of guns, but specify that Dublin did not regard decommissioning as a pre-condition for republican entry into talks.

the text was to be the subject of discussions between Dublin and London. Reynolds later explained:

> I said, 'If you're talking about a time frame, forget it. I can't sell that and the question of persuaders. We will argue if you like, but I'm not convinced that we will win the argument. That is asking the British to go a little bit further than the Brooke statement of no strategic interest and so on. There is no way we are going to adopt that role, and if you persist in this argument then forget that side of the discussion because we simply are not going to persuade the Unionists to do anything, they're going to have to make up their own minds.' My feeling was telling me that the British wouldn't run with what was in the document. I was prepared to put it forward but I was telling Sinn Fein that it wouldn't run for the reasons I outlined. I also said it was unbalanced – it was a nationalist document, and there was no balance whatsoever in it in relation to the Unionist position.

A senior Dublin source explained:

> The big difficulty as far as the Taoiseach was concerned was that the Provos were looking for a limit on the attainment of unity. In other words, they said, 'It doesn't matter what time you say, but do say some time, if it's a generation fine.' But Reynolds was saying he would not be able to sell the document either to the Unionists or to the British if you put a limit into it, because a limit of that sort is essentially a negation of the other statement that you are making, about consent. If you put a time frame in, you abolish consent and consent is one of the pillars of the document. You cannot say we will attain unity in a generation and at the same time say unity will be obtained only with the consent of the majority in the North. The two things are contradictory. One must go and the thing that goes is the time. That was a very long and heated argument. Reynolds said, 'There's no way, I'm not going to sell this document if you persist with the idea of a limit.'

The June 1993 document was less clear than its June 1992 predecessor about the idea of a timetable. It said the British government would introduce measures to give legislative effect to self-determination 'over a period to be agreed by both governments'. The language had become less stark but there was still ambiguity. Reynolds faced a stark choice: to abandon the whole idea of a declaration, or to try to persuade Major to accept the June 1992 document as a starting point for intergovernmental discussion. He decided to give it to Major. He also conceived the idea of impressing Major with its potential by taking the unprecedented step of personally flying to London, without ceremony, to hand the document to Major. It was an open secret in Dublin circles that Reynolds did not get on well with the British ambassador to the Republic, David Blatherwick – at one point, in fact, Reynolds cut short a meeting with him and told him to get out of his office. Instead of handing the document to Blatherwick, Reynolds proposed to fly to London himself. Spring's aide, Fergus Finlay, later recalled: 'Albert proposed going privately to London and handing over the document. He actually had in mind putting it to John Major on a kind of "take it or leave it" basis, as I understand it. He was going to go completely privately, completely anonymously and just appear to John Major in his den. Dick Spring felt very strongly that that was completely the wrong way to go about it and was almost certain to be counter-productive. It wasn't the handing over of the document that was at issue – there was a kind of ultimatum involved, a kind of "take it or leave it" which was Albert's style in these matters. It was Spring's view that he had to be restrained in the interests of keeping others on board. I think it was at that point that he said to Albert, "If you do that you're on your own." I don't think Albert ever forgave him for it.'

Reynolds abandoned the idea of going to London and instead Major had the British Cabinet Secretary, Sir Robin Butler, fly to Baldonnell military airport near Dublin. Reynolds himself went to the airport and personally handed Butler the document together with an explanatory note. According to Reynolds: 'I took full responsibility for it. I handled it myself and I delivered the document into the man's hands. It was a question of not taking any unnecessary risk – anything can happen. The confidentiality and the credibility attached to the whole operation in my view was paramount. Sir Robin and I had a cup of coffee at Baldonnell and we spoke about the document. It was in a sealed envelope and he was going to hand it to his Prime Minister when he went back.'

After this hand-over Reynolds, Hume and the republicans waited anxiously for John Major's response. Sinn Fein, according to Dublin sources, were very nervous at this stage; so was everyone else, for no one knew what John Major's response would be. This was a prime minister who had been narrowly missed by the IRA mortar-bombs in Downing Street, and whose 1992 general election victory had been marred by an IRA bomb in the City of London.

It was clear that parliamentary considerations would weigh heavily in Major's mind in deciding whether to take a chance and pursue the declaration path. He had won only a slender majority in the election, and by this point a group of dissident right-wingers in the Conservative party was threatening to rebel, principally on important votes concerning Europe. The parliamentary arithmetic meant the nine Ulster Unionist MPs, led by James Molyneaux, could be of great value to him, and might be vital to the survival of his government. A crucial vote on the Maastricht treaty was to take place in the Commons the following month, July 1993, and it was therefore obviously not in his interests to alienate Molyneaux. Since everyone knew the Ulster Unionist leader would strongly disapprove of any initiative based on reaching out to Sinn Fein, the chances of an immediately favourable response to the declaration idea looked decidedly slim.

Alienating Molyneaux, and thus possibly jeopardising his entire government, was just one of a series of risks which Major was now being pressed to take. Another huge risk lay in the fact that even if he accepted the declaration as it stood, there was no guarantee of the IRA ending its campaign. Going down the declaration path would in any event have meant laying aside decades of tradition in British policy. London's approach had evolved dramatically with the Anglo-Irish Agreement of 1985, but one fundamental plank was untouched even in that important change of course.

For more than two decades British governments had worked on the theory of finding the middle ground, establishing a devolved administration there, and patiently building up a consensus from the centre out. In this theory the extremes were to become gradually more and more isolated, and would finally wither away. This approach had many drawbacks, not the least of which was that it never worked. In 1974, the only time that the first hurdle was overcome and a power-sharing executive created, the whole experiment fell apart under loyalist pressure in less than six months. All other attempts to set up a centrist institution did not reach first base, but even so successive governments had maintained a deep philosophical commitment to the centrist approach. The Anglo-Irish Agreement had not departed from that approach in that the accord specifically stipulated that the Agreement's remit would be reduced if moderate Unionists and nationalists would agree to share power together.

Although Hume had been one of the architects of the Agreement, he was also the first major political figure to advocate a wider form of accord which might include the republican, and indeed the loyalist, extremes. Reynolds and Hume were now advocating a dramatic departure from the traditional approach, urging Major to lay aside the concept of building incrementally from the middle out and instead to opt for the new, untried, and politically hazardous idea of trying to draw the extremists into the political processes. Though Dublin did not know it at this point, Major had, when he took over from Mrs Thatcher, allowed the back-channel contacts with the IRA to proceed. However, as we shall see, it was in April 1993, two months before Reynolds handed the declaration to Sir Robin Butler, that the government effectively wound up the back-channel contact.

Blatherwick's ambassadorial reports to London must have reflected the fact that in Reynolds Britain was dealing with a politician who had been Taoiseach for little over a year. During that time he had managed to bring down his own government unnecessarily, scrambling back into power only because it had suited Spring to rescue him and give him a second chance. Blatherwick may well have offered the opinion, as he reflected on the Taoiseach who had ordered him out of his office, that Reynolds had become overheated and over-excited about the whole business.

But on the other hand Major was very much of the opinion that Northern Ireland was a serious problem which warranted serious attention. This was in itself quite unusual, for many prime ministers and other senior British politicians had throughout their careers attempted to devote as little time and energy to the issue as possible. Major was different. In his first months in office he took a conscious decision to pay serious attention to the problem. This went against what a senior British source described as the conventional wisdom that British politicians 'don't gain many credits on Northern Ireland and shouldn't take too many risks'. He immersed himself in the topic: in 1990, in his first Christmas in office, 'he took home a series of briefings, put a wet towel around his head, and started reading them'. He set about establishing relationships, first with Haughey and later with Reynolds. Unlike Mrs Thatcher, he did not see Anglo-Irish relations in adversarial terms, and saw value in lifting the relationship out of the Northern Ireland rut. He increased the frequency of Anglo-Irish summits, aiming not only to discuss Northern Ireland but also to find more common ground in approaches to European issues. He and Reynolds got into the habit of writing to each other and spoke frequently on the telephone, often calling each other at home.

Major also won an admirer in Reynolds's wife Kathleen, a formidable County Sligo woman who throughout this time offered her husband strong support but whose health was to cause him much concern. Reynolds was an old hand at coping with political pressures, but throughout this period anxieties about Kathleen's well-being were a great worry.

The concern had begun one evening shortly before Christmas 1991, just after Haughey had sacked Reynolds for trying to overthrow him. Reynolds and his wife arrived late at a Fianna Fáil function which Haughey was addressing: Haughey was on his feet making his speech when they got there, and they had to wait outside until he finished speaking. Their late appearance was interpreted by a number of newspapers as a deliberate slight on Haughey. The lateness was in fact caused by a very different reason. That evening, while showering in readiness for the function, Kathleen raised her left arm and discovered several lumps. Reynolds immediately called a doctor and arranged an X-ray for the following morning. She later saw a specialist, who told her she had breast cancer. When John Major found out about her condition he was so sympathetic and concerned that he became a big favourite in the Reynolds household. Reynolds said later: 'John Major phoned Kathleen a number of times when she was ill. He wrote a number of messages to her, and to both of us. She watched his general election campaign from her bed in April of 1992 – she was one of the few people who said he was going to win. She said that people were coming towards him all the time.' Kathleen Reynolds, in an interview conducted for this book, added: 'John Major seldom rang here without having a few words. He would always ask how I was. I am very fond of him: he's a very honest, genuine man, he's so human. Believe me I don't get bowled over by prime ministers and the like, and I could see this guy was sincere.'

On 11 June Hume made it clear that he would not allow the barrage of criticism to deflect him from remaining in contact with Adams. He did so by issuing a joint statement with Adams saying they had met again, felt they were making progress, and intended to continue the dialogue.

A week later came a simple handshake which carried enough symbolic force to send tremors through the political system, north-south relations and Anglo-Irish relations. It involved a figure who was technically supposed to be above politics. It happened when the Irish President, Mary Robinson, briefly shook hands with Gerry Adams while on a visit to west Belfast. Before becoming President, Mrs Robinson had been in the vanguard of those in Dublin who believed the Unionist cause should receive more sympathy. She had in fact resigned from the Labour party in 1985 because she disapproved of the Anglo-Irish Agreement, regarding it as unfair to Unionists. One of the principal themes of her term of office was that of reaching out to the dispossessed, the alienated and those on the fringes of southern society. She defined these mainly in social and economic terms, giving much attention to groups from poorer areas.

But it was plain that Sinn Fein and the republican community in the north also fell into the category of those who were marginalised and excluded from mainstream society, and the question arose of how the President should act towards them. This issue came to the fore in the middle of June 1993, when it emerged that she intended to travel to west Belfast to attend a function at which Adams would be present, and could be expected to shake hands with him. The purpose of the visit was not specifically to see Adams, but the fact was that Mrs Robinson would encounter representatives of dozens of west Belfast organisations, and inevitably Sinn Fein would be among these.

The visit was scheduled at what was politically a most sensitive time. Less than two weeks earlier Reynolds had sent the joint declaration draft to London, while Spring was busy trying to win friends and influence Unionists. The British government – though it had been in secret contact with the republicans – strongly took the line that they should be publicly shunned. The British were adamantly against the visit and the handshake. So was Spring, though Reynolds was more non-committal. Mrs Robinson was such a popular figure that any Irish politician knew he would cross her at his peril. An opinion poll at this time showed 93 per cent in the Republic thought she was doing a good or excellent job while the ratings for Reynolds and Spring hovered around the 30 per cent mark. Her presidency had been an outstanding success, catching and expressing the country's new and more open mood.

But talking to Sinn Fein was one of the most sensitive and difficult issues of the day, as the public battering of Hume had shown. Spring tried to talk Mrs Robinson out of the handshake but the President was insistent. The government had the power to prevent it happening but Reynolds declined to exercise it. Immediately before the visit Reynolds, accompanied by Spring, flew to London to see Major for what was clearly a crucial meeting, since the joint declaration was on their agenda. The entire visit was, however, overshadowed by British complaints about the presidential schedule. Major spent more than an hour pressing Reynolds to have her plans changed, while Mayhew and Blatherwick also applied heavy pressure. The Irish side were particularly irritated by Blather-wick, whom they regarded as exaggerating the importance of the issue, increasing tensions and making things worse. The British side handed over a paper expressing opposition to the visit: their views were passed on to Mrs Robinson but did not change her mind.

The visit duly took place, the President receiving a warm reception from hundreds of west Belfast people. Among the multitude who shook hands with her was Adams, bearing a lapel badge which identified him as a founder-member of the west Belfast festival. By that stage the media had been ushered out and the encounter was not filmed or photographed. They exchanged a few words and Mrs Robinson moved on. The incident led to a now-familiar torrent of condemnation from Unionists, and to criticism from a number of newspapers. The Dublin *Sunday Independent* fulminated: 'She should know that she has disgraced her office and tarnished her presidency beyond redemption. Mrs Robinson has shamed the people of this country gratuitously, unforgivably, indecently. She should now resign.' But a revealing sign of public opinion in the Republic, as opposed to political criticism and histrionic headlines, came when an opinion poll recorded 77 per cent approval of Mrs Robinson's action. This was a telling indication that the political establishment's position of ostracising the republicans was not necessarily supported by the population as a whole. In a newspaper interview in November 1994, just after the IRA cessation, Mrs Robinson said: 'It was a very difficult decision, one I thought deeply about. It was not easy to know whether you were doing the right thing. I underestimated what the media response would be afterwards. It was as though I had gone to Northern Ireland to shake Gerry Adams's hand. I tried to say that there was a story of local community vibrancy, of what was being done for young people, the drop-outs from school, the old people, but there was no interest in that. The only interest was on focusing on shaking hands with Gerry Adams. It was clear that it had been extremely important for those communities in west Belfast. In a small sense I think I helped them make the changes they were making.'

Adams later remarked: 'The president's day in west Belfast was an outstanding success. It sent a timely signal of the need to accord people respect; it was also hugely popular throughout Ireland.' The significance of the event was that it was the first public sign that at least some elements in the Republic were thinking of reaching out to Sinn Fein. And the opinion poll reaction showed a potentially deep well of support for such a course.

The fascinating – and unfortunately unanswered – question is whether Mrs Robinson knew of the behind-the-scenes work on the declaration. Reynolds, as Taoiseach, had regular meetings with the President to apprise her of political developments; it is not impossible that he kept her informed of the declaration work, and that this helped her resist pressure not to shake Adams's hand.

It was clear from an early stage that London regarded the joint declaration not as a potentially historic formula for peace but as an unwelcome hot potato. According to Reynolds, he had a preliminary discussion by telephone with Major a few days after giving Butler the declaration document, telling him: 'There's a document I'm putting before you, and I can tell you if it's acceptable to the British government, and we can proceed on the declaration on the lines laid out in that document, we can have a ceasefire in Northern Ireland – a permanent ceasefire.'

Major's initial response was that there were aspects of the document which he did not believe Britain could accept. Reynolds said later: 'He certainly named the one about the consent principle, that it appeared to him that the consent principle was not being accepted. And this question of "Brits out" on a given timetable – paraphrasing him, he said that was another trusty old demand of the IRA, it hadn't been changed, it might have been changed in flowery language, but it hadn't changed very much. He didn't see that as a runner. I said, "Whatever you may say about the couple of areas you may disagree with, there has been a marked progress in where they're coming from." He said they hadn't come far enough, or something like that. I said, "We're going to have to try and move it from there, bearing in mind that I'm going to have to input a balance into it from a Unionist point of view." '

When Reynolds flew to London to see Major later in June 1993 he sought to impress on him the potential of the declaration, the amount of work that had gone into it, and to argue that it contained much more potential for progress than any attempt to revive the Mayhew talks. Major was cautious. He agreed that London would talk about the text, but drew a careful distinction: his government would discuss it, but would not negotiate on it. Several meetings then took place, Butler and Chilcot representing London while O hUiginn and Nally represented Dublin. The British made observations on the declaration and the Irish side made a number of changes to the text to accommodate some of the points raised. Dublin believed, however, that the Westminster political situation was telling against them and holding up progress. In July 1993 a number of Tory right-wing backbenchers rebelled, refusing to support Major in key votes on Europe. Major was in real trouble in the Commons lobbies until Molyneaux and the Ulster Unionist MPs came to his rescue and in effect saved the government from defeat. Both Major and Molyneaux denied that any deal had been done to win Unionist support, but the widespread belief was that an understanding, whether formal or informal, had been reached between them. A government dependent on the Unionists, Dublin concluded, was even less likely to contemplate signing up for something as audacious as the declaration.

On the nationalist side there were different theories as to why Major was not moving faster. He seemed committed to doing something about the Northern Ireland problem, but he was by temperament a cautious man. In addition, he was obviously aware that a false move on his part could result in a withdrawal of Ulster Unionist support and, conceivably, the collapse of his government. Dublin sources had the impression that Sir Robin Butler was very sympathetic to the joint declaration approach but that Sir Patrick Mayhew disapproved of the whole strategy. It was also suspected that some in London were instinctively opposed to a proposal which had emerged from nationalist Ireland and over which they had no control. By September Reynolds was worried that Major was in the business of rejecting the declaration, and wrote a slightly desperate personal letter appealing to him to keep the initiative alive.

Private correspondence between prime ministers of different countries carries the highest security classification, but we have had access to secret files which include letters between Major and Reynolds. The text of the letter from the Irish Taoiseach to the British Prime Minister is as follows:

> First I would like you to know beyond equivocation or doubt that the paper which the two sides have been discussing is a paper which we have worked on here long and hard. As I think has been mentioned at earlier meetings the proposals have my own personal backing and input. And it has the backing, so far as we can ascertain through our intermediaries, of those who can produce peace on their side at least.
>
> Peace will be an achievement worth striving for. After 25 years of violence it would be on a par with any of our predecessors in this century, in fact a truly historic breakthrough. There are risks, but peace is within our reach if we play our cards right.
>
> The principle of consent on which you laid so much emphasis earlier is not an issue. The nationalist proponents now fully accept the idea subject to the sort of framework set out in the paper. What we are all hoping to achieve is not necessarily Irish unity or anything in that area within any limited timescale, but a period of stability, without violence or the threat of violence, in which both sides can put past bitterness behind them and work out an agreement on their future rationally and equitably.
>
> Peace, which could result from the present process, could transform the current climate and make that outcome not only possible but probable, certainly over the medium term. I will therefore ask you in all sincerity to continue to give the process your full and enthusiastic backing so that your people come together to work on the paper so as in the end to produce these results which I am sure the people of our two countries so devoutly wish for. I would hope that it would be possible for us to agree the terms of an understanding at our next meeting. Time is not on our side. Finally, if the Arabs and the Israelis can do it, why can't we?

By September both Hume and Adams were also impatient for some kind of response from London. On 17 September Hume went to Downing Street to meet Major, urging him to respond positively. He angered loyalists when he brusquely told reporters in Downing Street after the meeting that he did not care 'two balls of roasted snow' (an expression his mother had often used) about all the criticism of his talks with Adams. Hume, feeling he had not got far in his meeting with Major, then decided to act, with the intention of increasing the pressure on the British Prime Minister. At this stage it should be remembered that Hume was unaware of Dublin's direct contacts with Sinn Fein, and of Mansergh's unsuccessful attempts to re-negotiate parts of the declaration.

He was also particularly worried about the safety of his party members, for by this stage the Ulster Defence Association had launched a systematic campaign of attacks on the homes of SDLP members. A number of party figures were issued with firearms by the police for self-protection, though Hume himself refused to carry a gun or accept police protection. He told a party colleague: 'I can't argue non-violence and carry a gun, and I won't accept a bodyguard to maybe take a bullet for me.' He was warned by police in the Republic to stay away from his Donegal retreat after a car was seen acting suspiciously nearby, apparently scouting the house for a possible attack. Some SDLP members moved house while the homes of others were fitted with reinforced windows and doors and 'panic buttons' to summon security force help at a moment's notice. But it was impossible to give full protection to its hundreds of members, and it seemed only a matter of time before one of them was killed. The UDA made no secret of the fact that Hume was a hate-figure to them, claiming he was not interested in peace but was instead in the business of linking up with Sinn Fein to do down the loyalists. An *Irish Times* report gave an insight into the nature of the UDA:

> The six men on the UDA inner council are far less image-conscious than their IRA counterparts. They received the press in a dingy room in west Belfast, expressing their views on the Hume–Adams talks, loyalist killings, and the prospects for peace as they munched through six fish suppers. 'Would you like a chip, darlin?' one inquired, before launching into a tirade against the 'pan-nationalist front'. The UDA's south Belfast commander

read out a statement, handwritten on pale blue notepaper, warning of 'Britain's final act of betrayal'. The Hume–Adams statement had merely confirmed UDA fears that a sell-out was imminent. The villain of the piece was undoubtedly John Hume – described as an arrogant, patronising man, determined to amalgamate Ulster with a third world country [the south], who they warned would soon realise that he didn't 'walk on water'.

It was in this ominous atmosphere that Hume considered ways of injecting new life into the process, and talked some options over with his aide, Mark Durkan. Hume was so absorbed with the process that he even buttonholed Durkan on his wedding day, in September 1993, to discuss it. Hume said he and Adams were considering going public in order to open the process up, gain maximum public attention and generate political momentum. They were thinking of issuing a joint statement revealing that they had reached an understanding together and had been able to pass it on to the British and Irish governments. Durkan approved.

Hume rang Reynolds and put the idea to him. Reynolds, according to a senior Dublin source, 'advised him heavily against going public – moved heaven and earth to try to stop it. He foresaw that going public would make it more difficult for the British.' The annual Conservative party conference was coming up, Reynolds argued, and it was a bad time to be handing Major such a controversial document. But when Hume, tired of all the delay, was insistent, Reynolds urged him to say he was sending a report only to Dublin rather than to both governments. Hume agreed to this, though it was not the full story, since he had already informed London of what was in the joint declaration. On 25 September, therefore, he and Adams issued a joint statement saying they had made considerable progress, and had agreed to forward a report to Dublin. They declared: 'We are convinced from our discussions that a process can be designed to lead to agreement among the divided people of this island which will provide a solid basis for peace.'

Before this statement was issued public, political and media interest had been running at a high level: afterwards, it reached an even more intense pitch, dominating news bulletins in Britain and Ireland. It produced acres of newsprint aimed at shedding light on how the north's two nationalist leaders – one identified with violence, the other dedicated to peace – could possibly be on the verge of agreement. Wherever Hume went sheaves of messages were waiting for him from journalists clamouring for interviews; every newspaper he picked up carried extensive coverage, often accompanied by editorials critical of his actions. Even newspapers normally sympathetic to him pointedly questioned his judgement.

The Hume–Adams statement gave the public another little glimpse of the secret world of talks and contacts. It was by then firmly established in the public mind that Hume and Adams had been in contact, apparently fruitfully, but the bulk of the story remained hidden from view: the public, and the media, knew nothing of the years of talks between Adams and Hume, between Mansergh and Sinn Fein, or of Father Reid's activities as an intermediary. They had no inkling of the succession of draft declarations, and were in complete ignorance of the fact that the declaration had been passed to the British government.

In the absence of all this background information there were far more questions than answers, and nothing seemed to make sense. In public both Adams and Hume were infuriatingly delphic, while British and Irish government ministers and spokesmen were evasive and uninformative. The confusion deepened when, two days after issuing the statement with Adams, Hume left for the United States on a long-planned trip accompanying businessmen seeking new investment. The pressure on him had been considerable ever since April 1993 when Adams had been spotted entering his home; by September it was intense and unrelenting, and he was chain-smoking and plainly under heavy strain.

It was said that he would be making a report to Dublin, but all was confusion. Some newspapers stated that a report had been given to the Irish government; others that it shortly would be. Hume thought of meeting Reynolds before leaving for the US, but the Taoiseach was watching a rugby match and officials were reluctant to disturb him. Spring, meanwhile, was already in America.

Hume rang O hUiginn from Dublin airport before his plane left for the States, and they agreed he should meet Reynolds and Spring together when he returned from the US. The media kept asking when Dublin ministers would receive the report, unaware that they already knew what it contained. Sean Duignan's diary entry for 27 September gives a vivid picture of Dublin's reaction to Hume's move to up the ante: 'What's Hume up to? I have rarely seen Taoiseach or Mansergh so upset. And not a peep from John. Haven't a clue where he is. I keep issuing "we look forward to hearing what progress may have been made" rubbish. Either he's lost the head or he is crafty as a fox – or both? – because we're getting conflicting reports from the US quoting him as having already given Dublin the report, then that he'll give Albert the report when he gets back. Mansergh says we've got nothing from Hume or Adams. Still, nobody here wants a public row with John. So I go on as if everything is perfect. What a way to make a living!'

A Dublin source was later critical of Hume: 'He was going to be in the States for a fortnight and he didn't know what was going to turn up when he was away and he was afraid that the Taoiseach would then claim credit for everything that had happened, and he took this extraordinary step of making announcements in public about things that weren't really happening at all.'

Another Dublin source went further still:

> There was a sense of absolute fury. The Taoiseach, Martin Mansergh and everybody else were all totally almost devastated by what John Hume appeared to have done. He had blown up the whole Hume–Adams process to a point where it was almost impossible now to deal with the British about it. He went shaggin' off to the States and he gave an interview there, and the claims he made in it were seen as a million miles away from the truth – to the point where we were wondering, was he well or had the strain of the whole process finally got to him. The bottom line in the whole thing was that you could only negotiate with the British about the basic propositions that were already in existence provided they had no fingerprints on them – and suddenly there was Adams–Hume fingerprints all over them.

At this point Dublin decided to cut Hume out of the loop. One Irish source said: 'Hume couldn't keep his mouth shut. He nearly wrecked the whole process.' Another explained: 'The Brits were very keen on having this process hermetically sealed and the only way that they could ensure this was to make sure that the circles in which these discussions were going on were very, very limited and completely trustworthy.' Officially, therefore, Hume was sidelined from the process, which had moved into an intergovernmental phase; in public, however, he continued to act as a lightning-conductor for the whole process, drawing most of the flak, worried by the UDA's death threats against him and his party, and fearful that the carefully constructed opportunity for peace was slipping away.

On his return from the US Hume held a meeting with Reynolds and Spring. It was a cool encounter, for the southern politicians strongly disapproved of his action in publicising the fact that he had reached an understanding with Adams. A cautiously worded statement said afterwards that the Irish government would carefully consider what Hume had told them, and take account of it in their discussions with the British government. The statement was noticeably lacking in warmth.

London, too, continued to be angry, particularly with Hume. The document handed over by Reynolds in June was treated with kid gloves; quite a few, in particular Mayhew, advocated throwing it in the bin. London was far from convinced that the declaration approach would bear fruit, but above all they were concerned that the government should not be seen to be negotiating with Sinn Fein, even at one remove. The reality, of course, was that London had been fully briefed about the idea's origins, in particular by Hume; the reality was also that Britain had itself been in clandestine touch with the republicans for years.

In the second half of October, Major, Mayhew and other ministers and officials held a series of meetings on the declaration. They considered intelligence reports which were highly sceptical of the idea that the IRA could be induced to move towards a cessation. In the end, Mayhew's opinion prevailed. It was formally decided that pursuing the declaration path was a futile exercise and that Reynolds should be told, as politely and diplomatically as possible, to forget it.

Dublin was informed of this, Major writing a personal letter to Reynolds to tell him that the declaration idea was being rejected. Major's message was: 'After giving it very careful consideration, with all the intelligence at our disposal, we have very reluctantly concluded that it will not run at the present time.'

Sir Robin Butler, flew to Dublin in secret, meeting Reynolds and Spring and passing on the message that the Hume–Adams report was being taken off the British agenda. The governments, he suggested, should look to other ways of making progress: London believed that reviving the Brooke and Mayhew talks might bring the parties around the table again. The signs were that the declaration was dead, and was being placed on the shelf along with all the other failed initiatives.

That meeting was on 19 October; four days later a terrible act of violence took place in Belfast, starting a cycle of killing which brought Northern Ireland to the brink of despair. The month of October 1993 was one of the most awful, yet most crucial, months in the troubles. It began in confusion mixed with hope, then plunged into violence and near-despair, almost as black as any period of the troubles. The death-toll was the highest of any month since 1976. In retrospect, however, it can be seen as a time which helped lay the basis for the 1994 cessation.

10

DEATH ON THE
SHANKILL

'Suddenly there was this huge bang. My little
girl was underneath all that rubble. I was
screaming her name but it was no use. My little
daughter was dead'
    — woman who lost her daughter in IRA
bombing

'I saw the gun coming round the corner and
then I heard the bangs. They slaughtered my
innocent wife. We went out on a Saturday night
for a wee dance and they blew her to bits'
    — man who lost his wife in loyalist attack

'I really don't come across anyone now who
doesn't talk about how dreadful it is. You can
see the fear everywhere'
    — trade union official

'[If he thinks] we should sit down and talk with
Mr Adams and the Provisional IRA, I can say
only that that would turn my stomach. We will
not do it'
    — John Major

It was lunch-time on a Saturday, 23 October, an unusually warm
day for the time of year. The Shankill Road, the loyalist district
sandwiched between the Catholic districts of Falls and Ardoyne,
was busy. As one of the last surviving ribbon shopping thoroughfares
in the city, each Saturday there were hundreds of people shopping,
hundreds of men in its pubs, hundreds of families out for the day.
The Shankill is a hard-line loyalist district, one of the toughest in

Belfast and one of the heartlands of the Protestant paramilitary groups. The UDA, for example, the largest of the loyalist organisations, maintained an office above a little fish shop on the main Shankill Road. The way into the office was through a door, past a steel security gate and up a rickety flight of stairs.

There were scores of people in the vicinity of the fish shop that day – some inside, some standing or walking outside, some driving past in cars – when an IRA bomb inside the shop went off without warning. The old building which housed the fish shop and the UDA office instantly collapsed into a huge pile of rubble, sending a cloud of dust and dirt billowing across the road and into the air.

One of the shoppers on the Shankill that day was Mrs Gina Murray, a woman who had known much sorrow in her life. She had lost a child at birth and another in a road accident, and her husband had died from a stroke eight months earlier. Mrs Murray was with her thirteen-year-old daughter Leanne, who usually stayed close by her side, but Leanne, unusually, had gone into the shop to buy a tub of whelks. Mrs Murray said: 'Leanne had just left me to go in to the fish shop. Suddenly there was this huge bang. We ran screaming for Leanne. We couldn't find her. No one had seen her. There were people lying in the street covered in blood. My little girl was underneath all that rubble. We started clawing at it with our bare hands. I was screaming her name but it was no use. My little daughter was dead.'

Local men, police, firemen and ambulancemen tore at the rubble in a search for survivors, but the elderly building had collapsed like a house of cards, bringing heavy masonry crashing down on those inside. They used axes and crowbars and their bare hands, but they knew there was little chance of finding anyone alive. From time to time the rescuers would pause and call for quiet when they thought they had heard a groan or a scream from within the rubble. A deathly hush would fall over the crowd as they listened for signs of survivors: there were few such signs. A fleet of ambulances took away the injured as local people looked on, barely able to comprehend the scale of the disaster. Then, after a while, the ambulancemen began to bring out shapes wrapped in blankets as the wreckage of the fish shop began to give up its dead. Among the bodies in the blankets was that of Leanne Murray.

They also brought out the bodies of Michael Morrison, his partner Evelyn Baird, and their seven-year-old daughter Michelle. The couple left behind two orphaned children aged nine years and six months. They brought out the remains of the shop's owner, sixty-three-year-old Desmond Frizzell, well known for his gospel singing. With him they found his twenty-nine-year-old daughter, Sharon McBride, a health worker who was helping him out in the shop that day. A young RUC officer who arrived quickly at the scene said later:

> I was one of the first in. I remember an old man being recovered. His head was the first thing to appear from the rubble, and that was quite a frightening experience. I knew he was still alive because his eyes were blinking. An ambulanceman put an oxygen mask over his mouth, but by the time he left the rubble he had died. After he was removed we continued to remove rubble from where we were standing, but unknown to anybody we were standing on other bodies. As the rubble was being removed – and it will stay with me until I die – I saw a young girl's foot. I knew it was a young girl's foot because her shoe size was about 3 or 4. It poked through the rubble, and I wanted to stop digging then, because I knew I was going to see quite a horrendous sight: and in fact I did.

A paramedic who was one of the first on the scene told of being surrounded by distraught bystanders: 'I was being pulled here and there to look at injured people. The scene was horrific. There was one lady lying in the road with head injuries and half her arm was blown off. She later died. But the worst part for me was when we unearthed the body of a young girl. I will never forget seeing that face staring up out of the rubble.'

Alan McBride, husband of Sharon McBride, said that when he saw the rubble he knew no one would get out of it alive. 'I went crazy, shouting and crying,' he recalled. He went to the hospital, which he described as 'like the waiting room of hell – families in every corner of the room. They were waiting in line to be told their loved one had died. We were almost last in line and we weren't told until about 5 o'clock. Nothing can prepare you for being told your wife is dead. I just went crazy.' By the evening the rescue workers had found ten bodies in the wreckage of the fish shop. Two of the dead were little girls, aged seven and thirteen; another four were women. Fifty-seven more people were injured, some of them seriously. Some had glass in their faces; one woman lost one of her lips.

A woman who lost both parents in the incident said the following day: 'They say a mother's love is a blessing. I miss my mother already. To lose both our parents in one day – oh God, oh God. I am angry, I am bitter. I will never forgive them for this, never. I want to see Gerry Adams face to face. I want to tell him that the people who did this to my mammy and daddy are nothing but scum. I want to tell them they are evil bastards.'

The world turned on Gerry Adams and the republican movement and angrily asked what possible justification there could be for setting off a powerful bomb in a busy shopping district. The full facts emerged only slowly. Nine of the dead were uninvolved Protestant people going about their daily business: the tenth, it turned out, was an IRA bomber killed by his own device. The target, the IRA explained, was not the fish shop but the UDA offices upstairs, where they claimed a UDA meeting had been under way.

The IRA had designed a plan to kill the UDA members they believed were upstairs. Two IRA men, Thomas Begley and Sean Kelly, were dressed in white coats and hats to pose as fishmongers. Begley carried a box inside the shop. The idea was that he and Kelly would order staff and customers from the shop, then flee, leaving behind the bomb which would go off within seconds, demolishing the building and killing the loyalists in the UDA office. But the device went off prematurely as Begley set it down, blowing him to pieces: his mutilated body was removed from the premises in two body-bags. His companion, Kelly, was badly injured but recovered and was later jailed for life.

Forensic science experts reported, and republican sources have confirmed, that the timing device on the bomb could be set for a maximum of eleven seconds. But the IRA men did not have time to make their escape; nor did people in the fish shop; and in any case the UDA office upstairs was empty. The IRA had obviously planned the attack carefully, but the idea that a powerful device could be set off in a crowded shopping street without causing civilian casualties was close to absurd. Apart from the customers in the shop itself, people were continually walking past, and in the event two of those killed were not inside but in the street outside.

An IRA source later said: 'The opportunity appeared to exist to take out the command staff of the UDA. The idea was if you got the bomb in downstairs it would bring the heap down. The operation had to go through Belfast brigade to be approved by Northern Command. It was in line with IRA policy. There was supposed to be a short fuse on the bomb – enough time to clear the shop but not enough time for people to escape from upstairs. The lad who was planting the bomb, it appeared he made a mistake in priming it. There is a thin line between disaster and success in any military operation.'

A senior security source made a similar point when discussing the Shankill bombing: 'The difference between that being a disaster and a stunning success in IRA terms was very marginal. The bomb used was designed to direct the blast upwards, and it did – in the fruit shop next door the rows of oranges were hardly disturbed.' The source confirmed the IRA was correct in saying loyalist extremists had been using the building, but revealed they had stopped several weeks earlier when they became aware of security force surveillance on them.

The attack did not come out of the blue, for it was in effect the culmination of several months of increasingly desperate IRA attempts to assassinate leading loyalists. For months hardly a week passed without IRA gangs attempting to gun down or blow up those they believed to be associated with groups such as the UDA and UVF. But loyalist figures took more and more precautions as it became obvious that the IRA was intent on waging a sustained campaign against them, and the republicans were frustrated by the failure of literally dozens of unsuccessful murder attempts. One well-known UDA Shankill Road figure, Johnny Adair, had been the subject of six republican assassination attempts, and was the particular target of the Shankill Road bomb. Adair had openly boasted of killing Catholics and republicans. (In September 1995 he was jailed for sixteen years after admitting a series of terrorist offences.) He and the other loyalists had been so active that for several years they had claimed more victims than the IRA. Those killed by them included Catholics gunned down at random, such as those who died in the Ormeau Road betting shop shooting early in 1992. But in addition to such killings, which had been the standard pattern of loyalist violence for decades, the loyalists had increasingly turned their attention to targeting republican figures. While membership of the IRA was subject to the strictest secrecy, the emergence of Sinn Fein as a political party meant many republicans were exposed to public view.

Loyalists targeted them whenever they could. In the five years leading up to the Shankill bombing eighteen people with Sinn Fein connections were killed by Protestant extremists, an onslaught which mounted to the most intense and sustained assault ever seen on a particular political grouping. Three of the dead were Sinn Fein councillors while another councillor lost a brother and a son in separate attacks. Republicans alleged collusion by the authorities in many of the killings, while the IRA retaliated by killing up to fifty alleged loyalist extremists over the years. It was against this background of republican–loyalist violence that the Shankill attack took place.

The word loyalists used most to describe Thomas Begley was 'scum', but republicans made clear they regarded him as a soldier. He was brought up and lived only half a mile from the Shankill, in the back streets of the Ardoyne district which saw so many killings in the troubles. A memorial on the gable wall of a Sinn Fein office, a hundred yards from his home, bore a long list of IRA members and Catholic civilians killed in the immediate vicinity. When Begley died there were 121 names on the list, ranging from IRA members to elderly women killed by stray bullets during gun battles; his own name was later appended to it. To loyalists he may have been a mad bomber, but to many in his home district he was a young man intent on hitting back at those who had killed so many of his neighbours. 'Bootsie' Begley was a product of the troubles: born in 1970, the year after troops arrived in Belfast, he had never known life without them. Described by locals as a polite, shy young man, he left school at the age of sixteen without passing any exams. Like many young men in the district he had no permanent employment, finding only a few temporary jobs. His small bedroom, which he shared with one of his brothers, was dominated by a large wooden crucifix and a copy of the 1916 republican proclamation. *Sunday Tribune* reporter Brenda Power found in the room 'a home-made tape recording of him playing the drums and flute with the Carrick Hill Martyrs band and, resting close by, the only book in the room, a volume so handled and dog-eared that you must bend the paperback cover into shape to read the title. It was *The Shankill Butchers*, the gruesome account of the torture and murder of Catholics by a vicious loyalist gang. "He'd been reading that over and over," said his father.'

At Begley's funeral republican Belfast demonstrated that it accepted the IRA's explanation about the bombing, for he was given a hero's send-off. The sizeable cortège wound its way through the Catholic ghettos of north and west Belfast, followed by thousands of people and watched by thousands more. It took six hours to deliver the coffin from his home to the republican plot in Milltown cemetery. The crowds gave no inkling of believing that Begley had done anything wrong, apart from causing his own accidental death. Those present included men, women and children, many mothers pushing prams.

The funeral passed off without violent incident, but was marked by one brief but particularly ugly exchange. Mourners passing close to the Shankill Road encountered a small number of Protestant women waiting for the funeral of a young Protestant girl killed in the Shankill bombing. The Protestant women shouted at the republicans: 'You're yellow pigs, all of youse.' Most of the republicans took no notice but several cars containing men sounded their horns and in two cases men held up nine fingers, signifying the nine Protestants killed. One shouted: 'We got nine of youse – we can't kill enough of you bastards.' Sinn Fein stewards clearly disapproved of such gestures, hurrying the cars through and attempting to stage a dignified funeral, but the vicious taunts gave a revealing insight into the depth of hatreds within the adjoining ghettos.

The funeral was also marked by another electrifying moment when Gerry Adams took a turn at carrying Thomas Begley's coffin, an image reproduced on the front pages of most newspapers. The result was a huge outcry: how, it was asked, could this man speak of peace while shouldering the coffin of a bomber who had caused so many deaths? The Shankill attack appalled the world and seemed to snuff out all thought of a peace process: those identified with the idea were mocked and ridiculed and almost lost hope. Hume said in a television broadcast at the time: 'I know the risk I am taking in this. I am a human being and I was shattered by what happened, but I will do everything in my power to bring this to an end.'

Gerry Adams too was shattered by the incident, which came at a time when he and Hume were attempting to save the joint declaration process from being abandoned by Major. From a republican point of view the bombing was one of the IRA's most disastrous mistakes since Enniskillen, in that at a stroke it killed nine civilians, lost one of its own members, and brought fierce international condemnation upon itself. Adams used unusually strong language, saying the attack was wrong and could not be excused. None the less, he shouldered Begley's coffin. He knew very well that this action would associate him with the worst excesses of the IRA, and would wipe out his years of work to put some distance between Sinn Fein and the IRA, but in republican terms he simply had no choice. He was well aware that the powerful image of himself hefting the coffin would be on every television bulletin and in every newspaper; he knew the impact of that image on his projection of himself as a man seeking peace.

One of the most essential features of the republican attitude to the peace process, so important as to be really rule number one, was that if the republican movement was to move away from

violence it had to do so as a unified coherent entity. At all costs
the type of splits which had bedevilled republicanism, and caused
it so much damage, had to be averted. This vital consideration
helps explain why in August 1994 the doubters went along with
the ceasefire, and why in February 1996 those who disagreed
with the resumption of violence did not air their disapproval in
public. Thomas Begley had been part of the republican movement
and was carrying out IRA orders when he died: Adams disapproved
of the attack itself, but could not disown the volunteer. He had
carried the coffins of many IRA men during the troubles: his action
in carrying Begley's created a stir in Britain but none in Belfast. In
republican terms it would have been amazing for Adams to refrain
from doing so, amounting to a dramatic renunciation of the IRA.
It would have been nothing less than the end of him as a republican
leader. He therefore had no choice, even if his action meant the
collapse of the Hume–Adams initiative. Whatever the damage to
his political moves, Adams had to shoulder the coffin: for he and
Thomas Begley were part of the same republican movement. A
line of Seamus Heaney's, describing family duties, could have been
written for that moment: 'I shouldered a kind of manhood, stepping
in to lift the coffins of dead relations.'

A Dublin source explained the impact of the bombing of the
fish shop: 'The Shankill was the moment of greatest despair. It was
the only moment when both Albert and Martin Mansergh were at
a complete loss. They didn't know what to do next, or how to
proceed, or how to rescue the situation.' Reynolds later said he was
appalled by the Shankill bomb:

> I sent a message to Sinn Fein. I said, 'If I am to continue with
> the process this thing has got to stop. I can't on the one hand be
> preaching peace with all this stuff going on behind my back – I
> can't do it. There's no credibility attached to it, no point in trying
> to convince the British government to come with you.' I had
> always told Major: 'I won't let you down – whatever happens,
> I'll carry the can. You're not going to be held responsible if
> something goes wrong.' And here you had a guy with goodwill
> keeping it high on his agenda, giving it more time than any prime

minister had ever given to the Irish problem since Gladstone, and this was blowing up in his face. He was going to have to be accountable to the British public for this as well. He was put in an extremely difficult and delicate position. I was really annoyed with it – to be honest I thought for some time that it would probably blow the whole thing sky high.

According to Reynolds, Major was furious and seething when he saw the newspaper photographs of Gerry Adams carrying the Shankill bomber's coffin. Reynolds said later that Major could scarcely contain himself:

He said, 'What's this about? How do you expect me to continue with any process when I take up the papers this morning and in every paper on the front page is Gerry Adams carrying a coffin?' I said, 'Look, John, you have to understand that if the guy didn't carry the coffin he wouldn't be able to maintain his credibility with that organisation and bring people with him. And how am I to know, if he refused to carry the coffin, that he wouldn't be in the next coffin himself?' John Major said to me: 'It's fine coming from where you are coming from over there, but I have to contend with the British public that doesn't understand what you are saying, nor have any appreciation of it, but sees the bald facts in front of them as they are and it's extremely difficult to continue on, to try and do something in those circumstances.' I think in the end he had an appreciation of what I was saying. This is the problem, that you always have to explain, because they would see Gerry Adams as synonymous with the IRA – if a bomb went off in the Shankill, surely to God he knew the bomb was going to go off in the Shankill. I was convinced subsequently that he didn't know the bomb was going off in the Shankill.

A senior security officer, speaking later of the bombing, remarked: 'Anyone who would castigate Adams for carrying the coffin could have no concept of republicanism. If he were involved in a process to turn republicans away from violence, for him to have credibility there wasn't any way he could shun being closely identified with the funeral.'

At this point Northern Ireland descended into something close to sheer dread, for everyone knew that large-scale loyalist retaliation for the Shankill bombing was a certainty. The UDA warned publicly: 'John Hume, Gerry Adams and the nationalist electorate will pay a heavy, heavy price for today's atrocity.' Loyalist gunmen went on the rampage, killing six people in a series of sporadic shootings, and then attempted to match the Shankill death-toll. The attack came in County Londonderry, in a bar in the quiet mainly Catholic village of Greysteel, on a Saturday night. It was Hallowe'en, a week after the Shankill bombing, and around 200 people were waiting for a country-and-western band to take the stage.

The door opened and in came two men, wearing boiler suits and balaclavas and carrying an AK-47 rifle and a Browning 9mm automatic pistol. One of them called out, 'Trick or treat'. A woman, thinking it was a Hallowe'en prank, turned and said: 'That's not funny.' The man with the AK-47 shot her first, then walked through the lounge, firing as he went. The other gunman's pistol jammed after one shot, and he cursed as he tried to clear it. In all forty-five shots were fired in the attack. The man with the rifle emptied one clip of ammunition, reloaded and resumed firing. When they left, the walls and floors were splashed with blood from the nineteen people who had been injured. Eight of them died from their injuries, including Moira Duddy, a fifty-nine-year-old mother of six children; a nineteen-year-old girl, Karen Thompson, who was with her boyfriend, planning their engagement; and James Moore, the eighty-one-year-old father of the bar's owner. Seven of the dead were Catholics: the UDA had exacted its revenge for the Shankill bombing.

John Burns, a former member of the Ulster Defence Regiment, was on his way to the toilet when the gunmen came in. A seventeen-year-old girl who arrived at the scene said: 'When they came in through the door and shouted "Trick or treat" he started to laugh and shout, but then he was hit in the stomach. He was in a really bad way. John was lying there and he told me everything would be all right and told me to look after his daughter and make sure she was okay. I bent down and kissed him on the head and told him he was going to be all right, but I knew he was dying because he was so cold. It was awful. I have not been able to sleep. Every time I closed my eyes all I could see was the dead bodies.'

Another of the dead was Mrs Moira Duddy, who was fifty-nine years old and had six children. Her husband John later wept uncontrollably as he spoke of the attack: 'My good wife, my good wife. We went out on a Saturday night for a wee dance and they blew her to bits. They slaughtered my innocent wife. They were shot all around me and I never got a scratch. I'll never get over it. They shot into the wee lounge first. I thought he had finished but he loaded another magazine and the other one with him shot everybody in the big lounge. I saw the gun coming round the corner and then I heard the bangs. My wife and friends were on the floor. They blew the legs off her. They shot her through her heart, through the back. Thirty-three years of marriage, and it's nearly Christmas . . .'

James Moore, at the age of eighty-one, was one of the oldest victims of the troubles. He was the father of the pub's owner, and was at the bar ordering a drink. His granddaughter recollected: 'Granda was standing on his own. There were seven bullets fired at him and four of them hit him – it was no accident, not a case of being hit by a stray bullet. Granny is devastated. It will kill her, she just lived for him. They had been married almost sixty years. He was in hospital last year fighting for his life with a heart condition. He came through only to be murdered like that.'

A young man charged with the murders was televised on his way into court, yelling defiantly and laughing almost maniacally at relatives of the victims in a display of open, naked sectarian hatred. The man, after his subsequent conviction, would in 1995 repent and become a born-again Christian: but his performance at the time added yet another nightmarish dimension to the atmosphere of poison and fear. Twenty-three people had died in the space of a week; the local television news seemed to consist of nothing except news of more and more violence, the grieving bereaved, and threats of more to come. And funerals: a seemingly endless succession of multiple funerals took place daily as the victims, old, middle-aged and young, were buried. Social functions and other gatherings were cancelled as people stayed indoors and took extra security precautions. In the evenings many parts of Belfast, particularly Catholic districts, were virtually deserted, with pubs and clubs reporting a drastic drop in custom. Terry Carlin, a senior trade unionist, gave a flavour of the atmosphere at the time:

> It's hard to place it on a scale, but certainly it's the worst for very many years. I do think they are actually taking us back to the early 1970s. I really don't come across anyone now who doesn't talk about how dreadful it is. Everybody is frankly scared to talk to people of the other community or even talk to people of their own community, in case anything they said might be overheard and give offence. You can see the fear everywhere. I was talking to a taxi driver and he told me many of the guys have pulled out of the business. Among those who are left there is now an agreement that the Prods will only go into Prod areas and Catholics will only go into Catholic areas. When I went to mass on Sunday attendance was down by a third, and there were armed RUC officers on guard duty in the car-park. The priest said at the end of mass that police advice was for us to leave quickly, not to congregate chatting, just to get into our cars and get going. I've been living in Belfast since 1968 and it's the first time I ever heard that.

Within days of the Shankill bombing Dick Spring took an initiative designed to draw the focus away from the spiral of killings and to bring attention back to political activity. In a speech to the Dáil he set out six principles which included a commitment to consent, a promise to examine Articles 2 and 3 of the Irish constitution and a commitment that 'even in the aftermath of some of the most horrible crimes we have witnessed, we must be prepared to say to the men of violence that they can come to the negotiating table – if only they would stop the killing and the maiming and the hurting'. The six principles attracted much attention, but interest centred not on the appeal to men of violence but on the fourth principle, which appeared to offer a historic concession to Unionists. It said that Unionists had the right to withhold consent, which was very different from the usual formulation that a majority had the right to withhold consent, and which seemed to offer Unionists a whole new veto. Spring and his aide, Fergus Finlay, who together wrote the speech, had intended to reach out to Unionists, but did not mean to go so far. They had, it turned out, put the speech together in one intensive overnight session. Finlay himself explained later:

> After the Shankill bombing Dick Spring told me that, unless something was put together quickly that people could cling on to, the situation could develop into a tailspin. He and I stayed up a good deal of the night and wrote that speech, which tried to pull some things together and get a message across that despite the horror of Shankill some things had not changed. To be honest the one that we were most concerned to try and get right was the last one, indicating that it was still open to the Provos to come into politics and play a full and equal role in politics, despite Shankill. We were trying to express that in a way that wouldn't seem incredibly insensitive in the wake of Shankill, and particularly in the wake of Adams carrying Begley's coffin.
>
> Now we didn't consult the theological experts and so we used the phrase 'Unionist' when we should have used the phrases 'majority', and that caused a bit of a ripple. It was immediately seized on by the British – I don't think, to be perfectly honest, because of its huge historical or intrinsic merit but because I think they were looking for something to cling to at that stage, to keep the process alive. The process train was tottering on the edge of derailment, but hadn't actually been derailed, and the six principles at least got it back on an even keel.

The 'theological experts' referred to were the professional diplomats, such as O hUiginn and Nally, who in the normal course of events either wrote or carefully vetted government statements concerning Northern Ireland and Anglo-Irish relations. In this instance Spring showed the speech to Reynolds, who appears not to have noticed the unusual fourth principle and raised no objection to it; but it was not sent through the usual bureaucratic channels to be checked and as a result the *faux pas* went unnoticed. The press and politicians seized on it immediately, and Irish government press spokesmen had to scramble to explain that the fourth principle was more a slip of the pen than a historic concession. The need for this clarification tended to blunt the impact of Spring's move.

The six principles were generally interpreted as something of an overture to Unionist opinion. In this they were a reflection of the fact that Spring all along saw greater potential in the talks process than in the peace process. In the event they drew little constructive response from Unionist quarters, while northern nationalists criticised them as a move away from them and towards the Unionists. This was reflected by a Dublin source who said at the time: 'The principles were a conscious reaching out to Unionists. The entirely predictable kick in the crotch came back – in fact there were two kicks in the crotch, one from Unionists, one from nationalists.'

The British interest which Finlay referred to came in particular from Mayhew, who hoped the community revulsion against violence would create a window of opportunity for the resumption of inter-party talks. He and his officials mapped out several months of intensive efforts to find new areas of agreement, working in particular on the theory that the previous talks deadlock could be broken if the Republic gave significant new ground on Articles 2 and 3 of the Irish constitution. Major supported him by arranging meetings with the party leaders from Northern Ireland. Although the previous rounds of talks conducted by Mayhew and Brooke had not turned out well, the Shankill bombing and other violence seemed to have virtually removed all hopes of success from the declaration path. With Spring and Mayhew primarily interested in reviving the inter-party talks, the declaration seemed all but dead.

Reynolds, looking back on this period, said: 'It was dreadful. The risks were getting greater all the time from where I was coming from, all the time, if the thing didn't work. You had the two little Warrington children, you had Shankill, you had Greysteel and everything else. You were on a hiding to nothing with the general public. There would be no sympathy for your position and trying to do anything with people who would execute those sort of murders.'

The end of October brought an EC summit in Brussels, giving

Reynolds and Major an opportunity to meet face to face. It shaped up as a crunch meeting, for Major seemed on the point of rejecting the declaration process while Reynolds was anxious to salvage something from the wreckage. The communiqué which they issued after the Brussels meeting stands as a classic illumination of how free governments feel to mislead each other and the outside world.

For many months the two governments had been in direct touch with the republican movement. Yet in Brussels they solemnly and jointly declared: 'There can be no talks or negotiations between their Governments and those who use, threaten or support violence for political ends.' Both governments had been assuring the republicans that if they ceased violence there would, in Brooke's words, be a 'flexible and imaginative' response. Yet in Brussels they declared that 'there could be no secret agreements or understandings between governments and organisations supporting violence as a price for its cessation'.

The communiqué carefully stipulated that Reynolds had given Major an account of the Hume–Adams dialogue, but that no actual report had been passed to the British government. In fact, as will become clear later, Major was well aware of exactly what was under discussion. The key decision of the summit was expressed thus: 'The Prime Minister and Taoiseach agreed that any initiative can only be taken by the two Governments, and that there could be no question of their adopting or endorsing the report of the dialogue which was recently given to the Taoiseach and which had not been passed on to the British Government. They agreed that the two Governments must continue to work together in their own terms on a framework for peace, stability and reconciliation.'

In his diary entry Sean Duignan was more candid and forthright: 'Hume and Adams told to get off the pitch! Joint statement sent a clear message to Hume to butt out and leave it to the two governments . . . Brits happy at having dumped on Hume. Albert says to me it had to be done, that only the two governments can do the job, but I can see he's not happy.'

According to Fergus Finlay:

It was a very touchy, tense meeting: the Taoiseach, I think, went to Brussels to confront John Major. As I recall the general feeling in the Irish party was that we were heading for a complete and total impasse. I remember saying at the time that if you wanted to deliver Hume–Adams you may have to denounce them first, and I think that was a general view. The Taoiseach resisted that idea for quite a bit of the lead-up to that meeting, but I think in the end saw the sense of it. There was a very strong feeling that the publicity of September had left us with no choice – if you wanted to keep the process alive and the documents intact you had to take the fingerprints off them. The key issue was that the British simply would not negotiate with the document they had. There was no question of them negotiating if Adams was associating with it – even if it was Mandela–Adams or Gandhi–Adams.

In fact, in a couple of casual conversations I've had with Gerry Adams since the ceasefire it's fair to say that he actually recognised the necessity at that stage to do that.

Reynolds and Major met several times during the Brussels summit, with a number of short meetings culminating in an hour-long get-together. The meetings took place in the Irish delegation room for a very simple reason: Major always liked to talk over a cup of tea, and the British room had no tea-pot. A Dublin source recalled: 'John Major always wants a cup of tea wherever he goes, and he came to our room because there was a cup of tea available. It's one of the things that Albert and himself have in common, they drink endless cups of tea.'

There were two five- or ten-minute meetings, then Reynolds and Major met alone for around three-quarters of an hour. For the final quarter of an hour they were joined by Spring and Douglas Hurd, who was then British Foreign Secretary. Reynolds said later: 'As far as I was concerned, I would do what had to be done to get success at the end of the day. If that meant pushing John Hume aside, or Gerry Adams aside, that was okay. It would be queering John Major's pitch if he thought that I was a conduit for Gerry Adams and Sinn Fein. I assured him that the document I gave him was a document drafted by Martin Mansergh and backed by the

Irish government and that was it. I mean it had nothing to do, it wasn't just a transfer document from John Hume and Gerry Adams straight to John Major, no way, it was our own document.'

A Dublin source added: 'The feeling that I remember from the day was Adams's fingerprints. That was the phrase of the day – "we have to get those fingerprints off the document, they won't talk while Adams's fingerprints are on the document." Everyone looking at the communiqué could see it would be unwelcome in the nationalist community. That was accepted.'

A senior British source said:

> The process could not have succeeded if it was not in the hands of the two governments. Mr Major argued that if you had a process identified with one side it could never be acceptable to the other side: Brussels made it clear it was a process between the two governments. There was an obvious risk that Hume–Adams could cut across the efforts of the two governments while creating a lot of antagonism. After Brussels the two Prime Ministers said, 'Whatever Hume–Adams do, we, the two governments, are going to go on our own.' The Prime Minister could see that suspicion about Hume–Adams was making discussions between the two governments very difficult.

The crucial point about the Brussels summit was that the two governments came away with completely different versions of what had been agreed. London said they believed Reynolds had agreed to drop the peace process and concentrate instead on the inter-party talks process. Dublin, by contrast, said the real decision had been to dissociate the peace process from Hume–Adams but to continue the declaration work in another guise.

A Dublin source said at the time that Hume was 'incandescent with fury', but he added that there was reason to believe the substance of what Hume wanted to do would actually be achieved. He said London's position was 'not as clear-cut as we would want', but there was reason to be optimistic about the declaration process.

A completely contradictory view was evident in London. A Whitehall source said some weeks later: 'Our interpretation, and the shared interpretation at the time, was that it was a rejection of

Hume—Adams and a recommitment of both governments to moving forward in the talks process.' Another British source added: 'The view in London is that peace would have to result from a political process rather than precede it.'

One of the causes of this striking difference of opinion was the fact that key exchanges had taken place between Reynolds and Major alone, in a tête-à-tête with no officials present; the possibility exists that one or both of the prime ministers misunderstood what was being conveyed. Major himself made it quite clear he regarded the declaration work was over. In a dramatic moment on 1 November, a few days after the Brussels summit, he told Hume across the floor of the Commons: 'I listened very carefully to what the Taoiseach had to say . . . but I did have to make a judgement as to whether I thought the proposals reached by [Hume] at this time, in the fashion he proposed them, would actually lead to progress and to a settlement. I reached the conclusion, after having been informed of them by the Taoiseach . . . that it was not the right way to proceed.' Major also declared, in reply to Labour MP Dennis Skinner: 'If the implication of his remarks is that we should sit down and talk with Mr Adams and the Provisional IRA, I can say only that that would turn my stomach, and those of most honourable members. We will not do it.' His remarks, televised and widely reported, seemed to represent the demise of the peace process and the rejection of Hume's efforts. Clearly the two governments were unable to agree on what they had agreed at Brussels. With violence sweeping the land, the political processes seemed powerless to provide an agreed alternative.

II

VOLCANIC
ACTIVITY

'John Hume is clearly intent on sucking us into
an immoral relationship with active terrorists.
Mr Hume and Mr Adams have nothing to offer'
   — Irish newspaper columnist

'Having watched your brave attempts to bring
peace, only one phrase leaps to mind — don't
let the bastards get you down'
   — letter to John Hume from a Dublin woman

'Association with Hume–Adams is a kiss of
death for any text intended to secure acceptance
on both sides of the community. We need to
finesse this difficulty'
   — John Major, in private letter to Albert
Reynolds

Hume, under strain from the relentless pressure and criticism and
anxious to rescue an initiative which seemed on the point of failure,
launched into a series of meetings and television interviews to
promote the process. On 4 November he went to Downing Street
to meet Major, emerging to intrigue everyone by saying that the
Hume–Adams initiative could end violence 'within a week'. He
later recalled a singular scene which took place at one of his
meetings with Major, possibly at this encounter. According to
Hume:

I remember meeting Major in Downing Street and as I was about
to go out I caught him by the lapels. I just walked up to him,
smiling, caught him by the lapels, and I said: 'Prime Minister, let

me tell you something. Gladstone failed. Lloyd George failed. Churchill failed. The PM that brings peace to Ireland will go down in history more than a PM who puts VAT on fuel.' He laughed, and he said: 'You are right.' Privately I think that had a big impact on him.

One of the most poignant moments came when Hume attended the funeral of one of the victims of the Greysteel shooting. He was approached by the daughter of one victim, who told him: 'Mr Hume, we've just buried my father. My family wants you to know that when we said the rosary around my daddy's coffin we prayed for you, for what you're trying to do to bring peace.' The television cameras captured the scene as Hume nodded, held her hands, then turned away and broke down in tears.

The strain on him was intense. He chain-smoked, was pale and nervous and was clearly not sleeping properly. He had become the lightning-conductor for the whole declaration process, attracting extraordinary vitriol. Although Reynolds was trying to keep the process alive, he was doing so in private, within the Irish Cabinet and in negotiation with London. As far as the public was concerned he had, in Brussels, apparently given up on it.

Hume, however, was exposed to the full blast of public and media criticism. Those who genuinely feared this approach would lend credibility to the republicans at a cost to democracy were joined by others who had previously felt inhibited, by Hume's standing, from criticising him. He was lambasted by various senior southern Irish politicians for 'using Provo-speak'; for making common cause with paramilitaries; for playing political footsie with terrorists. Lawyers say some of the criticism was certainly libellous. A senior Unionist leader said he had 'sold his soul to the devil'. Another accused him of endorsing the republican 'Armalite and ballot-box strategy', deriding 'that mixture of pleading and pathos which he exudes as the background for his dreary and platitudinous monologues'. A British Sunday paper said he had lost all judgement and advised him to retire. The *Irish Times* noted: 'Mr Hume is on the highest of high wires, with no safety net and with a great many enemies who would only too happily see him plunge to his political doom.'

Criticism of Hume from London and from Unionists was familiar, but a new note was sounded in Dublin. Until that point Hume's high standing in both political and public circles in the south had made him a revered figure, almost above criticism. With the Hume–Adams initiative he had, however, launched himself in a new and controversial direction: suddenly he was no longer beyond criticism, and the floodgates burst. The heat and intensity of the attacks, and the debate on whether his approach might work, was vividly illustrated by the 3 October issue of the Dublin *Sunday Independent*. The broadsheet devoted more than seven pages to Hume, illustrating them with an emblem emblazoned 'Hume on a tightrope'. It included nine articles attacking him and two in his defence. In one cartoon he was depicted with what looked like blood on his hands. The issue was possibly the most extreme example of the verbal onslaught against Hume, but it reflected the tone of some of the discussions and intellectual circles at the time, and it gives a useful flavour of the debate.

The newspaper's headline was HOPES FADING FOR HUME–ADAMS BID TO ACHIEVE PEACE, while a front-page opinion by columnist Eilis O'Hanlon declared: 'For all the euphoria there is not yet the slightest shred of evidence to suggest the initiative has been worth even a fraction of the trouble it caused, or that we are even half a step closer to peace.' Page two of the paper featured two articles entitled 'A pan-nationalist comedy of errors' and ' "Breakthrough" a shambles of confusion and contradiction'. Another column by O'Hanlon asserted: 'The Hume–Adams process cannot be the way to make political progress. It is the problem, not the solution; and people in Ireland should stop fooling themselves that this is any way to accelerate the coming of peace. It is only making peace more difficult to find.'

Dr Conor Cruise O'Brien, the distinguished politician and journalist who all along was one of the process's severest critics, wrote: 'John Hume is dancing to Gerry Adams's tune . . . If we mess around with this stuff, even a little bit, we could end up by stimulating both the Provisionals and the loyalist paramilitaries into bringing their different forms of terror down here into our Republic.' Shane Ross, a journalist who was also an independent member of the Dublin Senate, reported: 'Unionists are rightly outraged that Hume, having apparently come to an agreement with terrorists, was now about to bounce the [Irish] government into a quasi-constitutional alliance. They see the SDLP leader as fuelling the flames of the loyalist terror gangs. They also suspect that Mr Hume would not shed tears at the prospect of the British army in bloody clashes with the Protestant paramilitaries. Mr Hume is now the main obstacle to any hopes of reconciliation.' He suggested Hume should step aside, to be replaced by his deputy Seamus Mallon.

A critical editorial was accompanied by a commentary by Michael McDowell, a senior member of the Progressive Democrats party, who wrote: 'The unreality of the Hume–Adams fiasco is underlined by the ludicrous pretence by Adams that he may be able to sell the idea to the IRA leadership.' In a long article illustrated by a cartoon depicting the SDLP and Sinn Fein as twin sledgehammers being used against the state of Northern Ireland, columnist Eamon Dunphy declared: 'John Hume has been evasive and illogical. He is increasingly irrational. He is clearly intent on sucking us into an immoral relationship with active terrorists. Mr Hume and Mr Adams have nothing to offer.'

Two columnists, by contrast, strongly defended Hume. Philosophy professor Richard Kearney wrote: 'Trying to persuade unconstitutional republicans to abjure violence and turn constitutional overnight is no mean task. We should be grateful to Hume for at least trying. If he succeeds, who will cry Judas? It is, I believe, far too easy for us sitting comfortably in our southern armchairs to scapegoat Hume. He is one of the most visionary politicians on this island, with the stamina to brave political storms, the audacity to break moulds, and the bravery to place himself at the cutting edge whenever Irish politics reaches a threshold or transition point between old and new ways of thinking.'

History professor Ronan Fanning sought to put the attacks on Hume in historical context, comparing them to the flood of criticism directed against Charles Stewart Parnell, the nineteenth-century nationalist leader who was first idolised but later savagely attacked after his involvement in a divorce case. Fanning wrote: 'Nationalist Dublin saw and seized its chance to drag John Hume between the wheels of its mills of mediocrity. It was a chance long craved. When the long-rumbling volcano of antagonism towards Mr Hume erupted in all its fury, the vomited debris revealed all the essential elements of anti-Parnellism. Mr Hume's outstanding characteristics, intoned one anonymous colleague, were vision, tenacity and ego-centricity. The same was said of Parnell. Others dwelt on the obsessive quality of Mr Hume's leadership. That too was said of Parnell. That John Hume was burnt out and had lost his touch after 25 years in the cockpit of northern Irish politics, that it was time he handed over the helm to his deputy leader, were other elements in the indictment. Such things were also said of Parnell. In the 1970s and 1980s, just like Parnell a century ago, John Hume enjoyed a monumental position as a leader in the history of Irish nationalism. Leaders are invulnerable for as long as they remain monumental. Failure alone flaws monumental leadership, and John Hume is now thought vulnerable because he is judged to have failed. The mockers are in full cry.'

The pressure of such criticism took its toll on the SDLP leader and he collapsed and was taken to hospital. At that point it all seemed to be over, with Hume ill in hospital and London evidently intent on shelving the declaration. Then came what turned out to be one of the defining moments of the troubles. On a high political level the initiative seemed dead, but there occurred an almost unprecedented surge of nationalist public opinion – a surge of indignation, anger at the treatment of Hume, a surge of hope. As far as grassroots nationalists were concerned, if John Hume said there was a chance of peace within weeks, that chance should be pursued.

In his bed in Londonderry's Altnagelvin hospital, Hume became aware of this as 1,169 letters, notes, get-well cards and other cards, most of them urging him to persevere, poured in. The postbag reflected a heartfelt desire for an end to the violence, and support for his efforts, providing a dramatic counterpoint to criticisms such as those of the *Sunday Independent*. The London *Independent* printed extracts from some of the cards and letters:

Catholic woman, north Belfast

After the recent massacres we were in total despair. Never in all the 24 years of the troubles was I so afraid, we were plain terrified, in the darkest hours of recent weeks we had one tenacious hope and voice – you.

Catholic woman, Belfast

The hope which you have implanted in our minds of 'the cessation of all violence' has caught like wildfire. It is on everyone's lips and has even invaded the minds of those who would oppose you.

Nun, Essex

It does cut through my heart as I watch the news and hear of murder after murder. So while you keep up the negotiations, I'll keep up the prayers.

Woman, Co. Dublin

I am 84 years of age and do not find letter-writing easy. The self-seekers jockeying for power and the limelight are not fit to polish your shoes. May God reward your efforts – I hope he is not on the side of the big battalions!

Nun, Dublin

Don't let the Bs get you down.

Man, Nottingham

How can there be any peace when those who are at the heart of the troubles are locked outside and made to feel alienated from normal political structures? Major and his squalid crew would do anything to save their parliamentary skins.

Man, Newport Pagnell

I am appalled that there are so many politicians at Westminster who are not prepared to listen and, worse, those who are intent on wrecking the process. I hope you will not be swayed by the baying of those who will not listen.

Woman, Rathmines, Dublin

I loathe, detest and despise all that Gerry Adams represents, but the sad fact is that he exists and must be acknowledged if it means peace.

Protestant woman, Belfast

My husband is a Methodist minister who is glad I'm sending you this note. I am ashamed I have never written before to say how I admire the way you have given of yourself.

Catholic woman, west Belfast

I said to my husband, my God, John Hume's in hospital. My handicapped daughter, who we always think knows very little, turned around and gave a big gasp and shook her head, so we are all with you.

West Belfast

We are fifteen families from west Belfast and we are writing to ask you not to give up on the peace talks with Gerry Adams. We have lost members of our families through British army violence and loyalist violence, no one has condemned this or gave us support in our bereavement only Sinn Fein. Our hearts are broke. The nationalist people have suffered badly, we all want peace and we want you to know we support you 100 per cent. Don't give up on us, you've given us hope.

The support came from nationalists north and south, from some Protestants and from some in Britain. The pressure, as far as Reynolds and his ministers were concerned, was simply irresistible: in effect the Irish government was forcibly told to stick with the Hume–Adams talks process; that there was promise in the initiative which should not be thrown away; and that it should make amends for slighting Hume. The Taoiseach's office was deluged with an unprecedented flood of angry letters and phone calls which accused him of betraying Hume and throwing away the chance of peace. The sentiment poured out of both parts of Ireland, cutting across party lines. A Belfast solicitor said: 'Sure we expected Major to do what he did, to humiliate Hume like that. It was the sight of our own in Dublin doing it too that got me so angry.' The most common comment was that Spring and Reynolds had 'hung Hume out to dry'.

The message was driven home at the Fianna Fáil ard-fheis which was held in Dublin on 7 and 8 November. Mentions of Hume's name drew thunderous applause, and ministers and TDs were buttonholed by delegates and told they should be supporting the SDLP leader. The *Irish Times* reported:

> Among much of the Fianna Fáil rank and file, John Hume obviously still has the stature of a demi-god. The SDLP leader could hardly have expected even his own party to give him the kind of accolades he was accorded this weekend on the floor of the ard-fheis. A motion calling for government support for the SDLP leader unleashed a wave of pro-Hume emotion that washed over the delegates and led to passionate declarations of belief in he Hume–Adams initiative. One delegate said Spring was being wishy-washy and that it was nothing short of a disgrace that the government showed no respect for the Hume–Adams proposals. How, he asked, could they be so cool about something that involved a possible end to violence? The mere mention of John Hume's name brought a round of applause. While there was no orchestrated challenge to Mr Reynolds's leadership, waves of dissent were washing about because of a perceived failure to champion the cause of sundered brethren in the north. There were loud voices warning against letting John Hume be hung out to dry.

The irony was of course that Reynolds was already working to keep the peace process alive, though after the Brussels meeting he was pretending not to. The sheer force of public opinion, however, left him with little choice: from that point on he not only had to pursue the initiative, but to be seen to do so. It was time to throw caution to the wind. By the final day of the ard-fheis, far from brushing Hume's fingerprints off the initiative, he was telling an Irish radio interviewer: 'John Hume was the first to say, "Look, the two governments should take up this initiative and run with it." We're doing that. There are elements of that initiative that indeed can provide the foundation on which a peace formula can be built.'

Two days after the ard-fheis a Dublin source said: 'Albert's gone wild for the peace, wild. He's catching a mood in the south. Hume has great credibility. That's quite a widespread feeling – wider than Fianna Fáil, it cuts across all parties. Albert's riding the peace train now. I think the Brussels communiqué had to be done – there's no way you can have it with Adams in the parentage, there's no way you can sell it. But it was too brutal, it could have been finessed much better. Now Albert is pushing it, I think catching the public mood and also with the political sense that if he doesn't the Brits will draw back. The file's in Downing Street – we have to keep it there, move it along, push it. If we go any slower the file drifts back to Stormont Castle [i.e. Mayhew's office] where it gathers dust.'

In fact, by this stage the two sides were so far apart that Reynolds was thinking of switching to 'Plan B' – a fall-back position in which, if no British–Irish declaration could be agreed, he would instead aim for a pan-nationalist initiative led by himself and including both Hume and Adams. On 10 November Reynolds delivered what became known as the 'Houston Declaration'. He bumped into two journalists at a concert given by American singer Whitney Houston in Dublin, and had a conversation with them. He believed he was speaking off the record but his remarks were carried in the papers: 'If it comes to it,' he said, 'I will walk away from John Major and put forward a set of proposals myself. I am not prepared to let this opportunity pass.'

By this stage the scope of the joint declaration was being extended. The original idea was to produce a text which would wean the republicans away from violence, and this remained its primary purpose; but the concept arose that it should be addressed to Unionists and loyalists as well. The Protestant community was notoriously insecure and fearful of political innovation, and people in both London and Dublin worried that a document addressed exclusively to republicans would spark off a wave of anxiety. Increases in loyalist anxiety often led to a rise in loyalist violence, which all sides were anxious to avoid. There were, in addition, interesting stirrings within the loyalist paramilitary underworld which some were hopeful of encouraging. The UDA was becoming if anything even more militant, with control of the organisation moving to a group of young Turks who had a real appetite for killing. Within the UVF, by contrast, some more thoughtful figures were emerging, with many ex-prisoners questioning the value of violence and expressing interest in exploring a political path. (The drop in UVF violence led UDA men to describe the UVF contemptuously as 'the peace people'.)

Dublin had long maintained a discreet network of private contacts with Protestant and Unionist figures including politicians, clergy and others, and two of these now came to the fore. One was Dr Robin Eames, who as Archbishop of Armagh was head of the Church of Ireland; the other was the Rev. Roy Magee, a Presbyterian minister based in east Belfast. Dr Eames, who had a reputation as a political prelate familiar with behind-the-scenes activity, had access to John Major. He was also known to be in close touch with many other sections of opinion, including important figures in the Ulster Unionist party. The party would not officially talk to Reynolds, but Dublin hoped to use Dr Eames as a line of contact to senior Unionists, and the churchman became a regular visitor to the Taoiseach's office. Reynolds related:

> He was a good balancing voice. It was obvious that he had a very clear view as to where he wanted to see his people going. I clearly recognised that he would have close contact with the leadership of the Unionist Party as well, and would be in a position – when I wasn't when I couldn't meet with them – to give me a very strong input as to what their views were, what their fears were and how those fears could be accommodated. I showed him drafts of the declaration. Certainly when I showed him the declaration he knew that it was for real and that I had very strong ideas as to how it could be accomplished. I gave it to him in my office, I let him read it a couple of times himself, gave him time to absorb it. I showed him where I was on the republican side, and I said I now needed to balance it up with input from him, and I invited him to give me a couple of paragraphs to balance the Unionist perspective in the declaration, which he did. He went away and thought about it and came back in a week or two.

Dr Eames, confirming Reynolds had shown him a declaration draft, said that as it stood it would have been rejected by Unionists. He said later: 'All the evidence of what was being proposed to me would have been totally unacceptable to the Unionist community. Taking the longer view there had to be a complete swing back to the legitimacy of the Unionist position. I believe it was at that point the principle of consent was born. I said, "Without this, this will never be satisfactory from a northern point of view." '

Reynolds also sought and received input from Mr Magee, a minister in east Belfast, where both the UDA and UVF had many members. He knew some of the most important paramilitary figures. In the early 1970s he had himself been involved in Unionist politics as a member of Ulster Vanguard, a hard-line loyalist grouping. He therefore had a track record of commitment to Unionism, though in his work in the 1990s all recognised his aim was ending violence. He was in touch with the CLMC – the Combined Loyalist Military Command, an umbrella organisation which represented the three major Protestant paramilitary groups, the UDA, UVF and the smaller Red Hand Commandos. One evening in late 1993 Mansergh, watching television, saw Mr Magee talking about the loyalist paramilitants and recommended to Reynolds that an approach should be made to him. Reynolds, aware of Mr Magee's contacts with the paramilitants, established a personal relationship with him, thus setting up yet another line of secret contact, this time between the Irish government and the extreme loyalists. Reynolds later recalled:

> Roy Magee used to come and see me in my own office. The two of us talked at length from time to time, with nobody present, no record kept, so there was a matter of trust between the two of us to build up a good relationship and to make others feel that their voices were being listened to in Dublin as well. Maybe every couple of weeks there would be telephone communication between my office and Roy Magee – it took some toing and froing. I became absolutely convinced that I could accept the messages coming from the loyalists, just the same as I would accept them coming from the other side. I was telling

Roy Magee that my view was, and my good feeling was telling me, that there was a distinct possibility of getting the IRA to call a ceasefire. I wanted to take the other side on board as well and see could we move them towards a ceasefire, as well. He was very straight-talking, open, very determined in where he was trying to go to. None of us could operate in isolation of each other. We all needed each other to make it happen. He appreciated that there was a genuine attempt being made by the Irish government, through me, to recognise the fears of the loyalist community and where they were coming from.

Although loyalist violence was running at a high level, Mr Magee assured Reynolds that opinion was changing and developing within the loyalist underworld. Reynolds believed that at least some of the loyalists wanted to move into politics. Mr Magee felt his dealings with Reynolds were valuable, but later said there had been one almost comic misunderstanding between them. He brought to Dublin a text from the loyalists which included six points including the right of free political thought, the right to pursue constitutional change by peaceful means and the right to equal opportunity. Reynolds, eager to show willing, said he agreed with all the points and would include them in the declaration. The misunderstanding arose because Reynolds assumed the points were what loyalists wished to be reassured about. In fact, however, they were points which the loyalists were prepared to offer to Catholics and national- ists. Mr Magee later explained: 'I presented six points. He assumed that what he was being told is what loyalists wanted written into a Bill of Rights. What they were saying was, "Here is what we would want to see written into a Bill of Rights to make sure nationalists would be comfortable." They were in fact conceding them, which is different.' The misunderstanding about these points went right through the system in Dublin. They were forwarded for inclusion in the text of the declaration and eventually incorporated in what was to become the Downing Street Declaration, where they may be seen today, a lasting reminder of how misapprehensions can occur in the most carefully constructed chain of communication.

Reports in the Dublin papers, such as 'the Houston Declaration' made it clear that Reynolds remained fully committed to the peace process. This was a source of great annoyance to John Major, whose view was that Reynolds had agreed in Brussels to shelve the initiative, and he despatched his private secretary, Roderic Lyne, to make this clear to the Taoiseach. Lyne, the son of an air vice-marshal, had joined Major's personal entourage, on secondment to the Cabinet Office, following a twenty-year career with the Foreign Office. In his career he had been primarily concerned with the Soviet Union and Eastern Europe, and had no direct experience with Ireland.

Although Lyne had a distinguished diplomatic career and played a prominent role in Anglo-Irish relations, a range of Irish sources later said he was regarded in Dublin as a source of friction in their relations with London. Whether this is because he was conveying from London messages which Dublin found unwelcome is a matter for speculation, though the same Irish sources speak highly of other British officials such as Chilcot and Thomas of the NIO. An informed British source said Lyne 'sometimes caused a few groans' among other officials such as Chilcot and Thomas. Whatever the reason, Lyne arrived in Dublin for what proved to be a disastrous meeting with Reynolds. Dublin sources said he was supposed to be simply a messenger, but that he spoke to Reynolds 'with astonishing freedom', and got into an argument with him.

Dublin tried to work out what was going on in London: they believed Butler and Chilcot were well-disposed towards the initiative, but that 'Sir P' – Mayhew – and others were against it. It was also acknowledged that Major had difficulties in trying not to alienate the Unionists, who were so important to him in the Commons. The understanding which Reynolds and Major thought they had arrived at in Brussels had collapsed within days, leaving the two prime ministers completely at odds. There followed an extraordinary series of crisis meetings with Butler, Lyne, Chilcot and Blatherwick arguing for hours with O hUiginn, Nally, Finlay and Mansergh – 'the atmosphere was volcanic at times,' said one of those involved.

It was a fraught time and relations were not always good: many in Dublin came to regard both Lyne and Blatherwick as irritants rather than conciliating influences while London made it very clear that it regarded O hUiginn as difficult to deal with. A Dublin source said: 'O hUiginn was champion of the broad nationalist position; he could also be rather abrasive in his manner.' According to Reynolds a British official raised the question of O hUiginn with him. He said he considered the representation carefully but decided it had no substance and dismissed it. O hUiginn stayed at the negotiating table. A Dublin source said of him: 'Sean is an absolutely superb negotiator. He understands the nationalist mind-set very well, and he never loses sight of his objective in negotiation – tremendously focused, fantastic focus.' Reynolds said he knew why the British found fault with O hUiginn – 'it's because he is so bloody good.'

On 10 November Irish officials flew to London for a meeting at the Cabinet Office with their British counterparts. The Irish stressed that there existed the best chance for peace in many years. If the next Major–Reynolds summit did not produce something adequate to the occasion, they argued, there would be a sense of anticlimax, and a vacuum which would benefit the men of violence. They said they understood the British need to distance themselves from the Hume–Adams label, but said the British should be careful not to distance themselves from Hume, who had a great influence for good.

The British team at the meeting was headed by Sir Robin Butler, who said the British government realised there was an opportunity, but added that they despaired of disassociating it from what the Unionists saw as its provenance. He said the British instinct was not to write it off, assuring the Irish they were looking at all possibilities. Archbishop Eames was privately rather upbeat, Butler conceded, but he added that London had doubts about the prelate's judgement of the Protestant community and questioned how much they could rely on him as a guide to Unionist opinion.

The British spelled out that their position was not based on the assumption that the IRA were war-weary: they had independent evidence that the republican movement was thinking seriously of peace, and they recognised there was an upsurge for peace in the community. They explained that the question in John Major's mind was not about rejecting the initiative but rather how best to exploit it in a way which was not provocative to Unionists. They pointed out that Unionists were worried and anxious about Hume–Adams, but said that if there was no other route, ministers would judge whether they should take the risk.

Interest in the initiative was kept alive when Major, speaking at the Lord Mayor's banquet in London's Guildhall, said Sinn Fein could join political talks if the IRA gave up violence for good. He added, however, that his government would never talk to organisations which did not renounce violence. The speech was interpreted by the British media as a new initiative by Major, but its exact import and direction was unclear. Dublin was encouraged by a number of the points made by Major, including the sense of urgency he imparted, his declaration that there might be a real opportunity for peace, and his use of language concerning the need for courage and to take risks. But while his statements carried echoes of recent pronouncements by Irish ministers, the speech was a masterpiece of subtle drafting which could be read in two entirely different ways. On one reading it gave the clear impression of sharing many of Dublin's concerns and endorsing many of its key points. At the same time, however, the text gave no actual commitment to signing up for any of the elements of the peace process, as Reynolds was urging Major to do. In fact Major, in listing the elements which gave grounds for hope, did not mention the possibility of any change of heart within the republican movement. The net effect of the speech, therefore, was to leave Mr Major's options open: he did not reject the Reynolds approach, but neither did he endorse it.

Yet if he did not show his hand in the Guildhall speech, the manner of its presentation to the media added to the general sense of momentum and maintained the expectation that something big could be on the way. But a complicating factor arose on 19 November, when the well-informed Dublin political journalist Emily O'Reilly published an internal Irish government document on the future of Northern Ireland. The document was part of ongoing work on what was known as the 'framework document' which Dublin and London were to publish in February 1995. It had no immediate bearing on the declaration initiative, but it showed that Dublin was pressing for a far-reaching say in the administration of Northern Ireland. Spring described the leak as an act of treachery. Its publication alarmed Unionists, raised concerns about the security and confidentiality of the Irish government, and did nothing to improve the fraught atmosphere. The following day the temperature rose still further when Hume and Adams issued a joint statement calling on the British government to respond to their initiative.

By this stage Unionist politicians including James Molyneaux, whose nine Commons votes were of such great potential import-ance to Major, were clamouring for the British government to drop the peace process. There were also allegations that the government had been in secret touch with the republicans: these were denied, on Major's orders, but he and Mayhew were uneasy at this stage that the back-channel might be exposed. One development which brought some sense of relief was the seizure at Teeside docks in England of a large haul of explosives and weaponry bound for the UVF. Unknown to the loyalists the plan to import the material had been known to the intelligence authorities for months, and was carefully monitored. Major was particularly annoyed by the Emily O'Reilly leak and by the latest Hume–Adams statement. After taking soundings in the Protestant community he judged that Reyn-olds's document had no chance of being accepted by Unionist opinion.

He also concluded that the document was indelibly identified with Hume–Adams – the association was, in his words, 'the kiss of death'. He therefore attempted to make a completely fresh start, and he had Butler, Lyne and other officials draw up an alternative document, using some of the language of the declaration but recast-ing it in a different light. Major conveyed the news of this new document to Dublin in the form of a personal and confidential letter to Reynolds on 25 November. The text is as follows:

It was good to talk to you last Saturday. I am sorry to have intruded on your weekend off. I hope that you and Kathleen were able to get some relaxation during your trip. If I may say so, I thought your interview with David Frost went very well.

Making no bones about it we have had an extremely difficult and depressing week. I need not labour the reasons why. I had allowed myself to feel a little optimistic after my meeting with Robin Eames on 18th November. But I'm afraid the following day's leak and the Hume–Adams statement on Saturday last had precisely the effect I feared when we spoke on the phone. I have spent all week trying to repair the damage through a series of meetings and public statements. I fear that I have had only limited success.

In the current political atmosphere there is clearly no hope of securing even tacit acceptance by the Unionist mainstream of a joint declaration along the lines of your draft. The text would be seen as deriving from Hume–Adams and thus would be assumed to be the product of negotiation with Sinn Fein. This is an impression which successive statements from Hume–Adams have done nothing to dispel.

As we've agreed all along, association with Hume–Adams is a kiss of death for any text intended to secure acceptance on both sides of the community. We need to finesse this difficulty. We must find another way of testing the ground for a cessation of violence. As we have gone so far with our work and have the summit hard upon us I do not think that we should abandon our efforts despite this serious setback.

Robin Butler will therefore be putting a proposal to you which results from my series of meetings this week and the most careful consideration at this end. Robin will explain our thinking fully. You will see that the text incorporates much of the substance of the joint declaration but in a different framework. This is a text which will certainly attract sharp criticism from many people in Northern Ireland. It goes as far as in my judgement the market will bear. I believe that our proposal would meet the central objectives of both governments and will show whether there is a genuine chance of securing a cessation of violence. I hope that you will agree and that we shall be able to issue the text as a joint statement after our summit meeting.

Reynolds and others in Dublin were furious. They had been working on the declaration ever since Hume had brought the first draft to Dublin in October 1991. It was in June 1992 that a document had emerged; it was in June 1993 that it was passed on to the British government, at Reynolds's meeting with Butler at Baldonnell airfield. In the following months the declaration had been altered in line with observations made by London. It was now November 1993, and Major was proposing to start all over again at the beginning. The day after Major's letter arrived, Butler travelled to Dublin with the fresh British proposal. He politely outlined the thinking behind it: Reynolds and his officials read it and listened, but quickly concluded it would not bring about a cessation of IRA violence.

The document in effect amounted to an abandonment of the idea of leading the IRA to a cessation, and was instead designed to help restart inter-party talks without the republicans. On self-determination it offered a new formulation: 'The British government acknowledge the people living in Ireland, north and south, should be free, separately, without coercion or violence, to determine whether a united Ireland should be established.' Dublin believed that this had no all-Ireland dimension to it and therefore stood no chance of gaining republican approval. The second critical sentence was meant as an overture to Unionists, setting out: 'The Taoiseach acknowledges the presence in the Constitution of the Republic, specifically Articles 2 and 3, of elements which are deeply resented by northern Unionists.' Irish government press officer Sean Duignan recorded in his diary Reynolds's reaction: 'Sir Robin Butler in from London. Produces alternative paper to Irish position paper, including proposals for unilateral changes to Articles 2 and 3. Albert gives him hell. Tells him he hasn't a clue. He also tells him that Major's proposal, which involves the two leaders finding some kind of "middle way", won't wash. Reynolds will not buy some kind of "sticking plaster" anodyne cover-up. Why bother to have the summit at all? Who is trying to bluff who?'

Reynolds's feelings were reinforced by the strongly voiced opinions of veteran diplomat Dermot Nally. One of those in the

Dublin decision-making circle said later: 'Nally came into his own at that point and told the Taoiseach that you couldn't negotiate with the British on that kind of basis. He said, "They always do this, this is the way they always behave." He described it as game-playing, and he told the Taoiseach that if he wanted the British to respect him he must not entertain that document at all, on principle. He said, "It doesn't matter what's in it at all – get it off the table." I've never seen Dermot so categoric and firm as he was that day.'

Reynolds said later: 'I was not prepared to start again on a new paper. Here we were after spending months and months and months, even sometimes spending weeks settling certain words of the declaration, and here was a proposal to start again. I mean I regarded it as a breach of faith.' He was about to draft a letter of rejection when news broke of the British back-channel to the republicans, and attention was drawn away from the declaration to the contentious question of the British government's secret contacts with republicans.

12

THE BACK-
CHANNEL

'This allegation belongs more properly in the
fantasy of spy thrillers'
   – British government statement responding
to allegation that it had been in secret contact
with republicans

'We've been in contact with the Provos. You
can read all about it in Quentin Thomas's file'
   – British official briefing another official after
the contacts were confirmed

'It was a spook freelancing'
   – Government source claiming a meeting
between Martin McGuinness and a British representative had not been authorised

'We have witnessed you being extremely nervous. I think we noticed you swallowing and
your syntax has gone to pieces several times'
   – Belfast journalist to Sir Patrick Mayhew,
who was defending the contacts

In the spring of 1993 one of the authors, Eamonn Mallie, had a
conversation with a public figure who remarked to him: 'Do you
know that there's a far bigger game going on in the background
than anybody knows?' He said he did not know exactly what was
happening; Mallie suspected he meant secret contacts between the
government and republicans. Reports of such contacts were a familiar source of rumour in Belfast: they cropped up with such regu-
larity, in fact, that they were largely disregarded. The fact that they
were routinely denied by the authorities, and went unconfirmed

by republicans, was generally taken as indicating they were without substance.

Some months later, when James Molyneaux hinted that such contact was taking place, few paid much attention to his words. But when, in the autumn of 1993, another source dropped a hint about the existence of such contacts, Mallie called the press office at the Northern Ireland Office and put the suggestion to them. On the same day, 1 November, a press officer said in response to the query: 'We have no knowledge of such talks or such meetings. The Secretary of State has made his attitude on talking to Sinn Fein very clear on many occasions.'

Half an hour later Mallie telephoned the press office at 10 Downing Street and posed the same question. The initial response from Jonathan Haslam, who was later promoted to become Major's chief press officer, was: 'It seems like fantasy to me. We have made clear our position on many occasions.' A more formal response was later given: 'We have made clear on many occasions that we don't speak to those who carry out or advocate or condone violence to further their political aims.' Haslam added in conversation that he had spoken to the NIO – 'they said this twaddle has been around a lot over the summer.' Mallie remarked to him: 'I hope this is not another Nixon [i.e. Watergate] story.'

On 11 November Mallie called DUP MP the Rev. William McCrea at his home in Magherafelt. McCrea said he had a source who had come to him and told him there had been contact 'right from the top of the government right to the top of the republican movement'. He said his source was on the inside and was very nervous but had agreed, after a series of phone calls, to pass on a copy of a document to him. On 12 November, on the strength of this information, Mallie wrote a story reporting on McCrea's claims, without mentioning his name, and noting: 'If the claim being made by the MP proves to be accurate it will come as a serious embarrassment to the government and particularly to John Major, who more than any previous Prime Minister has voiced his opposition to talking to Sinn Fein.' That evening Mallie was interviewed on Ulster Television about the story. Following the broadcast the NIO issued a statement which declared:

> No such meetings have taken place. The Secretary of State has said on many occasions there will be no talking to the IRA or any other violent group of people unless or until they have said violence is at an end and shown that they mean it. That remains the position. Simply repeating unsubstantiated gossip and rumour does not make it any truer. It serves only to produce more rumour. It is worth noting that this allegation lacks the essential details by which the truthfulness of any new story is judged – who, where, when, for a start. As such it belongs more properly in the fantasy of spy thrillers.

This amounted to a stinging and almost contemptuous rebuke. Mallie spoke to an NIO press officer to point out that he had not mentioned the IRA, but instead had carefully reported the MP's allegation that the contact was with Sinn Fein. The press officer, after checking, returned to say that the denial covered both the IRA and Sinn Fein. On 14 November Gerry Adams, in a series of television interviews, responded to questions about contacts: 'I'm not confirming or denying they did, but I would take with a pinch of salt the British government's denial.' This intriguing answer whetted journalistic curiosity on the issue. On 15 November, after further inquiries, Mallie wrote a story saying Sinn Fein sources confirmed republican leaders had on a number of occasions been in direct contact with government representatives.

That evening John Major, in a speech at the Guildhall in London, declared that he would 'never talk to organisations which did not renounce violence'. This followed his earlier pronouncement in the Commons that the idea of talking to Adams or the IRA 'would turn my stomach. We will not do it.' On 16 November McCrea rang Mallie at 10.30 a.m. to say his source had been in touch to say staff had been told to 'cover all traces' on the contacts. On the same day the BBC and others reported that Martin McGuinness was the key Sinn Fein figure in contact with the government. The next day McGuinness told a rally in Londonderry that he had been meeting government representatives. On the same evening McCrea phoned Mallie to say he had received a document: it had gone astray on its way to him but had just been retrieved. Mallie said: 'Put it on the fax to me, Willie.' Within minutes he had in his hands a document which strongly suggested that the idea of the government talking to republicans was not 'the fantasy of spy thrillers' but a reality. What came through on the fax was a 'speaking note' – the instructions given by Mayhew to a representative who was handing over a document to the republicans. It read as follows:

> The following instructions should be delivered orally to [the name had been deleted] when you hand over Annex C in written form. In handing over this written message – and you need make no bones about the fact that it is a written message that you are handing over – you should emphasise that this process is fraught with difficulties for the British Government, as must be obvious. They are nevertheless prepared to tackle these and accept the risks that they entail. But it must be recognised that all acts of violence hereafter could only enhance these difficulties and risks, quite conceivably to the point when the process would be destroyed. If that were to occur, the British Government would consider that a potentially historic opportunity had been squandered. The paper gives out substantive advice in response to the initial message. As it makes clear, we wish to establish whether this provides a basis for a way forward. We on our side are ready to answer specific questions or give further explanation.
>
> You should also emphasise to your interlocutor the British Government's acknowledgement that all of those involved share a responsibility to work to end the conflict. We agree on the need for a healing process. We wish to take a positive view of these developments and hope that it will be possible to continue to do. You should be aware that the above has been personally approved by SOSNI [the Secretary of State for Northern Ireland, Sir Patrick Mayhew]. In fact, all but the first sentence of the first paragraph is his own wording. In other words, it is not negotiable.

The piece of paper seemed genuine but there was no guarantee that it was not a fake. McCrea had passed it on in good faith, but the MP did not know the name of his source: it was always possible that the paper could be a hoax. With the paper in his pocket,

Mallie put it to Mayhew several times over the following days: 'Are you in contact with republicans?' On each occasion Mayhew denied that he was. By this stage Mallie was uncomfortably aware that some other journalists believed he was obsessed with the issue. On 22 November, as Mayhew took part in a tree-planting ceremony at Malone House in south Belfast, Mallie took to one side Jonathan Stephens, one of Mayhew's personal aides, and put the allegation to him. Stephens responded: 'Well, he [Mayhew] says it's not happening.' A press officer produced yet another government statement saying the government did not talk to supporters of violence. Mallie, in the hope of provoking a different response, gave the press officer a flavour of the document, mentioning the word interlocutor and quoting the phrase 'this process is fraught with difficulties for the Government'.

Mallie asked Mark Lyons of ITN to pose the now-familiar question to Mayhew. When Mayhew once again dismissed the issue Lyons followed up: 'What will you do if evidence emerges in the coming week to prove contacts are taking place?' Mayhew clasped his hands and said with a smile: 'We will have to look at any evidence.'

On 24 November McCrea was part of a DUP delegation which met Major in Downing Street. They were assured by the Prime Minister that he and his ministers had not been talking to the IRA. The document was in McCrea's pocket during the meeting, but he decided to say nothing at that point. Mallie, meanwhile, sought to authenticate his paper by approaching a number of people familiar with government documents. The consensus was that it seemed genuine, though there was no proof. He consulted Dublin journalist Mary Holland who, like Mallie, contributed regularly to the *Observer* newspaper. The *Observer*'s deputy editor, John Price, was immediately excited by the document and discussed it with the paper's political editor, Tony Bevins. Late that night Bevins approached Michael Ancram, one of Mayhew's deputy ministers at Westminster, and told him of their information. The government then moved quickly as it decided how to react to what was one of the most sensational revelations of the troubles.

By Friday morning 'everything went into overdrive', according to Andy Wood, the senior civil servant who has for many years occupied the sensitive post of head of information services at Stormont Castle. Wood, a canny Yorkshireman, was the veteran of dozens of political and security crises but would remember this as one of the most striking moments in his two decades as a press officer. Early on Friday morning Wood was in London, driving round the North Circular Road on the way to catch a plane for Belfast, when a call came through on the car phone from the NIO duty officer. He was told to report to the Old Admiralty Building at Whitehall. He knew immediately there was a crisis: 'I thought they were going to introduce "the big I",' he later recalled, meaning he believed internment was about to be brought back. The flap was in fact about the impending *Observer* revelation.

Wood rushed to the office. He recalled: 'Jonathan Stephens was the first guy I saw when I got into the office. He said: "We've been in contact with the Provos. You can read all about it in Quentin Thomas's file." At 7.40 a.m. I was given a file which read like the first draft of a Le Carré novel. I did a bit of speed-reading, then there was a discussion – where do we go from here?' A meeting was then convened. Around the table were Wood, Sir Robin Butler and Rod Lyne from the Cabinet Office, Gus O'Donnell, Major's press secretary, Sir Patrick Mayhew and his deputy, Michael Ancram, and Quentin Thomas, deputy to Sir John Chilcot, the NIO permanent secretary.

The ministers and officials wondered how one of the government's most highly classified operations had come to be publicly exposed. Most immediately, they discussed how to react when the *Observer* produced documentary evidence of the back-channel. There had been so many public denials of any such contacts by Mayhew that his and the government's credibility was clearly on the line. His brief had been to respond to questions by saying carefully that no one had been authorised to enter into talks or negotiations with the IRA, but he had occasionally overstepped this mark and categorically denied any line of contact. The government was therefore without even the fig-leaf of arguing that, in denying talks or negotiations it had been strictly and technically correct, even if extremely economical with the truth. Lyne argued that the story 'wouldn't run hard', meaning it would not attract much interest, since the Sunday papers would be preoccupied with economic stories. Wood believed it would have major play in the media and argued that they had little choice but to confirm the contact and engage in damage limitation – 'I argued we should shoot the fox,' he said later.

The outcome of the meeting was that they would wait to see how much of a stir the story caused. In the meantime Chilcot called Bevins of the *Observer* and spent some time putting as favourable as possible a gloss on the reasons for the existence of the back-channel. (It was Chilcot who had personally authorised the statement describing the allegations as fantasy.) Ulster Unionist party leader James Molyneaux was also contacted by the government and given advance notice that a disclosure was about to be made: it was not as bad as it sounded, he was told. On Friday evening everyone was intrigued when Molyneaux issued a statement warning that there would be a development over the weekend but saying people should await clarification. This was a reference to the *Observer* story, but the fact that he did not specify this caused wild rumours to circulate. Bevins by now had been in touch with a number of politicians and word was leaking out. The SDLP conference, taking place over the weekend, was ablaze with speculation.

When the *Observer* reached the streets late on Saturday night Wood had a statement ready – 'we were tooled up on the Saturday,' he said later. The statement insisted that no one had been authorised to talk or negotiate with republicans, and went on to make an assertion which was to prove controversial. It said that in February 1993 a message was passed on to the government from the IRA leadership: 'It was to the effect that the conflict was over but they needed our advice as to the means of bringing it to a close. The Government obviously had to take that message seriously.'

The confirmation of the back-channel generated intense interest and international publicity, and when Mayhew called a press conference on Sunday morning scores of journalists and camera crews hurried to Stormont Castle to hear his explanations. A flavour of the event was given in this report in the *Independent on Sunday*:

The old Sir Patrick Mayhew was a big, bluff character with a genial twinkle in his eye and a ready smile. Some in Belfast thought him perhaps a little patronising, but in general he was accepted as a man of rectitude and straight dealing, as indeed befits a former Attorney-General. The new Sir Patrick Mayhew made his first appearance at a Stormont Castle press conference last Sunday. Pale, tense and unhappy, he stumbled through his explanations of why he had been in protracted contact with Sinn Fein and the IRA.

His audience was not a receptive one, for it consisted of journalists who had repeatedly heard him denying such contacts. Absolutely untrue, he had insisted. His press officer had scoffed at one such report from journalist Eamonn Mallie: 'It belongs more properly in the fantasy of spy thrillers than in real life.' Sir Patrick, asked how he would react if somebody produced evidence of such contacts, had chortled condescendingly, 'I should be very interested to see it.' The production of that evidence last weekend – by Eamonn Mallie – introduced us to the new, grim, non-chortling Sir Patrick.

The press conference was unimpressed by his performance. 'We have witnessed you being extremely nervous,' one woman journalist told him with Belfast directness. 'I think we noticed you swallowing, and your syntax has gone to pieces several times.' He made a hurried, graceless exit after his ordeal, leaving his glasses behind.

Many of the points made by Mayhew in his defence were to be hotly contested by Sinn Fein, who described his version of events as a tissue of lies and in particular rejected his assertion that the IRA had ever said 'the conflict is over'. They were shortly to produce a very different version of events. Mayhew defended himself, at his press conference and later in the Commons, by placing the talks firmly in the context of this alleged message. He explained that it had come through a confidential channel of communication that had been in place for a long time, using intermediaries, though it had not been in use for many years.

It had been sent on behalf of the IRA by Martin McGuinness, he said. The cornerstone of his defence was that this was considered of such importance that the government had felt duty-bound to follow it up. He was adamant that the government had never bargained to secure an end to violence, maintaining that nobody had been authorised to undertake talks or negotiations. Messages had been sent back and forth, he said, but 'what had been said to the IRA in private is exclusively what has been said in public. They have been told in private that we have meant what we've said in public.' Mayhew repeated that because his communications with republicans had been in writing, he had been correct in saying no one had talked to the IRA. But, reacting to reports that there had been face-to-face meetings with the IRA, he admitted government representatives had twice met republicans. He insisted however that these had been unauthorised meetings. Members of his staff privately briefed the media that members of MI6, the Secret Service, had taken part in meetings without authority – 'it was a spook freelancing,' a senior NIO source told a group of journalists in a Stormont Castle corridor.

The government's credibility had clearly suffered a heavy blow, and Mayhew's position as a minister seemed in doubt. It was with much apprehension that he went to Westminster the following day to make a special statement in the Commons about the affair. In the event MPs gave him an unexpectedly easy ride, with Labour, the Ulster Unionists and the SDLP all refraining, for various tactical reasons, from staging an all-out attack. Any Conservative MPs who had doubts kept them to themselves, responding to the argument of the Tory whips that Mayhew's resignation would hand a ministerial scalp to terrorists. The only really outspoken critic was the Rev. Ian Paisley, who was escorted from the chamber after accusing Mayhew of issuing 'falsehoods'.

The *Irish Times* described how Mayhew's confidence grew at the despatch box as he realised he would survive the affair: 'Sir Patrick's body language was revealing. Clearly not at ease and keeping his head bowed as he read his statement, he continually played with his pen. Off came the top, then back on again, then into his jacket pocket and then out again. To accompany his denials that the government had deceived or misled the House, he undid his jacket buttons; as his colleagues cheered their approval, he did them up again. As he became confident of his colleagues' support he began to pause between sentences, waiting expectantly for the inevitable "Hear, hear".' A veteran journalist said later: 'I remember sitting in the Commons press gallery looking down on the scene and saying to myself, "Everybody knows the government's lying, but they've decided to let them get away with it because if they don't Mayhew will have to resign and the IRA will have won a huge victory." '

Mayhew announced that he was placing a copy of all correspondence through the back-channel in the Commons library to demonstrate that everything communicated in private had been consistent with the government's publicly stated positions. From his point of view, this proved to be a mistake. Sinn Fein responded to Mayhew with a series of angry press conferences and statements accusing him of wholesale deception and doctoring the record. They said the present series of contacts had begun not in 1993 but in 1990; that Martin McGuinness had never sent the 'conflict is over' message; that the allegedly unauthorised meetings had actually been authorised; that real negotiation had taken place. They accused Mayhew of changing some messages, withholding others and of simply forging more. They issued a sheaf of documents entitled 'Setting the record straight', including copies of what looked like authentic original messages. But at this stage the issue seemed to be fading, with the Commons having in effect given its consent to the operation of the back-channel.

The republican version told a very different story from Mayhew's version, but the widespread assumption was that Sinn Fein was bending the truth for its own propagandist purposes. Those who believed the government was not telling the truth kept silent.

Then out of the blue came a development so embarrassing that it led to Mayhew offering his resignation to Major. Sinn Fein issued a number of documents even before Mayhew placed his in the Commons library, and comparison of the two versions showed that vital parts had been altered by one or other of the parties. Someone was engaged in a major deception exercise, forging, omitting and doctoring documents. Each accused the other of fabrication. The embarrassment for the government arose when the two sets of documents were compared, for the republican versions looked internally consistent while the government material did not. For example, among the material published by both Mayhew and the republicans was a message in which the republicans had stated: 'We need clarification of the phrase "progressive entry into dialogue".' This phrase cropped up earlier in the republican documents, but it appeared nowhere in the government version, which was supposed to be a full record of all the back-channel exchanges.

On Tuesday, 30 November, the NIO was asked to account for the discrepancy. A spokesman said: 'We are checking this out.' The following afternoon, in response to the same query, a spokesman said: 'The only thing we can say at this stage is that the matter is being examined carefully.'

The government response, when it eventually came, was unexpected. Late on Wednesday night at an awkward time for media deadlines, too late for ITN's *News at Ten* or the first editions of the London papers, Mayhew announced that a number of 'errors' had come to light. He detailed twenty-two of these which, he said, had been caused by typographical and transcription errors. One of the amendments he announced was that the phrase 'progressive entry' should be inserted into the text. The other amendments thus meant that Mayhew's document had become identical to the republican version. The change meant this glaring inconsistency had been removed, but the manner in which the correction had to be made was seen as another blow to the government's credibility. Paisley accused the government of doctoring the documents – 'They made the changes so quickly they made very obvious mistakes that have exposed the fabrication,' he alleged.

Mayhew later confirmed that he had offered Major his resignation after the errors in the documents came to light. He said 'It is right that I formally offered my resignation. The Prime Minister felt that while the errors were unfortunate they were not a matter requiring ministerial resignation.' There were other textual inconsistencies in the British record, but because events in the peace process were moving so fast at the time few journalists, politicians or others had the chance to make a careful analysis of the two versions. Further examination casts more doubts on the government version.

A number of points can be cited as evidence in support of the theory that the documents were doctored not by the republicans but by the government. For example, the republicans asserted that at one stage the British offered to hold delegation meetings if the IRA would call a temporary ceasefire. The British maintained no such proposition was put forward. In a message, given in the British version, the republicans stated: 'In the course of that exchange you asserted the belief that a two-week suspension to accommodate talks would result in republicans being persuaded that there is no further need for armed struggle.' The British government continues to insist that no such suggestion was made, but instead of seeking to explain how the republicans could be so mistaken on such a vital point, a government note appended to the published document says simply that the republican understanding 'was incorrect'.

Another passage in a republican document, as given in the British documentation, is difficult to reconcile with the government's arguments. This states: 'We wish now to proceed without delay to the delegation meetings. In order to facilitate this step we sought and received a commitment which will permit you to proceed. . . . It is important that you understand how important a gesture this is.' Firstly, the use of the phrase 'the delegation meetings' clearly implies these had been the subject of discussion, but the phrase does not occur anywhere else in the British documents. Anyone reading the British documents therefore finds the phrase unexplained and puzzling. Secondly, the passage above is much more compatible with the republican contention that a two-week ceasefire was under discussion than with the subsequent British argument that talks could not be contemplated until violence had ended permanently. Republicans would never refer to the ending of the IRA campaign merely as 'a gesture': they would see it as a historical and momentous occasion.

Above all the government insists that the exchanges opened in February 1993 because an oral message arrived from Martin McGuinness which said: 'The conflict is over but we need your advice on how to bring it to a close.' McGuinness's version is that the exchanges in fact began in 1990, and that the initial approach came from the British side.

There are other difficulties with the British text, but now a much more telling piece of evidence has emerged to undermine the government's version of events. The fact is that, in an interview conducted for this book in 1995, after he had left government office, Peter Brooke readily confirmed that he had authorised the opening of contacts in 1990. In doing so he contradicted the official government assertion and confirmed the timetable outlined by Martin McGuinness. Since Brooke left Northern Ireland in April 1992, it is simply impossible to square the government's claim that the back-channel opened in 1993 with his confirmation of the republican assertion that it opened in 1990. As recounted earlier, Brooke confirmed that he had given the go-ahead for the use of the back-channel in 1990, on the advice of John Deverell of MI5. He said: 'We had a substantial debate about it. It was a debate which among other things discussed the identity, the process by which the linkage would occur. I mean – were we making statements which were not strictly true, in terms of responding to the House of Commons? I certainly believed, in the context of the conduit which existed, that we could continue to say that we were not in direct contact. The conduit was a voluntary one. There was somebody in place who had been involved for quite some time, and he had the advantage of retaining the confidence of both sides. It wasn't negotiation. It was not negotiation. I was not sanctioning a whole series of things – it was the opportunity to carry on conversation.'

Brooke could not remember in which month he had given the go-ahead, but was definite that it took place in 1990. Asked whether he had ever come across a message saying that the IRA wanted to surrender and wanted the government to help them, he replied: 'No, I certainly wouldn't say that. There is a mild mystery which if I ever have the time, I would take the time to unravel. I still believe that somewhere in the winter of 1991, perhaps February or March 1991, that Martin McGuinness made the comment somewhere, and I believe him to have made it through a press report, that he uttered a single sentence – "This is a difficult struggle to disengage from." Now the significance of that remark is that nobody would make that remark unless they were actually trying to think through how they did disengage. And therefore I regard it as a significant remark. But nobody's been able to find it.'

In the light of this, it seems reasonable to place more faith in the republican document than in those produced by the British government. The account which follows of the back-channel traffic therefore draws heavily on the republican documents, though it should be noted that these are also to be approached with some degree of caution: the fact that the British version is untruthful does not in itself guarantee the accuracy of the Sinn Fein version.

Although the republican documents contain no obvious and inexplicable inconsistencies, an element of mystery continues to surround Martin McGuinness's alleged 'conflict is over' message. When the British first said such a message had been sent McGuinness declared at a Belfast news conference: 'I don't believe there's a person in Ireland with a titter of wit who would believe that I handed such a document or oral communication to the British government.' Given his reputation for militancy, most people at the time thought it scarcely credible that McGuinness should deliver any such message. With hindsight, that still seems to be the case; yet it is a fact that the republicans did, in August 1994, declare a cessation of violence against the British on a unilateral basis. There is no direct evidence to support the British contention that McGuinness sent the message; in fact the weight of available evidence supports his claim that he did not. At the same time, however, it has to be noted in the light of the 1994 cessation that the violent conflict did at that point come to an end, if only temporarily.

Such a message could have been distorted in transmission; alternatively, it could have been deliberately distorted by the British government. It must be said that the 'conflict is over' message, as alleged by the government, seems as unlikely as ever: but it can hardly be ruled out that a perhaps more ambiguous signal was conveyed, perhaps by someone else.

According to the Sinn Fein version, the back-channel had existed for over twenty years but after the 1981 hunger strikes was not in use until reactivated by the British government in 1990. This was the first of a sustained series of overtures which included sending the republicans advance copies of Brooke's speeches, details of min- isterial discussions, and even confidential reports on the progress of the Brooke and Mayhew talks with the other parties and the Irish government.

Over the three years of contacts there were three distinct phases. In the first, which lasted from 1990 until February 1993, London actively courted the republicans, sending nineteen messages while Sinn Fein sent only one in response. Occasional meetings took place, sometimes in Northern Ireland and sometimes in London. In the second phase, between February and November 1993, the pace quickened with an average of a message a week passing back and forward as the possibility of 'delegate meetings' was explored. The third short phase followed before the back-channel effectively petered out in November 1993.

The back-channel opened with an approach from the British government representative who had been in touch with the republi- cans in earlier periods. He explained he was due for retirement and said he wanted to meet McGuinness to prepare the way for a new representative. This overture opened a line of communication which went from the authorities to 'the government representative' who spoke to a person known as 'the contact', who was in touch with Sinn Fein. The name of the contact has never been made known. In October 1990 McGuinness and the retiring representative held a meeting which lasted three hours. It was also attended by the contact. They had a general political discussion: McGuinness said very little and was non-committal about republican attitudes. In June 1991 the new British representative introduced himself to the contact, producing a letter from Brooke to verify his status. Over the next seven months the new representative initiated a series of meetings and occasional telephone conversations with the contact, giving him detailed briefings on government policy.

In January 1992 messages were passed back and forth on what Sinn Fein called 'the Irish peace initiative' – that is, the Hume–Adams talks. The British also, according to McGuinness, kept Sinn Fein informed of the progress of the Mayhew political talks, passing on, in October 1992, a detailed internal government report and assessment on the discussions. Part of this document, which appears to be genuine, suggested the government was intent on secretly writing a report by Sir Ninian Stephen, the retired Australian diplomat who was acting as independent chairman of the talks. Part of it suggested that Sir Ninian was not as independent as he seemed, saying: 'In preparation for its meeting with Sir Ninian on 21 October the HMG [Her Majesty's government] team is drawing up model Heads of Agreement which it believes stand the widest chance of being accepted by all concerned. These will be submitted for his use on a non–attributable basis, in an attempt to guide his consultations. The idea is to ghost-write Sir Ninian's report.'

This was followed, in December 1992 and January 1993, by meetings between the contact and the British representative, together with a series of phone calls, sometimes on a daily basis. Sinn Fein was pointedly unenthusiastic until the government representative indicated a face-to-face meeting was possible, and began to discuss the logistics of such a meeting. According to the republican account of a meeting between the contact and the representative in February 1993:

> He was very upbeat about the possibility of delegation meetings. He said that he and his colleagues had been working on this for two years. Major and Mayhew had discussed the republican struggle and the Christmas cessation. . . . Events on the ground [i.e. IRA violence] will bring an enormous influence to bear. The IRA needs to provide the space to turn the possibility of meetings into a reality. A suspension is all that is being required of them. The British believed that two or three weeks was a sufficient period to convince republicans [that the IRA campaign was unnecessary]. There would be an intensive round

of talks. Once started, people remain until decisions were arrived at. Reciprocation would be immediate; troops withdrawn to barracks, checkpoints removed, security levels determined by loyalist threat. Their side would probably be led, in such an event, by Quentin Thomas. The republican side could include whoever they wanted. Possibly plus three advisors.

The government offered to provide an aircraft to fly a republican delegation to Scotland, Sweden, Norway, Denmark or the Isle of Man. The republicans were eager for such meetings and told the government: 'We were pleased to receive this message and welcome the possibility of a meeting. We would like two representatives, Martin McGuinness and Gerry Kelly, to have an exploratory meeting with you as soon as possible.'

On 19 March 1993 the government despatched an important document to the republicans, setting out the broad British approach. It said that any dialogue could only follow a halt to violent activity, which it conceded could be an unannounced halt. If that happened, then progressive entry into dialogue could take place. The government laid out its position that 'in the event of a genuine and established ending of violence, the whole range of responses to it would inevitably be looked at afresh'. It said it had no blueprint for the outcome of all-party talks, and accepted the outcome could eventually be a united Ireland, though based only on consent.

But only four days after this, according to the republican record, a face-to-face meeting took place between the British representative, Martin McGuinness and Gerry Kelly. The message conveyed by the representative at this meeting, according to the republican note, was much more encouraging to the republicans:

Mayhew is now determined. He wants Sinn Fein to play a part not because he likes Sinn Fein but because it cannot work without them. Any settlement not involving all of the people North and South won't work. . . . The final solution is union [i.e. a united Ireland]. The historical train – Europe – determines that. We are committed to Europe. Unionists will have to change. This island will be as one. The two weeks [suspension] for talks proposed was repeated. He alleged that John Chilcot had instructed him to inform Sinn Fein that if this was agreed at six o'clock that clearance for meetings at the level of delegations would be forthcoming by one minute past six. Confidentiality was of the utmost importance. Only Major, Mayhew, Hurd and secretary to the cabinet [Butler] knew of all this.

A flurry of messages followed, but by early May Sinn Fein was asking: 'Some time has passed since we both agreed to proceed to delegation meetings. Are you still serious about this? Are there problems?' In reply, the British maintained that the continuing acts of IRA violence posed problems: 'We cannot conceivably disregard them. We gave advice in good faith taking what we were told at face value. It is difficult to reconcile that with recent events.'

On 10 May Sinn Fein sent to the British an important document setting out their position, together with a message confirming that the IRA had agreed to a two-week suspension. The republicans were by this stage taking the exercise extremely seriously, having established a small committee, chaired by Gerry Adams, to oversee the enterprise. The document declared: 'Dialogue and negotiations are necessary and inevitable if this conflict is to be resolved on a democratic basis. Pre-conditions represent obstacles to peace.' The road to peace, they insisted, lay through national self-determination by the Irish people. British sovereignty over the north was the cause of instability and conflict: republicans sought the end of British jurisdiction. Unionist concerns had to be addressed but Britain should persuade the Unionist community to reach accommodation with the rest of the Irish people.

The republicans were intensely interested in the idea of delegate meetings, agreeing to a two-week IRA suspension and pressing the British eagerly on logistical details: 'We need to agree agendas and formats for meetings etc. We have appointed a small secretariat to assist in this task. We would like you to nominate someone to liaise with M.McG [Martin McGuinness] on this. We also have a number of questions. They are to do with the mechanics of the sequence outlined by you. They are: Who will represent you? We need to know when the British government will be politically represented in this process and by whom? We need clarification of the phrase "progressive entry into dialogue". When will this start? Where is the proposed venue? It would be more practical and quicker if these details could be agreed directly with M.McG. If this is not possible we ask that you proceed through usual channel as soon as possible.'

In the event, however, the go-ahead never came from London. Instead, later in May the British government representative was in touch to say he had returned from a walking holiday to find that ministers had changed their minds. He was 'absolutely disgusted' with this, he said. According to the republican documents the representative gave the contact the following account of what had happened:

> The initiative of 10th/11th May had been very well-received by Chilcot and plans were immediately put in place to get approval from John Major. Mayhew had reservations, pointing out that he couldn't risk any announcements in the run-up to the local government elections. He stated that he was worried about an upsurge in support for the DUP [Paisley's party] at the expense of the Ulster Unionist party [Molyneaux's party]. It was pointed out to him that in reality it was unlikely that there would be enough time anyway for any formal discussions.
>
> The timetable agenda was agreed by Chilcot and Mayhew. That is, cessation followed with 1–7 days by logistics, followed by delegates meeting. It was the intention to put this to Major on Monday 17th May. Present at the meeting were Major, Hurd, Mayhew, Chilcot, Braithwaite★ and two other names which appeared to be secretaries or similar.
>
> The meeting was rushed and indecisive with Major asking questions on which he should have been more fully briefed, eg 1. What guarantees we have that this cessation can he held or will hold? 2. We need more evidence that what they say, they mean. Douglas Hurd had to leave for a meeting of Foreign

---

★British government sources, while not confirming the accuracy of this account, have confirmed that Sir Roddy Braithwaite was one of the small circle concerned with management of the back-channel. Sir Roddy, one of Britain's most senior intelligence figures, was then chairman of the Joint Intelligence Committee.

Secretaries on the Bosnian peace plan. On the whole the meeting was most unsatisfactory from an Irish point of view.

John Major adjourned the meeting to the following day and called in Kenneth Clarke [then Home Secretary] who was in buoyant, bombastic mood and advised John Major that the proposition was much too risky at the present time with the government under siege. If the republicans were sincere about their intentions then the Prime Minister should hasten slowly to adopt such a radical departure from their previous publicly successful anti-terrorist line.

Mayhew was wobbling between pushing for acceptance and wanting a safer longer period of cessation. John Major compromised by instructing his secretaries to draw up a programme which he would be able to announce in Parliament having previously, ie 24 hours before, informed church leaders and the heads of the main political parties that he was instructing the NIO to enter into dialogue with the republican movement. Major's plan involved a longer cessation, followed by private logistics [the two British government representatives] followed by his agreed statement at Westminster followed by dialogue.

The contact spent approximately one and a half hours in London listening to the British government representative, whose last remark was that he would like it known that everything that he had said to Sinn Fein representatives was the truth exactly as he had been instructed by Chilcot with specific reference to his famous one minute past six o'clock offer.

The British representative passed on a personal message in which he said: 'There is depression and anger here at our failure to respond to your brave and straightforward offer. None feel it more than I do for obvious reasons. . . . You have my word that all that was conveyed was done so honestly and accurately at the time. . . . I can only ask for patience for all our sakes.'

This account of the inner workings of a Cabinet committee may represent an extraordinary indiscretion on the part of the British representative, or the account may have simply been deliberately fabricated to mislead Sinn Fein. Either way, the message to the republicans was the same: that if the government was ever genuine about the delegate conference, it was no longer on offer. From this point on, according to the republicans, they received no positive or constructive communications from London.

The account of Cabinet proceedings, though superficially plausible, may have been a fabrication. It fits with the thesis that the Cabinet committee meetings did not take place as described, but were simply invented to remove the offer of delegation meetings, and instead dangle before the republicans the proposition of a longer ceasefire as put forward by Major. By September Sinn Fein was clearly disappointed and suspicious that the government was acting in bad faith. On 10 September it said in a message: 'The positive response by the leadership of the IRA underlined the willingness on the republican side to facilitate movement towards a real peace process. The rejection of this substantial gesture by you has not only prevented further movement but has damaged the project and increased the difficulties involved. This, and your present attempts to deny this aspect of the contact between us, can only be regarded with the utmost scepticism and must raise serious questions about your motives in all of this.'

The end of the back-channel came early in November when the republicans were surprised to receive a lengthy British document responding to a Sinn Fein message of 2 November. The surprise came because the republicans had sent no such message. The British document stuck firmly to the government's public position: a copy of the communiqué from the Major–Reynolds summit in Brussels was appended to it, together with the formally-delivered assertion: 'There can be no departure from what is said there and in particular its statement that there could be no secret agreements or understandings between Governments and organisations supporting violence as a price for its cessation. . . . It is the public and consistent position of the British Government that any dialogue could only follow a permanent end to violent activity.'

This formal missive effectively brought the back-channel traffic to a halt, leaving the republicans to wonder why the British had spent three years communicating with them, only to cut the link so suddenly. The favoured explanation on the republican side was that the key British change of heart had come around May, just as

John Major was hopeful of securing Ulster Unionist support in the key Commons votes on Europe. One interesting point, especially for those who believed the IRA was in the process of bombing its way to the conference table, was that the coolness on the British side appeared in the month after the Bishopsgate bomb in the City of London, an attack which caused widespread disruption and had tremendous political and financial impact. The timetable clearly shows, however, that the government, far from being galvanised by the bombing, effectively closed down any serious dialogue with the republicans shortly afterwards.

In the years of its existence the back-channel survived many acts of violence: on many occasions, in fact, the government used it to complain about IRA attacks. It began to function in Mrs Thatcher's time under Brooke, and was kept open by Major and Mayhew. It was not broken by the mortar attack on Downing Street, by the Teebane crossroads killings nor by the many other killings and bombings in Northern Ireland, Britain and mainland Europe. It was not broken by the deaths of the two children in the Warrington bombing; nor when, in a series of incidents, the SAS killed IRA volunteers.

So what then was its purpose? Given the lack of candour on the part of the authorities, any analysis of the government's motivation must necessarily be speculative. In opening the channel in 1990 Brooke and Deverell appear to have been motivated by a spirit of exploration. Brooke described it as 'essentially an intelligence process' and spoke of wishing to know what was happening on the other side of the hill. He and Deverell had noted the reports that a debate of some sort was going on within the republican movement, and wanted to find out more about it. It was not until 1993 that the back-channel was used by the British to put forward an actual proposition, the idea of a secret conference at which they would attempt to convince the republicans that their violent campaign was unnecessary. It was during this period that the channel really came to life.

There is no real indication, either within the back-channel messages or elsewhere throughout this period, that the British at

any point contemplated meeting the traditional demand for a declaration of intent to withdraw from Ireland. Given this, the central
question on the British mind must have been whether the IRA
would contemplate stopping without securing such a declaration.

Looking back, the idea of the delegate meetings may have been
a Machiavellian British scheme to test the readiness of republicans
to talk about ideas short of a British declaration of intent to withdraw. The account of ministerial discussions conveyed by the allegedly upset British representative was ostensibly part apology and
part explanation of why the delegate conference idea was no longer
on offer. But it also set out Major's idea for a longer cessation than
two weeks, a proposal which the republicans did not pursue. The
British may also have been concerned to test whether the approach
of impending talks would lead to a reduction of IRA attacks: if so
they were disappointed, for violence remained at a high level.

In the end, after dozens of messages and exchanges of documents
and a number of face-to-face meetings, the two sides never got
together for serious talks. Both laid out their positions in formal
documents, but much of the back-channel concerned the arrangements for talks, and no substantive negotiations took place.

The real negotiations throughout this period actually involved
Adams, Hume and Dublin, resulting in draft declarations which
were later forwarded to London. But quite a few of the messages
through the back-channels concerned Hume–Adams, and at one
stage the British appear to have passed back to the republicans,
presumably for verification, a document which had been conveyed
to them by Dublin. The exercise ended in November 1993, leaving
the republicans aggrieved by the whole three-year exercise. They
concluded that the British were not serious about staging talks with
them in advance of an end of violence, and were probably intent
on causing a split rather than opening serious negotiations.

If the republicans felt sore, so did many people who worked for
the authorities. The RUC, for example, only became aware of the
contacts a short time before the *Observer* broke the story. Within
the government itself, many were displeased and even shocked.
According to one source close to the NIO: 'When it all eventually

broke there was a great sense of almost anger, outside the very tight circle who know about it, that people who were dealing with the media or with their contacts had for such a long time been misled. Afterwards there was a tremendous internal debate about it – there were people who felt they had been made to look foolish or dishonest, because they'd been given certain assurances which weren't true.' After the disclosures, many were left angry at the thought that John Major, who had proclaimed to the Commons that the thought of talking to Gerry Adams would turn his stomach, had actually been maintaining indirect contact with him for years. And Albert Reynolds, who had been lectured so sternly by Major that association with Hume–Adams was the 'kiss of death', started taking a more cynical view of Britain's sensibilities.

13

THE DOWNING
STREET
DECLARATION

'December 3rd was the sort of meeting that
Paddy Mayhew calls a "shit or bust" day'
 – senior British source

'The British government agree that it is for
the people of the island of Ireland alone, by
agreement between the two parts respectively,
to exercise their right of self-determination on
the basis of consent, freely and concurrently
given, North and South, to bring about a united
Ireland, if that is their wish'
 – the   Downing   Street   Declaration,
December 1993

Albert Reynolds considered that he had properly informed Major
of his own contacts with the republicans, and felt Major should
have reciprocated. The day after the *Observer* story on the back-
channel appeared, Reynolds and Major had a forty-minute telephone conversation. The Taoiseach berated the Prime Minister on
two counts. He criticised him for his secret contacts with the
republicans, making clear he regarded these as double-dealing.

He also criticised Major for sending Butler over to Dublin with
a new document two days before the back-channel story broke and
only a week before 3 December, the date pencilled in for a prime
ministerial summit in Dublin. Reynolds told Major he would not
negotiate on the basis of the new document. Major explained he
was still concerned about the Hume–Adams fingerprints which

he felt were on Reynolds's document. His view was that the document would be rejected by Unionists and that, if published, could even cause a rise in loyalist violence. Reynolds replied that the amendments made after his discussions with Archbishop Eames and the Rev. Roy Magee had made it more acceptable to Unionists than Major believed. Major complained of Emily O'Reilly's leak of an internal Irish government document; Reynolds countered by pointing to the leak of the British back-channel. After the call Reynolds drafted a personal letter to Major reiterating his displeasure about the new document and pointedly referring to the revelation of the back-channel. The text of this letter is as follows:

> Thank you for your letter and for sending Robin Butler across to explain your position. The thrust of the draft document which you sent to me is completely altered from the one your and my officials worked over for some months which has the balance capable of achieving peace. I do not see any prospect of the new proposal working.
>
> At this stage we should not be trying to start again from scratch bringing to nowt 18 months of patient work. We will let you have our formal response after tomorrow's Cabinet meeting. As you know, the very first document sent to you in June was a proposal of the Irish Government and in the course of discussion our officials improved and refined it to take on board the many legitimate points made by your side. We have further incorporated a lot of material given to me by Archbishop Eames which would make the document more acceptable from the Protestant and Unionist side.
>
> We feel we have now gone as far as it is possible to go. As you know my objective is peace, not a propaganda exercise directed at the paramilitaries. I do not accept as credible the reason for not proceeding with the joint declaration as originally envisaged. With regard to fear of some indirect taint from Hume–Adams the weekend's revelations surely speak for themselves.
>
> As for the damage caused by the leak of the Irish paper [to Emily O'Reilly], again you now have experience of revelations emanating in the first instance, I understand, from the Reverend William McCrea who obviously had it from official contacts.
>
> I have spoken to a close confidant, who is in close contact

with the loyalist paramilitaries, who assures me that the language of loyalist backlash does not represent their views and their position. This person now knows of the contents of the document and in his judgement it would not lead to the feared backlash when it is explained in full.

In all the circumstances I still strongly believe that the only course of action is to rise above a multiplicity of attempts from various quarters to stop the initiative in its tracks. And we should not allow ourselves to be blown off course. The public at large in these islands and around the world will applaud our efforts. The prize is big enough to overcome present difficulties.

Hume, unaware of the new documents brought by Butler, was meanwhile separately pressing Major to act on the declaration. In a private letter to the Prime Minister, dated 29 November, Hume summarised the Hume–Adams document and wrote:

In the light of recent events I am writing to express my concern lest a major opportunity for lasting peace in Ireland will be lost. As I have made publicly clear I think it would be a serious and irresponsible error for any party to play party or personality politics with recent revelations or to seek party advantage. As you are aware, at our meetings in Downing Street I made clear that I was certain that the proposed joint declaration presented to you in June by Mr Reynolds would lead to a total cessation of its campaign by the IRA. Given my experience of the past 25 years, I do not make such statements lightly. I am available at the shortest notice if necessary to meet you if you require any clarification of the above.

A tense episode of brinkmanship followed. London was anxious for a summit on 3 December, but wanted the new British document to be on the table. The Irish said they would agree to the 3 December date only if the British document was withdrawn. After much argument the summit was given the go-ahead. Dublin believed there was a mutual understanding the new British document would not be discussed, though London appears to have had a different impression. This led to difficulties in the initial stages of the summit which was attended by Major, Mayhew and Hurd in Dublin Castle, formerly the seat of British power in Ireland. It was a vital summit: it was also a tense and bad-tempered summit. An Irish source recalled how it opened, in a drawing-room traditionally known as the King's bedroom:

> We sat across the table in the King's bedroom. It was a very nasty meeting, with a lot of angry toing and froing. We had a long session first, when they tried to discuss their document and we refused: the Taoiseach and Tanaiste did all the talking and played a kind of double act. Then there was a suggestion, I think perhaps from Major, that he and Albert should have a tête-à-tête, and they went off together. They were withdrawn for an hour or more, and they both came out looking very pale and very tense. I always remember us approaching the Taoiseach as they came out of the room. When he was asked how it went, he kind of half-grinned and he said: 'It went all right – I chewed his bollocks off and he took a few lumps outa me.'

According to a senior British source:

> December 3rd was the sort of meeting that Paddy Mayhew calls a 'shit or bust' day. Before the summit there had been briefings, which we thought were coming from Dublin, which had stoked up expectations. There were crunch points we had not agreed upon, and there was a lot of loose talking in the press, which created a certain amount of strain. We felt it was better not to negotiate through the media – Major had to spell it out to Reynolds that we were not going to succeed by negotiation through the media. In the build-up tension had risen. There was a lot of anguish about the back-channel: they wanted to get that off their chests and on our side there had been a lot of steam about leaks etc. The two Prime Ministers going off into a meeting alone was not the normal method of working, but they felt the need to speak with such extreme frankness that not even their closest advisors should be in the room when they did it. They got an awful lot off their chests.

Reynolds later recalled:

> One couldn't feel otherwise than betrayed, because here we were talking behind the scenes with the British government for quite some time and we were also talking behind the scenes with the republican movement as well, so with a revelation like this

naturally one would feel betrayed. If you're going along in good faith you expect all the cards on the table and you expect to know what's going on on both sides, when somebody was making a genuine effort to try and get a declaration that everybody could subscribe to. I felt that I was let down, that I should have been told. There was a straight head-to-head – straight talking between us. I made a case very strongly about these talks.

Others in Dublin also made their objections clear. While Reynolds and Major were closeted together the Irish government chief whip, Noel Dempsey, was giving interviews in which he spoke bitterly of the British 'dealing from the bottom of the deck'. The Irish Justice Minister, Mrs Geoghegan-Quinn, buttonholed Mayhew in Dublin Castle and made her feelings known. She said later: 'I think the most upsetting part of it was that time after time after time, at many Anglo-Irish conferences, they themselves initiated discussions about how much they hated the Provos and how they wouldn't be seen in the same place as them and all the rest of it. They talked like that on a regular basis and yet at the same time here they were talking to them behind our backs. They would have been better off not saying anything at all about it.'

Another Dublin source made a similar point: 'The real anger, the real frustration, arose from the sanctimonious way that they would condemn any contact with republicans, and the total hypocrisy of some of the things that they had been saying. The memories of those things came flooding back when you heard that they had been totally caught with their pants down.'

According to Reynolds, he and Major discussed the back-channel 'and then we parked that issue and got on to the next one, the question of the declaration'. He recalled later: 'The main business of the day was to try to bring forward the declaration and here we are faced with another major problem, the presentation by the British of another paper for consideration. I thought that wasn't the way to do business – if they had felt like that about it they should have tabled the paper much earlier. So it was either we go ahead with what we had, and try and finish it, or call it off. There was no point in going forward with a document that we knew wasn't going to work.'

He recalled going back into the main conference room with Major: 'You could cut the ice-cold atmosphere at that stage. It was knife-edge stuff, but it had to be done. There was no point me going forward with something that had no chance of success. John Major threw his hands up in the air a few times in desperation, threw his pen down on the desk at times. It was a tough head-to-head meeting, no question about it. There were times when it looked odds-on to collapse. It was a question of: "Are we going to do something that has a chance of success or are we going to just suspend all our actions?" That's basically where it came down to in the end.'

Mrs Geoghegan-Quinn recalls: 'There was a feeling that the Brits were trying to slide out and go a different road, and we weren't prepared to go down that road with them. The Taoiseach was absolutely clear in his mind, as were Mansergh and O hUiginn, that what he was saying was correct and proper. What the Brits were trying to do was the thing the Brits always do – they make an agreement with you and then on the twenty-third hour, they decide that they're going to change it in some way.'

The atmosphere in the conference room remained cool, with tetchy exchanges between Major and Reynolds. At one stage, after Reynolds had been speaking for some time, Major interrupted and said: 'Albert, this problem cannot be solved by homespun philosophy.' Mrs Geoghegan-Quinn recalled:

Major had a pencil in his hand and he interrupted and he said: 'No, Albert, that's not going to go.' And Albert said: 'Look, I'm telling you, this is the way it's going to be and you'll have to trust me and everything I've told you so far has turned out to be true.' Major came back at him and said no, it was going a bit too far as far as they were concerned, and they didn't accept that what Albert was putting forward would be bought by the loyalists. And Albert took his glasses off, put them down on the table, put down the pen that he had in his hand and said, across the table: 'Look, John, it's as simple as this: either you buy this and you buy into this or there is no deal and we are wasting our time here, and I've too many things on my agenda to be wasting time here to try and get this changed.'

Albert also said: 'I know that you are under pressure on either side of you. I know that there are people on either side of you telling you that what Albert Reynolds is saying is wrong. But I'm telling you that we've known each other for far too long to lead each other up the garden path and I'm telling you, this is it.'

And Major literally broke the pencil in two and says: 'Ah, this is a waste of time,' and Albert says: 'Well, fine John, you go ahead, off you go home. We'll go out and tell the journalists that there's no point in talking any more because the Brits won't do business.' Reynolds doesn't raise his voice but the man opposite did, and in raising his voice actually broke the pencil and threw it down on the table in a temper. Everybody was really just on tenterhooks.

Another source said of the meeting:

The Prime Ministers, I wouldn't say they were shouting at each other, but they were more than usually involved in points of detail which shouldn't have bothered them at all. There was no bad language, it never came to that, but it was obviously a meeting where what was being talked about shouldn't have been talked about at all in that sort of a gathering. The two Prime Ministers just seemed to feel that they had to display their muscles before their own audiences and that was just totally wrong and bad and unproductive.

They had come upon so many points of disagreement and so many points that they wanted to argue about. If you have a small meeting where the two people can talk one-to-one, or with one or two in support, then you can isolate the points where there is disagreement and you can reach agreement. But when you have a large meeting the points of disagreement seem to multiply and everybody feels that they have to intervene, and then the points of disagreement become real breaking points because of matters of pride – matters of national pride and personal pride, and people thinking, 'I'm right in what I say about this and I can't let myself down before the people sitting beside me' – that sort of consideration. The whole mood was bad. It certainly was the least productive of prime ministerial meetings.

Mrs Geoghegan-Quinn said that at one critical moment during the meeting Chilcot, apparently recognising that things were getting out of hand, wrote a note and passed it discreetly to Major. There was then a break, the two sides going off to separate rooms. She recalled:

> At the stage when we left the meeting we thought that was it – they're going to go home, they're just not prepared to allow him to do what he wants to do. Reynolds always believed that Major always wanted to do it, that he wanted to do the big thing, the big deal, that he wanted to be the Prime Minister that cracked this finally, but that he was not being let do it. Albert came out and said to us – he's so matter-of-fact and cool and calm about things – 'Oh well, that's it. It's up to him now what he decides.' We came back and resumed the meeting and it was agreed that the officials could go away and work on the basis of what we had put forward, and they would have this ready by December 15th, and that in between faxes would go back and forward.

The break in proceedings appears to have been the turning-point after which the atmosphere lightened considerably. According to a British source: 'The meeting broke because there was some point about whether they could live with something. That was a long break. At that point we were working out what we were going to say to the press: at the end the message was that we had a basis for continuing. When we resumed the meeting didn't produce an instant breakthrough but it was getting more constructive all the time because you were getting the angst out.'

Despite all the bad temper and rancour and difficulties, it was a key meeting with crucial results. Reynolds and Major retained their working relationship and, against all the odds, work on the declaration moved on. Officials worked through the details of the text while Major and Reynolds held another meeting in the margins of an EC summit on 10 December, and again on the following day.

The basic structure of what was to become the Downing Street Declaration had been settled: it was, after all the months and years of hopes and disappointments, optimism and set-backs, all finally coming together. There was to be a joint declaration which

Reynolds and Major would present together in Downing Street on 15 December, though almost until the last moment the two sides haggled and argued over the details. Every sentence, every word, every piece of punctuation of what was to become the Downing Street Declaration was scrutinised in the most minute detail, and was often contested between London and Dublin. Mansergh, O hUiginn, Finlay, Nally and Noel Dorr, the quiet but cerebral diplomat who headed the Department of Foreign Affairs, spent hours on end closeted in Mansergh's room. A Dublin source described the office as being 'festooned with pieces of paper, with drafts and re-drafts, commas and semi-colons and so on'.

In these final stages Dublin kept in contact with Unionist and loyalist opinion, taking the temperature in the Protestant community. By early December, as the Declaration was being finalised, Archbishop Eames and the Rev. Roy Magee were in almost daily contact with Reynolds's office. There were worries on all sides about the loyalist paramilitary groups, for though some leading figures in that underworld were clearly interested in a political path, others seemed as committed as ever to straight militarism. November had brought a lull in killings after Shankill, Greysteel and the other horrors of October, but the killings began again in December. In the two weeks before the declaration the UDA killed four Catholics and a Protestant in Belfast, while the IRA killed a soldier in County Armagh and two police officers in Tyrone.

Some high-level security figures, while not opposed to the declaration work, were apprehensive that the political moves could trigger another peak of violence. On 9 December a senior security source privately expressed some of his worries about the situation, saying the level of threat remained high from both the IRA and the loyalists. He believed the IRA was interested in reaching a settlement but added: 'The worry about that is that it could be too far for the loyalists. The scenario is that if they produce something that will take PIRA along, it may stir the loyalists up even more. But then if it doesn't take PIRA along, PIRA will go back to their full range of activities, and that will inspire the loyalists to even greater efforts. In other words, the outlook could be a bit bleak.'

The other worry, he said, was that Adams might bring most of the IRA along with him, but that hard-liners in places such as south Armagh might split off and form breakaway groups.

The final draft of the Downing Street Declaration was finally agreed in the early evening of 14 December. Shortly after 7 o'clock that night a senior British source said privately: 'The deal is done. The Irish are confident that it stands a chance of doing the trick with the IRA, that's the word we've got. It's not greatly different from last week's text, to be honest – there's a lot of disinformation flying around all over the place, lot of false briefing and people telling porkies [lies].'

Officials on both sides of the Irish Sea worked into the early hours to finalise the arrangements for the following day. In London Lyne and other officials laboured through the night to prepare for the press conference and draw up Major's statement and his script for a television broadcast.

On the morning of 15 December the Irish party flew to London, headed by Reynolds and including Spring, Mrs Geoghegan-Quinn and their officials. On the way over Irish ministers spoke among themselves of the Treaty negotiations which led to the birth of the southern Irish state after the First World War. A disagreement then between the delegation and Eamon de Valera, who had remained in Dublin, had led to a civil war in which one of the state's legendary founding fathers, Michael Collins, was killed. This time, although there were different views in the Cabinet, there would be no split. Mrs Geoghegan-Quinn recalled: 'We talked about the last time that emissaries were sent by De Valera and what happened to them subsequently. Dick Spring said: "At least this time we have the man with us so if it goes wrong we all go down." ' Reynolds later recalled: 'There was a great sense of history attached to it. We had finally come to agree upon a declaration that was going much further than the British Prime Minister or British government had ever gone before, and indeed than an Irish Prime Minister on behalf of an Irish government had ever gone before. This was the ultimate achievement of a lot of work behind the scenes, bringing a lot of people together, getting a lot of input and striking the right balance and finally getting acceptance by the two Governments, and hopefully to get a fair amount of acceptance throughout the communities and indeed from the paramilitaries as well.'

The atmosphere was optimistic but there was also an element of apprehension that even at the last moment something might go wrong. Some in the Irish party feared that they might be confronted with the familiar British tactic of attempting a last-minute re-negotiation. Reynolds said several times: 'Well, that's it, I've told him the bottom line. If they're not prepared to accept it I'm not signing it.' But nothing of the kind occurred. John Major met them at the door of 10 Downing Street, shook hands with each as they entered, and had them shown into the Cabinet Room.

Although the text had been agreed by this stage, there had been so many versions and so many alterations in the last-minute flurry – one draft was marked draft 15b – that the British and Irish officials double-checked their copies together. An Irish source explained: 'There had been so much drafting and re-drafting and dotting "i"s and crossing "t"s that we compared our clean copy with their clean copy, going through them word by word to make sure they were identical in every way. There was no problem.' Mrs Geoghegan-Quinn later described the scene in the Cabinet Room:

> On one side of the table you had Douglas Hurd and Patrick Mayhew with Major in the middle, and directly opposite them Reynolds, Dick Spring and myself. Then you had officials sitting on either side, as they would at a normal Anglo-Irish conference. It was great fun because Major came in and he said: 'I want to tell you Maire, you're Chancellor of the Exchequer for today', because I sat where the Chancellor would sit at a British Cabinet meeting. There was a lot of banter before we sat down and then a kind of an opening statement from Major as the host and a response from Reynolds. And then there was a drink of champagne, though I had orange juice and so did Albert [Reynolds is teetotal], and they went outside for the press conference. Then we went back in again and they finished their champagne.

Sean Duignan, Reynolds's press officer, felt Major was somewhat tense and nervous, and that the occasion had no atmosphere of celebration. He later wrote: 'I remarked to Martin Mansergh that the occasion had all the strained bonhomie of a shotgun wedding reception, but Mansergh said it was just their natural British reserve.' Duignan spotted one particularly reserved figure in the gathering – Mayhew, who held continuing doubts about the whole Declaration process. Duignan wrote: 'Sir Patrick made no attempt to conceal his lack of enthusiasm. He remained separate from the milling politicians and officials, gloomily staring out of windows for much of the time.' Mayhew's preference was for pursuing a talks process rather than the peace process. Only a few weeks earlier he had declared: 'While the talks retain so much potential, the priority must be to carry them forward, not cut across or duplicate them.' But he had failed to convince others that inter-party talks held such promise, and in the end had been overruled by Major. His lack of belief in the peace process was evident throughout this period.

When photocopies of the Declaration arrived in the Cabinet Room Fergus Finlay wanted a souvenir of the occasion. He recalled: 'When the copies had just rolled off the photocopier they were brought in. I grabbed the first copy and asked John Major and Albert to sign it. Maire Geoghegan-Quinn thought that was a great idea so she asked them too, and it ended up with everybody signing each other's copies for about twenty minutes. I went back to John Major and told him he had devalued the signature he gave me because now everyone had a signed copy. So he took my copy back and he wrote on it, "the first copy" and signed it again.'

Afterwards the Irish flew back to Dublin where Reynolds, Spring and Geoghegan-Quinn received a warm and prolonged standing ovation as they entered the Dáil. Reynolds recalled: 'I couldn't believe it. Politics is politics, but this certainly had lifted everybody above politics, and quite clearly everybody felt it was a tremendous breakthrough. Everywhere you went in the streets people were shaking your hand and saying "Well done, we hope it will bring results." '

Everyone waited anxiously for the reactions of the republicans, and the Unionists, to the document. The Declaration, when it made its public appearance, took some time to be absorbed, since it was much longer and more complex than the versions previously described. It contained nothing that could be interpreted as a British declaration of intent to leave. Rather, it had as its heart a serpentine sentence which intertwined the concepts of self-determination and consent. It read: 'The British government agree that it is for the people of the island of Ireland alone, by agreement between the two parts respectively, to exercise their right of self-determination on the basis of consent, freely and concurrently given, North and South, to bring about a united Ireland, if that is their wish.' It was in effect an ambitious attempt to construct a finely balanced double helix in which self-determination and consent were inseparable.

The Declaration contained many of the elements of the earlier drafts, incorporating much of their language. But it also had a long new section aimed again at assuring Unionists of their rights, and the commitment of both London and Dublin to the principle of consent. Some of this text had been provided by Dr Eames and Rev. Magee, including the six points which loyalist paramilitaries had put forward as concessions, but which Reynolds had miscon-strued as demands. Many of the elements republicans had pushed for were not there, but the two governments did formally confirm that democratically mandated parties which established a commit-ment to exclusively peaceful methods would be free to participate in the political processes.

For the IRA and Sinn Fein the Downing Street Declaration was a moment of truth, representing as it did the considered view of the British and Irish governments, hammered out over so many months. The fact that London and Dublin could agree on some-thing so substantial, within weeks of the horrors and despair of October, was in itself an achievement for politics and negotiation and a reaffirmation of the strength of the Anglo-Irish relationship. The Declaration was widely welcomed in Britain, the Republic and internationally; the Unionist community, after a period of uncertainty, decided not to take great exception to it.

Right through the peace process many in the Unionist com-munity were in two minds, and most of their political representatives attacked it strongly at many points. For one thing, the process served to focus attention on Hume, Adams and the Irish government, all of whom Unionists saw as their opponents. For another, some – though by no means all – of the leading Unionist politicians were by instinct confrontational, regarding politics as a field of conflict: over the years they had become almost comfortable with the violence, and seemed nervous about how they would cope with a peaceful Northern Ireland. Some loyalist politicians, and paramilitary groups, feared a powerful pan-nationalist front was in the making, and would eventually be deployed against them.

Unionist representatives suspiciously scrutinised the Declaration for signs of a sell-out. At Castlereagh council in east Belfast, normal business was abandoned and Unionist councillors spent almost three hours expressing opposition. There was talk of forcing – 'and I do mean forcing' – John Major to change his mind. The mayor declared: 'I'm getting fed up to the teeth with pussy-footing Unionists in Westminster.' A councillor ranted about 'mickey fenian pig-dogs'. Elsewhere, more moderate Unionists were in two minds. A Presbyterian clergyman said: 'Well the union is still there all right, but it's shrouded in shamrocks now, isn't it?' A Unionist MP, asked whether the union was weakened, replied: 'In essence yes, in practice no.'

For the Protestant community at large, the fact that IRA violence continued and even at times increased did nothing to ease community relations, and meant most Protestants and Unionists did not believe the IRA was heading for a cessation. A general Protestant consensus emerged, however, that the Declaration was not a particularly dangerous document.

The spotlight was therefore on the republicans. The two governments had declared, formally and publicly, that Sinn Fein could enter the political processes if the IRA gave up violence. Dublin had gone further, with its offer to establish the Forum for Peace and Reconciliation. The pressure on the IRA to respond positively was enormous. Unknown to the general public the republicans had been involved, over a period of years, in the process of formulating a statement which could end IRA violence. But the Downing

Street Declaration was not at all what the republicans had aimed at and hoped for when that process began. Much of the document was concerned with reassuring Unionist opinion, and in what it said on consent Reynolds had gone further than any previous Taoiseach in enshrining the right of a northern majority to say no to Irish unity. There was no trace of any British intention to withdraw; on the contrary, Dublin had joined in setting out a formal guarantee that unity could only come about by consent. The republicans, in their first draft, had wanted Britain to make a unilateral move committing itself to Irish unity and British withdrawal within an agreed period. That document suggested that the consent of Unionists was to be sought for such an arrangement, but did not make this a prerequisite. Here consent had been elevated to a point of the highest principle.

As often happened in the wake of agreed Anglo-Irish statements, the British embroidered the Declaration with a series of comments designed to reassure Unionist opinion. Major, for example, itemised for the Commons a list of things which had been suggested at various times for inclusion in the Declaration. He told MPs: 'What is not in the Declaration is: any suggestion that the British government should join the ranks of the persuaders of the value or legitimacy of a united Ireland; that is not there. Nor is there any suggestion that the future status of Northern Ireland should be decided by a single act of self-determination by the people of Ireland as a whole; that is not there either. Nor is there any timetable for constitutional change, or any arrangements for joint authority over Northern Ireland. In sum, the Declaration provides that it is and must be for the people of Northern Ireland to determine their own future.'

The British government has always maintained that ministers had never seen Hume–Adams and did not know its contents. As we have seen, however, Major, Mayhew and Chilcot were briefed at various stages about the Declaration work; and certainly Major's Commons statement displayed a detailed knowledge of many of the points which republicans had sought to have included in the

Declaration. London's official position was outlined by a high-level source:

> It's impossible to give a view [on the relationship between Hume–Adams and the Downing Street Declaration] because nothing was ever presented to the Prime Minister on what was the Hume–Adams text. The PM has never seen a Hume–Adams document. To what extent Albert Reynolds was reflecting Hume–Adams in what he presented, Albert Reynolds can tell you. As far as the British government was concerned, it didn't really matter where the Irish government got its ideas from. We took out that which we could not accept and put into it what we could accept. Albert Reynolds put forward a set of ideas which, over the course of several months, were negotiated and changed quite a lot. What you ended up with was a document, bits of which can be traced back to different people. A lot of people have claimed parentage of the document, but it came about through a genuine process of two sides putting in their own ideas and eventually hammering out a deal.

The British government continues to be anxious to present the Downing Street Declaration as something clear of any 'fingerprints' left by Hume–Adams. As we have seen, however, the Declaration was in effect the culmination of a line of documents which had input not only from Dublin but also from Hume, the army council of the IRA, loyalist paramilitary groups and Protestant clergymen.

Although the Declaration excluded the elements listed by Major, many in the republican camp were taken by surprise that he had taken part in any such exercise, for they had thought it unlikely that Reynolds could talk Major into making any announcement which so publicly and directly addressed republican concerns such as self-determination. A month earlier a senior republican had said privately: 'Major just hasn't the balls for it, hasn't the bottle for it. He's the wrong man in place at the wrong time.' But Major had co-operated in producing a declaration, and furthermore had addressed republican theory in a serious and substantive way, and one which had the approval and support of constitutional national-ism both north and south. He acknowledged Irish self-determination, subject only to the operation of consent, and formally declared that Britain had no selfish strategic or economic interest in Northern Ireland. Many republicans had assumed that Major's desire not to offend the Ulster Unionist party, with its nine Commons votes, would prevent him from going so far. But Major had handled Unionist leader James Molyneaux subtly and carefully, ensuring that he did not damn the Declaration out of hand. Major had thus achieved the feat of producing a Declaration which kept mainstream Unionism on board, while putting maximum pressure on the republicans.

The Downing Street Declaration in itself was clearly incompatible with traditional republican theory, yet Sinn Fein reacted not by rejecting it but by calling for clarification. The party announced it was setting up a peace commission to organise a process of consultations with as wide a range of opinion and individuals as possible before giving its definitive response. The Declaration had placed those republicans who wished to fight on indefinitely in a difficult position, for the document had in itself increased the odds against a military victory for the IRA. The two governments had jointly laid out a position of self-determination coupled with consent, and even the most militant had to recognise how slim were the chances of changing that through violence.

The two governments were generally judged to have made genuine efforts to tackle the issues which matter most to the republicans. A decision to fight on as before would clearly produce a wave of anger in nationalist Ireland, which would blame the IRA, and no one else, for continuing the conflict. Ed Moloney commented perceptively in the Dublin *Sunday Tribune*: 'To say no invites the risk of being isolated at least in nationalist Ireland, but to say yes could lead to division and defeat. If they say no and the IRA resumes its campaign, Dublin and London could launch a joint crackdown, including internment. A failure in 1971, internment this time might be much more potent. A yes answer on the other hand brings other problems, not least the prospect of dissension so severe that it might render the delivery of a positive answer impossible.'

A senior Dublin source said of the Declaration: 'It gave the Provos an involvement, an entry to the political process. It gave them the possibility of saying, "We can influence events, we can become involved in discussion." Its major achievement was that it did that without, at the same time, alienating the Unionists to a point where they would resort to open violence – in other words there was a balance in it. We did allow it to be diluted: the serious dilution as far as the Provos were concerned was the absence of the time frame and on the British acting as persuaders. But those points were simply non-negotiable for the British.'

On a pre-Christmas visit to Belfast Major brusquely brushed aside the republican request for clarification, declaring: 'There is a gauntlet down on the table. It is marked peace. It is there for Sinn Fein to pick it up. The onus is on them. There is no need for fresh negotiation. There is no need for any indecisiveness. There is no further clarification needed – we are not being drawn into negotiations. I am not playing that game.' While this was effective as a television sound-bite, it led to a stalemate which lasted for months. Sinn Fein said it would neither reject nor accept the Declaration without hearing explanation of some of its aspects: Major refused to explain any of it. On this sticking point a logjam extended into weeks and then months, with the pressure on Sinn Fein gradually lessening and momentum steadily draining from the process.

Reynolds took a different attitude from Major, promptly answering all questions addressed to him by the republicans. He later recalled: 'I felt, fair enough, if they are genuine questions that are being asked, let's answer them and get them out of the way and find out if it's a front for something else. I answered all the questions, took up all the arguments and disposed of them. The British were not as convinced as I was that the process could bring the results that I believed it could bring, and consequently they were choosing their steps very, very carefully. I disagreed with their point of view that clarification automatically led to discussion – it didn't.'

By January 1994 the euphoria which greeted the Declaration was fading as the clarification stalemate dragged on. Everything seemed as frozen as the winter: the IRA campaign, though reduced in intensity, showed no sign of ending. Dublin, in an attempt to encourage the republicans, took the highly symbolic step of removing the regulation which had for more than twenty years kept Sinn Fein spokespersons off the airwaves. Gerry Adams and others regularly appeared on television and radio from that point on, but the republican message remained the same: there must be clarification. At this point Hume, who was by this stage out of hospital, laid out a long and detailed analysis arguing that the time had come for the IRA to stop. The essence of his argument was that the Downing Street Declaration covered much the same ground as the Hume–Adams agreement, and that the arguments advanced by the IRA for maintaining its campaign had become redundant.

He said the IRA contentions that the British were in Ireland for their own selfish reasons, and were preventing the Irish people from exercising the right to self-determination, had been dealt with by the Declaration. Brooke's statement that Britain had no selfish economic or strategic interests in Ireland had been formally repeated in the Declaration, while the principle of self-determination was clearly accepted by London. While the British government had not used the word 'persuade', as republicans wanted, it had committed itself to encouraging agreement between the traditions. Republicans had repeatedly asked what the alternative was to 'armed struggle': this had been provided by the Forum for Peace and Reconciliation. Powerful sympathetic elements in Europe and the US would, he contended, support a new and peaceful nationalism.

Hume did not make it known at the time, but the statement carried in the newspapers was actually an edited version of a long letter which he wrote to Gerry Adams, sending copies both to Adams and to the army council of the IRA. He made additional points in this unpublished version:

> As promised, I am putting in writing to you my reasons as to why I believe that the Downing Street Declaration contains the substance of the proposed joint declaration that arose from our dialogue, finalised in what we have consistently described as the June document.

The Downing Street Declaration contains a clear affirmation of what our June document asked the British government to say in relation to its own interests. Given the words of our June document and given our joint public statements which made clear that any agreement among the divided people of our island must earn the allegiance and agreement of all traditions in Ireland and respect their diversity, is it not clear that the joint Declaration clearly accepts the fundamental principles that we proposed to them privately and publicly? Is whatever difference there is between our June document and the joint Declaration, and I see no difference in substance, worth the cost of a single human life?

. . . I am sorry that I have been so lengthy and perhaps wordy in my promised written response to you, but as we have both taken our dialogue and its objective so seriously and so genuinely since we began many years ago my hope, as I know yours is too, is that as we approach the 21st century it will be the first century in the long history of our island people in which physical conflict and its terrible consequences will be banished forever. I fervently hope that the serious dialogue now taking place within the republican movement will lead to the objective for which we have both worked so hard – lasting peace and justice.

Yours sincerely,

John Hume.

Adams's response was a disappointment to Hume. Warning that there were 'no quick fixes', he said there were differences between the Declaration and the Hume–Adams document and repeated that there could be no definitive republican response without clarification. The stalemate continued. There was, however, intensive activity on another front. Hume had spoken of the potential American power to be harnessed by peaceful Irish nationalists; in February 1994 Adams was given a taste of that power. Constitutional nationalists on both sides of the Atlantic combined to demonstrate that they had the power, given the right circumstances, to defeat all the influence that Britain could bring to bear.

14

ADAMS IN
NEW YORK

'You know, I've been fascinated by it for 25 years. I never dreamed that I would ever have an opportunity to do anything positive to help the process along'
– President Bill Clinton

'It was a win-win for the administration because if we gave the visa to Adams and he did deliver a cessation, fine. And if he didn't, he would be exposed as a fraud. In our view we thought we would win either way'
– Clinton aide Nancy Soderberg

'The conflict is ongoing. Every so often there will be something spectacular to remind the outside world'
– Gerry Adams, speaking after IRA attack on Heathrow airport

On 31 January 1994 Gerry Adams walked off a jet at a New York airport and for the first time stepped on American soil. It was one small step for the Sinn Fein president but a giant propaganda victory for his movement: it was also a crushing defeat for the British government, which for weeks had fought an intense diplomatic battle to keep him out of the US. The transatlantic drama, involving major figures in Britain, Ireland and the US, went right to the Oval Office of the White House, and was settled just days before the visit took place. President Bill Clinton spent half an hour listening to US Secretary of State Warren Christopher argue that letting Adams in would damage Anglo-American relations. But in the end Clinton overruled him and gave the go-ahead for the visit by saying simply: 'Okay, let's do it.'

To say that John Major was furious is an understatement. Major wanted Adams, Sinn Fein and the IRA isolated and ostracised, but the Irish government, John Hume and others argued for the use of the carrot rather than the stick. They believed an American visit would give the republicans a glimpse of the new vistas of support which could be available to them — but only if they gave up violence. In the event the impact of the short visit surpassed all Adams's hopes and all Major's fears. The republican leader was given a dream celebrity reception, being fêted like a movie star throughout New York, appearing on the most prestigious television shows and meeting many of the most influential people.

But despite all the British chagrin and dismay at the time, the visit would prove to have played a significant part in nudging the IRA towards the 1994 ceasefire. Peter Westmacott, a senior British diplomat based in Washington, lobbied hard to prevent the visit. He had a personal connection with Northern Ireland because a cousin, Herbert Westmacott, was a member of the SAS who had been killed by the IRA in Belfast in 1980. Westmacott defended his government's attitude: 'I don't think our opposition was short-sighted. The IRA was still involved in a full-blooded campaign, and we simply didn't think it was right to give Adams the visa he craved. It took another seven months before we got a ceasefire — meantime, we had Adams carrying the coffin of Begley.'

A Dublin source spelt out the opposite viewpoint: 'Our psychology was to give a bit and see if they would deliver. The British psychology was to box them in and then, when they're truly in the box, give a bit. They were using a colonial psychology. Clinton put the whole American weight behind the first model.'

It has always been the ambition of Irish nationalists to harness the huge political and financial power of the US, both in terms of the American administration and of the forty million people who describe themselves on their census forms as Irish-American. British governments, on the other hand, were always particularly sensitive to the old Irish-American accusation that Britain was a colonial power exploiting Ireland. British ministers and diplomats display distinct resentment at what they regard as the migrant Irish attempting to poison the wells of the special relationship between Britain and the US. According to one Irish observer: 'The British want to convince people that they are honest brokers, peacekeeping in Northern Ireland. But the basic assumption of many Irish–Americans is that they are effectively there as agents of occupation, active agents of injustice. That's what they're up against.'

Many of the millions of Irish–Americans are descendants of people who had left Ireland in painful and traumatic circumstances during and after the famine years of the 1840s. Their ancestors lived with the knowledge that they had survived while many left behind had died, and were thus more than usually susceptible to the traditional guilt of the emigrant. There was also a villain of the piece – the British, who in the over-simplified folklore of Boston and New York had deliberately neglected the Irish, refused to save them during the famine and were, right up to the present day, occupying part of Ireland. Over the decades this simplistic but potent image led to a measure of Irish–American support for Irish revolutionary movements. When the troubles began in 1969 the IRA were seen by some Irish–Americans as anti-colonial freedom fighters intent on driving out the British army of occupation. In the early 1970s this translated into large donations of dollars, sent openly to the republicans, as well as a surreptitious flow of arms shipments. The rifles which Danny Morrison spoke of in his 'Armalite and ballot-box' slogan came from America.

The picture changed in the mid and late 1970s, largely as a result of an initiative headed by John Hume and Irish diplomats. Hume impressed and befriended powerful Irish-Americans such as Senator Edward Kennedy and the late Tip O'Neill, then Speaker of Congress. He became the most influential Irish figure in Washington, particularly within the Democratic party. 'To see John at a Democratic Convention is quite something,' an envious British politician once remarked. 'He is fêted on all sides and can hardly move for his retinue of senators and congressmen.' Irish diplomat Michael Lillis, who was later to play a major part in putting together the Anglo-Irish Agreement, encouraged prominent Irish-American politicians to become organised in a new group, the Friends of Ireland. Their combined influence was enough to bring President Jimmy Carter to contemplate a large-scale aid package for Northern Ireland. Support for Sinn Fein and the IRA came back into prominence in 1981 during the hunger strikes and donations to the republicans soared, but this proved temporary.

The Irish government successfully interested President Ronald Reagan in the Northern Ireland problem. Irish diplomat Sean Donlon, who was by then Dublin's ambassador to Washington, persuaded Reagan to pay a four-day visit to Ireland in 1984 and, in each of his eight years as US President, Reagan spent St Patrick's Day at the Irish embassy in Washington. This association gave the Irish valuable political clout, with Reagan speaking publicly about Northern Ireland on at least fifteen occasions and frequently raising Anglo-Irish relations in conversations with Mrs Thatcher. He lent strong support to Dublin's efforts to persuade the British government to enter into the Anglo-Irish Agreement of 1985.

By the early 1990s a new phenomenon was emerging: corporate Irish-America. People of Irish descent had risen to some of the most powerful boardrooms of America, where they commanded large amounts of investment money and, very often, sizeable personal fortunes. Many wanted to do something for the old country; most of all they wanted, if they could, to rescue it from the long nightmare of violence. Some of these figures were collected together in 1991 by the then Irish ambassador to Washington, Dermot Gallagher, who established an 'Irish-American Advisory Board' which included significant figures such as Bill Flynn, chairman of Mutual Assurance of America, and businessman Chuck Feeney, reputedly a billionaire. A key figure here was Niall O'Dowd, a bearded journalist from Drogheda, County Louth, who in the 1970s emigrated first to San Francisco and later moved to New York, where he founded the *Irish American* magazine and the *Irish Voice*, both of which he publishes. A close associate of O'Dowd's was Bruce Morrison, a former Congressman who led a successful campaign to have the number of visas for Irish emigrants increased. In an interview conducted for this book O'Dowd recalled:

> I felt that the flag-waving had run its course. The sense I had was that of a time and a tide, a confluence of events. It had been obvious to me for some time Sinn Fein were looking for another, wider outreach in America. They had become ghettoised, and I was interested in developing a new approach. When the race for the Democratic nomination began we identified the potential of Clinton long before most people, and we felt it was worth reaching out to him. We wrote to him and got an immediate response. Following that contact I was asked to form a support group for Clinton in February 1992, and we put together a database of Irish-Americans to get resources behind Clinton. Around that time I made contact with Sinn Fein, and I came to Belfast to talk to them about the developing American scene. This was received with extraordinary enthusiasm – I knew nothing of other developments but I had a sense from them of a re-examination taking place. I met Clinton in September 1992 and raised the question of a visa for Adams with him then. From January 1993 I had a series of meetings with Sinn Fein about bringing America into the equation.

The republicans were excited about the prospect of having new doors open for them in the US. The money being sent to Belfast from its support groups had dwindled while the FBI had successfully infiltrated a number of arms-buying operations, in the process arresting valuable IRA personnel. The real action and the real power clearly lay in Washington and in corporate Irish-America, but the republicans were firmly excluded from both worlds. When O'Dowd arrived offering a possible entrée to such influential circles they jumped at the chance. They were so keen to have access to the world of influential Irish-American businessmen that in September 1993, when a group led by Morrison visited Ireland, they took an unprecedented step. Without any public announcement, the IRA ordered a ten-day ceasefire while the Americans were in Dublin and Belfast. The group met Adams, holding out to him the prospect of political and possibly financial aid if the republicans moved towards peace.

Bill Flynn was an example of the type of moneyed Irish-American who was anxious to help out his country of origin but who wanted nothing to do with violence. His father came from Loughinisland in Co. Down, a little village which would later figure in the saga of the peace process. Flynn was raised in the US in an environment which he described as Catholic and culturally Irish, and for thirty years he had regularly visited Ireland, north and south.

In a 1996 interview conducted for this book he said he had been approached by republican sympathisers who asked for his support. He recounted: 'I said I felt for the nationalist cause, but I could not support violence. They asked me what I was doing about the situation, and for the first time in my life I felt like a draft dodger.' In Ireland Flynn made the rounds of a number of organisations, seeking a positive way to become involved: he met the Peace People, the remnant of an organisation which had flourished in the 1970s, and held talks with Church of Ireland Archbishop Dr Robin Eames and the Catholic Cardinal, Dr Cahal Daly, as well as Reynolds, Mayhew, some loyalists, and Sinn Fein. According to Flynn:

> In our private meetings with Sinn Fein I said I, and corporate America in general, felt embarrassed and humiliated by the use of violence and could never support it. I said the time had come, in furtherance of their cause, to lay aside arms. I said they could do more with their mouths than with weapons. I spent a lot of time with Adams in Clonard monastery, and he introduced us to different groups. We thought then that Adams had to be convinced, but we now think Adams already believed that there was a world out there that cared for nationalists, and that he was using us to convince others.

Bill Barry, another of the group, was particularly impressed with Adams:

> I liked him immediately. I thought he was a real man, just in the way he comported himself. I didn't have great expectations so it was a surprise to find he was very much in control, he had charisma, his message was good. He couldn't have been more gracious.

At every meeting we had Bill Flynn would say, 'Put down the gun, stop the killing or we're out of here and you can forget about corporate America.' We went to Clonard monastery – those priests look at Gerry Adams like a son, it was a very warm and respectful relationship. Adams didn't propagandise us. I felt he was a guy who had been isolated internationally and who was looking for any help he could get.

Clinton's action in granting the Adams visa was all the more startling because it represented a radical change of heart on his part. He had made campaign promises to give Adams a visa and to send a 'peace envoy' to Northern Ireland, but once in office he dropped both ideas. In November 1993 he had brusquely turned down a previous application from Adams for a visa. A letter from Clinton to the then mayor of New York, David Dinkins, who had supported the application, closely reflected the British government's perspective: 'Credible evidence exists that Adams remains involved at the highest level in devising PIRA strategy. Moreover, despite his recent talks with John Hume, Adams still has not publicly renounced terrorism. The PIRA's October 23 bombing in Belfast [the Shankill Road bomb] that killed ten people – including two children – has underscored the brutal and terrorist nature of the organisation and undermined efforts to resume the political dialogue among the parties. My administration's policy continues to support the early resumption of political talks as the most promising way to seek peace.'

This was almost a mirror-image of the British government's attitude. The application had landed on the desk of a woman who was to prove a key figure in the Irish peace process, Nancy Soderberg. Ms Soderberg was third in command of the National Security Council (NSC) with special responsibility for Irish affairs. She knew a lot about Ireland before going to work at the White House, having worked for seven years as senior foreign policy adviser to Senator Kennedy. She had a long-standing friendship with Hume and regarded herself as '25 per cent Irish', having a Scots-Irish mother and a Swedish-American father. She became the key to the Clinton administration's Anglo-Irish policy.

In an interview conducted for this book, Ms Soderberg recalled: 'The administration didn't think that first visa application by Adams [in November] should be taken seriously and I was opposed to it because of his association with violence.' December, however, brought a White House reassessment of its entire Irish policy, which amounted to the most intensive review of its kind since the troubles began. One early sign of this came in late November when, at the suggestion of Dublin, Clinton telephoned Major in the run-up to the signing of the Downing Street Declaration, urging him to 'go the extra mile' in the peace process. Clinton himself was personally interested in the Northern Ireland problem. He had been a Rhodes scholar at Oxford in 1968, when the civil rights movement emerged, and he had closely watched the events of the time. In a 1995 newspaper interview he said: 'I was there when the troubles began, you know. I was living in Oxford. It occupied the attention of the country, obviously. And as someone who was there who had basically Irish roots, also Scottish roots, and on my father's side, English roots, I was sort of fascinated by it at the time. You know, I've been fascinated by it for 25 years. I never dreamed that I would ever have an opportunity to do anything positive to help the process along, but from the day the troubles began I just had a personal fascination with it.'

The Irish government did not back Adams's November visa application. But when he applied again in the wake of the Downing Street Declaration, Reynolds supported it even though IRA violence continued. He recollected: 'We believed it was very important because we always recognised that the Irish-American viewpoint weighed very heavily with the republican movement, and it was important to bring that on-side as an instrument to bring about a peace process. I made my position very clear to President Clinton personally and to his people in the State Department.' Bill Flynn, as chairman of the prestigious National Committee on Foreign Policy, had organised a one-day conference on Northern Ireland in New York, inviting Adams and other political leaders to attend. Flynn took out a full-page advertisement in the *New York Times* in which 220 leading Irish-Americans, including the heads of eighty-five leading corporations, voiced their support for the peace process. Hume added his support, as did Irish–American political figures such as Senators Chris Dodd and Daniel Moynihan, who in Washington terms were among Clinton's most important allies. So too did Senator Kennedy's sister, Jean Kennedy Smith, who had been appointed by Clinton as US ambassador to Dublin.

Of all those involved, reliable Washington sources say the key player was Senator Kennedy, who lobbied hard for it. O'Dowd explained the importance of Senator Kennedy: 'Nothing moves on Ireland in the administration without Kennedy having a say. If you want to get progress on Ireland you get to Kennedy and his aide, Trina Vargo.'

Nancy Soderberg recounted how a chain of communication was established from the White House to the Falls Road: 'We started getting indications in December from Congressmen and people like Niall O'Dowd that things were changing. He was convincing Irish–Americans that they wanted to end the violence, and I felt there was something changing. At first the British didn't really think we were going to grant the visa, but we started looking at it very carefully. We were going through Kennedy's office via Niall O'Dowd who was communicating with them. We wanted to have a sense of where Adams was on the issues.'

In the course of just a few weeks the Clinton administration's attitude veered from strong support for the British approach to one of backing Dublin's line. As the first post-Cold War president, he had more political manoeuvrability on the issue. British influence, while still considerable in Washington, had become less important in that Clinton was no longer as constrained by the strategic obligations of the special relationship. This made it easier for him to overrule the traditional State Department attitude that Britain was an important ally who if possible should not be offended by the US.

Adams was asked to meet the US consul in Belfast, Val Martinez, to be interviewed about his attitude to violence. Martinez sought assurances that he would renounce violence and support the Downing Street Declaration; Adams replied that he wanted to see 'an end to all violence and an end to this conflict'. According to Ms Soderberg: 'That report came back. There was middle of the road rhetoric. We wanted to make clear to him what sort of progress we wanted to see, if we gave him the visa, on the Downing Street Declaration and the violence.' By this stage Anthony Lake, Clinton's National Security Adviser, and the Vice-President, Al Gore, were involved in the decision-making process. Hume was also in contact with Kennedy's office, and Kennedy was personally lobbying for the visa. The British government, however, was dead against it, with Major's aide, Rod Lyne, regularly phoning Lake to argue the case against. The State Department, which worried about the effect of such a move on Anglo-American relations, was also opposed. Then on 27 January three hoax bombs were planted in San Diego, California which were reportedly claimed by the 'Southern California IRA'. They turned out to be practice grenades without explosives. No one in America or Ireland had ever heard of any such organisation, and the idea of the IRA causing bomb scares in California was absurd. According to Ms Soderberg:

> We went in to talk to the President. There was the President, George Stephanopoulos [a senior presidential aide], Tony Lake and myself talking about it. We had pretty much decided to give Adams the visa, but we decided if he renounced the San Diego violence it would push him down the road a little more to condemning violence. It was a win-win for the administration because if we gave the visa to him and he did deliver a cessation, fine. And if he didn't, he would be exposed as a fraud. In our view we thought we would win either way. I started talking to Niall O'Dowd directly. I called Niall and gave him a mission to get Adams to renounce the San Diego incendiaries. If he renounced it he would get the visa: we needed a statement. Adams showed he had a sense of humour. His reaction, when Niall called him and told him what he was being asked to do, was: 'Does this mean that I have to apologise every time an Irishman punches an Englishman in a bar?'

> Adams put out a press statement that night. It was a strong statement, and we took it into the President on Sunday morning. The President spoke to Secretary Christopher for half an hour.

Secretary Christopher argued the visa could damage British relations because of the ongoing violence. I argued on the phone to the President – Tony and I were walking him through the situation explaining the pros and cons, the win–win situation. He was concerned about the impact. We felt it could do some damage with Britain: we knew it would do some damage but not too much. But finally, the President said: 'OK, let's do it.' I thought it would help get peace in Northern Ireland. It was still part of the idea that with a push the violence should end. I called Niall O'Dowd and I said: 'Give me twenty-four hours.'

Of Clinton's interest in Ireland, she added: 'It was an instinct he had – while not getting involved politically when Northern Ireland came up, he'd always say he'd like to do more. He saw it as the last, longest remaining unresolved problem in Europe. He thought it was something we ought to be able to help.'

Clinton said later of his decision: 'Well, you know, I talked to Tony and Nancy, and then to people out around the country and I listened to all the arguments pro and con. I also listened to people in the administration who thought I shouldn't do it. And it occurred to me that it was one of those points when there had to be some tangible evidence that there could be a reward for the renunciation of violence and beginning to walk toward peace. Those kinds of things are always a judgement call. There's no rule book that tells you when this or that or the other thing happens. It was a judgement call. You asked me whether I think I did the right thing? I do.'

London was dismayed by the visit, and sections of the British media came close to apoplexy. They took the view that a front-man for terrorism had scored a resounding propaganda victory. Dublin, by contrast, had a different mind-set, regarding the episode as a boost for the peace process. Adams had indeed received a spectacular welcome in the States; but the main point was that he had been given an insight into the power of Irish-America and of the goodwill that existed towards him there. The important thing in Dublin's eyes was that he was welcomed not as a dedicated terrorist but because he was seen as the man who was going to stop the terrorism. Dublin saw the whole exercise as providing Adams with an incentive to move toward peace, though within weeks came an event which raised the most serious doubts about the whole process.

On an evening in March 1994, people in and around London's Heathrow airport were startled by a series of loud bangs around the Excelsior hotel near the airport's northern perimeter. Shortly afterwards a vehicle in the hotel car-park burst into flames. Security personnel at the airport were already on the alert, for a series of telephone calls, made with a recognised IRA codeword to confirm their authenticity, had warned of an impending mortar attack on the airport. Two mortars had landed on the northern runway, while two others fell short. None of the four had exploded and no one was injured in the incident. The burning vehicle was found to contain mortar tubes which had been used in the manner of the attack on Downing Street in February 1991.

Because of the threat of terrorist attack from the IRA and other terrorist groups Heathrow, like other airports, maintained a high level of security. The incident demonstrated, however, that even such a tightly guarded target was still vulnerable to attack. But it also left the security forces puzzled. For one thing, a high proportion of IRA mortars usually exploded, yet none of these had gone off. For another, the IRA campaign in the wake of the Declaration had been running at a relatively low level, and this was a dramatic escalation. Most baffling of all, the IRA seemed to have thrown all caution to the winds by firing mortars which could have hit an aircraft, causing multiple civilian casualties. Incidents such as the Enniskillen bombing showed such attacks had a devastating effect on IRA support: why, then, were the terrorists deliberately risking a repetition?

Security was stepped up at Heathrow, but two days later the authorities received a jolt when a second mortar attack took place. This time, again after a series of warnings, mortars were fired from tubes buried in rough ground on the southern side of the airport. Four landed near Terminal Four, one of them hitting the ground only 40 yards from a stationary Jumbo jet. But again no one was injured, because none of the mortars exploded. There was an outcry as the government was questioned on why this second attack had not been prevented. It turned out that while there had been a general search of the area around the airport, it was surrounded by many acres of unused land, not all of which had been intensely examined. The mortar tubes had been placed in the ground prior to the first attack, and set off by a timing device.

Two days later there was near-incredulity when the same thing happened again. Another four mortars, again activated by a timing device, were fired towards Terminal Four, one landing on the roof of the building. The tubes had been partially buried in scrubland and camouflaged with wood, leaves and relaid turf: all the searches had missed them. Once again, however, it appeared something had gone wrong with the detonating mechanism, for none of the devices exploded.

When the reports of the first and second attacks came in, many of those who believed in the peace process were dumbfounded. Although the hoped-for cessation had not arrived, Reynolds and others in Dublin continued to hope: he had just said publicly that he would be patient in awaiting a reply. That response seemed to be an indiscriminate attack on a major international airport, used daily not only by the British public but by travellers from all over the world. The effect of a mortar bomb exploding inside a crowded terminal, or hitting a Jumbo jet, was almost too horrendous to contemplate.

For a moment the peace process appeared to be at an end. Yet when the full facts began to emerge, the attacks took on a different aspect. Although the mortars contained Semtex plastic explosive, it turned out a key component had been doctored so that they would not explode. It was a conspicuous example of the IRA's ingenuity in conceiving and executing slyly clever attacks. A senior RUC officer told the *Belfast Telegraph*: 'In military terms this is powder-puff stuff, and it is quite obvious what they are up to. The Provos are piddling about. If they really wanted to cause death and destruction they could do it – it's second nature to them. What they were doing at Heathrow is hinting at the potential. They're having a good laugh, and keeping morale high back here in Belfast.' Although Mayhew claimed publicly that the mortars had been designed to explode, both security and republican sources have since confirmed the IRA had ensured they would not go off. The whole thing had been an incredibly elaborate hoax, designed to frighten and pressurise the British government without actually killing anyone. It had in fact been more of a threat than an actual attack, an attempt by the IRA to use violence in a finely tuned and almost forensic way to strengthen their political position.

The Heathrow attack may have caused concern to the British government, but it had also cancelled out many of the propaganda gains made by Adams in the States, where the incident conjured up the spectre of another Lockerbie. It severely dented the image which Adams had presented in his New York visit a month earlier. His reception then was based on the assumption that he was a man of peace: but Heathrow had all the appearance of an act of war.

The republicans clearly saw themselves as being involved, as they moved towards cessation, in a finely orchestrated blend of violence, politics and propaganda. The first half of 1994 saw them attempting to extract maximum political advantage and leverage from the final stages of their violent campaign. But they may have been too clever by half at Heathrow, for the subtlety of the attack was not widely appreciated. The fact that the mortars were designed not to explode was not widely publicised, Mayhew's claim that they were supposed to go off went uncontradicted and criticism of the republicans mounted. Furthermore, Adams made the mistake of saying, in a radio interview: 'The conflict is ongoing. Every so often there will be something spectacular to remind the outside world.' He apparently wished to project that he was speaking more in sorrow than in anger, but his words were taken as a threat. He claimed his comment had been 'taken completely out of context and misreported and misinterpreted', adding: 'The peace process is not finished. I have always said there were no quick fixes, that building a developing peace process is going to be difficult and problematic. At times perhaps there are going to be aspects of it that look confusing, but all in all the peace process is not finished. It's going to be difficult but I think it can be done. We need cool management and calm heads. The process will go through various phases and it will have ups and it will have downs and it will have difficulties.' However, the Heathrow attacks, together with other incidents such as the IRA killing of an RUC detective in Belfast and a beating administered to an SDLP councillor in Crossmaglen, combined to sap much of Sinn Fein's recently enhanced status.

The following month, under heavy pressure from all points of the political compass, they declared a three-day ceasefire to mark Easter. In republican terms this was a highly meaningful development, since it came at the most significant part of the republican calendar and because it was the first openly declared ceasefire for many years. It set a new precedent and as such it was a real landmark for their movement. Adams wrote to a number of Irish-American figures assuring them of the significance of the move. He also gave an indication of how difficult things were within the republican movement, telling at least one of the Americans that the three-day ceasefire 'did not come easily'.

The importance of it was privately recognised by both governments, but as far as the rest of the world was concerned it was a derisory gesture which did nothing to make up for the credibility lost over Heathrow and it was widely dismissed as too little too late. A Dublin source commented at the time: 'I think it's the minimum that can be discerned by the naked eye – anything else and you'd need an electronic microscope. If they were trying to put pressure on London without unsettling their own soldiers, I don't think it's enough to put real pressure on the British, and they've still used the C-word – ceasefire.'

But the short ceasefire was followed by yet more militarism, with a particular show of strength by the IRA. The organisation had repeatedly threatened drug-dealers, and on 25 April scores of IRA members were involved in a large-scale series of attacks. They killed a west Belfast man they alleged was a drug-dealer, and shot sixteen others in the legs. It was another moment of severe doubt for those who hoped the republicans were serious about going political.

The month of May brought a change of heart from the British

government, which dropped its objections to clarifying the Downing Street Declaration and published a lengthy 'amplification'. This broke no particularly new ground, but it threw the political onus back on the republicans. Furthermore, the responses were phrased in a measured, non-confrontational tone, without name-calling or belligerent language and the net result was to place even more pressure on the republicans. The six-month clarification argument had bought them valuable breathing-space, but when London did clarify, it did so seriously and in some detail, winning applause from Dublin and other nationalist sources. The government's responses clearly did not amount to re-negotiation of the Declaration, but they made explicit some points which were welcome to republicans. They directly addressed several areas of Sinn Fein concern by stating that no section had a veto on progress, recognising the validity of Sinn Fein's electoral mandate, making clear that the Declaration did not have to be accepted in its entirety, and specifying that constitutional change could be placed on the table in future talks.

Until Christmas 1993 most observers agreed that Adams and other republican leaders had often displayed deft day-to-day tactical skills. At many points in 1994, however, they left an impression of uncertainty and of following no clear policy. Within the movement Adams's stock was high and his arguments tended to prevail, but opinion was by no means unanimous in favour of a ceasefire. Many still preferred militarism and doubted whether a non-violent strategy would work; others would accept a ceasefire but wanted violence to continue until the last moment, in order to make it clear that calling a halt should not be interpreted as a sign of weakness. The result was to create an appearance of indecision. The sterile clarification argument had its uses, but it helped create a vacuum in which killings by both loyalists and republicans continued. Each set of IRA violence carried political penalties by disillusioning those who tried to bring the republicans out of the cold. The continuing loyalist campaign, meanwhile, helped poison the atmosphere against peace.

Throughout the spring of 1994 Sinn Fein held a series of

'peace commission' hearings, inviting opinions on the Declaration. In all it received 228 submissions, mainly from the nationalist community: eight-five of the submissions, or 37 per cent, called for either an ending of the IRA campaign or a three-month ceasefire. One influential voice was privately advising republicans that the IRA's campaign had run its course and should be brought to a close. This was the late Paddy McGrory, a Belfast solicitor respected both by republicans and by the Belfast legal establishment. This was manifest at his funeral late in 1994 which was attended both by the Lord Chief Justice of Northern Ireland, Sir Brian Hutton, and other judges, but also by Gerry Adams and senior republicans.

McGrory was himself a republican, though a non-violent one. A solicitor who appeared in many IRA cases during the troubles, he came to international prominence in Gibraltar, where he appeared at the inquest for the three IRA members killed there by the SAS in 1988. His performance as the sole Irish lawyer pitted against a battery of British legal representatives was praised by many observers. For many years he acted as legal representative for Gerry Adams and other well-known republicans, who respected him despite his opposition to violence. He put his views down on paper several times and sent them to Adams, who paid great attention to them. The following is an edited extract from his previously unpublished documents:

> There is nothing wrong with parsing and analysing the Downing Street Declaration, looking all the while for hidden meanings. It is an exercise which has to be done, if only by way of minesweeping, since nobody in this world is so adept as the British civil service in the laying of documentary booby-traps. But it should also be viewed from a distance, providing a wide-angle perspective in which the true nature of the document can often more clearly reveal itself. Many documents, especially in the political sphere, can exude, however faintly, what I have been accustomed to describe as a perfume.
>
> The Declaration presents a clear appearance of a Unionist document. Many observers have pointed to seven separate assurances to the Unionists that their support of the union will be upheld, and to the fact that nationalist identities and allegiances

are given no such legitimacy. But an intelligent Unionist, contemplating this document, would be better served by reliance on his nose, rather than his eyes – and if he did, he would smell a rat. I suspect that intelligent and perceptive Unionists have looked behind the statement that Britain has no selfish strategic or economic interest in Northern Ireland and will have begun to look at their future accordingly. For all its Unionist looks, this document emits a scent of rejection, though, for all that, it could hardly be described as nationalist or republican.

There is no room for doubt that the Declaration concedes the Irish have a right to self-determination, without external interference. The importance of this simply must not be underestimated. It is a departure from an attitude of the British towards Ireland which has endured for centuries. It is sad to reflect on the human suffering, the grief and misery which would have been avoided had Britain acknowledged the existence of this right even a century ago. And it must rank as the greatest achievement of the modern republican movement that it has wrung this acceptance of Ireland's essential nationhood from the British.

A pledge to the Unionists that they will never be coerced into a United Ireland changes its character depending on whether that pledge comes from a British or an Irish source. When the pledge comes from a British source, that is external interference with the Irish right to self-determination, and constitutes a veto. When the pledge comes from an Irish source, however, that is merely the Irish exercising their right to self-determination in the way they have freely chosen, and without any external interference. The Irish, as they are entitled to do, are by their own wish conferring a concession on a section of the nation. What strikes me about the document is the air of impermanence about almost everything in it save only the acceptance that the right of self-determination reposes in the Irish people. That is a statement of a fact, and there can be no going back on it.

The most important decision is not acceptance or rejection of the Declaration, but a decision as to whether more is likely to be gained for the republican cause by armed struggle than might be won through political means. Only madmen make war for fun, and the republican struggle has been waged for a specific political purpose, and only because of the total failure of conventional politics to advance the Irish cause.

293

I hold the view that armed action is unlikely to secure any significant political advance, and certainly nothing to compare in importance with the political achievements to date. And the grave danger is that it could undo spectacular recent gains. Will political activity achieve more? I think it probably will, given the climate that has been created, and the status and credibility which the republican movement now enjoys. I believe that peace now will garner a rich harvest of support for the republican movement, such as it has not known for decades. Conversely, I think failure of the movement to seize this hour will in all probability mean a virtual collapse of Sinn Fein electoral support, and a rejection of the republican position all over Ireland and in America. I believe the tide is at the flood, and is beginning to ebb. This is the hour.

McGrory's words were written in the spring of 1994. The IRA was indeed moving towards cessation, as he advocated. But it was doing so extremely slowly and it was using violence along the way; and so too were the loyalist paramilitary groups.

15

TUAS – TOTALLY UNARMED STRATEGY

'There was utter chaos – people screaming, grown men crying, wives, girlfriends, mothers not knowing whether their sons were in the bar. They couldn't have killed six more inno- cent, more decent people'
– County Down councillor after loyalist attack on Catholic pub

'Father, would you please say a prayer for those who killed him?'
– widow of one of the victims, speaking to her priest

'It's fair to say that at that stage the Taoiseach was the only one sitting around the Cabinet table who believed that this could be pulled off after Letterkenny'
– former Irish Justice Minister

'The leadership has now decided that there is enough agreement to proceed with the TUAS [totally unarmed strategy] option'
– internal republican document

Loughinisland was the sort of little place that looked as though the world had passed it by. A mere twenty miles from Belfast, it was none the less a million miles away from the troubles. It nestled in County Down's pretty, fertile drumlin country, one of a surprising number of places virtually untouched by the violence. Veteran journalist David Dunseith said of it: 'It's a very quiet place. It's hardly even a village, it's barely a hamlet. You would drive through it on a day out and you'd say to yourself, "Ach, this is a lovely wee part of the world." It's the sort of place where some old fella is sure to wave at you as if he's known you all his life. Community relations are very good, people mix very well, they're in and out of each other's pubs.'

In Belfast on 16 June, gunmen from the Irish National Liberation Army drove along the Shankill Road and, spotting a group of loyalists, opened fire on them. When the gunfire died away three men lay dead or fatally wounded, not far from the spot of the Shankill fish shop bombing. The men included two members of the Ulster Volunteer Force, one of them, Trevor King, an important UVF figure. Everyone knew there would be retaliation: it came two days later, with the UVF staging a carbon-copy of the UDA's Greysteel pub attack. The target, chosen very much at random, was Loughinisland.

At 10.20 p.m. on a Saturday night UVF gunmen burst into O'Toole's, a tiny Catholic pub in the village. Most of those in the bar were watching football on television – the Republic of Ireland was playing Italy in a World Cup soccer match. The gunmen fired repeatedly into their backs. Within seconds customers who had been cheering the Irish team were dead and injured as the scene in the pub was transformed from one of enjoyment to a nightmare. Bodies were piled on top of each other, blood running freely on the floor. Afterwards local people sobbed in the street outside as word emerged about who had been killed and injured. Six Catholics lay dead, one of them, at eighty-seven years of age, the oldest victim of the troubles. The owner and seven regulars escaped the slaughter because they had just flown out to Romania on a charity mission to help rebuild an orphanage.

The scale of the carnage, together with the fact that Loughinisland had previously been sheltered from the violence, increased the impact of the attack on the little community. Shock, incomprehension and disbelief mixed with grief. To the rest of Ireland and Britain it seemed as if the peace process and the Downing Street

Declaration had come to nothing. A councillor stood outside the bar and said:

> When I arrived there was utter chaos – people screaming, grown men crying, wives, girlfriends, mothers not knowing whether their sons were in the bar. A man was in there with his son and his son-in-law. All he could do was cradle their heads and try and comfort them. The son-in-law died at the scene, his son died on the way to hospital. I have been at their home this morning. There's children crying, they've lost their father. There's an old man of eighty-seven who came in for a quiet drink. His nephew brought him along just to give him an evening out; they'd have come in regular. They're both dead. We have a local man, a well-known fella who worked in the local car place here, came home from holidays yesterday morning. His wife dropped him off, didn't realise he was going to meet his death. The six people they've killed, I know them personally and they couldn't have killed six more innocent, more decent people.

The owner, Hugh O'Toole, flew back from Romania and broke down in tears as he surveyed his bloodstained pub. He wept openly and was barely able to speak. 'It's destroyed me,' he said. Local people spoke of the dead. Barney Green, aged eighty-seven, was a pipe-smoking character who enjoyed a game of whist. He died simply because his nephew, Dan McCreanor, a fifty-nine-year-old bachelor, took him, as a treat, down to O'Toole's bar to watch the match. Dan died too. Emma Rogan, seven, and Tony Rogan, eight, became children without a father when the UVF bullets cut down Adrian Rogan, known to everyone as Frosty, who worked in a local scrapyard and was one of the most popular men in the district. Canon Bernard Magee told mourners at the funeral that his wife Clare had cried uncontrollably that night. 'What am I to say to the children?' she kept saying. Another casualty, Malcolm Jenkinson, fifty-two, left three children and a wife, Ann, who worked in a psychiatric hospital. The priest at his funeral said her grief was very intense, but after saying the Rosary she had asked him: 'Father, would you please say a prayer for those who killed him?' Eamonn Byrne's wife Marie gave birth a few weeks before his death to their fourth child, a child which would never know its father.

The Loughinisland attack was to be the last of the large-scale multiple murders before the IRA and loyalist ceasefires. But nobody knew that at the time; and even if they had, it was little consolation to the families and friends of the innocents who died, shot in the back, as they watched a football match on television.

Pessimism became almost universal during June when a large-scale Sinn Fein conference in the County Donegal town of Letterkenny sent out a message which was interpreted as ruling out a ceasefire. The purpose of the meeting was to hold an internal review of the state of the peace process, but the media built up expectations that an IRA ceasefire was to be announced. Before the Letterkenny meeting the republicans sent word to Reynolds that the occasion would probably be interpreted as a rejection of peace. They reassured him that this was misleading, and that the process was still on course. According to Bertie Ahern, Reynolds confided to him that 'it wouldn't come out too good but not to mind it too much'. This advice was also passed on to British officials at a meeting in Dublin. According to one source: 'Mansergh told the British that Letterkenny would be very bad, ostensibly, but that they weren't to lose heart and that they should try to avoid rebarbative [i.e. dismissive] comment.'

Sinn Fein delegates from all over Ireland assembled in Letterkenny on the weekend of 23 July, under the gaze of media from all over the world. Although Adams made a neutral speech, a number of motions critical of the Downing Street Declaration were passed. The media, concentrating on these, exuded disappointment, telling the world in their reports that the Downing Street Declaration had been rejected and that the peace process looked dead. But a republican source commented:

> The media didn't see the background to the picture. Reynolds knew we were going to try to move it forward. The British succeeded in making the issue of peace dependent on a yes or a no to the Declaration, and the conference was interpreted as a rejection of Downing Street and the peace process. Actually,

the issue of an unarmed strategy [i.e. a cessation] did not come up at Letterkenny. On the surface it was about the Declaration, but the real story of Letterkenny was an expression of confidence in the leadership's political strategy. Its importance was internal – less to do with Downing Street and more to do with keeping the activists abreast of the republican strategy. In the course of all this Hume–Adams was read to delegates a number of times. There were questions and answers on Hume–Adams. People asked for paragraph 4 to be read and re-read. No one in that hall had any problem.

As Sinn Fein realised the impression which was being given, a senior republican approached a journalist in the car-park of the hotel and said: 'Be careful in what you're saying. There could be a silver lining in there.' But Letterkenny was followed by a wave of criticism, with many supporters of the process deeply worried. Nancy Soderberg tracked down Niall O'Dowd, the Irish–American journalist who had lobbied for a visa for Adams. On holiday in Kerry, he listened as she delivered a sharp transatlantic lecture, berating him for having assured her a ceasefire was on the cards: after Letterkenny it no longer seemed possible.

John Hume and his wife Pat and two friends were on holiday in Bordeaux, where they were joined by a senior SDLP member, Sean Farren, and his wife. After Letterkenny, Hume issued a hopeful public statement, but Farren later recalled: 'John was on edge. On the Monday after Letterkenny when we visited him he was reassuring me but he was still anxious. He was on the phone several times and there were phone calls from the Department of Foreign Affairs. We went for dinner in Royanne but he kept leaving the table and didn't really engage in much discussion.'

The only other person who reacted positively to Letterkenny was Reynolds who, relying on the private reassurances from Sinn Fein, urged people not to lose faith in the process. The vibrations from Letterkenny were so bad, however, that even Reynolds had serious doubts. Sinn Fein would be proved right in the private forecast that a ceasefire was on the way, but many republicans were still not convinced that one should be called. Reports from the

Garda Special Branch were, according to Justice Minister Mrs Geoghegan-Quinn, extremely unpromising:

> They had great hopes for Letterkenny, but the information coming back from them was that it was a huge disappointment. The word was that the hawks were creating a lot of difficulties for Adams. It's fair to say at that stage the Taoiseach was the only one sitting around the Cabinet table who believed that this could be pulled off after Letterkenny. He got terribly annoyed after Letterkenny – he got really, really annoyed, he was seething. He sent a very straight message to these boys – 'You get up and deliver the goods or you go home and we forget all about this.' I think that they thought at that point that they were dealing with somebody who would give them anything that they wanted, and would be prepared to stick his neck out for them on any issue. They suddenly discovered that he just wasn't prepared to go down a particular road and he was giving them a very direct message – 'This is it and if you don't deliver, forget about it, don't come back to me any more.'

Another Dublin source confirmed that no one else at the Cabinet table now thought the peace process would succeed, explaining:

> I think that all fourteen members of the Reynolds–Spring Cabinet were extremely sceptical of the process, extremely sceptical that the Provos would come on board. That's not to say they weren't supportive and it's not to say they didn't play their role – Maire Geoghegan-Quinn particularly was sceptical, but she played an active role whenever she could in supporting the project, and so too did Dick Spring. There were times when Albert felt alone because nobody else was sharing his optimism, but the reason nobody was sharing it was because he wasn't telling them what he knew. Letterkenny was always presented as the lowest point in the peace process and the moment when Albert was most on his own. But he and Mansergh had clearly been briefed about what was going on, that it would be no more than a hiccup, to the extent that they were able to tell the British that in advance of Letterkenny. So it was hardly surprising that they were able to keep their spirits up when others felt the whole process had been rejected.

Reynolds remembers it as one of his darkest moments: 'I was saying one thing and everybody was saying the opposite to me, including a lot of members of my own party, members of government. Everywhere you went you read nothing but negative stories in the media. Everybody said it was over, that it was going nowhere, that it was foolish in the extreme to have expected it to have happened in the first place. A certain amount of it gets to you, but you have to put it aside and soldier on.'

Things looked so bad by this stage that even Father Reid was experiencing self-doubt. According to one close to him: 'He was beginning to search his conscience as to whether he could remain a channel. He was like an ambassador but he started to wonder whether he could continue if they were not serious.'

The republicans may have made a number of miscalculations during the first part of 1994, but on one point they were as successful as usual – that of leaving the outside world as uncertain as ever of their true intentions. Many of those who had hopes for the peace process lost heart and experienced increasing doubts throughout 1994 as the violence went on and the Downing Street Declaration did not elicit a definitive republican response. The British government, through its large security apparatus, poured a great deal of resources into intelligence agencies tasked with divining exactly what the republicans were up to; in the event, all the signs are that despite all the political and intelligence resources at their command, London failed to pierce and penetrate the highest levels of the republicans. Penetration was sometimes achieved at lower levels, often enabling the security forces to foil planned IRA operations and lay SAS ambushes; but working out what was going on in the top echelons of the IRA and Sinn Fein, the republican brain, was a different matter.

The person with the most openly and frequently voiced faith in the process was Hume, whose message in countless radio and television interviews was that a real chance existed for peace. In Dublin hopes were high at the beginning of the year, but optimism faded as the weeks passed. By March Spring, concluding that a permanent IRA cessation looked unlikely, was suggesting that a short stoppage of the campaign would be looked on as a welcome start. But by July, as we have seen, Reynolds was the only person in the Irish Cabinet who still clung to the belief that a complete cessation could be achieved. None the less, episodes such as Heathrow and Letterkenny were enough to undermine the strongest faith. Intelligence reports reaching the Irish Cabinet provided no comfort at all for Reynolds, as Mrs Geoghegan-Quinn later recalled:

> We got a full report from the Gardai in relation to who was strongly on the hawk side, and who was strongly on the dove side, in relation to supporting or not supporting. The word back to us was that Gerry Adams certainly had a very tough battle on his hands to win them over because they were very sceptical. They didn't believe that the loyalists were going to buy into anything and they didn't want to be seen buying into it first, and they just didn't see any light at the end of the tunnel and they just wanted war.
>
> Adams sent people like Pat Doherty to do a lot of touring around the country, speaking in favour [of a cessation], but being very clever at meetings in always waiting to get the pulse of the meeting first before committing himself. It was interesting to see the reports coming back – in certain parts of the country Doherty would have been very strong and vociferous in favour of having a ceasefire. In other areas, where obviously the organisation was against it, he would still be looking for a ceasefire, but in a very different kind of way, kind of playing to the gallery. Obviously he had to mind his back. The word back on the security front was that there was no sign of a ceasefire, that they were having a lot of difficulty in certain areas in convincing people. The area where the greatest difficulty was going to be was Fermanagh and South Tyrone.

The British assessment of the chances of a cessation was even more pessimistic than that of Dublin. Throughout this period the British government was intensely sceptical of the whole proposition that the republicans could be induced along a political path. Few in authority in London or Belfast really believed, in 1993 or 1994, that the republicans were serious about moving in the direction of peace.

Brooke, in his thoughtful way, had spoken in 1989 of the government being flexible and imaginative in the event of a cessation, but after Mayhew succeeded him in 1992 the possibility was given little public credence. At that point the idea of making any kind of pitch to the republicans, even at the very basic level of saying that an abandonment of violence would eventually lead to the conference table, was one that more or less faded from currency. In the rare speeches and statements in which the concept was mentioned during Mayhew's term it tended to be raised in a challenging and confrontational way, rather than presented as any kind of serious and considered offer. Throughout 1993 various British sources made it clear they did not for a moment believe the IRA was moving towards a cessation. It was emphasised to journalists and others that the preferred British approach was via the inter-party talks route: Reynolds's talk of peace was seen as at best a distraction and at worst something which might interfere with the task of putting the inter-party talks together again.

Instead, Mayhew seemed interested almost exclusively in the traditional model of isolating Sinn Fein and the IRA by constructing a deal with moderate unionist and nationalist elements. One of the great frustrations for Mayhew was that a key element of this model was of pressing Hume and the SDLP to thrash out an agreement with Unionists. Hume made it very clear, however, that he favoured instead concentrating on attempting to end the IRA campaign. Mayhew in other words wanted to start talks without the republicans, and to reach an agreement which would eventually isolate them. The approach of Hume and Reynolds, by contrast, was based on a belief that such talks were unlikely to succeed while violence continued.

Hume's persistence in pursuing the declaration path caused Mayhew and others in the NIO to resent his attitude. Government sources regularly alleged throughout this period that Hume was an unreasonable leader who was deliberately preventing more moderate elements in his party from reaching agreement with Unionism. Journalists were regularly briefed by the NIO that Hume was an obstacle to inter-party agreement. On one occasion it was said of him: 'He runs his party like Mussolini.' This frame of mind may have contributed to the relative lack of British interest in exploring currents within republicanism and considering whether advantage should be taken of them. Another factor in preventing the British from reading the situation more astutely than they did lay in the general perspective from which they viewed republicans.

The Irish government may have actively disliked and condemned the republican movement, but in Ireland there were many precedents for republicans putting away their weapons and becoming absorbed into politics. Reynolds's own Fianna Fáil party, for example, had begun life as a revolutionary movement – its founder, Eamon de Valera, had once been sentenced to death by the British. One of its leaders had famously described it as 'a slightly constitutional party', yet in time it had gone on to become the Republic's largest political party. This familiar process of absorption was what Ruairi O Bradaigh had warned of when he declared in the 1986 abstention debate: 'Haughey, FitzGerald and Spring will say, "We waited sixty-five years but we have them at last." ' It was therefore ingrained in the Irish psyche that one of the most effective ways of dealing with violent rebels was by engulfing and enveloping them in the political process, thus helping them evolve into politicians.

On the British side, however, few displayed any enthusiasm for such an approach. It was certainly the case, in a number of former British possessions, that figures once branded as terrorists, who had seen the inside of British jails, had in time gone on to become accepted as politicians and even statesmen. But in the Irish peace process the prevailing British response was one of condemnation, scepticism and a deep disbelief that republican leaders could be genuine. Major thought Reynolds was talking voodoo when he spoke of a possible IRA cessation; Mayhew was convinced that if only Dublin would move on Articles 2 and 3, the inter-party logjam would be broken and a generous Unionist response would result. Where constitutional Irish nationalists were prepared to welcome the republicans as prodigals, London persisted in viewing them as incorrigibles. Dublin saw Adams and his associates as seeking an

honourable exit from violence; London viewed it as, in all likeli-
hood, a trap.

It was perhaps not surprising that London should take a sterner
and less flexible attitude, given that the IRA had been killing British
soldiers and attacking Britain with such violence for a quarter of a
century. Any government had to take account of British public
opinion, and the IRA was certainly hated by many in Britain. The
Sun may have been exaggerating when it declared that the two
most hated words in the English language were 'Gerry Adams' but
there was some truth in the assertion.

There were also additional reasons telling against any British
attempt to reach out towards the republicans. The violence was
maintained right until the end while the Major administration
was forever looking over its shoulder at its own backbenchers and
indeed at the Unionist MPs whose support it was anxious to gain.
There appears to have been little in the intelligence reports reaching
ministers to suggest that the republicans' professed desire for peace
should be paid more attention than it was. According to senior
security sources it was only in 1992 that the intelligence community
began to take the stirrings within the republican movement
seriously. That community has only limited hard information on
the innermost workings of Sinn Fein and the IRA, and many of
its conclusions about the republicans were (and are) based not on
hard fact but on guesswork – well-informed guesswork, but guesswork none the less. This lack of accurate intelligence was not
crucial in the run-up to the 1994 cessation but, as we shall see, it
was critical in the February 1996 ceasefire breakdown. At the latter
point the intelligence agencies did not warn that such a breakdown
could be imminent: the government thus thought it could keep
the pressure on Sinn Fein, in the mistaken belief that the ceasefire
could bear the strain.

The fact that so much was open to speculation led to various
theories within the intelligence world. Some, looking at the continuing violence, simply thought the republicans were not serious.
Others thought Adams was serious about peace but was unable to
persuade the hard men. Still others thought that he had most of

the hard men on board but was above all else determined to avoid a split, and would therefore not move unless and until opinion in his favour was virtually unanimous. Some of this was reflected in March 1994, when a British government source said: 'Some pretty careful assessments were made before we took things to where they are now. There is confidence that Adams is serious, but he doesn't yet speak for the whole movement by any means. The odds seem to be slightly tipped against him being able to deliver the republican movement in the short term. But the movement can't ignore the Declaration and maybe at some stage, if Adams could deliver Tyrone and Fermanagh and south Armagh, or felt he could marginalise them, then we might be taking things forward.'

Another government source, speaking around the same time, reported that opinions differed within departments but added: 'The consensus seems to be that if Adams could carry them he would go for it, but he's not prepared to do it unless he's certain that they'd nearly all fall in behind him. My guess is that his main preoccupation is to maintain the unity of the movement. He'd want the vast majority as opposed to a bare majority, I'd have thought, to minimise the sort of blood-letting that could occur. He's obviously got his own position to think about and his own life to think about.'

There is some evidence of differing opinions between the NIO and other government departments, with the suggestion that Chilcot and Thomas had considerably more hope for the Downing Street Declaration than did Mayhew, their political master. In February a Whitehall source spoke of the NIO being highly optimistic and not discouraged by Sinn Fein's failure to accept the Declaration, commenting: 'The NIO will look for beams of light in anything Adams says at the moment.' This is supported by an independent source with considerable knowledge of the NIO who said later that the feeling within the department was that some sort of ceasefire 'was a probability rather than a possibility if the circumstances could just be got right'. This source said there was considerable optimism on this point within sections of the NIO for most of the time.

The public was given a series of assessments by the RUC Chief Constable, Sir Hugh Annesley. In April 1994 he said: 'I believe we are entering the final stages and all terrorist violence will have ended in three years.' Later that same month he warned that the prospects for more violence were high, adding: 'My personal view is that the Downing Street Declaration is unquestionably a watershed, both in security terms and politically, in that it has to some degree forced the IRA into a cul-de-sac. I think it leaves the IRA wondering where to go and I have no doubt that that debate within their circles continues.'

In July he was noticeably more upbeat, saying that intelligence reports indicated a majority within the republican movement favoured the ending of the IRA campaign. Annesley said he believed the republicans were genuinely considering the idea of peace, though there were many shades of opinion within the republican movement. He added: 'There are those who would say, "We won't touch it at any price," and those who would probably say, "Yes, let's go for it." I think the way forward lies perhaps somewhere between the two.' On 22 August, nine days before the cessation announcement, he said he was 'just optimistic' about the peace process.

An intelligence source said later that they were aware of different views at different levels of the republican movement. According to this source, the republican leadership believed that an unarmed strategy, which would allow the development of a consensus within nationalism, would deliver more than IRA violence. Underneath this level, many 'middle-rankers' were sceptical of this but ready to give the leadership the benefit of the doubt. This was however subject to the stipulation that the IRA should remain intact structurally, with no hand-over or decommissioning of weapons. At the bottom end of the scale, he continued, were the volunteers who believed, as always, that the only way to deal with Britain was to 'hit them hard and keep hitting them, because it is the only thing that will move them'.

Momentous developments and changes were indeed taking place within the republican movement for, despite most outward appearances, it was moving towards a cessation. Years earlier one of its leading figures, Danny Morrison, had spoken of wielding a ballot paper in one hand and an Armalite in the other: now the leadership had concluded that the time was fast approaching when it could no longer utilise both, and had to opt for one or the other.

Reynolds, anxious to ensure that the IRA opted for nothing less than a full cessation, sent Mansergh to meet Father Reid. The two men met in early August, over breakfast at the Aherlow House hotel in County Tipperary. They discussed what ceasefire terminology would allow Dublin to give an unqualified welcome to an IRA announcement, and to welcome Sinn Fein fully into the political processes.

The IRA was heading for a ceasefire, but in the run-up to that point there would be a last-minute wave of violence tailored to achieve maximum political effect. A large part of this final flourish took the form of attacks on loyalist targets. In the case of two of those who died it may well have been a simple desire for communal revenge, for they were rumoured to be linked with the killing of five Catholics in an Ormeau Road betting shop in 1992. Joe Bratty and Raymond Elder, who were both members of the UDA, were ambushed by the IRA on the Ormeau Road just a few hundred yards from the betting shop on 31 July. They attempted to run away when they saw two men with rifles approaching them, but both were shot down. The gunmen then stood over them and pumped more bullets into their bodies, hitting Bratty eighteen times. The IRA also launched a fierce attack on the home of the Rev. William McCrea, the Democratic Unionist MP who had been Mallie's source for the document which unearthed the existence of the back-channel. The IRA's motive appears to have nothing to do with McCrea's part in this, but because they regarded him as one of the most extreme of unionist politicians. Up to forty shots were fired at his home, narrowly missing eleven people who were inside at the time. McCrea claimed he was the real target of the attack, and that his life had been saved because he was late coming home from a church service: he said he had been delayed 'by the hand of God'. In other incidents the IRA bombed three pubs in loyalist areas of Belfast in a twenty-four-hour period. No one was injured, but the attacks could hardly have been more provocative: in one case a holdall containing a bomb was left in the hallway of a bar just yards away from the scene of the Shankill fish shop bomb.

The other fatal attack came when the IRA shot and killed Ray Smallwood with three shotgun blasts outside his home in Lisburn, County Antrim. Most observers could not understand why Small-wood should have been singled out for assassination, for in the year before his death he had become the most prominent political spokesman for the UDA. He was a leading member of the Ulster Democratic party which had emerged as the UDA's political voice. It was therefore difficult to comprehend why the republicans, if they were intent on pursuing a political path, should have made a point of killing a loyalist who was apparently thinking along the same lines. It has since become known that the IRA unsuccessfully plotted to kill another leading Ulster Democratic party spokesman, Gary McMichael. In his UDA career Smallwood had been involved both in violence and in dialogue. He was one of the UDA team which shot and almost killed the former nationalist MP Bernadette McAliskey (née Devlin), in 1980. Arrested at the scene, he served a lengthy jail sentence for his action.

But in his latter years he had also become interested in political activity. He had been in frequent touch with Father Alec Reid, Father Gerry Reynolds, the Rev. Ken Newell and other members of the cross-community group, and had introduced them to members of the UDA's ruling inner council. According to Mr Newell, a strong bond had developed between Smallwood and his group, his commitment to peace impressing them. Members of the group were most upset when he was killed. Following his death they went to the loyalist Tonagh estate in Lisburn, where he was being 'waked'. According to Mr Newell: 'Loyalist paramilitary leaders were there, and Father Gerry Reynolds led the entire gathering in prayer. John White, Davy Adams and Joe English [all prominent loyalists] were there. It was quite stunning for me to see a Catholic priest leading everyone in prayer around the table.'

The priests complained bitterly to republicans about the killing.

Although Smallwood was interested in politics, it is now known that he was not a straightforward 'dove'. Several of his associates later confirmed that within loyalist circles he had argued strongly against loyalist groups following the IRA on to any ceasefire. One of Smallwood's colleagues said at the time that his killing represented 'a final fling, a final show of strength and a final bloodbath before Sinn Fein go to the talks table'. He was probably correct, though there may have been more to it than that.

It is known that one adviser to the republicans, who favoured a ceasefire, argued that the activities of the loyalist paramilitaries could be turned to the advantage of republicans. Loyalist violence was running at a high level, this argument went, and if the IRA were to call a ceasefire then loyalists might continue their violence and thus come into direct confrontation with the RUC and British army. In this circumstance the IRA could enhance its standing by acting as defenders of the Catholic community, while the loyalists and security forces could be left at each other's throats. If the IRA was indeed following this theory, then the attacks on loyalist targets make more political sense. An identical theory was later advanced independently by a senior security analyst who said: 'There was an element in republicanism saying, "Let's hit these loyalists so that they have to retaliate, and then we will hit back, then turn off the tap so the government is left only with loyalist violence to deal with."'

There were other killings too: a part-time member of the security forces was shot dead at his County Down shop on 8 August, and a major Dublin criminal figure, Martin Cahill, was killed in Dublin on 18 August, the IRA alleging he was in league with the UVF. Sinn Fein speeches and statements, on the other hand, spoke incess- antly of working towards peace and seeking a political way forward. The sheer number and length of republican statements had grown wearisome, for so many of them were long, densely written and packed with so many generalities that they were difficult to interpret with any confidence.

It was in mid-August that Danny Morrison, who had been in prison for several years and thus largely out of public view, made a brief but revealing reappearance. Freed from the Maze on parole, he launched his novel, *On the Back of the Swallow*, at a Falls Road bookshop. Journalists who attended the event were less interested in the merits of his book than in what he had to say about what was happening within republicanism. Questioned about this, his replies cut through the carefully employed fog of verbiage and obfuscation thrown up by Sinn Fein and, in a few succinct sentences, laid out the debate which was engrossing the movement. With his customary directness Morrison explained: 'The republican movement vowed years ago there would never be another ceasefire until the British government gave a clear-cut decision to withdraw. We have moderated that position and we have shown an attempt to unblock the logjam. The British government has made no similar response but let's hope it shall. Now the republican movement is talking in different time-scales because we're accepting the reality of the situation. Republicans are now attempting to explore whether or not the possibility exists of an unarmed strategy which can bring us a just settlement, however defined.'

Listening to Morrison was Richard McAuley, Gerry Adams's modest but quietly effective press aide, who was afraid Morrison was going too far in drawing back the veil. He said later: 'I sweated more during that press conference over what Danny was saying than I had during the whole of the time he was in prison.' The unarmed strategy mentioned by Morrison was exactly what the IRA was moving towards. In republican circles it was referred to as TUAS – 'totally unarmed strategy'.

The key to the republican analysis and strategy was spelled out in a confidential paper, sometimes referred to as the TUAS document, which was circulated within the IRA and Sinn Fein in the summer of 1994. (The document is reproduced in full as Appendix 3.) It laid down that the movement's goal remained 'a united 32–county democratic socialist republic', and that its strategic objectives were to build the strongest possible political consensus involving Sinn Fein, the Irish government and the SDLP, on the basis of what it called the Irish peace initiative, reinforcing this with support from the US and Europe. In a few vital sentences it spelt out in a nutshell the Adams approach:

After prolonged discussion and assessment the leadership decided that, if it could get agreement with the Dublin government, the SDLP and the Irish-American lobby on basic republican principles which would be enough to create the dynamic that would considerably advance the struggle, then it would be prepared to use the TUAS option. The leadership believes there is enough in common to create a substantial political momentum which will considerably advance the struggle at this time. The leadership has now decided that there is enough agreement to proceed with the TUAS option.

In other words, the IRA campaign was to be brought to an end because republicans were not strong enough on their own to achieve their objective, but believed progress could be made through the fashioning of a new nationalist alliance. The document referred approvingly to the attitudes of Hume, Reynolds, Clinton and the Irish-Americans, and made a list of encouraging factors:

Hume is the only SDLP person on the horizon strong enough to face the challenge. Dublin's coalition is the strongest government in 25 years or more. Reynolds has no historical baggage to hinder him and knows how popular such a consensus would be among grassroots. There is potentially a very powerful Irish-American lobby not in hock to any particular party in Ireland or Britain. Clinton is perhaps the first U.S. President in decades to be substantially influenced by such a lobby. At this time the British government is the least popular in the E.U. with other E.U. members. It is the first time in 25 years that all the major Irish nationalist parties are rowing in roughly the same direction. These combined circumstances are unlikely to gel again in the foreseeable future.

It sought to reassure those who might fear betrayal: 'It has been stated from the outset that this is a risky strategy. TUAS has been part of every other struggle in the world this century. It is vital that activists realise the struggle is not over. Another front has opened up and we should have the confidence and put in the effort to succeed on that front.'

It was the conclusion which for so many years so many people had been working, hoping and praying for. It raised many thorny questions for the future: Would the IRA grassroots accept it? Would it cause a split? Would the violent loyalists follow suit? Would the republicans get enough from a political path to prevent disillusionment and a drift back to armed conflict?

In other words, republicans were acknowledging that the combined pressure which the IRA and Sinn Fein could bring to bear was not enough to bring about British withdrawal and a united Ireland — at least, not in the way which republicans had traditionally envisaged. The IRA, with its Libyan-supplied weaponry, its quarter-century of experience in waging terrorist war, its units in Ireland and in England, had done serious damage and could inflict much more, but it could not win the war. It had killed more than 1,700 people without achieving its objective. The phenomenal destruction caused by the two City of London bombs in 1992 and 1993 must have given the IRA pause for thought and caused it to consider whether Britain might yet be brought to its knees by such attacks; but at that moment the conclusion was that they would not force the British out, and that it was time to try another way.

16

CEASEFIRE

'Do you want to keep the party alive or people alive? Whatever you think, I'm going to the end of the road. You can get rid of me if I am wrong'
   — John Hume responding to critics within the SDLP

'There will be a complete cessation of military operations'
   — IRA ceasefire statement

'On the day it was announced I was emotional; there was a lot of doubt and apprehension. We were going into a new phase of uncertainty but we trusted the leadership'
   — veteran republican activist

The leaders of Sinn Fein and the IRA have taken a policy decision not to disclose to writers, journalists or other researchers the full inside story of all the twists and turns of the process which led first to the August 1994 ceasefire and subsequently to its collapse in February 1996. A range of republican sources were helpful in piecing together parts of the picture, and research for this book has unearthed much previously unknown material, but there are almost certainly more secrets yet to be uncovered. This means that any analysis of republican thought processes may be less than complete, but even at this historically comparatively early stage some tentative conclusions can be drawn.

With hindsight, early 1992 can be seen as the period when a new approach crystallised within the republican leadership. The violence would continue for almost two years, but at the same time

Adams and his associates can be seen to be pursuing other avenues. The publication of 'Towards a Lasting Peace' in February 1992 was a very obvious sign of this. Republicans were consciously modernising their analysis and examining long-unchallenged assumptions. Adams spoke of interim phases and interim arrangements; Gibney spoke of peace and negotiation. The document defined the IRA campaign as an option of last resort, invited those who condemned it to come up with an alternative and spoke of 'an effective unarmed constitutional strategy'.

The logic ran: republicans were not strong enough on their own, and therefore needed to link up with non-violent nationalism in the form of Dublin and the SDLP. Such groups were clearly not going to build any common platform on a demand of British withdrawal, and were certainly not going to form any platform at all while the IRA campaign persisted. Rationally, therefore, the only hope for republicans to enter any new alliance was on the basis of abandoning the demand for speedy withdrawal, and of ending the IRA's campaign. The republicans were also rethinking their analysis of why Britain remained in Ireland, and of the place of Unionists in Irish politics. Consideration of both questions led them to conclude that traditional republican theory was inadequate. Britain no longer looked like a colonial power, but the IRA was left fighting an out-dated anti-colonial war. Unionists could not have a veto over all political movement, but none the less they had considerable rights.

The pivotal figure in all this was Gerry Adams. Denounced by most politicians in Britain and Ireland, those who met him face to face came away impressed by his sincerity. Hume was so convinced he was genuine that he continued their dialogue for years. Michael Lillis, the former Irish diplomat, found him 'very concentrated, very sincere, very serious'. Fianna Fáil deputy Dermot Ahern, who met him in 1988 in a Dundalk monastery, felt Adams and other republicans wanted to get off the hook of violence. It was in the spring of 1992 that the Rev. Ken Newell, after eighteen months of meetings, concluded that 'Sinn Fein were prepared to make peace' and became convinced Adams wanted to end the war.

Adams was the central personality in the peace process, but he was surrounded by a cadre of associates who thought the same way. If senior republicans such as Martin McGuinness, Mitchel McLaughlin and Pat Doherty ever disagreed with Adams on the vital issues, they gave no sign of it in public. Indeed when the momentous change of direction came no senior member of Sinn Fein showed any real sign of dissenting from it, and most could be seen working hard in support of it.

One senior republican close to Adams portrayed the process as spanning a decade:

> A political strategy was being discussed over a ten-year period, and implicit in the discussion was the possibility of developing an unarmed strategy. This came out in the Sinn Fein–SDLP papers in 1988, for example, when Sinn Fein challenged those who opposed armed struggle to put an alternative in its place. There was no vote on the ceasefire, but year after year Sinn Fein conferences voted for changing positions – on abstentionism, on 'Scenario for Peace', on 'Towards a Lasting Peace'. In that sense there was a vote for change within Sinn Fein. The ceasefire didn't just drop out of the air. This process has been leadership-led and leadership-driven, but consultation took place. People were prepared for change: discussions and dialogue were taking place all the time.

The idea of a cessation was a historic one. Since 1970 the IRA had been prosecuting a determined war against the British. Many of its members had been born and grown up in war, and had never known anything else. A generation had been raised on the belief that the IRA was the cutting edge of Irish nationalism, that the only thing the British understood was force and that, without the gun, republicans would be at the mercy of the hostile British and the even more hostile loyalists. Gerry Adams commanded immense respect throughout the movement, but his role, and that of Sinn Fein, had generally been viewed as an adjunct to the IRA campaign. Abandoning that campaign to rely entirely on Sinn Fein's political influence was a leap in the dark. There were hopeful signs for republicans, as outlined in the TUAS document, but there were also many unpromising portents. The British government, for example, had often appeared uninterested in the peace process. In its secret talks with Sinn Fein it had misled them, let them down and, in republican eyes, acted in duplicitous bad faith.

Meanwhile Unionism looked, to republicans, as adamantly opposed as ever to the concept of a united Ireland or to the idea of reaching any agreement with republicans. The Rev. Ian Paisley had won more than half the Unionist vote in European election contests. The Ulster Unionist party, while less stridently extreme than Paisley, showed no signs of seriously attempting to reach accommodation with the SDLP, let alone Sinn Fein.

The republicans would obviously have preferred to end the IRA campaign in a way which put British policy firmly on an all-Ireland course, setting the scene for the ending of the union within a reasonable time-scale. Plainly, however, the Downing Street Declaration did not do that, nor did it commit London to acting as effective persuaders in favour of Irish unity. Paddy McGrory's contention that the document was bad news for Unionists was interesting but unproven. The cessation was to be a unilateral gesture: the republicans had reached no agreement or understandings with the British government, and did not pretend they had.

The question hung in the air: how much leverage would a non-violent republican movement have? Sinn Fein was assured of a seat at the Dublin Forum for Peace and Reconciliation, and entry into the political processes in the south. All the major parties in the Republic had, however, signed up for the Downing Street Declaration with its emphasis on consent, and there seemed little immediate prospect of Sinn Fein changing minds on that fundamental point. Crucially, the near-universal endorsement of the Declaration meant that the vital issue of self-determination had been decided on, signed, sealed and delivered, before the Forum was ever convened. There already existed a strong constitutional nationalist consensus that self-determination could not be separated from consent: in practice it was accepted that Northern Ireland would be part of the United Kingdom for the foreseeable future. Reynolds had been given a standing ovation in the Dáil for negotiating an essentially partitionist settlement, so there was little prospect of the Forum providing the 'dynamic' sought by the republicans.

But set against all these points was the crucial republican assessment – 'that republicans at this time and on their own do not have the strength to achieve the end goal'. The leap in the dark was therefore about to be taken.

One of the highest priorities of the republicans, as the move towards cessation gathered momentum, was to avoid a split in the ranks. Although the rupture with O Bradaigh in 1986 had not been a particularly serious one, the old guard taking only a small number of people with them, it was a reminder of the type of fissures which had always bedevilled the republican movement. The brain – the leaders of Sinn Fein and most of the leaders of the IRA – had become convinced that the campaign of violence had run its course, but that message had to be sent out to other parts of the body. This was a sensitive, delicate process, for this was a movement whose central and indeed defining component was an army, and that army was about to be ordered to stop fighting. The movement was a far-flung body with many constituent parts. The IRA has many layers, including the ruling army council and a structure of brigades and 'active service units'. Sinn Fein had many branches and was also important, but in addition significant parts were played in different ways, by various other components, including prisoners held in the north, the south, in England and on the continent; by the families of those in jail; the families of those killed; and by many former IRA activists who are respected and whose opinion counts in their local communities. The task of explaining the proposed new unarmed strategy to people so accustomed to militarism was lengthy and often difficult. It took so long, in fact, that by the time the cessation was declared many had lost all faith in the process.

The cessation, was, however, on its way, and the IRA had by this stage decided the terms on which it would come. Military operations would cease, but the IRA would be free to continue with measures which it defined as 'policing' – that is to say, carrying out punishment beatings of alleged drug-dealers and others it deemed guilty of 'anti-social activities'. It also felt free to go further on occasion and actually kill such people.

The IRA would continue to exist and to recruit, train, raise funds, and carry out surveillance on possible targets, in case the ceasefire did not lead to inclusive talks and negotiations on a new political settlement. It would not decommission, destroy or hand over a single ounce of explosives, a single gun, or a single bullet since these would be acts of capitulation to the British. It was to be a disengagement from armed conflict, but it was not to be a surrender.

By August the decision to call off the campaign had been taken but was not yet generally known. By that stage many had concluded the IRA must never have been serious; some assumed Adams was sincere but had not been able to sell a cessation to the hard men; many were simply tired of waiting.

Such feelings were to be found within Hume's party, the SDLP. Hume had been the driving force in the party since its foundation and its leader since 1979. He was widely admired in the ranks, and over all the years there had never been even the suggestion of a leadership challenge. His leadership was still not in question, but doubts about the wisdom of persevering with the peace process had steadily mounted. Many in the party were accustomed to viewing politics in primarily institutional terms, which is to say their first priority was the well-being of the SDLP as a party. Sinn Fein, viewed from this perspective, were not only supporters of violence but also the SDLP's most direct rival for votes, and the sight of their party leader consorting with Adams and issuing joint statements with him sowed confusion and unease. The trauma of the many loyalist petrol-bomb attacks on SDLP homes added an extra dimension, for the UDA made it clear these were as a direct result of the Hume–Adams relationship.

For many months the party's other three MPs – Seamus Mallon, Eddie McGrady and Dr Joe Hendron – had both publicly and privately made no secret of the fact that they did not share Hume's commitment to the process. As the months passed with no sign of a ceasefire tensions rose, finally coming to a head on 18 August.

On that day Mallon issued a lengthy press statement saying baldly that it was clear there would not be a total cessation of IRA violence. If the republicans did not end their violence, he declared, they should be 'removed from any further involvement in the process of creating peace'. This was a direct contradiction to the approach Hume had been pursuing for so many months. At 5 p.m. that day SDLP constituency representatives met in south Belfast, and as they gathered in party headquarters all were aware it would be a meeting of the greatest importance.

By this stage Hume's health had improved after his stay in hospital in late 1993, but he remained under intense pressure. Parts of the Dublin media continued to pillory him on an almost weekly basis, and as the violence continued the view had grown that he had staked his reputation on a process which appeared to have failed. The Mallon statement now represented a direct and open challenge to his political judgement. The following account of the meeting came from a reliable SDLP source who attended it. Its important points have been verified by a number of other party members.

> There appeared to be a lot of self-doubt at the meeting. They seemed to lack confidence to go with a political process in which we hadn't been involved before and which was a radical change for us. The problem was that people had built up false expectations of the Letterkenny conference. There was a fear that the SDLP was being strung along, though a number of people firmly believed we should not waste a chance of bringing about the ending of violence.
>
> At the outset of the meeting Hume said he had been given an assurance there would be an announcement about a ceasefire within weeks. Joe Hendron, who was chairing the meeting, spoke of his deep anxiety after Letterkenny. He invited Seamus Mallon to say something but Seamus bounced the ball back to Joe, saying he wasn't prepared for play just yet. Frank Feely [who was close to Mallon] started talking. He said this was too dangerous and unwise to continue. John Hume went into recoil mode. He folded his arms, looked down at the table and then he asked Feely to listen to himself and what he was saying.
>
> Donovan McClelland said he was utterly confused – people in

his area were getting fed up with the lack of progress, and frustration was developing because we were not engaging in discussions with the other constitutional parties. Sean Farren came in and he talked about the Letterkenny meeting. He was concluding the signals from Letterkenny had not left much hope or point in continuing on. He emphasised his worry that the SDLP was losing credibility among its moderate voters, felt we could be losing out because we were continuing in a bilateral mode with Sinn Fein only. Sean said there wasn't much hope left, felt Adams was not in a position to deliver the extremes in the republican movement, but he said that on balance, based on John's advice, we should wait a bit longer.

Hendron spoke of dangers and of the attacks there had been on his house and other people's homes. Eddie McGrady came in, and was in neutral mode – he did nothing to wreck anything, but he said time was running out. Joe Byrne argued that the outcome of Letterkenny was being misread, and was really for internal Sinn Fein consumption, what he referred to as a conditioning process for their own people. Dr Alistair McDonnell questioned whether the republicans were capable of reforming themselves into a peaceful movement.

Mallon then came in very strongly and said this whole thing was being largely conducted by the leader – the MPs were not being apprised, and he said he believed the thing was dead, the whole process of engaging with Adams was dead. He said he felt we were being taken for a ride, being mocked and laughed at.

Then John cut in, pulled the handbrake, outlined a number of instances when he had kept the MPs informed. He said he'd called with Mallon on the way to Dublin to inform him of what was going on. It was obvious Seamus, Eddie and Joe had been fairly well informed – none of them contradicted John on any of the material facts of the instances when he kept them informed. Then John really revved up and said he believed they would deliver peace. He said, 'I will continue because I believe what we are engaged in is not contrary to any of our party policies. Look, we should continue to exhaust the process as long as there is even a slim chance of ending the misery.'

I remember him being emotional – when you see him clenching his left fist you know he is displaying all his deep conviction and zeal. He also intimated he was deeply shocked at what he had been hearing from a number of speakers because he had not deviated one iota from party policy. He felt he had no apology to make to anybody for what he was doing. I remember him saying one of the duties of a leader of a political party is to take risks, especially risks which that leader felt could lead to an improved situation. He said he believed personally that Adams was sincere in the talks he'd been having with him. He said he believed the leaders of Sinn Fein were sincere, and he felt he had a duty to stay with the process in order to help them to make this momentous decision about ending the violence. He said he'd stick with it.

At another point someone said: 'We are giving the Provos too much space, too much time,' and the question of the potential danger electorally was raised. Hume replied: 'I cannot believe what I am listening to. Tell me, are people here afraid of peace?' I was worried John's nerve was being tested to the limit. Seamus was agitated and so was John. John asked: 'Do you want to keep the party alive or people alive? Do you realise what we're looking for here? This is about getting peace – this is about ending killing – this is about a chance of ending this misery and surely we should do everything in our power to help to bring that situation about.' At one point he said: 'Whatever you think, I'm going to the end of the road. You can get rid of me if I am wrong.'

The meeting ended in an atmosphere which was described as 'very, very charged'. One prominent member said: 'I was relieved we still had a party left after the meeting. It was the tightest meeting I was ever at.' Afterwards Hume, looking like a man who had been mauled, was driven back to Londonderry by Mark Durkan, who later recalled: 'He was very badly bruised. He was talking about quitting – whatever way it went, he was quitting. He said people were afraid of peace. I told him not to be going on like that. I told him the cessation would take care of a lot of things.'

Hume said later: 'The party was under enormous pressure because of the talks, party homes were being attacked and I had been asking them to wait for the IRA response. I understood the tensions and we had a very strong meeting. I said, "If I fail I will apologise – but I will apologise for failing, I will not apologise for trying." '

In the run-up to the cessation announcement Father Alec Reid was particularly anxious that nothing should go wrong at the last moment. He bombarded Reynolds with telephone calls day and night, trying to ensure everything passed off smoothly. He often visited Reynolds at his Dublin flat, as Kathleen Reynolds recalled later:

> Father Reid was nearly the cause of the breakup of our marriage. You wouldn't be in bed an hour when he would ring. He was a very insistent man – he had been so long trying, that once he got some light at the end of the tunnel he was going to make sure he held on to it. I had very little space to myself now. There were nights leading up to the ceasefire when Albert had practically forgotten he was a married man at all. He didn't know if I was in the bed or if I was there at all. Quite often I'd sit up to 2 o'clock in the morning, and he'd come in with his briefcase and his mind was away.
>
> Poor Father Reid, he'd never eat. I used to give him a cup of tea; all he ever took was a cup of tea. Poor Jean Kennedy Smith [the American Ambassador] was trying to get a holiday in France but Albert was on the phone to her night, noon and morning. I worried for Albert all the time. I didn't know what to believe: I was reading Conor Cruise O'Brien's columns, and he kept talking about civil war. I was kind of believing Conor Cruise O'Brien and I was listening to Albert: I didn't know what to think.

Reynolds, who could see the *Sunday Independent* attacks were upsetting his wife, took to hiding the paper from her.

Adams and his associates had almost everything in place for a complete cessation, but one vital area remained to be covered, the republican network in America. The republicans, anxious to avoid any chance of a split in the US, wanted their supporters there to hear about the cessation at first hand from someone they trusted. They therefore wanted to send to the US Joe Cahill, a veteran Belfast republican figure who had been associated with the IRA for more than half a century. In the 1940s he had in fact been sentenced to hang for the murder of a policeman: his sentence was commuted, but a colleague was executed. He was one of the first commanders of the Provisional IRA in Belfast in the early 1970s, and in 1973 had been arrested in the Atlantic on board a ship carrying weapons bound for the IRA. Reynolds later described his importance: 'They needed him because he had the stature and he had acceptance in the States to take the supporters through a change of direction. This was a huge move for them and consequently they weren't going to take any chances of a split in the United States.' Cahill himself said later: 'I had to be there to secure the base as the announcement was being made.' At this point the question of Cahill getting into the States assumed central importance: if he was kept out, it was said, there would be no ceasefire.

The British, however, became aware of Cahill's application for a US visa and strongly opposed it, thus sparking off a rerun of the Adams visa battle. This time Nancy Soderberg did not favour allowing Cahill to enter the States: like everyone else she had been disappointed after the Letterkenny meeting, and was increasingly sceptical of the ability of Adams to deliver a ceasefire. One problem was that the peace process had lost much credibility after Letterkenny. Another was that Cahill's terrorist record was so long and so striking.

A week before the IRA cessation Ms Soderberg was on holiday in Madrid when the telephone rang. It was Jean Kennedy Smith who told her: 'We are going to have a ceasefire – Cahill must get a visa.' Ms Soderberg recalled: 'I said, "Yeah, I'll believe it when it happens." I said we were not going to give any more visas. The entire administration agreed with me – no more visas until the ceasefire happened. I flew to Los Angeles and the phone rang there – it was Jean Kennedy Smith, again advocating that Joe Cahill needed to get a visa.' By now Father Reid was ringing Reynolds, sometimes repeatedly throughout the night, emphasising the importance of allowing Cahill into the States. Reynolds was in turn on the phone to Nancy Soderberg, applying pressure on her to convince Clinton. Reynolds recalled: 'When things were looking bad on the Cahill visa Nancy came back to me on a number of occasions, phoning me to say, "I don't think we can cross this hole for you." I said, "Well, we don't have peace if we don't have this," and she said, "You put me in a terrible position." And I said: "You always told me you were 25 per cent Irish – I need that 25 per cent Irish, all of it, every bit of it to be put to work in this case. We can't take no here – this has to be yes or we all fail." '

Reynolds was also in touch with the US State Department, who indicated that there was so much opposition from different Washington elements, including the Justice Department, the Attorney-General's Office and the State Department itself, that it would take the President himself to overrule them all. Reynolds subsequently spoke directly to Clinton. According to Reynolds:

> I asked them to tell the President that if he was going to make a negative decision to talk to me before he made it. He spoke to me from Martha's Vineyard [in Massachusetts], saying that giving a visa to Gerry Adams hadn't gone down very well in the States. He wasn't going to give Cahill a visa. He said people in America had expected a much faster response from Adams. I assured him that he had done the right thing, and we wouldn't be at the position now if he hadn't done it. The President asked, 'Have you read this man's [Cahill's] CV? You can understand the opposition from the Justice Department you know, to let some-body in with a CV like that?' I said: 'I haven't read his CV but I can well imagine, you know – there are no saints in the IRA.' I said: 'I believe you should handle it like this, give him a visa for a week and extend it afterwards if the ceasefire decision comes through, and if it doesn't, that's it.'
>
> He said, 'You're as convinced as that?' and I said, 'Yes, I wouldn't be putting that to you if I didn't believe it.' He said: 'Okay, tell those people to attend at the US embassy at 9 o'clock in the morning and we'll certainly sort them out.'

An announcement of some sort was clearly on the way from the republicans, but its exact terms were still unclear. A senior Dublin source, speaking on 15 August, said the Irish government believed the IRA might retain the right to strike back in a defensive capacity. This would make it very difficult to allow the republicans into politics, he said: 'I suspect it will be good but not necessarily good enough.' Bertie Ahern recalled seeing Reynolds at a reception in Dublin on 26 August: 'They were all talking about a ceasefire, a prolonged ceasefire – six months. Reynolds was adamant that a short ceasefire was no "f—ing good". I remember him waving his hands saying, "That's no use, that'll get us nowhere." The message he was sending out was it had to be permanent.'

Reynolds gave the same message to a delegation of Irish-Americans, led by Niall O'Dowd and Bruce Morrison, when he met them in Dublin in the same day. The Americans were travelling on to Belfast to meet Adams and Sinn Fein, and Reynolds gave them a clear message to take with them. He later recalled: 'I made it clear that we wanted a ceasefire for good or not at all. I didn't want it couched in any language that could be misinterpreted, that one meaning could be taken out of it by one person and another meaning by another. We were either going to go on the road to peace or stay on the road to violent conflict.'

The Americans met Adams, McGuinness and other Sinn Fein figures in Belfast. They arrived prepared for an argument on whether the ceasefire should be temporary or permanent, but instead Gerry Adams delighted the Americans by telling them there would be a complete cessation. O'Dowd recalled: 'The one thing I remember was how well Adams looked. He looked like a man who had a decision through and was happy with it, ready to move. I've never seen Adams so on top of things, so upbeat. The mood was one of great joy, great sense of accomplishment.'

On 28 August, a Sunday, Hume and Adams issued a statement saying they were convinced significant progress had been made and announcing: 'It is our informed opinion that the peace process remains firmly on course. We are, indeed, optimistic that the situation can be moved tangibly forward.' This provoked the latest of the hundreds of Unionist criticisms of Hume, with Molyneaux accusing him of 'supping with the devil'. But this was, ironically, the day the republicans let it be known that a complete cessation was on the way. Reynolds was informed of the decision, and given an advance copy of the announcement. He passed on the news to Clinton and to Major. He recalled: 'I said to the republican movement that I thought it was only courtesy to advise both John Major and President Clinton in advance of any statement that was going to be made. I rang John Major at his home in Huntingdon. I told him I believed there was a ceasefire on the way. He said he hoped I was right. He would be surprised if we got a permanent ceasefire, very surprised, he said, because that was not the sort of intelligence that was being given to him.'

A senior British source described Major's perspective: 'He believed it was going to happen but he didn't know when. He'd seen some evidence that it might happen but he was cautious. When the Irish government said it was going to come soon he was cautious and said, "Let's wait and see." When Albert rang up in advance and told him an IRA ceasefire was going to happen his reaction was, "Let's wait and see if it happens and if it holds. Let's not count our chickens before they are hatched." '

Three days later came the announcement. Just after 11 a.m. excited journalists and newsreaders read out an IRA statement which proclaimed: 'Recognising the potential of the current situation and in order to enhance the democratic process and underlying our definitive commitment to its success, the leadership of Oglaigh na hEireann [the IRA] have decided that as of midnight, 31 August, there will be a complete cessation of military operations.' Few people in Ireland have forgotten where they were when they heard the news that after twenty-five years of conflict and more than 3,000 deaths the IRA, one of the world's most formidable terrorist organisations, had decided to call a halt. Irish-American businessmen Bill Flynn and Bill Barry were at the American embassy in Dublin. According to Barry: 'The whole embassy staff were called together in the rotunda and the ambassador, Jean Kennedy Smith, announced there had been a ceasefire. Somebody said: 'That is what diplomacy is about.' Niall O'Dowd was in the workout room at Dublin's Berkeley Court hotel. He recollected: 'When the radio broke the news of the ceasefire I just broke down and cried. I was very proud of what Adams and those guys had done. I picked up the phone and told them I was proud of them, and told them America would not let them down.' In Washington Nancy Soderberg, his line to the Clinton administration, celebrated in her own way by going to her office at 4.30 a.m. and making a stream of phone calls. She was particularly gratified to receive calls of congratulation from the State Department, telling her she had been correct in pressing for the Adams visa.

According to a senior intelligence source, the British authorities were aware for two weeks in advance that an announcement was on its way, though they believed it would come two days earlier than it did. They also were surprised that the IRA announced a complete cessation rather than a ceasefire which was time-limited or qualified in some way. Annesley later described the RUC's reaction: 'We sat in this office day in and day out on the approach to that declaration, and when it came I have to say that the term used, a complete cessation of military operations, was significantly in excess of what we had expected. I think the expectation in the office here probably was something more of an open-ended cease-fire and therefore we were at least surprised to see that it was couched in those terms.'

When the announcement came Reynolds was attending a meeting of Fianna Fáil deputies which he had called to discuss domestic business. A tribunal into the beef industry, which had caused such political controversy and had in fact brought down the previous Reynolds administration, had just published its report. Mrs Geoghegan-Quinn recalled the scene:

> There was a great expectation. You see on the one hand you had the beef tribunal thing, people wanted to hear about what was in it and what wasn't in it, but on the other hand there was an air of expectancy that something big was about to happen. Then word began to filter into the room that the Provos were about to announce a ceasefire. The whole atmosphere was just electric: I mean everything else was forgotten about. Even people who couldn't stand Albert Reynolds were all of a sudden just terribly emotional about the whole thing.
>
> Suddenly there's a knock on the door and a piece of paper with the Taoiseach's name on it was handed in. Albert was on his feet talking. He says 'Excuse me', puts the glasses on, opens the note, closes the note, puts it down and announces that the Provisional IRA have announced a ceasefire. He then went on to read the text, and he said as he was reading it out, 'I hope to

Christ this is what they have released to the papers – this is what they told me they were going to be releasing.'

Everybody jumped to their feet, everybody clapped and screamed and roared, shouted, whistled and everything. I mean it was like, what do you say, a crucial goal in a nail-biting game and people, you know, there were tears in people's eyes. People were hugging each other, couldn't wait to get to him. He was in a mêlée just surrounded by people and people acknowledging the fact that after Letterkenny he was the only one that believed.

Brian Lenihan spoke, Bertie Ahern spoke. All of us in that room knew that we had, as a party, grown out of a war, grown out of a civil war and all that that entailed. You knew that the founder of our party, Eamon de Valera, had played such a crucial role in the civil war himself, had been involved with guns and with war over a period of time, and then had decided that he was putting them to bed and was going to go down the democratic process. All of those kinds of emotions were there – people remembered their fathers having been in that room and having worked on this problem over years and years.

John Hume had been told of the impending cessation several days earlier. He was sitting in the studios of BBC Radio Foyle in Londonderry, waiting to go on air when the news broke. Once he heard it he gave the thumbs-up sign, which had a particular significance in Londonderry. After Hume was televised using the sign in Downing Street, it had become a signal of approval for the Hume–Adams initiative, with people using it when they spotted him in the streets.

Sean Duignan described in his diary the scene in government offices:

Major rings, cautious and even sceptical, and Reynolds tells him: 'We did it together.' Albert says afterwards: 'John Major doesn't believe it's for real.' He also talks on phone to Hume. They are curiously cool and careful with each other. Is it vanity, rivalry, jealousy? 'Posterity,' says Bart [Cronin, a government press officer]. 'They're already jostling for their place in the history books.' Champagne with Dick, who is generous with praise: he made his contribution. I hope Albert and Hume stick together. Hume is my hero, the man who started the movement, but Albert took the ball and ran with it.

In republican areas it was a moment of great uncertainty. Many wondered whether Sinn Fein had reached some secret deal with the British government, but word was quickly circulated that no such deal had been done. It was an IRA initiative: the leadership that had argued that their predecessors had two decades earlier been conned by the British into going on ceasefire were now following the same path. Furthermore, they were doing so with no agreement whatever with the British. It was a huge step, undertaken unilaterally.

In west Belfast a platform was quickly rigged up outside Sinn Fein offices. Loudspeakers blared out republican tunes while a crowd gathered, uncertainty clear on their faces. Adams was cheered when he arrived with Martin McGuinness, and someone thrust a bouquet of flowers and a bottle of champagne into his hands. The crowd was in no doubt: it was over. What was completely unclear, however, were the terms on which it had finished, and what the future might hold. Adams was cheered when he praised the IRA, said the prisoners would be released, and promised them they would one day get their republic: the people of west Belfast, he said, remained undefeated despite all Britain had thrown at them. But he did not pretend the IRA or Sinn Fein had won a victory: in fact when he said that 'the core issues have not yet been resolved' he was saying nothing was settled, that they had not yet won their demands, and that they had dropped the idea of winning them by means of the IRA campaign.

Within the IRA and Sinn Fein all realised that it was nothing less than a historic moment. There were feelings of relief that it was all over, but also feelings of worry and anxiety as members wondered how successful an unarmed strategy could hope to be.

The psychological adjustment which hard-line republicans had to make was described by Martin Meehan, whose quarter-century of commitment to militancy was a legend both within and outside the movement. Meehan, who came from north Belfast, had been in the IRA right from the start of the troubles: a grainy old black-and-white photograph shows him with Adams, both wearing black berets, walking alongside the coffin at an IRA funeral.

He was in charge of one of the IRA's most active sections and was linked, by repute, with some notorious republican acts of violence, such as the killings of three off-duty teenage Scottish soldiers in 1971. Meehan had been imprisoned on numerous occasions and was acknowledged by the authorities as one of the hardest of the hard men, a living symbol of republican resistance. When internment without trial was brought to an end in 1975 he was the very last IRA suspect to be released from Long Kesh prison. In an interview for this book he described his reaction to the cessation:

> On the day the ceasefire was announced my feelings were for the IRA volunteers – the men and women who suffered, and particularly for those in jail, who included my own son. I was emotional; there was a lot of doubt and apprehension. I thought of all the sacrifices. We were going into a new phase of uncertainty but we trusted the leadership. We had men and women in the leadership who we could trust not to sell us short: it wasn't blind faith.
>
> Before the ceasefire, for two to three years everyone knew there was going to be some sort of ceasefire and talks. I personally had believed that we would achieve the objective of a united Ireland militarily, by driving the British army into the sea. But in the latter years I realised that this could not happen by military means alone, but by a combination of tactics, manoeuvres and political direction. It was difficult for people like myself. It was a mental thing for me to overcome – for twenty-three, twenty-four years you are fighting, and then in a short two to three years you come to the conclusion that there are other ways.

Martin Meehan, the quintessential republican hard man, would never apologise for anything that he and his movement had done in twenty-five years of his armed struggle. He remained proud of what he saw as the IRA's achievement and victories. But he and his associates had been persuaded that there was another way of pursuing their goal, a way which need not involve a campaign of terrorism. It was a moment of bright promise which may yet prove to be a historic turning-point: tragically, however, it was not the end of the troubles.

17

BOMBSHELL

'We offer the loved ones of all innocent victims over the past twenty-five years abject and true remorse'
— loyalist ceasefire announcement

'In my view he [Adams] was a brave man. He led them across that Rubicon. The whole of Ireland and the whole of the world is grateful to him for having done it'
— Peter Brooke

'If the hard men say, "What did Gerry Adams do, we have called a ceasefire but got nothing sufficient in return?" then Mr Adams will take a long walk on a short plank'
— Sir Patrick Mayhew

'We sued for peace, the British wanted war. If that's what they want we will give them another twenty-five years of war'
— IRA leader

'We will give blow for blow'
— response from loyalist paramilitary groups

Though it was clearly a major development, the cessation statement was received in many quarters with suspicion rather than celebration. The British government was cautious, pointing out that it had not included the word 'permanent'. Unionist politicians warned that it was a delusion and a trick rather than a genuine move, but most nationalists and republicans instinctively felt that the troubles really were over. Albert Reynolds moved quickly to demonstrate his faith in Gerry Adams, meeting him and John Hume within a

333

week of the ceasefire for a historic public handshake aimed at sealing and consolidating the peace. Reynolds and Adams had seen each other countless times on television and had sent messages to each other, but until that moment had never actually met. Reynolds recalled the occasion:

> I think Adams felt a bit nervous when he walked into my office. He showed that sense of nervousness about it, coming into the office and sitting down, talking. But I was certainly impressed: he was very quiet and soft-spoken, probably not what I expected. I was expecting a more robust approach, the aggressive type of approach that you see at times on television. But that wasn't it, it was a different kind of manner. Then Hume comes in and it was a great day for Ireland. Everybody had tea. Adams walked around, a cup of tea in his hand. We had buns. It was very upbeat and celebratory as an occasion.

The occasion was conceived primarily as a photo-call, to broadcast to the world the image of the republican entry into the political system. But a few hours before it took place, Hume, in his room in Jury's hotel in Dublin, mapped out on the hotel's notepaper a joint statement in which the three leaders of nationalism declared themselves 'totally and absolutely committed to democratic and peaceful methods of resolving our political problems'. Reynolds agreed the statement, though Adams suggested a small change, which was accepted. The three men then went outside where, as Reynolds recalled, they faced dozens of television cameras:

> Outside, on the steps, I shake hands with Gerry, I shake hands with John. Somebody shouts that we have to have it all together, and the two hands came and I put mine on top of them. This was the coming together of those who had driven the peace process. I can understand people who lost their loved ones and relatives feeling a bit sick when they saw me shaking hands with Gerry Adams on the steps. But if that handshake was to ensure that no more loved ones were going to be killed on either side, somebody had to do it. I felt honoured to have the opportunity of doing it.

As the weeks passed and the ceasefire held, another momentous occasion came. In October 1994, the loyalist paramilitary groups followed the IRA's lead. In a community centre in north Belfast, a man called Gusty Spence announced that for the loyalists, too, the violence was over. It was another electric moment, filled with historic echoes, for Spence had once been a hero for violent loyalists, after being jailed in the 1960s for one of the first sectarian assassinations.

Like many other loyalists, Spence had mellowed in prison and become a firm supporter of peace. The loyalist announcement set a new tone by including an unexpected note of apology, as Spence offered 'the loved ones of all innocent victims over the past twenty-five years abject and true remorse'. This new note confirmed the emergence from that violent underworld of militant loyalism of a new political element whose role was to be analogous to Sinn Fein's role in the republican movement. Groups such as the UVF and UDA remained, and retained their capacity for violence, but now they adopted a ceasefire and sprouted new political wings. The UVF produced the Progressive Unionist party, with articulate new spokesmen such as David Ervine and Billy Hutchinson, while Gary McMichael and the Ulster Democratic party spoke for the UDA. Some of these political loyalists had for months been in close touch with reconciliation workers such as Father Reid and Father Reynolds.

The loyalist ceasefire announcement took six weeks in coming, but when it did it came not in a spirit of suspicion but of generosity and goodwill. This was to the astonishment of almost everyone, since only months earlier loyalist violence had been raging at a high level, and the appetite for war had seemed strong. But many of the new spokesmen were ex-prisoners, who had learned the hard way the cost of violence, and had looked for other ways forward. Some had served life sentences, spending a dozen or more years behind bars, on their release becoming involved in community work. A number had discreet contacts with republicans whom they had met in jail, had come to know individual IRA members, and were convinced the IRA cessation was genuine. This hidden network of relationships helped to break down barriers of mistrust between the two sides. The old loyalist paramilitary rhetoric of bluster and belligerence gave way to a new language of compromise. In October 1994, for example, David Ervine told a conference:

> The politics of division see thousands of people dead, most of them working class, and headstones on the graves of young men. We have been fools: let's not be fools any longer. All elements must be comfortable within Northern Ireland. We have got to extend the hand of friendship, we have got to take the peacelines down brick by brick, and somehow or other we have got to introduce class politics. You can't eat a flag. Unionism, I believe, has got lost against a background of violence, which was preceded by a background of patronage and suppression. Edward Carson said, 'Look after the minority.' We didn't – and have we suffered for it. We have got to appeal to the Catholics, because Catholics, at least some of them, have shown their willingness to be Unionist. Unionism is a wholly legitimate philosophy which has the right to be heard, but we have found ourselves friendless. We're going to have to be honourable with each other's aspirations. That means I will concede not my nationality but my friendship.

The sight of the previously violent loyalists embracing the peace process with such unexpected and evidently genuine enthusiasm was as welcome as it was surprising. It gave the process a huge boost, for many had assumed that the loyalist groups would pose an active threat. Instead, they became a force for moderation, anxious for talks with the government and others, and presenting a much more open-minded approach than mainstream Unionist politicians. Ulster Unionist MPs by contrast claimed the ceasefire was a ruse, making repeated predictions that it would break down either in January 1995 or at Easter of that year. MP William Ross urged the British government to ignore the calls for concessions to republicans 'from all sorts of do-gooders and fools across the world'. The Rev. Ian Paisley, meanwhile, declared that Protestants faced 'the worst crisis in Ulster's history since the setting up of the state'. He told his party conference:

> Are we going to agree to a partnership with the IRA men of blood who have slain our loved ones, destroyed our country,

burned our churches, tortured our people and now demand that we should become slaves in a country fit only for nuns' men and monks' women to live in? We cannot bow the knee to these traitors in Whitehall, nor to those offspring of the Vatican who walk the corrupted corridors of power in Dublin, in Europe and in Washington. In the propaganda war we must excel, answering the lies with truth, and smoking out from their lairs the media skunks, cleansing their putrid odour from the face of Ulster's earth.

Most people, however, did not subscribe to the theory that the IRA cessation was a trick, believing or hoping that it offered a new opportunity for lasting peace. The days and weeks after the announcement were marked by a swirl of competing feelings within the republican camp, including hope, fear, nervousness and uncertainty. It gradually became clear, however, that there was widespread approval for the IRA move. The republican community – the IRA, Sinn Fein, and their supporters – had maintained a war for a quarter of a century, and there was no real doubt that the violence could have been sustained. Yet the decision to stop was a popular one in almost all quarters. Within the leadership of the IRA there were those who had doubts, but the majority of republicans welcomed the cessation of violence. As it emerged that the republican movement was united in the decision to call off the campaign, and that Reynolds and Hume were welcoming Sinn Fein into the nationalist mainstream, the predominant emotion was one of relief.

Some of that sense of relief turned to irritation, and then by stages into a much more sour and dangerous anger, when it gradually became clear that the British government was not intent on making the type of 'flexible and imaginative' response which had been promised by Peter Brooke. In the early weeks of the ceasefire Major and Mayhew repeatedly called on republicans to use the word 'permanent' in relation to the cessation: the republicans would not, though they used a variety of formulations with the aim of conveying that the IRA had no intention of resuming its campaign. After some time, the British government announced that it was making a 'working assumption' that the cessation would last.

Mayhew explained: 'We were denied an explicit assurance of permanence, yet the peace was holding, and we wanted to build on it.'

Within weeks of the cessation, in fact, the British government had made a private assessment that the start of all-inclusive round-table negotiations was probably two years away. A senior British source said at the time:

> Bringing all concerned to the table for full negotiations on a political settlement will take, at our first rough guess, two years. Obviously that assessment will have to be updated as things happen. But the goals for the next two years are to have completed negotiating most of the peace process, downscaling or demilitarising the security effort, getting Sinn Fein up to scratch and all of that. Then, after that, you start the equally tricky process of negotiating a political settlement. If we play our cards very carefully and don't let either the republican side or the loyalist side get completely disillusioned then we're into a proper negotiated peace. But there's many a slip 'twixt cup and lip, there are minefields all over the place, and it will need a lot of very careful handling.

Such an approach was received with near-incredulity by republicans and nationalists, illustrating the eternal cultural, psychological and temperamental gap which exists between Britain and Irish nationalism. The Irish, regarding the cessation as genuine and a historic opportunity, wished to move with all speed to enfold the republicans into the political system before any of the IRA hard men had the chance to have second thoughts. Most nationalists wanted and expected talks to start within a few months, but in contrast to this attitude the British government exuded scepticism and suspicion, refusing to concede that in stopping their killings the republicans had done anything commendable. There was no question of acknowledging that the IRA had done something admirable and of making a reciprocal gesture; rather, the onus was still on the IRA to prove that its change of heart was genuine and irreversible.

This British attitude, which took shape within weeks of the cessation announcement, was to prevail throughout the seventeen months of the ceasefire. The republicans were to receive no public credit for the ceasefire, and were to be kept under constant pressure to prove their bona fides and to make more concessions. To the British this was proper and prudent caution; to the republicans it was minimalist, begrudging and ungenerous. It was almost as though the British and the republicans were playing a game of chess, but could not agree on whose turn it was to move.

From the very beginning, Dublin sources saw dangers in the British approach. Speaking in September 1994, a senior Dublin source said, in a comment which, with the hindsight of 1996, seems almost eerily prophetic:

There are a lot of worries that our British friends don't seem to quite understand what's happening. The thing of making a fetish of the word 'permanent', when the whole tenor of the thing was plain to see, seems odd. This gratuitous stuff from the British doesn't actually reassure the Unionists. There is growing concern at the inability of the British to actually read the potential of the present situation, and their capacity for getting impaled on ritual-istic side issues. We can't for the life of us see the need to inject all these negative notes that nothing can be done until something is somehow proven. I don't know where British pragmatism has gone to.

You have to say that Adams has taken the greatest risk of all, and then it's very dangerous if the British seem to confirm that once the heat is off they may start getting tough and playing hardball again. We don't actually doubt that the cessation state-ment means what it says, and that the present Sinn Fein leadership are basically irretrievably identified with this policy. The only danger would be that they're upset by failing to deliver on the ground. We keep saying to the British, 'Look, these guys are sincere, they intend it to be permanent. Whether it does in fact become so is a matter of history – and you're not spectators in that, you have a leading role to play one way or the other.'

An awful lot of things could still go wrong. We're not saying there's a big wave of protest waiting in the wings or anything like that. It's just that in the long-term everyone, including Adams, has a constituency, and if you get that massively wrong something happens. We're not saying it's happening as yet, but if it goes on long enough people begin to wonder what the hell is happening. It's not at the point where there's any real danger as yet, but on the other hand if everything were to continue in this vein indefinitely then something would give eventually. We don't deny the British the right to be prudent, but there's a certain point where this argument is absolutely circular. It can't be permanent until they say it is; the longer the British take to say it's permanent the more they undermine the chances of it becoming truly so.

Dublin pressed ahead with the approach of welcoming the republicans into politics, with the first meeting of the Forum for Peace and Reconciliation, as promised in the various declarations, taking place in late October.

Viewed from London, however, things looked very different. John Major was a Conservative prime minister who, in spite of his undoubted personal commitment to working for peace in Northern Ireland, had never shown a full grasp of republican psychology. He had visited Northern Ireland frequently but when he walked around Belfast he was, understandably enough, surrounded by bodyguards. An IRA mortar bomb, fired into Downing Street, had missed him by a matter of yards. While he had established working relationships with constitutional nationalists such as Albert Reynolds, he had never spent an evening with an Irish republican. During the seventeen months of the ceasefire he never, so far as is known, talked to any member of Sinn Fein. He had gone along with the peace process reluctantly, in response to unremitting private and public pressure from Dublin and from Hume. His intelligence agencies, which had failed to forewarn him that a complete cessation was on the way, clearly had an incomplete understanding of the republican mindset and psyche. His Northern Ireland Secretary, Sir Patrick Mayhew, displayed no instinctive feel for the situation, and harboured the deepest doubts about the whole enterprise.

Other factors prevailed on Major to respond to the cessation with the utmost caution. The Unionist community was clearly uncertain and nervous about the future, and although many grassroots Protestants welcomed the ceasefire, most of their political representatives found it an unsettling experience. One Unionist politician remarked privately: 'Our people like the peace, but they don't like the peace process.' James Molyneaux and other Unionist politicians recommended handling the cessation as gingerly as a suspect bomb; and Molyneaux had valuable Commons votes which in some circumstances could be crucial to the Major government's survival.

Major's majority throughout this period was tiny and dwindling, and the Tory backbenches contained a number of potential right-wing rebels who greatly undermined the government's security of tenure. At every stage of the peace process Major had to look over his shoulder, aware that a false move could endanger his administration. It is not the case, as some nationalist critics would claim, that his approach was dominated by the desire not to antag-onise the Unionists or the restless right – he took a number of actions which were most unpopular with Unionist MPs – but government sources nonetheless readily confirmed in private that the potentially perilous parliamentary arithmetic was a factor Major could not afford to ignore.

Within weeks of the ceasefire it became obvious that the 'cess-ation of military operations' did not mean that the IRA would be entirely inactive. Since the 1970s the IRA and other terrorist groups had punished alleged wrong-doers in republican areas by 'kneecap-ping' them – shooting them in the legs – or by beating them. After the cessation the kneecappings ended but the beatings continued. Scores of youths and men who were said to be joyriders, burglars or 'anti-social elements' were beaten savagely, often with sticks and iron bars. Many suffered broken limbs. Such actions served a number of purposes for the IRA and for the loyalist groups who carried out similar assaults in Protestant areas. They helped maintain paramilitary authority in the ghettos, showing that the IRA had not become a toothless tiger; and they were also popular with many in the ghettos as a brutal but immediate form of communal retribution against miscreants.

It also emerged, in October 1994, that the IRA was still watching members of the security forces, and continued to size up potential targets for attack in both Northern Ireland and Britain. A London security source said: 'Adams is under pressure from hardliners, and they are reappraising the vulnerability of certain targets which appear to have reduced security. If the ceasefire ended tomorrow they would go for a big target in the City. We're continuing to monitor suspects and sympathisers because they are still assessing targets.'

November 1994 brought a moment of crisis when a postal worker, Frank Kerr, was shot dead during an IRA robbery in Newry, County Down. The ceasefire seemed in doubt, but the IRA leadership quickly issued a statement saying it had not sanctioned the robbery and had granted no one permission to use arms. It added that responsibility for the incident lay with 'an identified problem in the IRA chain of command' which it said had been rectified. It added: 'We have established that Frank Kerr was shot in the midst of an intense scuffle with one of our volunteers and we take this opportunity to offer sincere apologies to his family and friends.' The killing caused real alarm in Belfast, London and Dublin. In the Republic, Maire Geoghegan-Quinn, as Justice Minister, had made it clear that several dozen IRA prisoners could expect early release as a response to the cessation. The murder of Frank Kerr, however, clearly raised a fundamental question about the IRA's commitment to the ceasefire. Mrs Geoghegan-Quinn later recalled:

Immediately after the ceasefire I sat down with the Secretary of the Department of Prisons. We went through the whole list of all the Provo prisoners and looked at how much had they served, what their period in prison had been like, their conduct and all that. A number were to be let out before Christmas to show the goodwill of the Irish government, and we started on that straight away. Then I'm in a car going to a function somewhere in Dublin and the message comes into Garda headquarters that this shooting has happened in Newry. The Secretary of the Justice Department rings me to say that the word is out that the Provos were involved, that while they feel it mightn't have been an official act of the Provos, that most definitely there was evidence to suggest that some element of the Provos had been involved.

I said to him, 'We'd better cancel the releases immediately.' On the mobile phone I rang the Taoiseach's office, asked where he was, and they told me he was at a function. I rang his security car, got one of his security men who told me he couldn't tell me the location – it later turned out he was in a hospital having his blood checked. I said I couldn't care less where he was, bring the mobile phone to him. I said: 'Even if he's in the loo bring it to him. I need to talk to him now.' So I told him what had happened. Before I had a chance to tell him the releases had been cancelled, he said: 'Cancel the releases.' I said I'd already done that.

It was an enormous blow. It really hit in the pit of your stomach and I know that he was very angry about it. Father Reid made almost immediate contact with Martin Mansergh to reassure him that this had not been officially sanctioned in any way, and had been done by people who hadn't looked for official sanction.

Within weeks of the Newry killing came another event which shook the peace process, and which indeed in the longer term had even deeper implications for it: the fall of Albert Reynolds. Following the ceasefire, the Fianna Fáil leader's standing had never been higher. Hailed as the hero of the peace process, he was seen as the Taoiseach who had succeeded where all his predecessors had tried and failed. Yet within a few months of his moment of glory, he became embroiled in a controversy concerning a Catholic priest accused of molesting children in Northern Ireland. Allegations that someone in authority in Dublin had attempted to prevent the priest's extradition from south to north grew into a full-scale crisis. When this undermined confidence in the Reynolds administration, Dick Spring withdrew the Labour party from the coalition, the government fell, and Reynolds resigned. Rarely can such a political triumph have been followed so quickly by political oblivion. The country could scarcely believe it and nor could Reynolds himself. There was a catch in his voice as he spoke his last words in the Dáil as Taoiseach: 'It's amazing. You cross the big hurdles, and when you get to the small ones you get tripped.'

There was some initial trepidation that the fall of Reynolds might be destabilising, but the peace process at that point looked so steady that the worry quickly receded. Although the details of Reynolds's efforts to convince John Major to back the peace process, as outlined in this book, were unknown to the general public, it was widely appreciated that he had been a key figure in helping to bring about the cessation. But the general view was that peace had come to stay, and that the process was robust enough to survive such domestic political turbulence.

The makeup of the next Irish government was not immediately known: it seemed certain that Spring's Labour party would be back in government, but for some weeks it was unclear whether he would form a new coalition with Bertie Ahern, Reynolds's successor as leader of Fianna Fáil, or make an arrangement with Fine Gael under its leader, John Bruton.

In the end, Spring opted for a three-way coalition with Bruton and a smaller left-wing party, Democratic Left. It was an outcome which caused Sinn Fein hearts to sink. The republican TUAS (totally unarmed strategy) document, it will be recalled, had cited Reynolds as one of the factors which had led to the IRA cessation: 'Dublin's coalition is the strongest government in twenty-five years or more. Reynolds has no historical baggage to hinder him . . . It is the first time in twenty-five years that all the major Irish nationalist parties are rowing in roughly the same direction.' Now, suddenly and unexpectedly, John Bruton was Taoiseach, and looked likely to row in a very different direction.

The new Taoiseach had been a frequent critic of the peace process. His party, Fine Gael, had a strong law and order tendency and, for reasons stretching back for decades, was bitterly anti-IRA and anti-Sinn Fein. The party in general and Bruton in particular lacked the empathy with the republican tradition which Reynolds had displayed. On the day of the IRA cessation in August 1994, Bruton told the Dáil: 'I saw a member of my own party, also a member of this House, murdered by the IRA. That experience stayed with me and I will carry it to my grave. It makes it difficult for me sometimes to accept people's good faith. I hope other members of the House will realise that it is difficult for me.' (The murdered man Bruton referred to was Billy Fox, a Fine Gael Senator killed by republicans in 1974.)

Within minutes of Reynolds's resignation, Bruton was on his feet in the Dáil giving an assurance that the peace process would be safe with him. He said: 'I have had to ask him [Reynolds] difficult questions but I hope he understands that is my job, and I do so in order to ensure that the peace process may be more durable, having been tested more carefully.' Despite such assurances, however, it was obvious that Bruton was unlikely to pursue the process with the same commitment as Reynolds.

Bruton had for many years in opposition pursued a policy of reaching out to northern Unionists – so much so that Reynolds had once referred to him as 'John Unionist'. His theory was that if concessions were made to Unionists they in turn would relax some of their attitudes, thus making political accommodation more possible. Reynolds had, as we have seen, made some moves towards Unionists, and during negotiations on the Downing Street Declaration had closely consulted with the Rev. Roy Magee and Archbishop Robin Eames. But he had concentrated on the republicans, encouraging them along the political path and persuading the British to move some way towards meeting them. Acting on a theory formulated by Hume and O hUiginn, his approach had been to deal in the first instance with the IRA and Sinn Fein, in the belief that the achievement of a ceasefire would make a later accommodation between nationalists and Unionists easier to achieve.

The republicans had looked to Reynolds to fight their corner with the British, commending him for in effect acting as one of the leaders of a broad nationalist front. Bruton, by contrast, was so anxious to impress Unionists that he had come to regard himself as a leader who should speak for both traditions in Ireland. He had earlier worried both Sinn Fein and the SDLP by declaring: 'We have got to re-think our whole attitude to Northern Ireland. We must say that we have no special relationship with anybody there on the basis of religion or ethnic origin alone.' Bruton, in other words, had moved away from the traditional view that an Irish Taoiseach had a particular duty to sponsor and speak for the interests of the northern nationalist minority. It was Reynolds's commitment to this role which had helped bring the ceasefire about.

Bruton's partners in government also worried the republicans. Spring, who would continue as Foreign Minister, had never obstructed the peace process, but prior to the ceasefire had not been one of its most enthusiastic supporters. (He would, in fact, become much more closely identified with it, but this was not known at the time.) Another source of republican concern was the fact that the third party in the new coalition was to be Democratic Left, under the leadership of Pronsias de Rossa. This party had its roots in the old official republican movement, which had parted company with the Provisional republicans in the early 1970s. The split had been a bitter one, with a number of deaths in violent feuds in Belfast in its early days. De Rossa's party had long since left the gun behind, but the passing years had done little to lessen the real hatred between his movement and Sinn Fein. His presence in the Irish government, along with that of Bruton, represented in Sinn Fein eyes the cabinet from hell.

All this was a source of dismay to Adams and his associates, who had sold the cessation idea to the IRA on the basis that Sinn Fein would be taking its place within a powerful broad coalition, with all nationalist parties 'rowing in roughly the same direction'. Bruton would not set out to derail the peace process, but he clearly would never have the same enthusiasm for it as Reynolds. The republican fears were to be borne out, for within months Bruton would indeed set off in a different direction, thereby seriously undermining the peace process in republican eyes.

As the months passed, day-to-day life in Northern Ireland steadily improved. Army patrols became less and less frequent, while the RUC visibly relaxed. Police officers went on the streets without their flak-jackets and their rifles. Armoured Land Rovers were increasingly replaced by saloon cars and even motor-cycle patrols. Many cross-border roads which had been closed for decades were re-opened, while in a number of areas of Belfast peaceline barriers were unlocked. In the new more relaxed atmosphere hundreds of southerners ventured north for the first time in years, to shop and visit places they had only ever seen on television. Dozens of conferences were held to discuss the political future, how the economy could be re-built, and how a peaceful society should be policed.

By December 1994, Sinn Fein representatives had met Reynolds and Bruton and were in regular contact, through meetings at the Dublin forum, with almost every major political figure in the Republic. It was not until 9 December, however, that a Sinn Fein delegation led by Martin McGuinness first met British government officials at Stormont. There were five such meetings. Sinn Fein pressed to meet a government minister, but the British resisted. The republicans sought movement on a range of issues, including the transfer of IRA members jailed in Britain and early release for all republican prisoners, and, above all, the opening of all-party talks.

The British were in no hurry to convene talks, however, and in any case a number of other events intervened to cause delay. The formation of the new Bruton-led Irish government had taken a number of weeks, holding up publication of what was known as the 'framework document', which was eventually published in February 1995.

This document was a booklet, published jointly by the British and Irish governments and largely written by Dublin diplomat Sean O hUiginn, in which they set out a joint vision of the future. The lengthy document depicted a future in which Northern Ireland would clearly remain part of the United Kingdom, and stressed the importance of Unionist consent. But it also stipulated that the Irishness of nationalists should be formally expressed through an increasing Dublin input, most visibly through new cross-border institutions. Unionist politicians took strong exception to the document, refusing to accept it even as a basis for negotiations, while nationalists, by contrast, welcomed it. Sinn Fein refrained from detailed comment, though one senior republican privately described it as 'brilliant'.

Although some Unionist politicians, in particular MPs David Trimble and John Taylor, angrily denounced the framework document, it was noticeable that much of the Unionist grassroots took a more relaxed view of its approach. Once the dust had settled after its publication, Northern Ireland seemed destined for a period of intensive negotiations. Those who expected and hoped for this were to be disappointed, however, for the year that followed was dominated not by negotiation but by a protracted argument about the IRA's weapons. The British government was eventually to reduce its emphasis on the issue, but for the rest of 1995 the question of decommissioning was the centrepiece of debate.

The matter of what should be done with illegal weaponry once violence has been halted is obviously one of the most important issues in conflict resolution. During 1995, however, the peace process virtually stalled on the question of when arms decommissioning should take place. The issue of what to do with weapons in the event of an end to violence had cropped up in 1993, during Martin Mansergh's talks with Sinn Fein, but it had not been emphasised. It had been mentioned in the 'Steps Envisaged' document sent by Reynolds to Sinn Fein in the spring of that year, though only in the last of its seven paragraphs. It was also addressed by Dick Spring who, on the day that the Downing Street Declaration was published in December 1993, said that establishing a permanent cessation meant handing up arms. Sean Duignan recalls Dermot Nally saying to him at that point: 'He [Reynolds] must stop talking of stiffer security measures, or the handing over of guns. They [Sinn Fein/ IRA] will walk away if we persevere with that kind of talk.'

In the wake of the IRA cessation, Major and Mayhew repeatedly called on the organisation to give up its weapons, and journalists regularly pressed Gerry Adams on this point. Adams delivered what was to become the familiar republican response: 'I think the whole issue of decommissioning of weapons obviously has to be part of finding a political settlement, and there couldn't be a political settlement without that. But I don't think there's any point in anyone trying to leap ahead on any of these issues. Let's get a political settlement and of course let's get all of the guns out of Irish politics.'

In essence, the Reynolds administration took much the same

view, regarding decommissioning as an important point to be dealt with during round-table negotiations. The issue was discussed at an Anglo-Irish summit at Chequers in October 1994, but Dublin tended to dismiss suggestions that the British might be intent on turning it into a sticking-point. A Dublin source said at the time: 'There was some discussion on the arms issue, but our people thought it was on a fairly realistic basis – you never quite know. If you wanted to isolate Sinn Fein I suppose it would be a great thing to give them an exam they couldn't pass, but we were fairly satisfied that wasn't the game plan.'

In March 1995, however, important adjustments were made to the positions of both governments. Mayhew, during a visit to Washington, said of the IRA: 'It is still in being, still maintains its arsenal, is still recruiting, targeting and training, still seeking funds, still carrying out punishment beatings.' He went on to lay down three new conditions which would have to be met before Sinn Fein could be admitted to all-party talks. Republicans would first have to demonstrate a willingness in principle to disarm, and, second, come to an understanding on the practicalities of decommissioning. Then, in what came to be known as 'Washington 3', he insisted on 'the actual decommissioning of some arms as a tangible confidence-building measure' in advance of talks.

To begin with, Washington 3 was not generally regarded as being critically important. It was a very clear requirement, yet the government had laid down such conditions before, only to move away from them at a later stage. As the months passed, however, London continued to insist on it, making republican entry into talks directly dependent on the decommissioning of some weapons. Yet practically everyone in Ireland knew that it was impossible to conceive of the IRA giving up guns in advance of talks. The first two Washington pre-conditions posed no real problem for the republicans, but to insist that guns had to be decommissioned before negotiations began was indeed to set them an exam they could not pass.

As already noted, the IRA had disengaged from armed conflict but had not surrendered. It had agreed to the Sinn Fein recommendation for a cessation, but had made it clear that it ruled out any handover of arms, since this would be an act of capitulation to the British. There was also a great deal of historical baggage: Irish insurgents had never in the past handed over their weapons in the wake of conflicts, and the IRA was not about to start now. The organisation itself, it will be recalled, had sprung from the vicious ghetto fighting of 1969, when the previous IRA leadership was bitterly accused of leaving Catholic areas unarmed and undefended against loyalist incursions. The men who had banded together in the wake of the battle of Bombay Street simply would not disarm, particularly since the loyalist groups made it clear they had no intention of giving up their weaponry. This was widely understood on all sides, and was later, in January 1996, to be reflected in the report of an international body which considered the decommissioning question. The report concluded:

> After careful consideration, on the basis of intensive discussions with the governments, the political parties, religious leaders, the security forces and many others, we have concluded that the paramilitary organisations will not decommission any arms prior to all-party negotiations. That was the unanimous and emphatically expressed view of the representatives of the political parties close to paramilitary organisations on both sides. It was also the view of the vast majority of the organisations and individuals who made oral and written submissions. It is not that they are all opposed to prior decommissioning. To the contrary, many favour it. But they are convinced that it will not happen. That is the reality with which all concerned must deal.

That report appeared after ten months of deadlock on decommissioning, but the British government was aware from the beginning that it was not realistic to expect any handover of weaponry. For one thing, it has now been established that the security forces' advice to ministers was not only that it would not happen but that it was unnecessary to elevate decommissioning to an all-important pre-condition. The practical point, put forward by the security forces on the ground, was that since so much of the IRA's armoury was home-made and improvised, not even a complete handover of all weapons would guarantee that the organisation could not wage another violent campaign.

The British government knew this from the start, but its stance was partly due to a desire to keep the republicans under pressure, thus reflecting the concerns of Tory and Unionist MPs. There could be no round-table talks before decommissioning started, ministers argued, because Unionists simply would not go to them and this would retard rather than advance the peace process. A senior government source said in May 1995: 'A lot of these hardline positions have been forced out of ministers by domestic Westminster and Whitehall considerations. It's so bloody stupid, but people have to listen to them [Conservative backbenchers] because of the weakness of the government, unfortunately. I mean, the last thing the PM would want would be a major backbench revolt on his Northern Ireland policy.'

The same source, looking back in March 1996 in the wake of the breakdown of the ceasefire, observed: 'I think it was very much backbenchers and Unionists, very much. The PM felt that the government couldn't deliver in political terms unless there was some requirement for some concession by the republicans in terms of their arms. I think he genuinely believed that. As far as I know, nobody gave him any indication that the republicans would hand over guns. Certainly, there was clear information and advice from Belfast, from people like the Chief Constable, saying, "They won't, and it doesn't matter anyway." '

Dublin's initial reaction to Mayhew's Washington 3 speech illustrated that the approach of John Bruton was going to be very different from that of Albert Reynolds. One Dublin source described how the Irish watched the evolution of the British attitude on decommissioning:

> In discussions between us and the British on the Downing Street Declaration the idea of handing in guns as a pre-condition never came up, was never raised. The whole question of weapons, if referred to, was always seen as a downstream issue. Decommissioning was formally raised, though not as a pre-condition, at the Chequers summit [in October 1994]. It was raised by Major

as an issue to be addressed. Albert Reynolds and Dick Spring agreed to establish a committee to address ways and means of decommissioning. It was discussed in the context of unfinished business. If a weapon were handed in, would it have to be forensically tested? Major said: 'That's an issue that it would be hard to talk about in public' – meaning they didn't want publicity about it. The next time the guns issue really surfaced was in the Washington 3 speech. Initially, the speech wasn't taken seriously. Nobody knows why it became an issue. After that we spent a long time trying to find a way around it.

According to Albert Reynolds, the British government gave no indication, in the many contacts prior to the IRA cessation, that decommissioning was to be a pre-condition for negotiations. Reynolds later wrote: 'Quite correctly, in my view, the British government was not at that stage formally insisting or placing any emphasis on an arms handover prior to Sinn Fein's participation in talks. They well knew that it would have tipped the delicate balance of the debate in the IRA against a ceasefire, for which they, the British government, would then have been blamed.'

Reynolds's approach, as we have seen, was, whenever possible, to ease the republicans into politics and maintain pressure on the British. But Bruton, in responding to the Washington 3 speech, momentarily took a line closer to the British. Rather than opposing the new pre-condition, Bruton called for a gesture on decommissioning, thus helping to establish Washington 3 as a firm position. He later adjusted his stance, but British sources thereafter frequently quoted Bruton's original reaction, together with some earlier remarks by Dick Spring, in support of their argument for decommissioning.

It was not until May 1995, more than eight months after the cessation, that Sinn Fein representatives met British ministers. First Martin McGuinness met Mayhew's deputy, Michael Ancram, in Belfast, then later that month Adams met Mayhew at a conference in Washington. Just before the meetings, Adams, sipping coffee in a west Belfast republican club, his ever-present minders watching the door, outlined his view of the state of the peace process. He said:

> If they want to talk about decommissioning, fair enough, we have said for months we'll talk about any issue. But I don't think there is any possibility of any armed group unilaterally surrendering its weapons at this time. If the British had been – and when the British are more generous – I think all of these things, I'm speculating on this, become more possible. But it's bizarre for the British to make that objective a condition or an obstacle, and there's an onus on Dublin, on Irish-America and on the US administration to avert a potential crisis over this.
>
> For six months we've thought that this was the ambush up the road. I'm using that term advisedly – that the ambush up the road was that the British would seek to protract what John Major called the process of decontamination of Sinn Fein. The British are still at war with us. For the British, negotiation is war by another means, and the British are still trying to defeat the republican struggle. Maybe the IRA initiative [the cessation] took them by surprise: maybe they're still trying to come to terms with it. Would you like to have been the head of British military intelligence, called in on the first of September and asked, 'Why didn't we have a report of this?' So maybe the British are wrong-footed by all of this.
>
> I don't think that the British are a monolith. I think the broad British establishment wants a settlement and there are probably different tendencies within it. Undoubtedly, some would like to see a settlement which would be fundamental, and which would indeed bring about the end of the union. Others would not countenance bringing about an end to the union, they want to see it preserved. And in between those two poles there are a range of other opinions who will settle, understandably enough from their point of view, on the best terms and in the best general interest, as they see it, of their side. Then in the middle of all of that you have the military and intelligence – the spook constituency – who obviously want very little change in the situation. Now those tendencies probably, like the rest of us, argue out the toss, argue out what way to go, what way not to go.
>
> So one then deals with it on the basis that you have to

build a dynamic in the peace process which moves the British establishment, with all its disparate tendencies, to a settlement which is in the best interests of the Irish people. Everyone, in my view, is making this up as we go along. There's no blueprint for this process, there are no modalities for this process.

If we can manage it properly, we can move the situation in ten years' time into one where the union will have ended, or there will be an agreement for a timespan in which it will end. We can have whatever transitional measures are required to move us into a new all-Ireland situation, which may be short of the goals of Sinn Fein, but would be perfectly in keeping with our primary objectives at this time. The benign scenario is that. The malign scenario is that the Brits footer about, mess about, and the peace process breaks down.

The meeting between Adams and Mayhew took place during a conference in the US. It took place in Suite 6006 of the Washington Sheraton hotel, which was besieged by reporters and camera crews. The first republicans to arrive in the room were Mick Conlon, from north Belfast, and Adams's press aide, Richard McAuley. According to McAuley:

When we got to their room they appeared confused about the meeting and were talking about moving it to another location. I made it clear that wouldn't be a good idea, arguing that it would be a media farce. Following a phone call, it was agreed we would stay put. I said to Mick, 'I'll go and get Gerry, you wait here' – I thought it was better keeping one of our people in the room. Conlon was surrounded by so many British civil servants and diplomats, and as I left the room he said: 'I'm beginning to feel like a bit of a hostage.' They all laughed. While I was out of the room, Mick started talking to the British ambassador, Sir Robin Renwick, about fly fishing in Donegal. Renwick was telling Mick the best fly fishing in the world was in Alaska and Mick said, 'Maybe some time we could share a fly in Alaska.'

Then Adams arrived and a handshake took place between Sir Patrick Mayhew, Balliol and the 4th/7th Royal Dragoon Guards, and Gerry Adams, of the Falls Road and Long Kesh prison camp. During the meeting Adams and Mayhew did all the talking.

Mayhew wanted movement on decommissioning; Adams replied that he too wanted to see the gun taken out of politics; the ground they covered was familiar to both. No coffee was served and no jokes were cracked, but there were no raised voices and no awkward moments. In the corridor outside, McAuley afterwards explained the approach taken by Adams: 'From the very beginning Gerry made a strong bid to engage at a personal level. We knew what they were likely to say: they knew what we were likely to say. We wanted to try to get just a wee bit beyond that by trying to get through to Mayhew. That's the first time the guy has talked to republicans, so here was an opportunity at a personal level to engage and to get this guy hopefully going away thinking, at the back of his head, that these people are human.'

But Mayhew, by all accounts, established no real personal contact or rapport with Adams. In fact one observer said later: 'Any time you mention Gerry Adams to Mayhew, he bridles, he bristles, he looks down his nose, his lip curls.' The decommissioning deadlock remained unbroken and the peace process, though intact, moved at a snail's pace: Mayhew, according to one report, approvingly described it as a slow bicycle race. Dublin anxiously tried a number of ways to end the stalemate. On 21 June, for example, Dick Spring wrote to John Bruton setting out his view of the problem: 'The essential difficulty as I see it is that the British government, already in a vulnerable position, is afraid of movement away from its Washington tests, because there is nothing to protect its flank. On the other hand, those who believe that the British government has the power to persuade the Unionists to engage in dialogue in the absence of progress on decommissioning are suffering from a delusion. And our own best assessment suggests that the Sinn Fein leadership is powerless to force the issue with their hardliners, even assuming they want to.'

Spring went on to suggest that one way of getting the British off the hook of Washington 3 was by the two governments setting up an 'international commission for peace and disarmament in Ireland', consisting of three persons, probably an American, a Swede and a Canadian. He added, 'An American chair would be best, as he/she would be best placed to exert moral pressure on the Provisionals.' He cautioned Bruton, however, that the commission idea would only be viable if the British really wished to find some way round Washington 3. Spring's letter went on: 'While I have no way of gauging Sinn Fein's reaction to such an idea, I have reason to believe that the loyalist paramilitaries would cooperate with it. The Ulster Unionists, in the person of Ken Maginnis, put forward a slightly similar idea some time ago (although Mr Maginnis's ideas included an unconscionable time-span, like five years, in which Sinn Fein would remain in the cold). And the British government (depending on who one talks to!) say they have no objection in principle to this approach, provided it leads to visible gains.' Bruton did put the idea forward, though it was to be some months before the two governments agreed on the commission.

In the meantime, almost everyone relished the continuing peace. Although both loyalist and republican punishment beatings continued, the atmosphere everywhere was much more relaxed. The army all but disappeared from the streets, parking restrictions eased and security roadchecks were reduced dramatically. An army base in the Falls Road was bulldozed. The RUC operated what one observer called 'the third ceasefire' – adopting a low-key approach, refraining from large-scale arrest and search operations. Prince Charles, paying the first formal royal visit to the Republic for eighty years, was greeted with great goodwill in Dublin.

Although Sinn Fein's way into talks remained blocked, Gerry Adams had shaken hands with Bill Clinton, Nelson Mandela, British ministers and almost every major political figure in the Republic. The new loyalist parties remained enthusiastic for politics, and there were no real signs of strain on the loyalist ceasefire. The ceasefires had not, however, been underwritten by an agreed political settlement, so an element of uncertainty was always in the air. This grew in the summer of 1995 when, as so often, the loyalist marching season increased tensions. Disturbances at a major Orange demonstration at Portadown, County Armagh, in July, were followed by trouble in Belfast and Londonderry in mid-August. There was also extensive rioting in Belfast when the government announced that it was freeing Private Lee Clegg, a British paratrooper jailed for life for the murder of a girl travelling in a stolen car.

In the republican community, irritation over the long–running decommissioning controversy was compounded by what was seen as a lack of movement on the issue of prisoners. The Irish government had granted early release to several dozen IRA prisoners, and the republicans pressed the British government to follow suit. London did respond in the autumn of 1995, but on a scale which republicans characterised as derisory. Instead of taking a new approach, the government simply increased remission rates from one-third to one-half. Since the one-half rate had been in force until 1989, republicans regarded this as the most minimal of moves and were distinctly unimpressed. They said, and the NIO did not demur, that under the new arrangements two-thirds of the 500 republican prisoners would still be in jail in the year 2000. They said that by the year 2000 only forty republicans who would not in any case have been released could expect to be freed. Republicans complained bitterly that the only prisoner to gain early release was Private Lee Clegg.

Another major irritant for the republican community was the reluctance of the Home Office to transfer IRA personnel jailed in Britain back to Northern Ireland. Although a decision in principle to return such prisoners had been taken some time earlier, in practice the Home Secretary, Michael Howard, usually declined to do so. During 1995, much republican concern centred on Patrick Kelly, an IRA prisoner held in England who suffered from skin cancer, and who was alleged to be denied proper treatment. A republican declared at a public meeting in Belfast:

> For a lot of people in our community the whole peace process is a very abstract thing. If you're talking about tangible, concrete measures that would consolidate and move the thing forward, the issue of prisoners is one that can be easily identified and easily measured. To have seen no response from the British government is not only very disheartening, it's making people very angry and very frustrated. If we can't get treatment for Patrick Kelly for

skin cancer, what does that say about the British government's approach to the broader issues?

Michael Howard also generally took the toughest line within the cabinet committee overseeing policy on Northern Ireland. A government source claimed: 'He is probably the hardest-line man in saying they're criminals and should be treated as criminals. He's one of that top group of ministers who is very influential in that he represents a significant strand in the party, both in parliament and in the country. The Northern Ireland Office certainly always believed he should have moved further and a bit more quickly on some of the prisons issues. But I think his natural instincts are to take a hard line and not to be in the business of what he would call concessions.'

By August, the ceasefire was showing signs of increasing strain, with Adams and other Sinn Fein figures repeatedly warning that the peace process was in crisis. Adams used the publicity from international trips to create a sense of momentum in the process, but he could not manufacture movement on the part of the British government. A source close to him said during August: 'There's a political vacuum. We need an inclusive agenda. We've had a strategy of alternative initiatives – the Dublin government, Hume, going to Washington, South Africa and so on. The trouble is, it's a year on, people aren't interested in Gerry going to Washington any more.' In private, republicans complained more and more about Bruton who, they said, was expending too much effort on attempting to reassure Unionists when he should have been concentrating on easing the stresses within republicanism.

A senior Dublin source worried about the effects of the protracted decommissioning wrangle, saying in September: 'A permanent stand-off is going to unravel the ceasefire. If you have a total stalemate for a long time, Adams and company are going to have to be more and more on the defensive. Some IRA people will be looking at it all very formally and saying, "Well, there were supposed to be talks and there aren't talks. We just regard the deal as having been welshed on and therefore it's back to square one." I think it would unravel not necessarily because of a malicious sudden decision, but eventually at some point the strains would just get too much.'

September brought a significant development when James Molyneaux stepped down as Ulster Unionist leader and was replaced by David Trimble, a former law lecturer who was the most hardline of the five leadership candidates. Most political elements were dismayed by his election, since he was regarded as a militant who was not amenable to compromise. A government minister recounted his reaction to seeing Trimble described in a British newspaper as a moderate: 'I was having my breakfast when I read that,' he recalled. 'Nearly puked up my Frosties.'

Trimble pursued an unremittingly hard line and, like Molyneaux, favoured a glacially slow peace process. He reflected the view that arms decommissioning must begin in advance of round-table talks, but he then intrigued ministers by indicating that he would be prepared to sit in an elected assembly with Sinn Fein, even if no arms had been handed in. From then on, the idea of an election figured prominently on the British government's agenda. Bruton, meanwhile, made various overtures to Trimble, hoping to strike up a rapport and build bridges with Unionism. Spring, on the other hand, took a different line. Before the ceasefire, he had been regarded as having reservations about the peace process, and certainly about the pace set by Reynolds in pursuing a cessation. With Bruton eager to establish a new relationship with the Unionists, however, Spring in effect became the guardian of the peace process, seeing his first priority as the maintenance of the ceasefire. Thus Spring, whom Unionists had once preferred to Reynolds, came to be described by Unionist MP John Taylor as 'the most detested man in Ulster'.

Bruton, meanwhile, by refusing in October a request for a three-way meeting with Hume and Adams, illustrated that he did not regard himself as involved in a nationalist consensus. Bruton privately came up with a series of notions aimed at reassuring Unionists. At one meeting with the SDLP he floated the idea that nationalists should be required to have something more than a simple majority in Northern Ireland in order to achieve Irish unity. Mark Durkan of the SDLP, who was present, responded sarcastically: 'Why don't you make it fifty-five per cent, Taoiseach? Then you could market it as Britvic 55.' The SDLP felt strongly that the priority should be the safeguarding of the ceasefire, and that any overtures to Unionists could wait until the peace was secure.

It was late in November, following a lengthy and complex Anglo-Irish negotiation, that the two governments finally reached agreement on a three-man international body, along the lines suggested by Spring, to report on the decommissioning issue. Chaired by former US Senator George Mitchell, it included Harri Holkeri, former Prime Minister of Finland, and a Canadian general, John de Chastelain. It was asked to report in January 1996.

Although the two governments agreed to set up the body, they were still very much at variance in their overall approaches. Spring's concept was that a commission would only be of use 'if it were clearly understood by the British as a way of helping them to set aside Washington 3, or seeing it as being met'. But although a target date for talks was set for the end of February, London gave no indication that it intended to drop Washington 3.

Agreement on the international body was hurried through at the last moment in advance of a major event: the visit to Belfast, in late November 1993, of President Bill Clinton. The American President, proud of his contribution to the peace process, came to celebrate the absence of violence – unaware that, a short time later, the ceasefire would break down. In Belfast and Londonderry he was given a rapturous reception, his visit turning into a huge communal celebration of peace as he delivered the message that the violence must be over for good and that formerly violent prodigals should be welcomed into politics. He declared: 'You must be willing to say to those who renounce violence that they are entitled to be part of the democratic process.'

Within weeks of the visit and the celebrations, however, came ominous signs that the IRA ceasefire was under increasing strain, as four alleged drug dealers and petty criminals were shot dead on the streets of Belfast. Responsibility for the killings was claimed, in telephone calls, by a previously unknown group styling itself 'Direct Action Against Drugs', but few doubted the IRA was involved. There had been previous killings of alleged drug dealers in April and September 1995, but no one had chosen to make a major political issue of these.

The spate of killings led to worries that a return to full-scale violence was under way, but these dissipated as the attacks petered out. Although there were once again bodies on the streets of Belfast, many presumed that the murders were a passing phenomenon which could be classed as 'policing operations' and thus did not represent a breakdown of the IRA ceasefire.

The next major development came on 22 January 1996, when Senator Mitchell's international body delivered its report. The report said that prior decommissioning would not happen, and went on to suggest that decommissioning could take place in parallel with political negotiations. It also set out a comprehensive list of six anti-violence statements which it recommended that all those engaged in negotiations should formally accept.

Some of Mitchell's six principles, as they came to be known, would clearly be difficult for republicans to accept; so too would any requirement for parallel decommissioning. But on the other hand, the Mitchell report seemed to dispose of prior decommissioning, and, within a few hours of its publication, Adams issued a welcome for it. He declared: 'It provides a basis for moving forward so that all matters can be settled to the satisfaction of all sides as part of the process. It points to a possible avenue into all-party talks.'

On that same afternoon, however, Major rose in the Commons, thanked Mitchell for his report, and then in effect overturned it. Rather than opting for the parallel decommissioning path, he said the road to talks lay either through prior decommissioning or by the holding of an election in Northern Ireland. David Trimble was delighted at this new tack, since it appeared Major was directly responding to his call for elections, but republicans and nationalists were furious for a number of reasons. Dublin, Hume and the republicans all wanted to get into talks as soon as possible, but it would clearly take months to organise and stage an election. There was also, republicans complained, no guarantee that the British government or Unionists would not in the interim come up with some additional pre-condition which would further postpone the opening of talks. Furthermore, the election gambit obviously meant that the government was reacting to Unionist pressure, an allegation which Hume angrily levelled at Major across the floor of the Commons. Trimble had made it clear that he had in mind an election of a body which would then occupy centre-stage in the peace process. Such a body would inevitably have a Unionist majority and could thus be expected to be under the effective control of a Trimble–Paisley coalition. For republicans this conjured up their worst nightmare, a reversion to a form of Unionist domination in which Sinn Fein would come under the loyalist thumb and would once again be treated as second–class citizens. Dublin and Sinn Fein joined Hume in accusing Major of being motivated not by a desire to advance the peace process but by the hope of winning Trimble's nine votes. Major hotly denied this but his relations with Dublin reached a low point and accusations of bad faith filled the air.

A Dublin source pointed to Major's slender parliamentary majority and to the fact that Trimble's votes potentially had the power to keep the Conservatives in office: 'Major's going to have great trouble keeping his ducks in a row over the next few months. No matter how he tries or wants to, I really doubt whether he has the capacity to take any kind of bold initiative at the moment. That's why he wants the election – it's sort of cost-free. Trimble likes it, it keeps everybody busily occupied. Weapons are a serious subject but they were used in a blatantly tactical way, I think essentially to buy time and space. And now I think Major looks to the election to do the same thing.' A British government source essentially agreed when he said:

I think we're in this impossible position, with Number 10 in this business of trying to play a balancing game so the Unionists don't feel the nationalist front is running away with it. The Tory backbenchers and the Unionists still have a key role to play in terms of the balance in parliament. That's going to be with us this side of a general election, and it's always going to create these sorts of difficulties. You can take it that the NIO and Number 10 do not always see eye to eye. That's a tension that's been there from the start, with, in general, the NIO being prepared to take more risks than the PM, who has all these other considerations. The classic example is that on some things connected with prisons the government has not moved as far as the NIO would have liked, mainly because of Michael Howard and Tory backbenchers.

On 7 February, Mayhew was taken aback when, at a meeting in Dublin, Spring came up with a new proposal for talks along the pattern of those in Dayton, Ohio, which had advanced the Bosnian peace process. The proposal envisaged all parties being present in the same building, though without necessarily facing one another across a table, while British and Irish intermediaries moved between the various parties. This was welcomed by Hume but described by Michael Ancram as 'at best premature'. The arguments over an election continued, Mayhew commending the idea as 'not a hurdle but a door opening to the conference chamber'.

Such was the state of politics and of the peace process when, on the evening of Friday, 9 February, after a confused series of warnings, a huge bomb concealed in a lorry detonated in the city of London, not far from the giant Canary Wharf building in London's docklands. That blinding, destructive blast claimed two lives, wrecking not only scores of buildings but the peace process itself.

Most participants in the peace process were sent into shock by the explosion. The British and the Irish, the Unionists and the nationalists, the Americans and the rest of the world looked astonished and aghast at the wreckage, wondering why it had happened and whether it meant another generation condemned to live through a terrorist war. There had been periodic warnings from Adams and other Sinn Fein figures of a crisis in the peace process, but most had dismissed this as crying wolf in the hope of increasing republican political leverage. The seventeen months and nine days of the ceasefire had been punctuated by occasional violence, the terrorist groups had not disbanded, but the general sense had been that a corner had been turned and there would be no return to full-scale terrorism.

Yet suddenly the terror had reappeared. There were two men dead, damage ran into millions of pounds, it seemed there was a return to war, and no one had a ready explanation for exactly why it had happened. Among those who had not known that the bombing was being planned were Sir Hugh Annesley, Chief Constable of the RUC, and Gerry Adams, President of Sinn Fein. In the aftermath of the attack, they and everyone else asked themselves two questions – what had gone wrong, and whether it could be put right.

The bomb had a galvanic effect on political activity. The two governments and other parties launched into a round of meetings. Hume suggested a referendum on peace and talks. London and Dublin discussed the idea of an election, Dublin softening its attitude. There were meanwhile three other smaller explosions in London, one of them killing an IRA member when a bomb went off prematurely. Spring's idea of proximity talks gave rise to a series of contacts involving the governments and the parties. Major and Bruton, at an Irish summit, set a firm date of 10 June for the opening of all-party talks, specifying that Sinn Fein could take part if the IRA declared another ceasefire. Adams was allowed into the US for St Patrick's Day in mid-March, but because of the ceasefire breakdown he was not received at the White House.

The initial assumption was that the docklands bombing had been triggered by Major's insertion of an election into the peace process. It later emerged, however, that the lorry used in the attack was being prepared as early as late November. This meant that even as President Clinton addressed cheering crowds in Belfast an IRA team was at work on the vehicle.

Hume and Adams went together to meet seven leaders of the IRA, pressing them for another cessation. Adams later gave a report of the meeting:

> We asked what had ended the cessation. The consistent bad faith of the British government and the placing of new pre-conditions were seen as evidence that the British were waging war by other means, and that they were seeking to fracture Irish republicanism

and to split the IRA. The open provocation of the punitive attitude to Irish prisoners, alongside the release of British paratrooper Lee Clegg and the attitude of the RUC on the ground, were all irritants. However, it was the absence of real negotiations which undermined the cessation.

There was also criticism of the Irish government's role. John Bruton responded, it was said, more to the British agenda and made no significant attempt to advance an Irish agenda in Ireland, in Britain or internationally. He seemed more content to manage the situation than to build upon it. Mr Bruton's call for the IRA to make a gesture on arms last March, his refusal to meet John Hume and myself in October, his support for the Unionist election proposal and his public rejection of any nationalist consensus approach undermined the second element on which the cessation was based. Once this basis was removed, through the breaking of the consensus and the reneging on negotiations by the British, the collapse of the peace process became inevitable.

In other words, the analysis outlined in the TUAS document had been undermined: Hume and Irish-American opinion had remained solid but Albert Reynolds's successor was more concerned with accommodating Unionists than republicans. And, crucially, the British had not convened all-party talks. A senior republican source said, months before the ceasefire ended: 'The bottom line here is no big complex philosophical thing. The requirement is inclusive dialogue.'

Because the ceasefire was a unilateral move by the IRA, with no negotiations or discussions with the British before it was declared, the organisation was in effect free to decide on its own terms and conditions. It had gradually become clear that the IRA would remain in being, continuing to recruit and train, raise funds, and carry out surveillance on possible targets in Northern Ireland and England. It would not decommission, destroy or hand over a single ounce of explosive, a single gun. In essence, the deal was that the IRA would remain in the background, though the expectation was widespread that as time passed it would gradually become redundant and would, hopefully, eventually wither away.

During Reynolds's period of office the cessation went reasonably well from a republican point of view, and Sinn Fein was pleased with the framework document of February 1995. But from then on Major's approach was to maintain pressure on Adams and Sinn Fein, and not to pressurise the Unionists. The decommissioning impasse, the absence of all-party talks, and the continuing lack of movement on ancillary but important issues such as prisoners, combined to increase the heat on Adams. The fact that Bruton went along with much of this approach heightened the strains within republicanism even more. By contrast, Spring regarded this as a high-risk strategy and argued for a lessening of the pressure. According to a senior Dublin source:

> We were practically on our knees to the British asking them to, for God's sake, watch the psychology of it. The psychology was very simple on their side: the IRA were in the box and the British pronounced confidently they could never go back to violence again – problem solved. We kept telling them that it wasn't going to be like that, that there was a psychological dimension and they were getting it wrong, one thing after the other. We were dealing with people who genuinely were a bit illiterate in terms of the currency of politics in Ireland. They were very reckless in the weight they put on the process.

One British reaction to such arguments was to attack the messengers. Journalists were briefed by London to the effect that John Bruton was an amenable man but that Spring and his principal Anglo-Irish official, Sean O hUiginn, were unreasonable and unhelpful. 'O hUiginn in particular was given almost a demon status by them,' one journalist recalled. Spring, asked on Irish radio about the British briefings, replied, 'That's been an old British tactic down through the years. It's not just an Irish experience; we have seen this in many parts of the world. The British set out to divide and conquer. They have made attempts before to divide us and they have not succeeded.'

John Major played the cessation as a long game, allowing seventeen months to go by without acceding to the republican demand for talks. He was plainly as shocked as everyone else when the ceasefire came to a sudden end. Since he would have made every effort to prevent its collapse, it is obvious he did not appreciate the true state of opinion among the leadership of the IRA. Some would say the British never got fully to grips with the republican mindset: one senior Dublin source said with some bitterness that the British 'didn't know why the ceasefire started and don't know why it finished'.

Some indications of the British assessment of the peace process can be seen in a succession of comments from official sources during the cessation. In January 1995, Annesley was upbeat, saying in an interview: 'There is very little doubt in my mind that the leadership of the republican movement were determined to go for the peaceful route when they announced the ceasefire, and I don't think the leadership has wavered in that in the interim months, and the ceasefire on their side has held very, very strongly.' Two months later he said he remained 'optimistic on balance.' In May he declared: 'I am still of the view, having access to all the intelligence reports, that the leadership want to go down the peace road, want to go down the political road. I accept there are pockets of resistance — some considerable pockets of resistance — to that. My opinion at the moment, on all the intelligence coming to us, is that the peace process will hold. That is just on balance.'

A government source, speaking in the same month, said there was far less republican dissent about the cessation than had originally been anticipated. He added: 'There is a belief that Adams and McGuinness see this as as big a prize as we do, and therefore they're prepared to put up with a surprising amount of hassle — at some risk, one must say — in order to keep their side of the process on the move.' By late June, however, after the decommissioning deadlock had developed, the same source was less confident: 'I think even those of us who were most optimistic are all treading a bit carefully at the moment. We're all a little bit worried — things do seem to be as fragile as they've been since the process really started.' A month later he added: 'The feeling is that if it does make it through the twelve-month barrier, it's going to be very difficult to unravel it.' Then in February 1996, only days before the docklands bomb, Annesley delivered an upbeat assessment which once again exposed the limitations of the intelligence organisations. He said he did not believe the IRA leadership was planning a return to violence, adding, 'Are they intent on doing anything to breach the ceasefire? On the intelligence patterns at the moment, the answer is no.'

As some of these comments indicate, the authorities at various points believed that the IRA ceasefire was under strain. Yet they always resisted the Dublin argument that the peace could be shored up by creating greater momentum on issues such as talks and prisoners. As one Dublin source put it during this period: 'The ceasefires are a dynamic: you need a certain dynamism to hold them and they have to be underpinned by political negotiation. The fact that they are so popular doesn't necessarily mean that they are therefore irreversible.'

Although the British government did not act in accordance with this theory, some elements privately subscribed to it. A number of government sources say that some senior officials at the Northern Ireland Office argued on many occasions for a more flexible attitude, but were overruled by Number 10. Perhaps most surprising of all, Mayhew – regarded by republicans as a paragon of British stiffness – once, in an unguarded moment, revealed that his private view was very different from his public projection. Addressing sixth-formers at a London school in January 1995, he did not realise that a reporter from the local *Ham & High* newspaper was present and spoke with unusual frankness. He said he did not trust Gerry Adams but added that 'if Mr Adams were replaced that would be a disadvantage' since his ability to control republican hard men was the key to ensuring the ceasefire was maintained. Mayhew went on: 'To some extent we have got to help Mr Adams carry with him the people who are reluctant to see a ceasefire, who believe they might be betrayed by the British government. If the hard men say, "What did Gerry Adams do, we have called a ceasefire but got nothing sufficient in return?" then Mr Adams will take a long walk on a short plank, and be replaced by someone much harder.'

Peter Brooke, Mayhew's predecessor as Northern Ireland Secretary, went even further, openly praising Adams. In a BBC interview in January 1995 he said: 'In my view he was a brave man and I hope he will be justified. He led them across that Rubicon, in my view that was a courageous step. He had a leadership role to perform, he performed it and I think the whole of Ireland and the whole of these islands and, arguably, the whole of the world is grateful to him for having done it.'

One unanswered question, given this analysis, is why the authorities did not seek to make life easier for Adams rather than subjecting him to continuous pressure. And the most crucial question of all is whether Adams can do it again.

The army council decision to disregard Adams's advice to maintain the process, and instead to bomb London, was a serious blow to the authority of the Sinn Fein president, who had personally invested so much in the process. It showed that he was not, at that point at least, the dominant figure in the republican leadership. The docklands bomb blew away years of his work of convincing the movement of the benefits of politics, and of persuading the outside world of the movement's bona fides and good intentions. It left the world to wonder whether the IRA could be serious about peace, and left a huge new deposit of distrust which will not be easily dispelled.

Those who were always sceptical of the ceasefire will argue that the IRA was never serious, and that the resumption of violence proves the government and the Unionist parties were right to react to it with the utmost caution. Those who believed in the cessation will by contrast contend that it was faulty intelligence and analysis, married to excessive caution, which contributed to its breakdown.

As this book goes to press, in April 1996, there are both ominous and hopeful signs on the horizon. One IRA leader has declared: 'We sued for peace, the British wanted war. If that's what they want, we will give them another twenty-five years of war.' Loyalists have warned in response: 'We will give blow for blow.'

It is a tense and dangerous moment, but there are also grounds for hope. If there is a return to war, it will be against the wishes not just of the always peaceful majority, but of a majority in both the republican and loyalist communities. There is little appetite anywhere for another quarter-century of death and destruction, of injuries, prison sentences, of ruined and wastes lives. The IRA ceasefire came to a violent end but during its seventeen months many people, even many of the hard men, bade a psychological farewell to terrorism. This book details a peace process which at many points looked dead in the water, yet which time after time was revived against all the odds. The hope is that it can happen again.

APPENDICES

Appendix 1

Draft declarations

Draft 1 was written by John Hume in October 1991. It is reproduced on pages 118–9.

Draft 2 was drawn up, also in October in 1991, by John Hume, Charles Haughey and Dublin officials.

Draft 2: A Strategy for Peace and Justice in Ireland

A Joint Declaration by the British Prime Minister and the Taoiseach.

The British Prime Minister and the Taoiseach acknowledge that the most urgent and important challenge facing the people of Ireland, North and South, and the British and Irish Governments together, is finally to overcome the legacy of history and to heal past conflicts and differences, recognising that past failures to settle relationships between the people of both islands satisfactorily has led to continuing tragedy and suffering.

They believe the development of closer European unity, which will result in the effective removal of borders, fundamentally changes the nature of British-Irish relationships and removes the basis of the historic conflict still taking place within the confines of Northern Ireland. These developments, and the fact that both parts of Ireland will in the future be the only considerable territory in the Community without land links to the other countries and regions, will intensify the need for both parts of Ireland to be

371

united in their approach to all major issues, which affect the future of all the people of Ireland, North and South, in the context of the new Europe.

Both the British Prime Minister and the Taoiseach are convinced that the ending of conflict and healing of division can make a huge positive contribution to the future welfare and prosperity of both parts of Ireland, as well as bring to an end the last remaining divisions in a European Community that has already ended more deep and bitter quarrels. Both of them recognise that the ending of division can only come about with the agreement and co-operation of the people North and South. They therefore make a solemn commitment to use all their influence and resources to create an atmosphere which will foster agreement and reconciliation, and to promote intensive co-operation at all levels to strengthen the process of agreement and achieve closer unity of purpose.

The British Prime Minister reiterates on behalf of the British Government that they have no selfish, strategic, political or economic interest in Northern Ireland, and that their sole interest is to see peace, stability and reconciliation established by agreement among the people who inhabit the island. The British Government acknowledge it is the wish of the people of Britain to see the people of Ireland live together in unity and harmony, born of agreement with respect for their diverse traditions, and with full recognition of the special links and the unique relationship which exist between the peoples of Britain and Ireland.

The Taoiseach, on behalf of the Irish Government, accepts that the exercise of the democratic right of self-determination by the people of Ireland as a whole cannot in practice be achieved except with the agreement and the consent of the people of Northern Ireland and that it must, consistent with justice and equity, respect the democratic dignity and the civil rights of both communities, whether majority or minority. The Irish Government would, accordingly, commit themselves to working, in the spirit and on the basis of the Report of the New Ireland Forum, to create institutions and structures, which while respecting the diversity of the people of Ireland would enable them to work together in all the areas where there is substantial common ground. This would help to build the trust necessary for an agreed future leading to a closer form of unity by agreement. Such unity would, of course, require institutional recognition of the special links that exist between the peoples of Britain and Ireland as part of the totality of relationships, while taking account of the newly forged links with the rest of Europe.

In order to promote these aims the Taoiseach has indicated to the British Prime Minister his intention of establishing a permanent Irish Convention in order to consult and advise on the steps required to remove the barriers of distrust which divide the people of Ireland and which stand in the way of the exercise in common self-determination on an equal basis. The Convention would be open to all democratic parties in Ireland, who share the objective of a united Ireland achieved peacefully through democratic self-determination, or who wish to share in dialogue about Ireland's political future and the welfare of all its people.

Note:
If the British Government are unable to accept a Joint Declaration, the Irish Government will proceed to set up the Convention with the further objective of planning and implementing the policies required to persuade the British Government to adopt this strategy and these objectives.

Draft 3: Document sent to John Hume and the Irish government by the republican movement, February 1992

Draft of a declaration which Sinn Fein suggests should be made jointly by the British and Dublin governments

The British Prime Minister and the Taoiseach acknowledge that the most urgent and important issue facing the people of Ireland, north and south, and the British and Irish governments together, is to remove the causes of conflict, to overcome the legacy of history and to heal the divisions which have resulted, recognising that past failures to settle relationships between the people of both islands satisfactorily has led to continuing tragedy and suffering.

The development of closer European Unity will intensify the need for Ireland to be united in its approach to all major issues, in the context of Europe and beyond.

Both the British Prime Minister and the Taoiseach are convinced that the securing of a comprehensive political settlement, with the consequent ending of conflict and the healing of divisions, can make a huge positive contribution to the future welfare and prosperity of Ireland and its people, as well as bring to an end one of the last remaining divisions in Europe. Both of them recognise that the ending of division can only come about through the agreement and co-operation of the people, north and south, and that the present constitutional arrangements have inhibited the development of this process. They therefore make a solemn commitment to create a new political framework, encompassing all the people of the island and, in this context, to use all their influence and resources to foster agreement and reconciliation among the people of Ireland and between the peoples of Ireland and Britain.

The British Prime Minister reiterates, on behalf of the British government, that they have no selfish, strategic, political or economic interest in Northern Ireland, and that their sole interest is to see peace, stability and reconciliation established by agreement among the people who inhabit the island.

The British government acknowledges also that it is the wish of the people of Britain to see the people of Ireland live together in unity and harmony, with respect for their diverse traditions, independent, but with full recognition of the special links and the unique relationship which exists between the peoples of Britain and Ireland. The British government, consequently, commits itself to such unity (within a period to be agreed) and to use all its influence and energy to win consent for this policy.

The Taoiseach, on behalf of the Irish government, accepts that the exercise of the democratic right of self-determination by the people of Ireland as a whole would best be achieved with the agreement and the consent of the people of Northern Ireland and that it must, consistent with justice and equity, respect the democratic dignity and the civil rights of both communities. The Irish government would, accordingly, commit itself to working in the spirit and on the basis of the Report of the New Ireland Forum, to create institutions and structures which, while respecting the diversity of the people of Ireland, would enable them to work together in all areas which affect them in common. This would help to build the trust necessary to end past divisions, leading to an agreed and peaceful future. Such structures would, of course, include institutional recognition of the special links that exist between the people of Britain and Ireland as part of the totality of relationships, while taking account of newly forged links with the rest of Europe.

Given the British government's commitment to facilitate this process, by removing the constitutional barriers to peace and reconciliation, the Taoiseach has indicated to the British Prime Minister, his intention of establishing a permanent Irish Convention in order to consult and advise on the steps required to realise the unity of the Irish people by removing the barriers of distrust which presently divide the people of Ireland and to develop adequate guarantees and safeguards for all sections of the Irish people, north and south. The convention would be open to all democratically mandated political parties in Ireland who share the objective of a United Ireland, or who wish to share in dialogue about Ireland's political future and the welfare of all its people.

Draft 4: Extract from April 1992 Hume–Dublin Draft

The Prime Minister reiterates, on behalf of the British Government, that they have no selfish, strategic, political or economic interest in Northern Ireland, and that their sole interest is to see peace, stability and reconciliation established by agreement among the people who inhabit the island. The British Government accepts the principle that self-determination by the Irish people collectively could take the form of agreed independent structures for the island as a whole. They affirm their readiness, subject to the necessary consent of a majority in Northern Ireland, to introduce the measures to give legislative effect on their side to such an arrangement as soon as it is formally established that that condition has been fulfilled. They acknowledge that it is the wish of the people of Britain to see the people of Ireland live together in unity and harmony, with respect for their diverse traditions, and with full recognition of the special links and unique relationship which exist between the people of Britain and Ireland.

Draft 5: June 1992 Sinn Fein draft (also known as 'Hume–Adams')

Draft of a declaration which Sinn Fein suggests should be made jointly by the British and Dublin Governments

1 The Taoiseach and the Prime Minister acknowledge that the most urgent and important issue facing the people of Ireland, north and south, and the British and Irish governments together, is to remove the causes of conflict, to overcome the legacy of history and to heal the divisions which have resulted, recognising that past failures to settle relationships between the people of both islands satisfactorily has led to continuing tragedy and suffering.
2 They consider that the development of European Union fundamentally changes the nature and the context of British–Irish relationships and will progressively remove the basis of the historic conflict still taking place in Northern Ireland. The challenges and opportunities of European Union will, of themselves, require new approaches to serve interests common to both parts of Ireland.
3 The Taoiseach and the Prime Minister are convinced of the inestimable value to both their peoples of healing divisions in Ireland and of ending a conflict which has been so manifestly to the detriment of all. Both

recognise that the ending of divisions can come about only through the agreement and cooperation of the people, North and South, representing both traditions in Ireland. They therefore make a solemn commitment to promote cooperation at all levels. It is their aim to foster agreement and reconciliation, leading to a new political framework founded on consent and encompassing the whole island.

4 The British Prime Minister reiterates, on behalf of the British Government, that they have no selfish, strategic, political or economic interest in Northern Ireland, and that their sole interest is to see peace, stability and reconciliation established by agreement among the people who inhabit the island. The British Government accepts the principle that the Irish people have the right collectively to self-determination, and that the exercise of this right could take the form of agreed independent structures for the island as a whole. They affirm their readiness to introduce the measures to give legislative effect on their side to this right (within a specified period to be agreed) and allowing sufficient time for the building of consent and the beginning of a process of national reconciliation. The British Government will use all its influence and energy to win the consent of a majority in Northern Ireland for these measures. They acknowledge that it is the wish of the people of Britain to see the people of Ireland live together in unity and harmony, with respect for their diverse traditions, independent, but with full recognition of the special links and the unique relationship which exists between the peoples of Britain and Ireland.

5 The Taoiseach, on behalf of the Irish Government, considers that the lessons of Irish history, and especially of Northern Ireland, show that stability and well-being will not be found under any political system which is refused allegiance or rejected on grounds of identity by a significant minority of those governed by it. He accepts, on behalf of the Irish Government, that the democratic right of self-determination by the people of Ireland as a whole must be achieved and exercised with the agreement and consent of the people of Northern Ireland and must, consistent with justice and equity, respect the democratic dignity and the civil rights of both communities.

6 The Irish Government accordingly commits itself to working in the spirit and on the basis of the Report of the New Ireland Forum, to create institutions and structures which, while respecting the diversity of the peoples of Ireland, would enable them to work together in all areas of common interest. This will help to build the trust necessary to end past divisions, leading to an agreed and peaceful future. Such structures would, of course, include institutional recognition of the special links that exist between the peoples of Britain and Ireland as part of the totality of relationships, while taking account of newly forged links with the rest of Europe.

7 In light of their joint commitment to promote the foregoing objectives, the Taoiseach has indicated to the Prime Minister his intention of establishing a

376

permanent Irish Convention to consult and advise on the steps required to remove the barriers of distrust which at present divide the people of Ireland and which stand in the way of the exercise in common by them of self-determination on a basis of equality. It will be open to the Convention to make recommendations on ways in which agreement, as defined in the Forum Report, and respect for the rights and identities of both traditions in Ireland, can be promoted and established. The convention will be governed by the authority of Bunreacht na hEireann, and the institutions established under it. It will be a fundamental guiding principle of the Convention that all differences between the Irish people relating to the exercise in common of the right to self-determination will be resolved exclusively by peaceful, political means.

8 The convention will be open to all democratically mandated political parties in Ireland which abide exclusively by the democratic process and wish to share in dialogue about Ireland's political future and the welfare of all its people.

Draft 6: Extract from June 1992 Hume–Dublin draft

The British Prime Minister reiterates, on behalf of the British Government, that they have no selfish, strategic, political or economic interest in Northern Ireland, and that their sole interest is to see peace, stability and reconciliation established by agreement among the people who inhabit the island. The British Government accept the principle that the Irish people have the right to self-determination and that the exercise of this right collectively could take the form of agreed independent structures for the island as a whole. Such an agreement, to be achieved over a period and allowing sufficient time for the building of consent and the beginning of a process of national reconciliation, would have to be freely negotiated and agreed to by the Irish people, North and South. The British Government affirm their readiness to introduce the measures to give legislative effect to the exercise of the right of self-determination on that basis. The British Government will use all its influence and energy to win the consent of a majority in Northern Ireland for an agreement between all the people of Ireland on their political future, which recognizes both the unity of Ireland and the special links and unique relationship which exists between Ireland and Britain. They acknowledge that it is the wish of the people in Britain to see the people of Ireland live together in unity and harmony with respect for their diverse traditions, recognizing that the whole island of Ireland has a right to independence based on agreement.

Draft 7: Extract from October 1992 Hume–Dublin draft

The British Prime Minister reiterates, on behalf of the British Government, that they have no selfish, strategic, political or economic interest in Northern Ireland, and that their sole interest is to see peace, stability and reconciliation established by agreement among the people who inhabit the island. The British Government accept the principle that the Irish people have the right to national self-determination and that the exercise of this right collectively could take the form of agreed independent structures for the island as a whole. Such an agreement, to be achieved over an acceptable period and allowing sufficient time for the building of consent and the beginning of a process of national reconciliation, would have to be freely negotiated and agreed to by the Irish people, North and South. The British Government affirm their readiness to introduce the measures to give legislative effect to the exercise of the right of self-determination on that basis. The British Government will use all their influence and energy to move forward the process of national reconciliation and to win the consent of a majority in Northern Ireland for an agreement between all the people of Ireland on their political future, which recognises both the unity of Ireland and the special links and the unique relationship which exist between Ireland and Britain. They acknowledge that it is the wish of the people of Britain to see the people of Ireland live together in unity and harmony with respect for their diverse traditions, recognising that the whole island of Ireland has a right to independence based on agreement. For their part the Irish Government are committed to making substantial progress towards a new and agreed Ireland within a generation.

Draft 8: Extract from March 1993 Hume–Dublin draft

The British Prime Minister reiterates, on behalf of the British Government, that they have no selfish, strategic, political or economic interest in Northern Ireland, and that their sole interest is to see peace, stability and reconciliation established by agreement among the people who inhabit the island. The British Government accept the principle that the Irish people have the right to national self-determination and that the exercise of this collective right democratically could take the form of agreed independent structures for the island as a whole. They affirm their readiness, in cooperation with the Irish Government, to establish a procedure to reach agreement on how the right of self-determination could be exercised democratically and collectively, allowing sufficient time for the building of consent and the beginning of a process of national reconciliation. The progress of this procedure will be reviewed within a specified time to be agreed and, as necessary, regularly thereafter. The British Government affirm their readiness to introduce the measures to give legislative effect to the exercise of the right of self-determination on that basis. The British Government will use all their influence and energy to move forward the process of national reconciliation and to win the consent of a majority in Northern Ireland for an agreement between all the people of Ireland on their political future, which recognises both the unity of Ireland and the special links and the unique relationship which exist between Ireland and Britain. They acknowledge that it is the wish of the people of Britain to see the people of Ireland live together in unity and harmony with respect for their diverse traditions, recognising that the whole island of Ireland has a right to independence based on agreement. [For their part the Irish Government are committed to making substantial progress towards a new and agreed Ireland within a generation.]

Draft 9: *Extract from June 1993 document drawn up by John Hume*

The British Prime Minister reiterates, on behalf of the British Government, that they have no selfish, strategic, political or economic interest in Northern Ireland, and that their sole interest is to see peace, stability and reconciliation established by agreement among the people who inhabit the island. The British Government recognise and accept that the people of Ireland have the right collectively to self-determination. We regret that the people of Ireland have been divided on how to exercise that right and we regret in particular the heavy price that the people of Ireland, particularly the people of the North, have paid for that division. We also regret any mistakes or failures by past British Governments that may have contributed to that division.

However, the past is over. Let us look to the future.

We would naturally, as we believe would the whole world, like to see the people of Ireland reach agreement on the exercise of self-determination. We have already made clear that if such agreement took the form of Irish unity that we would legislate for it. Whatever form such agreement takes we would therefore naturally endorse and we underline that it must be a matter for the collective agreement of the people who inhabit the island. Indeed we will do all in our power to encourage such agreement and in particular to persuade the people of Northern Ireland that such agreement is in their best interest as well as everyone else's. We are more than willing to take immediate and appropriate steps to create the conditions and climate for such agreement providing for consensus and reconciliation. We have no doubt that any such agreement should reflect and give clear expression to the common interests in today's world of the people of Ireland North and South, respecting their diverse traditions and recognising the special links and unique relationships which exist between the peoples of Britain and Ireland.

The British Government deeply regrets the failure of successive British Governments to achieve agreement on all relationships to the satisfaction of the people of Ireland. We will do all in our power to succeed this time.

Draft 10: Extract from May 1993 agreed document

The British Prime Minister reiterates, on behalf of the British Government, that they have no selfish, strategic, political or economic interest in Northern Ireland, and that their sole interest is to see peace, stability and reconciliation established by agreement among the people who inhabit the island. The British Government accept the principle that the Irish people have the right collectively to self-determination, and that the exercise of this right could take the form of agreed independent structures for the island as a whole. They affirm their readiness to introduce the measures to give legislative effect on their side to this right over a period and according to procedures to be agreed by both Governments and allowing sufficient time for the building of consent and the beginning of a process of national reconciliation. The British Government will use all their influence and energy to win the consent of a majority in Northern Ireland for these measures. They acknowledge that it is the wish of the people of Britain to see the people of Ireland live together in unity and harmony, with respect for their diverse traditions, independent, but with full recognition of the special links and the unique relationship which exists between the peoples of Britain and Ireland.

Draft 11: This was identical to Draft 10, except that the phrase 'and according to procedures' was removed

Appendix 2

Extract from paragraph 4 of the Downing Street Declaration:

'The British government agree that it is for the people of the island of Ireland alone, by agreement between the two parts respectively, to exercise their right of self-determination on the basis of consent, freely and concurrently given, North and South, to bring about a united Ireland, if that is their wish.'

Appendix 3

The TUAS (Totally Unarmed Strategy) document circulated by the republican leadership in summer 1994

The briefing paper of April deals with strategic objectives and events to that date in more detail than this paper. However, a brief summary is helpful. Our goals have not changed. A united 32–county democratic socialist Republic.

The main strategic objectives to move us towards that goal can be summarised thus. To construct an Irish nationalist consensus with international support on the basis of the dynamic contained in the Irish peace initiative. This should aim for:

a The strongest possible political consensus between the Dublin government, Sinn Fein and the SDLP.
b A common position on practical measures moving us towards our goal.
c A common nationalist negotiation position.
d An international dimension in aid of the consensus (mostly U.S.A. and E.U.).

The strategic objectives come from prolonged debate but are based on a straightforward logic: that republicans at this time and on their own do not have the strength to achieve the end goal. The struggle needs strengthening;

381

most obviously from other nationalist constituencies led by SDLP, Dublin government and the emerging Irish-American lobby, with additional support from other parties in E.U. rowing in behind and accelerating the momentum created.

The aim of any such consensus is to create a dynamic which can:

1 Effect [*sic*] the domestic and international perception of the republican position, i.e. as one which is reasonable.
2 To develop a northern nationalist consensus on the basis of constitutional change.
3 To develop an Irish national consensus on the same basis.
4 To develop Irish-America as a significant player in support of the above.
5 To develop a broader and deeper Irish nationalist consensus at grassroots level.
6 To develop and mobilise an anti-imperialist Irish peace movement.
7 To expose the British government and the unionists as the intransigent parties.
8 To heighten the contradictions between British unionist and 'Ulster Loyalism'.
9 To assist the development of whatever potential exists in Britain to create a mood/climate/party/movement for peace.
10 To maintain the political cohesion and organisational integrity of Sinn Fein so as to remain an effective political force.

Present British intentions are the subject of much debate and varied opinion. However, what can be said is that sometime preceding the Downing Street Declaration of December '93 a deal was done with the U.U.P. to keep the Conservatives in power. This becomes an obstacle to movement.

The D.S.D. (Downing Street Declaration) does not hold a solution. Republicans are not prepared to wait around for the Brits to change, but as always we are prepared to force their hand. It is nonetheless important to note that there has been no recent dialogue between the Brit government and Republican representatives since November '93. The republican position is that if the Brits want to talk they should do it through normal political channels.

At the end of the April briefing it states: 'Our (strategic) objectives should guide all our actions. Given that these are our guidelines we must now look at what our options are and what initiatives we can undertake.'

After prolonged discussion and assessment the Leadership decided that if it could get agreement with the Dublin government, the SDLP and the Irish-American lobby on basic republican principles which would be enough to create the dynamic that would considerably advance the struggle, then it would be prepared to use the TUAS option.

We attempted to reach such a consensus on a set of principles which can be summarised briefly thus;

1 Partition has failed.
2 Structures must be changed.

3 No internal settlement within 6 Counties.
4 British rule breaches the principle of N.S.D. [national self-determination].
5 The Irish as a whole have the right to N.S.D. without external impediment.
6 It is up to the Dublin/London governments with all parties to bring about N.S.D. in the shortest time possible.
7 The unionists have no veto over discussions involved or their outcome.
8 A solution requires political and constitutional change.
9 An agreed united and independent Ireland is what republicans desire. However an agreed Ireland needs the allegiance of varied traditions to be viable.

Contact with the other parties involved have been in that context. There are of course differences of opinion on how a number of these principles are interpreted or applied.

In particular: on British rule breaching the principle of N.S.D.; on the absolute right of the Irish to N.S.D. without external impediment; or interpretation of what veto and consent mean; on the issue of timescales.

Nevertheless, differences aside, the leadership believes there is enough in common to create a substantial political momentum which will considerably advance the struggle at this time. Some substantial contribution factors which point towards now being the right time for an initiative are:

Hume is the only SDLP person on the horizon strong enough to face the challenge.

Dublin's coalition is the strongest government in 25 years or more.

Reynolds has no historical baggage to hinder him and knows how popular such a consensus would be among grassroots.

There is potentially a very powerful Irish-American lobby not in hock to any particular party in Ireland or Britain.

Clinton is perhaps the first U.S. President in decades to be substantially influenced by such a lobby.

At this time the British government is the least popular in the E.U. with other E.U. members.

It is the first time in 25 years that all the major Irish nationalist parties are rowing in roughly the same direction. These combined circumstances are unlikely to gel again in the foreseeable future.

The leadership has now decided that there is enough agreement to proceed with the Tuas option. It has been stated from the outset that this is a risky strategy. Its success will depend greatly on workload. All activists must be pro-active. Those who continue their present work need to double effect. If you find yourself idle help in another field.

Tuas has been part of every other struggle in the world this century. It is vital that activists realise the struggle is not over. Another front has opened up and we should have the confidence and put in the effort to succeed on that front. We have the ability to carry on indefinitely. We should be trying to double the pressure on the British.

For various reasons, which include the sensitivity of discussions up to this point, communication up and down the organisation has been patchy. Since we are now entering a more public aspect to the initiative communication should be a less encumbered matter and therefore more regular than before.

Appendix 4

Schedule of meetings between Albert Reynolds's envoy, Martin Mansergh, and Sinn Fein leaders

(All meetings took place in Dundalk except that of 25 October 1993.)

4 May 1988 (with Dermot Ahern) – met Gerry Adams, Pat Doherty & Mitchel McLaughlin

20 June 1988 (with Dermot Ahern) – met Adams, Doherty & McLaughlin

(Meetings from this point on were with Martin McGuinness & Aidan McAteer, unless otherwise stated.)

14 October 1992 (with Fr Alec Reid & Fr Gerry Reynolds)

22 October (approx) 1992

3 February 1993

April 1993

10 June 1993 (with Fr Reid) – met Gerry Adams & Tom Hartley

25 October 1993 (with Fr Reid) Dublin – met Gerry Adams & Aidan McAteer

23 February 1994 (with Fr Reid)

July & August 1994 (with Fr Reid) – series of meetings

INDEX